What America Owes the World
The Struggle for the Soul of Foreign Policy

For two hundred years, Americans have believed that they have an obligation to improve the lot of humanity. This belief has consistently shaped U.S. foreign policy. Yet within this consensus, two schools of thought have contended: the "exemplarist" school (Brands's term), which holds that what America chiefly owes the world is the benign example of a well-functioning democracy, and the "vindicationist" school, which asserts that force must sometimes supplement a good example. In this book, H. W. Brands traces the evolution of these two schools as they emerged in the arguments of the most important public thinkers of the last two centuries. This book is both an intellectual and moral history of U.S. foreign policy and a guide to the fundamental question of America's relations with the rest of the world – a question more pressing than ever in the confusion that has succeeded the Cold War: What does America owe the world?

H. W. Brands, the Ralph R. Thomas Professor of History at Texas A&M University, has degrees from Stanford University, Reed College, Portland State University, and the University of Texas at Austin. His previous books include *The Specter of Neutralism, Inside the Cold War, The United States in the World, The Wages of Globalism, The Reckless Decade,* and *T.R.: The Last Romantic.*

What America Owes the World

The Struggle for the Soul of Foreign Policy

H. W. BRANDS

CAMBRIDGE
UNIVERSITY PRESS

CAMBRIDGE UNIVERSITY PRESS
Cambridge, New York, Melbourne, Madrid, Cape Town, Singapore, São Paulo

Cambridge University Press
The Edinburgh Building, Cambridge CB2 8RU, UK

Published in the United States of America by Cambridge University Press, New York

www.cambridge.org
Information on this title: www.cambridge.org/9780521630313

First published 1998

A catalogue record for this publication is available from the British Library

Library of Congress Cataloguing in Publication data
Brands, H. W.
What America owes the world : the struggle for the soul of foreign
policy / H. W. Brands.
p.   cm.
Includes bibliographical references and index.
ISBN 0-521-63031-2 (hardcover)
1. United States – Foreign relations – Philosophy.   2. United
States – Foreign relations – Historiography.   I. Title.
E183.7.B694   1998
327.73 – DC21   97-38837
                                                      CIP

ISBN 978-0-521-63031-3 hardback
ISBN 978-0-521-63968-2 paperback

Transferred to digital printing 2008

Contents

Preface

If a single theme pervades the history of American thinking about the world, it is that the United States has a peculiar obligation to better the lot of humanity. Call it a Puritan survival, or a sport from the Lockean roots of natural-rights philosophy, or a manifestation of American exceptionalism; but for whatever reasons, Americans have commonly spoken and acted as though the salvation of the world depended on them. From the moment John Winthrop planted his "city on a hill" as a self-conscious example for the whole world to see; through the era when the American revolutionaries cast their conflict against Britain as a blow for the unalienable rights of *all* men; to the day when Abraham Lincoln defended the war for the Union as a struggle to guarantee that government of the people, by the people, and for the people not perish from the (entire) earth; to the day when Woodrow Wilson called for a crusade to make the world safe for democracy; to Franklin Roosevelt's extrapolation of the Atlantic Charter to the Pacific and Indian oceans; to John Kennedy's pledge to pay any price and bear any burden in the defense of the liberty of Berlin and other Cold War hot spots; to George Bush's assertion of the need for Americans to secure a "new world order"; to Bill Clinton's dispatch of troops to Bosnia to enforce an American-brokered peace in that broken and bleeding land – which is to say, from the beginning of American history to the present – this sense of obligation to suffering humankind has been a persistent theme in American thought, speech, and writing about the world.

Yet there has been decided disagreement regarding the precise nature of this obligation. On one side have been those who hold that the United States owes the world merely the example of a humane, democratic, and prosperous society. These exemplarists, as they might be called, have argued that perfecting American institutions and practices at home is a full-time job. To try for more, as by meddling in the affairs of other nations, would not only not do much good for the nations meddled in, since societies have to solve their problems themselves, but could jeopardize American values at the source. In attempting to save the world, and probably failing, America would risk losing its democratic soul.

On the other side of the debate have been those who contend that America must move beyond example and undertake active measures to vindicate the right. In a nasty world, these vindicators say, the sword of wrath must complement the lantern of virtue. Evil goes armed, and so must good. Human nature is too recalcitrant for mere example to have much lasting effect, and until human nature changes – a development most vindicators anticipate about the time of the Second Coming – military might, even if it doesn't necessarily make right, certainly can restrain wrong.

Neither the exemplarists nor the vindicators have overlooked American self-interest as a critical factor in shaping U.S. relations with the world. Quite the contrary: Each side has consistently upheld its position as affording the largest likelihood of securing America's national interest. Further, the two sides have commonly agreed on the nature of the long-term American interest. With exceptions few enough simply to prove the rule, both the exemplarists and the vindicators have desired to see other regions of the world look more like America – if not always the imperfect America of the present, then the ideal America of their dreams.

The parting of the ways occurred in the matter of how to get there from here. The exemplarists, often but not always less satisfied with America's present condition than the vindicators, asserted that Americans must concentrate on improving their own society. In doing so, the exemplarists argued, Americans would simultaneously provide the greatest service to humanity, which, seeing heaven approach nearer to earth in the middle latitudes of North America than anywhere else, would be motivated to adopt America's methods of social organization. The vindicators rejected such thinking as utopian. While not denying America's imperfections, they held that the imperfections of the rest of world were far greater – so much greater, in fact, as to necessitate forcible American efforts to close the imperfection gap. If Americans didn't bring the world up to their own standard, the world would bring Americans down to its. In vindicationist views, not even Hobson would have called this a choice.

The present volume delineates the debate between the exemplarists and the vindicators as part of what might loosely be called an intellectual history of American foreign policy. It begins with a chapter on the eighteenth and nineteenth centuries, when the two sides staked out and initially articulated their positions. It tightens the focus at the 1890s, when Americans themselves first focused on foreign affairs on a regular basis. From that point, the book identifies particular individuals as emblematic of particular stages and facets of the debate. Some of the individuals – Walter Lippmann, Charles Beard, George Kennan, Hans Morgenthau, Reinhold Niebuhr, William Appleman Williams, Norman Podhoretz, Jeane Kirkpatrick – addressed directly the central question of what America owes the world. The contribution of others – Brooks Adams, Lincoln Steffens, Herman Kahn – lay more in shaping the context in which the debate took place. Contributing also to the context, and to the debate itself, were the numerous individuals who dissented from, assented to, and otherwise commented upon the thoughts and writings of the marquee characters; many such are included below as supporting actors.

The employment of individuals to carry the story forward is only in part a literary device; it is also a reminder that ideas always come attached to people. And people come with their own agendas, temperaments, and personal histories. Sometimes these ancillary elements matter as much as the ideas themselves in influencing audiences.

This said, the emphasis here is on the ideas – on the debate over America's obligation to the world – rather than on the individuals. Still less is the emphasis on the policies the debate helped produce. Histories of American foreign policy are legion; histories of the intellectual precursors of policy are far rarer. And histories of the moral aspects of those precursors – of this issue of America's obligation – are, remarkably, so much rarer as to be essentially nonexistent. It is this lack that the book in hand has been written to help remedy. How presidents and other policy-makers responded to the public debate is an interesting and important question, and one calling for a volume or two for each presidential administration. But it is not the basic question here.

After two centuries (four, counting from Winthrop), the debate over what America owes the world is as contentious as ever – which strongly suggests that the competing arguments are evenly matched, or nearly so. To recapitulate and analyze those arguments as they have been developed by some of the best minds in American history will hardly settle the matter. But it may facilitate an intelligent continuation of what might fairly, and at only minor risk of melodrama, be called the struggle for the soul of American foreign policy.

1

Exceptionalists All!
The First Hundred Years

I

The exemplarists started the debate when John Winthrop proclaimed that the Puritan settlement on the Atlantic's western shore would be a model for the entire world. If the experiment in government by the godly succeeded, its light would illumine humanity; if it failed, all would know. Yet unalloyed exemplarism wasn't a necessary consequence of Puritanism per se. A more vigorous vindicator than Oliver Cromwell would be difficult to conceive. Had Winthrop and associates enjoyed the capacity to do what Cromwell did, they never would have left England. For Winthrop, exemplarism was the refuge of the weak.

It remained so for Americans for a century and a half. Until the inhabitants of Britain's North American colonies wrested sovereignty from London, they were in no position to impose their notions of politics, social order, or anything else on the world at large. To be sure, they leaned heavily on neighboring Indians and somewhat more lightly on the French, Dutch, and Spanish they encountered in the colonial borderlands. Yet without a national government, Americans had no foreign policy distinct from Britain's, and so small was their voice in the formulation of British policy that few bothered to raise it.

Though Thomas Jefferson didn't share many habits of mind with John Winthrop, the author of the Declaration of Independence agreed that Americans were uniquely placed to set a pattern for the earth's less favored denizens. In describing the causes compelling the colonies to separation from Britain, Jefferson expressed a view re-garding the nature of government that at least implicitly held America forth as a beacon to the world. In Jefferson's phrasing, *all* men, not simply Americans, possessed unalienable rights to life, liberty, and the pursuit of happiness. And when *any* form of government, not just Britain's peculiar mix of crown and parliament, became destructive of the people's welfare, they were justified in abolishing it. Thus the American revolution became an exemplary blow for liberty everywhere.

One might have thought setting a good example would satisfy the citizens of a small country far from the focus of international affairs. But such was American self-confidence that independence had hardly been secured before certain individuals and factions began arguing for a more ambitious program. When the French went to war in 1793 to preserve their revolution, Jefferson showed a slight vindicationist streak. He and his followers sympathized with France's predicament, and although the Republicans hardly applauded the bloody turn events in France had taken, they judged the general direction of the revolution worthy of American support. Jefferson saw republican France's battle with the monarchies of Europe as part of the abiding struggle between freedom and slavery. The "liberty of the whole earth," he said, depended on the outcome of the European contest. Americans could not stand idle. James Madison likewise cheered the French for their efforts at "compleating the triumphs of Liberty." With Jefferson, Madison contended that right and virtue required the United States to honor its obligations under the Franco-American treaty of 1778 and succor France in that ally's hour of need.[1]

Alexander Hamilton and the Federalists roundly rejected the Republicans' reasoning. The Federalists denied that the fate of France should be identified with the fortunes of liberty. But even granting that premise they denied, equally vehemently, that the United States ought to take an active part in the French struggle. At Hamilton's urging, President Washington declared neutrality in the European war. Hamilton went to some lengths to defend the dubious argument that the French revolution had voided the 1778 treaty. By overthrowing the monarchy with which the American government had concluded the pact, Hamilton said, the French people themselves had nullified it.

---

[1] Lawrence S. Kaplan, *Jefferson and France* (New Haven, Conn., 1967), 51; Madison to Roland, April 1793, in Thomas A. Mason et al., eds., *The Papers of James Madison* (Charlottesville, Va., 1985), 15:4.

Yet Hamilton's fundamental point was that the United States had troubles enough of its own, and therefore shouldn't shoulder the burden of other people's problems. Instead it should concentrate on setting an example. Such a course would yield the greatest benefit, to foreigners as well as to Americans.

They will see in us a people who have a due respect for property and personal security, who in the midst of our revolution abstained with exemplary moderation from every thing violent or sanguinary instituting governments adequate to the protection of persons and property; who since the completion of our revolution have in a very short period, from mere reasoning and reflection, without tumult or bloodshed, adopted a form of general Government calculated, as well as the nature of things would permit, to remedy antecedent defects, to give strength and security to the nation, to rest the foundations of Liberty on the basis of Justice, Order and law.[2]

Hamilton's exemplarist view strongly marked Washington's farewell address, a matter unsurprising in light of Hamilton's large role in writing the piece. "Observe good faith and justice toward all nations," the retiring president counseled. "Cultivate peace and harmony with all." In this way would the United States simultaneously serve the cause of America and of humanity. "It will be worthy of a free, enlightened, and at no distant period a great nation to give to mankind the magnanimous and too novel example of a people always guided by an exalted justice and benevolence."

The example would produce its benefits only if United States remained distant from the affairs of foreign countries, Washington said. Adherence to any single power would disqualify America in the eyes of that power's rivals. More perniciously, it would corrupt the example. "History and experience prove that foreign influence is one of the most baneful foes of republican government." Entanglement abroad inflamed faction at home. "Excessive partiality for one foreign nation and excessive dislike of another cause those whom they actuate to see danger only on one side, and serve to veil and even second the arts of influence on the other. Real patriots who may resist the intrigues of the favorite are liable to become suspected and odious, while its tools and dupes usurp the applause and confidence of the people to surrender their interests."

[2] Harold C. Syrett, ed., *The Papers of Alexander Hamilton* (New York, 1972), 16: 18–9.

Providence had so situated America as to enable it to perfect its institutions on its own. "Why forego the advantages of so peculiar a situation? Why quit our own to stand upon foreign ground? Why, by interweaving our destiny with that of any part of Europe, entangle our peace and prosperity in the toils of European ambition, rivalship, interest, humor, or caprice?"[3]

II

Why indeed? Jefferson asked during his own presidency. Responsibility and Napoleon tempered Jefferson's enthusiasm for things French, and, having pronounced Americans all Federalists as well as all Republicans, he proceeded to follow Federalist advice. The republican experiment in France had fizzled, as evidenced by Bonaparte. Prospects elsewhere appeared dim. Under the circumstances, Jefferson declined to stake American safety on the success of revolution abroad.

Of equal significance in shaping Jefferson's opinion, the new round of war between Britain and France threatened to draw the United States more fully into Europe's affairs than even the most ardent vindicator could desire. With France and Britain both violating American rights, securing the survival of republicanism in its North American birthplace posed sufficient challenge to Americans. Alone of the nations, America preserved the values of equality and self-rule that some day would revolutionize human society; in the future, Americans might export these values once more. But for the moment they must concentrate on keeping them safe at home. Jefferson's embargo, which in a sense was exemplarism carried to an extreme, demonstrated how thoroughly he had adopted the exemplarist philosophy. Though the embargo brought thunderous abuse upon his administration, Jefferson urged his compatriots to tend their own business in a world bent on destruction. "A single good government," he wrote, "thus becomes a blessing to the whole earth."[4]

Conversion to exemplarism likewise claimed Jefferson's successor.

---

[3] James D. Richardson, ed., *A Compilation of the Messages and Papers of the Presidents* (Washington, 1896), 1:213–24. See also Felix Gilbert, *To the Farewell Address* (Princeton, N.J., 1961).

[4] Norman A. Graebner, ed., *Ideas and Diplomacy: Readings in the Intellectual Tradition of American Foreign Policy* (New York, 1964), 86.

More tangled in the coils of European power politics even than Jefferson, Madison longed for the opportunity to cultivate America's garden in peace. Like Jefferson, he had underestimated the difficulties of transplanting republicanism to foreign soil. With the mature Jefferson he held that setting a good example for other nations would satisfactorily discharge America's obligations to the world. "The free system of government we have established is so congenial with reason, with common sense, and with a universal feeling, that it must produce approbation and a desire of imitation," Madison wrote. "Our country, if it does justice to itself, will be the workshop of liberty to the Civilized World, and do more than any other for the uncivilized."[5]

The same European wars, however, that enmeshed the United States and helped move Jefferson and Madison to exemplarism also touched off a series of revolutions throughout the western hemisphere that prompted the further development of vindicationist arguments. Sympathy for French republicans during the 1790s had included a desire on the part of many to send American aid, official or otherwise, to France, but even the most enthusiastic American supporters of *liberté* recognized the limits of American assistance and understood that help from the New World would probably play no more than a marginal role in freedom's struggle for survival in the Old. The situation of the Latin American republics was different. They were closer to home. They were smaller. Their fate, while of concern to the great European powers, was not of such significance as to trigger a war to the death among the great powers. Consequently, Americans could entertain the idea of strongly influencing, perhaps determining, the Latin Americans' future.

The idea initially arose in the context of diplomatic recognition of the revolutionary regimes. Henry Clay argued for early recognition. In 1818 Clay, then speaker of the House of Representatives, averred that the United States couldn't but have "the deepest interest" in the independence of Latin America. The countries of the south, he said, once free, would "be animated by an American feeling and guided by an American policy." They would "obey the laws of the system of the New World, of which they would compose a part, in contradistinction to that of Europe." The Latin American governments had taken the United States as their inspiration. "They adopted our prin-

[5] Ibid.

ciples, copied our institutions, and, in some instances, employed the very language and sentiments of our revolutionary papers." Now they looked to the United States for assistance. The least the United States could do was adopt a "just neutrality" between the struggling nations and their colonial overlords. This required immediate diplomatic recognition.[6]

Clay subsequently amplified his argument, contending that the countries of the western hemisphere should and did form a realm separate from that of Europe. In a much noted speech at Lexington, Kentucky, Clay urged the formation in the two Americas of "a sort of counterpoise to the Holy Alliance"; this counterpoise would comprise those hemispheric states pledged to "national independence and liberty." American support for such a realm of democracy must begin with "the force of example and moral influence," but it mustn't stop there. In the cause of Latin American independence, the United States should employ "all means short of actual war."[7]

Even as Clay's forthright statement of the vindicationist position compelled the exemplarist Monroe to develop a riposte, a fresh controversy complicated the issue. In 1821, Greek nationalists rebelled against the local enforcers of the writ of the Ottoman sultan. The Greek war for independence deeply moved large numbers of Americans. The well-educated elite, versed in the Greek classics, felt a natural affinity for the birthplace of Western culture; the wider body of Americans who knew Plato only second-hand nevertheless understood that American democracy echoed Athenian precursors. The overwhelming majority of Americans who subscribed to the Christian faith interpreted the struggle by the Greek Christians against the Muslim Turks as a tenth Crusade.

Like the Latin American freedom fighters, the Greek insurgents appealed to Americans for support. They solicited donations, consulted with the aging Jefferson for advice on establishing a government, and followed American precedents in writing a constitution. They also forwarded a proclamation justifying their struggle to Edward Everett, the editor of the influential *North American Review* and a long-time supporter of Greek independence. Everett published the manifesto, which, after praising the United States for embracing

---

[6] James F. Hopkins, ed., *The Papers of Henry Clay* (Lexington, Ky., 1961), 2:519–25.

[7] Arthur Preston Whitaker, *The United States and the Independence of Latin America, 1800–1830* (Baltimore, 1941), 344–5.

the ideals enunciated by the ancient Greeks, appealed to the Americans for assistance. "It is for you, citizens of America, to crown this glory in aiding us to purge Greece from the barbarians. . . . It is surely worthy of you to repay the obligations of the civilized nations and to banish ignorance and barbarism from the country of freedom and the arts."

Everett, responding to the petition, asserted that it couldn't fail to wake Americans to the obligation their country had to take an active role in humanity's salvation. The Greek appeal "must bring home to the mind of the least reflecting American the great and glorious part which this country is to act in the political regeneration of the world." Everett called for swift recognition by the United States of the revolutionary government in Greece. And individual Americans, in their capacity as private citizens, could do more. From England, Germany, and France, brave young men had gone out to join the Greeks in their epic contest; Americans might do the same. Those unable to offer their bodies to the cause could contribute their wealth. Every form of assistance counted. "The experience of our own revolutionary war is so recent that we ought to have felt how precious would be any aid from a distant land, however insignificant in amount. Who does not know that there were times in our own revolutionary war when a few barrels of gunpowder, the large guns of a privateer, a cargo of flour, a supply of clothing, yea, a few hundred pairs of shoes for feet that left in blood the tracks of their march, would have done essential service to the cause of suffering liberty?" American communities should follow the example of London, which had taxed itself to support the freedom struggle. "Let Boston appropriate ten thousand dollars for the same object; New York and Philadelphia and Baltimore and the cities of the South in proportion to their means will heartily unite in the cause."[8]

Daniel Webster added his sonorous voice to Everett's call. Webster stopped shy of calling for volunteers or passing the collection plate to back the Greeks, but the Massachusetts congressman, later twice secretary of state, thought the support provided by diplomatic recognition a necessity. The heroes of Hellas deserved no less. Webster, then at the top of his oratorical form, declaimed:

I cannot say, sir, that they will succeed; that rests with Heaven. But for myself, sir, if I should tomorrow hear that they have failed, that their

[8] Edward Everett, "Affairs of Greece," *North American Review*, October 1823.

last phalanx had sunk beneath the Turkish scimitar, that the flames of their last city had sunk into ashes, and that naught remained but the wide melancholy waste where Greece once was, I should still reflect, with the most heartfelt satisfaction, that I have asked you in the name of seven millions of freemen, that you would give them at least the cheering of one friendly voice.

Other commentators, however, refused to be swept over by the tide of emotion for Greece. Against the vindicationist approach of Clay and Everett and Webster, such exemplarists as John Randolph of Virginia resisted American involvement in affairs so far from the United States. Randolph thought the Greeks should look to America's example rather than America's assistance, diplomatic or material. "Let us say to those seven millions of Greeks," Randolph declared, " 'We defended ourselves, when we were but three millions, against a Power, in comparison to which the Turk is but as a lamb. Go and do thou likewise.' " Diplomatic recognition would lead to exchange of envoys, which would provoke retaliation by Turkey; inevitably the United States would be drawn into the maw. "To entangling alliances we must come, if you once embark in projects such as this."[9]

An even sterner warning against the enthusiasms of the vindicators came from John Quincy Adams. Monroe's secretary of state, a master (and not overly modest) diplomat who nonetheless recognized the limits of his ability to manipulate the world balance of power, countered the arguments of the vindicators with the single most succinct and compelling exemplarist statement ever. Speaking on the forty-fifth anniversary of American independence, Adams answered any who would have the United States intervene in the affairs of foreign countries, even for the noblest purposes. Once America assumed responsibility for the welfare of others, Adams said, she would endanger the interests of her own people.

Wherever the standard of freedom and independence has been or shall be unfurled, there will her heart, her benedictions, and her prayers be. But she goes not abroad in search of monsters to destroy. She is the well-wisher to the freedom and independence of all. She is the champion and vindicator only of her own. . . .

She well knows that by once enlisting under other banners than her

[9] Paul Constantine Pappas, *The United States and the Greek War for Independence, 1821–1828* (Boulder, Colo., 1985), 68, 71.

own, were they even the banners of foreign independence, she would involve herself beyond the power of extrication, in all the wars of interest and intrigue, of individual avarice, envy, and ambition, which assume the colors and usurp the standard of freedom. The fundamental maxims of her policy would insensibly change from liberty to force. . . .

She might become the dictatress of the world. She would no longer be the ruler of her own spirit.[10]

III

Adams's statement silenced the vindicators momentarily, but Americans' insatiable land hunger soon afforded them opportunity for rebuttal. While several varieties of material interest provided the principal impetus for the acquisition of Texas, California, and Oregon, uniting the cotton planters, cattle ranchers, fur trappers, and China-traders was an overarching conviction that bringing new territory under the American flag was tantamout to "extending the area of freedom," in the favored phrase of the day.

Yet opinions differed as to how freedom's area might best be extended. The doctrine of Manifest Destiny definitely allowed the possibility that American expansion would happen through the voluntary adherence of America's neighbors to what Congressman Luther Severance of Maine called "our bright and shining example as a pattern republic." Indeed, the desire of Texans to annex themselves to the United States seemed to confirm the power of the American example. The high priest of Manifest Destiny, John O'Sullivan, denounced the very idea that America's example required any armed assistance. "Nothing upon earth, or above or below the earth, can be farther from the genius and principles of this Republic than the acquisition of territory by military conquest," O'Sullivan asserted. "The attempt would be as monstrous as it would be new in our history, and short-lived indeed would be the power and influence of those who should undertake it. They would be looked upon as the worst of traitors, striking at the life of their country and laying the foundation for its speedy and certain ruin."[11]

---

[10] Walter LaFeber, ed., *John Quincy Adams and American Continental Empire* (Chicago, 1965), 42–6.

[11] Albert K. Weinberg, *Manifest Destiny: A Study of Nationalist Expansionism in American History* (Baltimore, 1935), 102; Frederick Merk, *Manifest Destiny and Mission in American History: A Reinterpretation* (New York, 1963), 110–1.

Yet O'Sullivan didn't have the field to himself: many Manifest Destinarians weren't above giving destiny a hand. The more self-conscious of these vindicators described democratic expansion, by force if necessary, as a defensive measure. Senator Daniel Dickinson of New York characterized the Oregon issue as a contest "between two great systems, between monarchy and republicanism." Only one system, Dickinson said, would survive. The *American Review* adopted a similar position, accusing the British, in the matter of Oregon, of deliberately and threateningly throwing up barriers to "the progress of republican liberty." The New Orleans *Jeffersonian Republican*, asserting the necessity of taking Texas, claimed that unless American sovereignty was pressed to the Rio Grande, there would develop on the country's southwestern frontier an influence "highly dangerous to our prosperity and inimical to the spread of Republican institutions."[12]

The more ebullient of the vindicators put the case for democratic expansionism more forthrightly. The *New York Herald* declared:

American patriotism takes a wider and loftier range than heretofore. Its horizon is widening every day. No longer bounded by the limits of the confederacy, it looks abroad upon the whole earth, and into the mind of the republic daily sinks deeper and deeper the conviction that the civilization of the earth – the reform of the governments of the ancient world – the emancipation of the whole race, are dependent, in a great degree, on the United States.

Others, not quite ready to take on the redemption of Europe and Asia, nonetheless conceived an American obligation to regenerate Mexico. Numerous commentators deplored Mexican "misgovernment" and advocated strong measures of reform, including war and perhaps annexation. "I would not force the adoption of our form of Government upon any people by the sword," Senator Herschel Johnson of Georgia said at the outset of the conflict with Mexico. "But if war is forced upon us, as this has been, and the increase of our territory and consequently the extension of the area of human liberty and happiness shall be one of the incidents of such a contest, I believe we should be recreant to our noble mission if we refused acquiescence in the high purposes of a wise Providence." The *Boston Times* ap-

---

[12] Weinberg, *Manifest Destiny*, 110–1.

plauded the prospect of American conquest of Mexico, deeming it a wonderful boon to the degraded Mexican people.

The "conquest" which carries peace into a land where the sword has always been the sole arbiter between factions equally base, which institutes the reign of law where license has existed for a generation; which provides for the education and elevation of the great mass of the people, who have for a period of 300 years been the helots of an overbearing foreign race, and which causes religious liberty and full freedom of mind to prevail where a priesthood has long been enabled to prevent all religion save that of its own worship, – such a "conquest," stigmatize it as you please, must necessarily be a great blessing to the conquered.

That the fighting against Mexico ended without accomplishing the revitalization of that country simply encouraged the apostles of Manifest Destiny to advocate more of the same. An editor for the *United States Democratic Review* asserted, "Mexico is in a state of suspended animation. She is in fact dead. She must have resurrection. She must be electrified – restored. This American Republic is strong enough to do anything that requires strength. It is vital enough to inject life even into the dead."[13]

Ranting like this last cries for discounting. Rascals have long called on heaven to cover their crimes, and Americans intent on expanding their country's domain by any means necessary were no exception. Yet the fulsome nature of the rhetoric oughtn't obscure the fact that millions in the United States, almost certainly a large majority, sincerely believed that by enlarging the sphere of American sovereignty they were contributing to the betterment of the human race.

IV

Where American sovereignty was out of the question, Americans contented themselves trying to roll back the still-encompassing ocean of monarchy. Federalism and its closet monarchists were long dead, and the heirs of Jackson robustly affirmed revolution as an agent of human progress. But as before, they differed regarding the degree of assistance the United States should supply to revolutionaries abroad.

---

[13] Graebner, *Ideas and Diplomacy*, 157; Weinberg, *Manifest Destiny*, 179, 183; Merk, *Manifest Destiny and Mission*, 122.

A new round of revolutions, in Europe in 1848, demonstrated that the exemplarists and vindicators continued to be as far apart as ever.

At the center of this latest controversy was Louis Kossuth, the Hungarian nationalist who came to America seeking support for Hungary against its Russian oppressors. A dashing figure and a shameless showman, Kossuth paraded triumphally across the country, holding rallies, raising money, and appealing for an American policy of "intervention for nonintervention," by which he meant American intervention to force Russian nonintervention. He asked President Fillmore to recognize Hungary's independence, to warn the czar against further aggression, and to dispatch American warships to the Mediterranean to keep the Russians in line.

Kossuth's cause caught fire among a sizable portion of the American people. Many observers accepted his claim that upon the fortunes of Hungary hung the future of liberty in Europe. Gamaliel Bailey, editor of the reformist *National Era*, demanded intervention, taking the Bible rather than Washington's farewell address as his text. "Love thy neighbor as thyself," Bailey exclaimed. "This is the fundamental principle of Intervention." The New Testament preached intervention: Witness the story of the good Samaritan. "The Apostles were Interventionists – the fathers of the Church were Interventionists – philanthropists and reformers, all who have written, spoken or acted so as to elevate Humanity, have been Interventionists." Bailey concluded, "Intervention in behalf of Freedom, Justice and Humanity is the maxim of Democracy; Non-intervention, except to limit them, is the demand of Slavery."

Pierre Soulé, the Louisiana senator who had fled France during the 1820s after promoting an anti-Bourbon brand of republicanism, embraced Kossuth literally and rhetorically. "We boast exultingly of our wisdom," Soulé declared. "Do we mean to hide it under a bushel, from fear that its light might set the world in flames?" Let the burning begin, he cried, for the fires of liberty would cleanse the earth of corruption. "Onward? onward! is the injunction of God's will as much as Ahead! ahead! is the aspiration of every American heart." The momentum of democracy would shatter all in its path. "Attempt not, therefore, to stop it in its forward career, for as well might you command the sun not to break through the fleecy clouds that herald its advent on the horizon."

The vindicators failed to carry the country, however, once the initial flutterings over Kossuth subsided. While no person of stature opposed the principles Kossuth represented, more than a few questioned whether America possessed responsibility or capacity to impose those principles on a refractory world, especially on a part of the world so far from America's borders. Erstwhile vindicator Henry Clay put the exemplarist case best. The aging Kentucky statesman, his youthful energy gone, confidence in America's future shaken by the deepening sectional schism, life itself ebbing, summoned Kossuth to his bedside. Clay grasped Kossuth's hand and wished him luck. "God bless you and your family! God bless your country! May she yet be free!" But Clay declared that America must not make Hungary's struggle her own. "If we should involve ourselves in the tangled web of European politics, in a war in which we could effect nothing, and in that struggle Hungary should go down, and we should go down with her, where then would be the last hope of the friends of freedom throughout the world?" Intervention was the counsel of imprudence, Clay said. Far better that Americans concentrate on securing liberty and democracy at home – that "we keep our lamp burning brightly on this Western shore as a light to all nations" – than to hazard "its utter extinction amid the ruins of fallen or falling republics in Europe."[14]

V

During the quarter century after 1850, while the sectional crisis, the Civil War, and Reconstruction consumed the country, few Americans had much thought to spare for international relations. Most vexed themselves instead over the survival prospects of republicanism in America. The Civil War constituted a grand vindicationist project by the North against the South, although only convinced Confederates placed the effort in the realm of foreign affairs. An interested observer might have expected the victorious Unionists, full of confidence and fielding perhaps the world's strongest army, to embark on vindicationist adventures around the hemisphere, or at least the continent, but with the exception of frightening the French out of Mexico, they did no such thing. As would happen fifty years later, fighting a war, even successfully, left Americans psychologically, morally, economically, and politically weary of other people's troubles. It was

[14] Donald S. Spencer, *Louis Kossuth and Young America: A Study of Sectionalism and Foreign Policy* (Columbia, Mo., 1977), 53, 93–4, 108–9, 138–9.

precisely this fatigue that finally caused Washington to withdraw its troops from the South and return control of that region to its prewar ruling class.

Enthusiasm for foreign dealings didn't vanish entirely during the third quarter of the nineteenth century. Filibusters traipsed across Central America, Southern slaveholders agitated to annex Cuba, and adolescents of "Young America" projected their fantasies abroad. Of substantive matters, Matthew Perry's opening of Japan in 1854 had more to do with American trade than with American ideals, but many Americans, especially those of a vindicationist frame of mind, encountered little difficulty convincing themselves that the first might lead to the second. William Henry Seward, the most Asia-oriented American diplomat of the nineteenth century, said of Japan a few years later that the positive effects of Perry's visit were already evident. The secretary of state expressed particular approval of the efforts the Japanese were "wisely making to accommodate their political and civil institutions and customs to the commercial movements of the age and to the principles and policies established by the law of nations."[15]

Seward's minister to Japan, Robert Pruyn, put the vindicationist case more strongly. Progressive influences had entered Japan as a result solely of American coercion, Pruyn claimed. "No conviction of public good nor respect for other nations" had opened Japanese doors to the West. Rather, "the silent but no less potent utterances of bayonet and wide-mouthed cannon burst away the barriers of isolation." American strength was required to keep the doors open. "Our foothold here can be maintained only by a firm attitude and with the hand on the sword." Americans had embarked on a noble venture in remaking Japan; their resolve mustn't slacken until the job was finished – which might take some time. "The entire framework of society and government must be remodeled," Pruyn declared.[16]

Seward complemented the opening of Japan with acquisition of Alaska, a territory he perceived as a natural waystation on the route to Asia. Although most proponents of the purchase stressed the commercial opportunities it afforded, Charles Sumner, the leader of the Senate fight for approval of the Alaska treaty, placed the transaction

---

[15] Ernest N. Paolino, *The Foundations of the American Empire: William Henry Seward and U.S. Foreign Policy* (Ithaca, N.Y., 1973), 172–4.
[16] Ibid.

in broader context. By drawing Alaska under the Stars and Stripes, Sumner said, the United States would accomplish another major step in "the extension of republican institutions," an objective he portrayed as "a traditional aspiration" of the American people. "The Republic is something more than a local policy," he declared. "It is a general principle, not to be forgotten at any time, especially when the opportunity is presented of bringing an immense region within its influence." Sumner saw the removal of the czar's authority from North America as the most recent in a succession of victories for liberty. "We dismiss one other monarch from the continent. One by one they have retired – first France, then Spain, then France again, and now Russia – all giving way to the absorbing Unity declared in the national motto, *E pluribus unum*."[17]

Some contemporaries of Seward, Pruyn, and Sumner judged the vindicators' self-confidence smug and unwarranted, especially in light of the travail America had recently experienced at home. Orestes Brownson put the case for a modest exemplarism more succinctly than most. Brownson, a career convert who left the Presbyterian church for Universalism, Universalism for Unitarianism, Unitarianism for his own church, and his own church for Roman Catholicism, touching transcendentalism and socialism along the way, and who reported the multi-stage hegira in various journals of the era, including *Brownson's Quarterly Review*, accounted the Civil War cause for caution in American foreign affairs. Americans had shown themselves incapable of solving their own problems peaceably, he said, and therefore were in no position to force their views on others. "The Union will fight to maintain the integrity of her domain and the supremacy of her laws within it, but she can never, consistently with her principles or her interests, enter upon a career of war and conquest. Her system is violated, endangered, not extended, by subjugating her neighbors, for subjugation and liberty go not together."

Brownson had no doubt that America stood at the edge of a brilliant future, with the slavery controversy now settled. Nor did he question that the country would continue to grow. "The American people need not trouble themselves about their exterior expansion. That will come of itself as fast as desirable." But expansion must result from the attractive power of the American model, not from force. Americans should work on improving their own institutions

[17] Charles Sumner, *Complete Works* (New York, 1900, 1969), 15:41–3.

and leave it to Providence to handle the rest, which Providence would. "Let them devote their attention to their internal destiny, to the realization of their mission within, and they will gradually see the whole continent coming under their system."[18]

VI

The humility Brownson displayed was rare in America in the Gilded Age. The archetypes of the era were the Social Darwinists. These American adherents of the ideas of Britain's Herbert Spencer first applied the paradigm of survival of the fittest to domestic life, rationalizing why John Rockefeller was richer than ten thousand of his workers combined. Yet their theories extended readily to the contest among nations. Why was America wealthy and powerful? they asked. Because America was better adapted to survival in the modern period, they answered.

John Fiske explained the situation in a widely read and frequently pirated piece called "Manifest Destiny." In this 1885 essay, Fiske described the preeminence of the United States in the world as the result of a unique melding of Anglo-Saxon racial superiority and American political aptitude. Noting the expansion of Anglo-Saxon influence during the previous three centuries, Fiske predicted a continuation of the trend.

The work which the English race began when it colonized North America is destined to go on until every land on the earth's surface that is not already the seat of an old civilization shall become English in its language, in its political habits and traditions, and to a predominant extent in the blood of its people. The day is at hand when four fifths of the human race will trace its pedigree to English forefathers, as four fifths of the white people in the United States trace their pedigree today.

While Fiske deemed Anglo-Saxons in general admirably suited to the governance of large territory and numbers of people, he held that the American branch of the race had approached nigher to perfection than any other. The key to America's special success lay in the concepts of representative democracy, which ensured a government answerable to the people, and federalism, which provided a balance

[18] O. A. Brownson, *The American Republic: Its Constitution, Tendencies, and Destiny* (New York, 1865), 436–9.

between local and national interests. The United States, Fiske asserted, had pioneered these twin ideas and developed them to their present superlative condition in America. Together they produced an effect no less revolutionary in politics than the introduction of steam power or electricity in manufacturing.

Overbrimming with this vitality, Americans would extend their influence and institutions across the globe. The United States a century hence, Fiske predicted, would embrace "a political aggregation unmeasurably surpassing in power and in dimensions any empire that has yet existed." American power would flow most readily into the backward regions of the earth, but not even Europe would be exempt. In the face of America's enormous economic productivity – another manifestation of American national fitness – the old, tired regimes would give way. "The pacific pressure exerted upon Europe by America is becoming so great that it will doubtless before long overcome all these obstacles." While Americans would benefit, the world would benefit more as the United States spread its empire "from pole to pole" and "from the rising to the setting sun."[19]

Though Fiske spoke a mouthful in covering the earth with an American empire, others were no less ambitious. Josiah Strong, the general secretary of the American Evangelical Alliance and, like Fiske, a regular on the lecture circuit of the expansion-minded, matched his lay brother's confidence, phrase for glowing phrase. To be sure, Strong warned of perils littering the road to America's destiny. Unchecked immigration might swamp the country and dilute its vigor; Romanism or Mormonism might divert the righteous; socialism might enervate the nation's productive forces. But hazards overcome would merely heighten the glory of the victory. And that glory would dazzle even the most optimistic. "I believe it is fully in the hands of the Christians of the United States," Strong proclaimed, "during the next ten or fifteen years, to hasten or retard the coming of Christ's kingdom in the world by hundreds, and perhaps thousands, of years. We of this generation and nation occupy the Gibraltar of the ages which commands the world's future."[20]

Evangelicals like Fiske and Strong were sometimes slippery in explicating just how the American millennium would arrive. At times

[19] John Fiske, "Manifest Destiny," *Harper's*, March 1885.
[20] Josiah Strong, *Our Country: Its Possible Future and Its Present Crisis* (New York, 1885, 1891), 227.

they seemed to talk an exemplarist game, suggesting that the force of American example, combined with the smiling oversight of the Protestant Christian God, would suffice to convert the world to American institutions and practices. Yet they thoroughly subscribed to the Algerite notion that luck comes to those with pluck, and that God helps those who help themselves. Considering the means by which the Anglo-Saxons had helped themselves to North America and the other parts of the globe then under Anglo-Saxon sway, the Social Darwinists' vision of a world empire implied vindicationist policies of the most vigorous, not to say brutal, nature.

Ultimately, it was the vindicationism in the Social Darwinist view that stuck. Fiske and Strong might sometimes soft-pedal the struggle that would be required to reshape the world, in order to make the vision as broadly acceptable as possible. But the entire Darwinian scheme rested on the premise of struggle, as its more blunt-spoken proponents made plain – and its critics recognized. Max Nordau complained in the *North American Review* of the advantage Darwinist ideas conferred on the proponents of militarism in an age beguiled by science. "The greatest authority of all the advocates of war is Darwin," Nordau wrote. "Since the theory of evolution has been promulgated, they can cover their natural barbarism with the name of Darwin and proclaim the sanguinary instincts of their innermost hearts as the last word of science."[21]

William Graham Sumner's innermost heart may not have been inordinately sanguinary, but no one made the struggle for civilization plainer or used blunter speech in depicting it. Sumner, the single most influential Social Darwinist in America, railed at the charitable efforts of persons who dared to tamper with the unfettered operation of free-market capitalism, arguing that melioration merely encouraged the poor in their shiftless ways. "It may be said," he wrote in 1883, "that those whom humanitarians and philanthropists call the weak are the ones through whom the productive and conservative forces of society are wasted. They constantly neutralize and destroy the finest efforts of the wise and industrious, and are a dead weight on the society in all its struggles to realize any better things."[22]

---

[21] Richard Hofstadter, *Social Darwinism in American Thought, 1860–1915* (Boston, 1955 ed.), 171.
[22] William Graham Sumner, *What Social Classes Owe to Each Other* (New York, 1883), 20–1.

When Sumner addressed issues of war and peace, he applied the same dismal view of humanity and the same hard-hearted calculus. Writing during the 1890s, while the great powers scrambled for colonies and spheres of influence across the globe, Sumner summarized the struggle for territory in vivid terms.

Earth hunger is the wildest craving of modern nations. They will shed their life blood to appease it. It gratifies national vanity and economic expansion both at once. No reasoning can arrest it and no arguments satisfy it. At the present moment the states of Europe are carving up Africa as they carved up America in the eighteenth century. They set about the process ten years ago with most commendable deliberation, and with an attempt to establish rules of order for the process; but they are already snarling and growling at each other over the process, like hungry tigers over their prey.

Sumner growled himself at the idea of territorial expansion, not because of the conflict it entailed but because it lessened population pressure at home. "When there is plenty of land, the penalties of all social follies, vices, and ignorance are light." Yet, misguided or not, expansionism was changing the face of the globe. It produced "a collision of the civilized and the uncivilized," in which the latter almost always fell beneath the crushing weight of the former. Of the nations beyond Europe and North America, only Japan had managed to join the modern world on terms approaching equality. Predictably, Sumner held that sympathy for peoples and countries that couldn't make the transition was as wasted as sympathy for the domestic poor. "The inevitable doom of those who cannot or will not come into the new world system is that they must perish. Philanthropy may delay their fate, and it certainly can prevent any wanton and cruel hastening of it; but it cannot avert it because it is brought on by forces which carry us all along like dust upon a whirlwind."[23]

Sumner didn't quite say that war, the form the whirlwind most commonly assumed, was a blessing to humanity. If nothing else, war's great destructiveness too often failed to discriminate between what deserved saving and what required liquidation. Nonetheless, war had played a vital role in the evolution of nations. "While men were fighting for glory and greed, for revenge and superstition, they

---

[23] Albert Galloway Keller and Maurice R. Davie, eds., *Essays of William Graham Sumner* (New Haven, Conn., 1934), 1:187–9, 195.

were building human society. They were acquiring discipline and cohesion; they were learning cooperation, perseverance, fortitude, and patience. . . . War forms larger social units and produces states. . . . The great conquests have destroyed what was effete and opened the way for what was viable." States mustn't enter into war lightly, and politicians who proposed war for partisan purposes were no better than criminals. All the same, wars would come, even to the most honorable nations and individuals. Prudence dictated accepting this fact and making the most of it. "War is like other evils; it must be met when it is unavoidable, and such gain as can be got from it must be won." In any event, war would work its effects regardless of the reasons and intentions of those responsible for starting it. "We must remember that the motives from which men act have nothing at all to do with the consequences of their action."[24]

VII

Sumner went too far with this last statement. Few Americans, at any rate, would have accepted it. During the 1890s, American exemplarists and vindicators remained as divided as ever over the proper role for the United States with respect to the world. While the Social Darwinists and other vindicators made their case boldly and vigorously, the exemplarists weren't about to yield without a fight, as the imminent, and indeed incipient, debate regarding an American overseas empire would demonstrate. But if the exemplarists and the vindicators disagreed on the question of enlightenment versus compulsion in foreign policy, the two sides generally concurred on the more philosophical notion – and here parted company with Sumner – that while consequences might not mirror motivations exactly, a significant causal relationship between the two existed.

Without faith in such a connection, Americans would have found it virtually impossible to sustain the belief – which nearly all of them held – that they had something unique to offer the world. They intended to do good for their fellow human beings, and they expected their accomplishments to reflect their intentions, at least approximately. Most Americans in the 1890s, following their forebears, accepted that God – perhaps working through the Darwinian device of

[24] Albert Galloway Keller, ed., *War and Other Essays by William Graham Sumner* (New Haven, Conn., 1911), 15–6, 35.

natural selection – had specially blessed their country. Most retained the belief that this blessing imposed on them a special obligation to promote the welfare of the human race. After slightly over a hundred years of national existence, Americans still perceived themselves as harbingers and agents of a better future for the planet. Providence smiled on America, as before. While it continued to do so – and few forecast frowns – Americans would continue to have a duty to share their blessings. And they would continue to quarrel over how the sharing might best be accomplished.

2

Brooks Adams:
Marx for Imperialists

I

As the nineteenth century drew to a close, two ideas seized American politics. The first was progressivism, which posited a need for reforming the American system of governance to correspond to the changed economic and social conditions wrought by industrialization. The second was imperialism, which proclaimed a civilizing mission for America to the world at large. To some degree, imperialism was simply the manifestation in foreign affairs of the progressive mindset. The progressives intended to remake American society in their own image, as a paragon of education, efficiency, and middle-class values; in the bargain, they would consolidate their political power at the expense of urban bosses and others beyond the pale of their approval. The imperialists aimed to accomplish a similar double-play in the territories the country acquired abroad: While uplifting the benighted, America would secure access to markets, investment opportunities, and positions strategic to the defense of American interests.

Not surprisingly, the personnel of the two movements overlapped. The first progressive president, Theodore Roosevelt, epitomized American imperialism in word and deed. Woodrow Wilson, whose presidency marked the progressive apogee, was no less an imperialist than Roosevelt, although it took Wilson, America, and the world some time to recognize that fact. Imperialist-progressives occupied humbler positions as well – in the cabinet departments and Congress, in the colonial administrations of the Philippines and Puerto Rico, in editorial offices around the United States, in academia, and wherever people pondered how the planet might be improved.

But the overlap was far from complete, and a sizable contingent of progressives rejected the imperialist program from the start. Embracing the exemplarist perspective, they contended that the United States must order its own affairs before presuming to refashion humanity at large. Where imperialist progressives detected a dovetailing between reforms at home and abroad, between bringing good government to Manhattan and good government to Manila, anti-imperialist progressives perceived a contradiction. Overseas adventures, the latter contended, would distract the American people from efforts to solve domestic problems and would encourage the forces of reaction. Empire required a large army and navy; empire fostered a constellation of values antithetical to democracy; empire had ruined Rome; empire would ruin America.

II

Brooks Adams had empire – Rome in particular – on the brain. The Adamses of Brooks' generation felt themselves heirs of a dynasty in decline. The glory days of the clan lay in the era of great-grandfather John, who had played a central role – *the* central role, the family could contend – in the most exciting political experiment in history. The tide had begun to ebb even as John left the presidency. His defeat at the hands of the democrat Jefferson and the scoundrel Burr – it was easy to get the adjectives confused – indicated the country's turn to notoriety at the expense of quality. Significantly, grandfather John Quincy's greatest success came during service as an appointed official, rather than an elected one. Quincy's term as president was as unfortunate as his father's, and his ouster, at the hands of the democrat-scoundrel Jackson, more ignominious. Father Charles Francis never received even a cabinet post. When Charles returned to the United States from London after a stint as ambassador during the Civil War, he discovered that America's industrial revolution was eliminating entirely what scant respect for the better classes the country's democratic revolution of five decades before had somehow spared.

Unlike brother Charles Francis Jr., thirteen years his senior, who served with distinction at Antietam and Gettysburg, Brooks Adams missed the fight to save the Union. Unlike second brother Henry, ten years older and already an adult when Lincoln entered the Executive Mansion, Brooks gained no practical experience from his father's posting as ambassador to Britain. Brooks did tag along during the

postwar adjudication of the *Alabama* claims in Geneva, but he im-
bibed insufficient enthusiasm for the law to last him more than a few
years at the bar back home. Ennui ensued, and by the late 1870s, as
the specter of his fourth decade approached, he was casting about for
another vocation. He contributed frequently to the *North American
Review*, conveniently edited by Henry and family friend Henry Cabot
Lodge. In 1877 he ran for the Massachusetts legislature. That he lost
by two votes and subsequently discovered that a pair of uncles had
cast their ballots for his opponent didn't improve an increasingly
dyspeptic disposition.

Unable to concentrate on his work, Brooks bolted Boston for Europe, the Levant, and points east. Travel soothed him somewhat, but
mostly it convinced him to devote his energies to unraveling the mys-
teries of human existence. Because he lacked direction in his own life,
he sought to discover direction in the life of the species. Because he
inhabited an age impressed with the rationalism of scientists and en-
gineers, he attempted to apply the scientific model to the development
of civilization. His first book, *The Emancipation of Massachusetts*,
was an effort, as he explained to Lodge, "to follow out the actions of
the human mind as we do the human body." He added, "I believe
they are one and subject to the same laws."[1]

Explicating and refining these laws became Adams's obsession,
and the effort carried his investigations far beyond the history of
Massachusetts. During the 1890s, the money question convulsed
American politics. Silverites demanded the remonetization of their
favorite metal; goldbugs denounced bimetallism as theft. To Adams,
the debate brought echoes of an earlier era. "I can see myself now,"
he recalled afterward, "as I stood one day amidst the ruins of Baalbek, and I can still feel the shock of surprise I then felt, when the
conviction dawned upon me, which I have since heard denounced as
a monstrous free-silver invention, that the fall of Rome came about
by a competition between slave and free labor and an inferiority in
Roman industry."[2]

The revelation at Baalbek provided the inspiration for Adams's
Law of Civilization and Decay. The book owed much to the notions
of the Social Darwinists, yet Adams was a Darwinist with a differ-

---

[1] Arthur F. Beringause, *Brooks Adams: A Biography* (New York, 1955), 82–3.
[2] Brooks Adams, "The Heritage of Henry Adams," introduction to Henry Adams,
   The Degradation of the Democratic Dogma (New York, 1919), 89.

ence. He was both more specific, in that he emphasized economic issues, and more general, in that he tied human evolution to the physical laws that governed not merely life on earth but the universe as a whole. Henry Adams attempted to summarize the thesis of what by the most favorable estimate was a challenging book.

On your wording of your Law, it seemed to me to come out, in its first equation thus, in the fewest possible words:

All Civilisation is Centralisation.
All Centralisation is Economy.
Therefore all Civilisation is the survival of the most economical (cheapest).

Darwin called it fittest, and in one sense fittest is the fittest word. Unfortunately it is always relative, and therefore liable to misunderstanding.

Your other formula is more difficult.

Under economical centralisation, Asia is cheaper than Europe.
The world tends to economical centralisation.
Therefore Asia tends to survive, and Europe to perish.[3]

This was a fair if incomplete assessment of what Brooks was up to. The book was clearly the work of an amateur historian, though one with broad interests. Ranging enormously across the terrain of human civilization, from republican Rome to imperial China and back to industrial Europe, Adams conducted a tour that sometimes left the reader stranded and gasping in a desert of abstractions. He ambled through decades, then leaped centuries in a sentence. He rarely offered guideposts at twists in the road, and he almost never stopped to summarize and gather the threads of the argument.

Adams implicitly confessed to confusing his readers: He reissued the book just months after its first appearance, with an interpretive preface. This 1896 edition was the one that gained widest circulation and attracted greatest attention. On its first page, Adams asserted that "the value of history lies not in the multitude of facts collected but in their relation to each other, and in this respect an author can have no larger responsibility than any other scientific observer." Presenting himself as the impartial inductivist, Adams explained that his

---

[3] Henry Adams in Charles A. Beard's introduction to Brooks Adams, *The Law of Civilization and Decay: An Essay on History* (New York, 1895, 1896, 1943), 35–6.

examination of the past had "forced" him to certain conclusions, the most noteworthy involving "the exceedingly small part played by conscious thoughts in moulding the fate of men." Adams was familiar with the work of William Graham Sumner, whose disdain for conscious human motives might have rubbed off. Or perhaps Adams arrived at his determinist conclusions independently. Whatever the case, Adams judged that "at the moment of action the human being almost invariably obeys an instinct, like an animal; only after action has ceased does he reflect." These involuntary, yet controlling, instincts divided men into distinct types. "Impelled by fear, one type will rush upon an enemy, and another will run away; while the love of women or of money has stamped certain races as sharply as ferocity or cunning has stamped the lion or the fox."

Further, instincts, like other biological traits, were strongly hereditary. "If these instincts be transmitted from generation to generation, it is plain that as the external world changes, those who receive this heritage must rise or fall in the social scale, according as their nervous system is well or ill adapted to the conditions to which they are born." Getting personal, Brooks added, "Nothing is commoner, for example, than to find families who have been famous in one century sinking into obscurity in the next, not because the children have degenerated" – perish the thought! – "but because a certain field of activity which afforded the ancestor full scope has been closed against his offspring."

Adams modestly outlined his project as an attempt "to classify a few of the more interesting intellectual phases through which human society must, apparently, pass, in its oscillations between barbarism and civilization, or, what amounts to the same thing, in its movement from a condition of physical dispersion to one of concentration." His theory, he said, was based on "the accepted scientific principle that the law of force and energy is of universal application in nature, and that animal life is one of the outlets through which solar energy is dissipated." Human thought and feelings were particular outlets for solar energy, and on their path to dissipation they took two forms primarily: fear and greed. Fear, which stimulated the imagination, gave rise to superstition and belief in the invisible, and it ultimately produced a priesthood. Greed fostered aggression, which found release first in war but eventually in trade.

For the ambitious among his readers, Adams connected social institutions and solar energy to other grand, more encompassing hy-

potheses like one postulating that "the velocity of the social movement of any community is proportionate to its energy and mass, and
its centralization is proportionate to its velocity." Those impatient
with such nebulous formulae could content themselves following Adams's argument tracing the evolution of human societies along an
axis leading from fear to greed as the dominant intellectual and psychological force. While societies were emerging from barbarism, Adams said, the ruling class identified with the priesthood, the group
that exploited humanity's instinctive fear of the unknown and uncontrollable. Gradually, as the realm of the known and controllable grew
larger, fear diminished and with it the hold of the priests on the
popular imagination. Greed emerged as the primary motif, and a new
ruling class, expert in the manipulation and satisfaction of greed,
came to the fore.

The transition resulted in a net loss to society. The honest martial
virtues of the age of semi-barbarism and of the transition period gave
way to the decadent qualities of the counting house. Adams devoted
considerable space to demonstrating the greater virility of warriors
compared to those who came after. Describing the Romans during
the last days of the western empire, he wrote, "They lacked the martial and amatory instincts. As a general rule one salient characteristic
of the later reigns was a sexual lassitude yielding only to the most
potent stimulants." The situation grew worse as the traders took
over. "Women seem never to have more than moderately appealed
to the senses of the economic man. The monied magnate seldom ruins
himself for love, and chivalry would have been as foreign to a Roman
senator under Diocletian as it would be now to a Lombard Street
banker." Indifference bred – so to speak – infertility, and greed-
directed societies gradually lost their ability to reproduce.

Summarizing this aspect of his thesis, Adams described "a progressive law of civilization," with each stage of development typified by
specific intellectual, moral, and physical traits and with each transition marked by particular changes. As the commercial class of merchants and bankers replaced the priests and warriors, certain evils
befell society. "The economic supersedes the martial mind, being superior in bread winning.... Nature begins to sift the economic
minds themselves, culling a favored aristocracy of the craftiest and
subtlest types; choosing, for example, the Armenian in Byzantium,
the Marwari in India, and the Jew in London." The process continued: "As the costly nervous system of the soldier becomes an encum-

brance, organisms which can exist on less successively supplant each other, until the limit of endurance is reached. Thus the Slavs exterminated the Greeks in Thrace and Macedonia, the Mahrattas and the Moslems dwindle before the low caste tribes of India, and the instinct of self-preservation has taught white races to resist an influx of Chinese."

The end of this twin process of selection – in favor of the effete and cunning, against the virile and brave – was inescapable. "When nature has finished this double task, civilization has reached its zenith. Humanity can ascend no higher."[4]

III

There was considerably more to Adams's account of human history than this. What provoked the greatest controversy at the time of publication was his lengthy analysis of the role of money through the ages, with conclusions that bolstered the silverites in their attack on gold – to the consternation of Adams's own class. But for those concerned with the general trend of world civilization, Adams's centuries-spanning theory was the essential issue. It left little room for optimism. Theodore Roosevelt declared in a review that "few more melancholy books have been written." Roosevelt, as a sound-money man, accounted Adams unreliable on the currency question; as an advocate of a strong military, he thought the author exaggerated the demise of the soldier; as a believer in the ability of individuals and nations to shape their destinies, he rejected Adams's determinism. All the same, he was compelled to concede that Adams's theory contained "a very ugly element of truth."[5]

Alfred Thayer Mahan's reaction was similar to Roosevelt's. By the mid-1890s, Mahan was well on his way to becoming the prototype of that class of defense intellectuals that would proliferate with the permanent mobilization of American society four wars hence. Already he enjoyed an unparalleled reputation as America's Clausewitz of the waves, and his books were read avidly in admiralties around the world. Samuel Clemens, in his days as a lecturer, used to offer sponsors a choice of dozens of titles for talks; one amazed host asked how he managed to have so many topics ready. Easy, Clemens re-

---

[4] Brooks Adams, *Law of Civilization and Decay*, 57–60, 333–34, 339–40.
[5] Theodore Roosevelt review, *Forum*, January 1897.

plied: The titles varied, but the lectures didn't. So it was with Mahan. In fact, unlike the novelist, the navalist didn't always bother much about changing titles. In *The Influence of Sea Power Upon History*, *The Influence of Sea Power Upon the French Revolution and Empire*, *The Interest of America in Sea Power*, *Sea Power in Its Relations to the War of 1812*, several other books and scores of articles, Mahan pounded home a single point: Who owned the waves won the wars.

Like Roosevelt, Mahan denied the determinism that characterized Brooks Adams's work. The United States could learn from history, Mahan declared, and it could act on what it learned and thus shape the future. Explaining America's near brush with disaster in the War of 1812, for example, Mahan attributed early losses to "the deeply mortifying condition to which the country was reduced by parsimony in preparation." In the modern era, American preparation must include construction of a navy adequate to the far-flung interests of a nation of traders, acquisition of rights to naval bases and coaling stations located conveniently in the oceans frequented by American vessels, and development of a frame of mind – "a Twentieth-Century outlook" – eager to project American power across the globe. Such preparations wouldn't come cheap, but the alternatives would prove far dearer in the long run. If the United States made the necessary investment, Americans needn't fret for a moment about going the way of Rome.[6]

IV

But the Roman question wouldn't be settled so easily. In 1898, in no small part as a consequence of the activities of Mahan and Roosevelt, the American military trounced the forces of Spain. The Spanish-American War, by extending the American reach deep into the Caribbean and projecting American power far across the Pacific, catapulted the United States to global influence, and in doing so compelled Americans to consider carefully the issues of the evolution of empires and civilizations Brooks Adams had been investigating. It also drew the line between exemplarists and vindicators more distinctly than ever.

[6] A. T. Mahan, *Sea Power in Its Relation to the War of 1812* (New York, 1905), 1: vi; idem, *The Interest of America in Sea Power, Present and Future* (New York, 1897), 217.

Among the exemplarists of the day, Carl Schurz claimed the longest experience. Since the 1860s, Schurz, a German refugee of the
revolutionary class of 1848, had been expostulating against expansionism. He opposed the acquisition of Santo Domingo in 1869 on
grounds that it was racially unassimilable by a nation with racial
problems enough already; twenty-five years later he castigated the
expansionist project of annexing Hawaii, contending that those islands, far from strengthening America, would become America's
"Achilles' heel."[7]

When the Spanish war raised the prospect of annexing the Philippines and Puerto Rico, Schurz argued that such an extension of
American rule would combine the worst aspects of seizing Santo Domingo and Hawaii. If the Hawaiian Islands were vulnerable, the Philippines, thrice as far away, were completely indefensible. If Santo
Domingo included unassimilable races, Puerto Rico and the Philippines together embraced a cultural cacophony – "Spanish-Americans,
with all the mixture of Indian and negro blood, and Malays and
other unspeakable Asiatics, by the tens of millions."

In Schurz's view, an imperial course would thoroughly corrupt the
United States. The annexationists spoke of spreading American values across the oceans; instead they would eviscerate American values
within America itself. Already American troops in the Philippines
were killing Filipinos; already the government in Washington had
fallen into deception to cover its course. To President McKinley's
claim that the Filipinos were to blame for the fighting, Schurz responded, "When we hear him say to the people such things, we fairly
hold our breath and bow our heads." The continuing conflict in the
Philippines, Schurz contended, was nothing less than a war of conquest. It would unleash emotions and social forces that would wreck
the foundations of the American republic. "What a democracy based
upon universal suffrage like ours needs most to ensure its stability is
an element of conservative poise in itself. This can be furnished only
by popular faith in the principles underlying the democratic institutions; by popular reverence for high ideals and traditions; by popular
respect for constitutional forms and restraints." In attempting to create an imperial democracy, the McKinley administration was destroying the basis for faith, reverence and respect – and therefore the
basis of democracy itself. "The only motive forces left in such a de-

---

[7] Carl Schurz, "Manifest Destiny," *Harper's*, October 1893.

mocracy will be greed and passion. I can hardly imagine any kind of government more repellent than a democracy that has ceased to believe in anything."

Schurz found the situation utterly discouraging. Not long after the Senate rejected his counsel and ratified the treaty ending the war with Spain and annexing the Philippines and Puerto Rico, he reflected, lamenting, on his half-century in America.

Can you imagine the feelings of a man who all his life has struggled for human liberty and popular government, who for that reason had to flee from his native country, who believed he had found what he sought in this Republic, and thus came to love this Republic even more than the land of his birth, and who at last, at the close of his life, sees that beloved Republic in the clutches of sinister powers which seduce and betray it into an abandonment of its most sacred principles and traditions and push it into policies and practices even worse than those which once he had to flee from?[8]

William Graham Sumner joined Schurz – albeit from a different direction – in asserting that annexation of overseas territory would ruin America. "The notion that gain of territory is gain of wealth and strength for the state, after the expedient size has been won, is a delusion," Sumner wrote in 1896. "What private individuals want is free access, under order and security, to any part of the earth's surface, in order that they may avail themselves of its natural resources for their use, either by investment or commerce." The American government should concentrate on assuring access – in the case of Hawaii, then the object of discussion, by a treaty guaranteeing free trade. To claim sovereignty over lands far from American shores would merely multiply the republic's responsibilities without enlarging its privileges. "This confederated state of ours was never planned for indefinite expansion, or for an imperial policy." Stretching America's borders across the Pacific would threaten American security and necessitate measures "disastrous to democracy." History attested to the fact. "If we had never taken Texas and Northern Mexico we should never have had secession."[9]

Sumner subsequently decried the war with Spain, placing its pater-

[8] Robert L. Beisner, *Twelve Against Empire* (New York, 1968), 27–34.
[9] William Graham Sumner, "The Fallacy of Territorial Extension," *Forum*, June 1896.

nity in politics and its progeny in cynicism. "It was a move of partisan tactics in the strife of parties at Washington." The uproar precipitating the conflict demonstrated the corrosive effect of imperialist schemes on political dialogue in America. "Whenever a voice was raised in behalf of deliberation and the recognized maxims of statesmanship, it was howled down in a storm of vituperation and cant. Everything was done to make us throw away sobriety of thought and calmness of judgment and to inflate all expressions with sensational epithets and turgid phrases." The people of America had yet to demonstrate they could manage their own affairs; to engage the engines of empire would make resolution of America's domestic difficulties only harder. Meanwhile, such a course would betray the vision that had inspired the founding fathers – not to mention preclude the low-tax, laissez-faire utopia of Sumner's Social Darwinist dreams. The imperialist brief, Sumner said, rested on appeals to "national vanity" and "national cupidity"; its advocates appeared entirely ready to throw the Constitution "into the gutter." Their professions were seductive but utterly wrong-headed. "They are delusions, and they will lead us to ruin."[10]

A variety of other public thinkers, including William James, E. L. Godkin, David Starr Jordan, Charles Eliot Norton, and Henry Demarest Lloyd, lent their voices to the anti-imperialist chorus. Samuel Clemens satirized "the Blessings-of-Civilization Trust" and was joined in his sneers by Ambrose Bierce.[11]

Fewer bookish types aligned themselves with the imperialists: Most of those who supported annexation liked to consider themselves men of action, even if their participation was primarily vicarious. Theodore Roosevelt had a foot in each camp – of action and reflection – but as one whose efforts at the Navy Department had played a signal role in sending Commodore Dewey to Manila, and who had participated personally in the conquest of Cuba, his enthusiasm for annexation came as no surprise. Roosevelt denounced as scurrilous the charge that acquisition of the Philippines constituted imperialism. There was nothing "even remotely resembling 'imperi-

---

[10] William Graham Sumner, "The Conquest of the United States by Spain," *Yale Law Journal*, January 1899.

[11] Mark Twain, "To the Person Sitting in Darkness," *North American Review*, February 1901.

alism'" in American actions in the Philippines, he shouted. Expansion, yes, much like America's historic expansion across North America; but imperialism, no. Roosevelt asserted that Americans mustn't apologize for desiring to secure American interests abroad. The United States had a large foreign trade that needed defending; this required control of strategic positions such as the Philippines offered. In any event, to argue against acquisition was to deny fate. The war had happened. American forces had seized the islands. "The question now is not whether we shall expand – for we have already expanded – but whether we should contract. . . . We have hoisted our flag, and it is not fashioned of the stuff which can be quickly hauled down."[12]

By no means the least consideration was that American sovereignty in the Philippines would benefit humanity. American expansion advanced the frontier of progress, Roosevelt avowed; to plant the American flag overseas was "to bring civilization into the waste places of the earth." The Filipinos would gain directly. "The peoples whose administration we have taken over shall have their condition made better and not worse by the fact that they have come under our sway." As for the world at large: "Every man should realize that it is for the interests of mankind to have the higher supplant the lower life."[13]

Henry Cabot Lodge joined Roosevelt in vigorous assertion of the vindicationist position. The historian-turned-senator had discovered Mahanism about the same time Roosevelt had, and throughout the 1890s he pressed for adoption of a "large policy" for the United States. During an 1895 dispute with Britain over the boundary of Venezuela, the Massachusetts Republican distinguished himself for a broad construction of the Monroe doctrine and for a rousing advocacy of American involvement even beyond the western hemisphere. It was eat or be eaten, he declared. "The modern movement is all toward concentration of people and territory into great nations and large dominions. The great nations are rapidly absorbing for their future expansion and their present defense all the waste places of the earth. It is a movement which makes for civilization and advance-

[12] Howard K. Beale, *Theodore Roosevelt and the Rise of America to World Power* (Baltimore, 1956), 68–70.
[13] Warren Lester Lashley, "The Debate over Imperialism in the United States, 1898–1900," Ph.D. dissertation (Northwestern University, 1966), 110–1.

ment of the race." As one of the great nations of the earth, the United States "must not fall out of the line of march."[14]

Lodge defended annexation of the Philippines as both securing an American foothold in the Far East and benefiting the Filipinos. He rejected the anti-imperialist argument that the Filipinos ought to be able to decide for themselves whether to accept the blessings of American rule, and that their armed resistance indicated disapproval. The Filipino rebels, Lodge asserted, hardly represented mass opinion in the islands. "The insurgent force, as an effective force, and the insurgent rebellion, as an effective rebellion, existed solely because of the victory of Admiral Dewey." Nor did the anti-imperialists' claim that the United States had somehow stolen sovereignty from the Filipinos stand up to examination. "There was no sovereignty there whatever except the sovereignty of Spain, and we succeeded to the sovereignty." Americans daily displayed their fitness to rule the islands, contrary claims of oppression and mistreatment notwithstanding. "There has never been an act of oppression against the Filipinos by any American soldiers or by the American forces of any kind in the Philippine Islands. . . . Their oppression exists solely in speeches in the United States Senate." If America had erred in dealings with the Filipinos, it had erred on the side of leniency. "They have been treated with the utmost consideration and the utmost kindness, and, after the fashion of Orientals, they have mistaken kindness for timidity." Critics of American policy, by spreading untruths and inflaming the insurgency, did neither the Filipinos nor America any service. The sooner calm replaced passion, the sooner the United States could turn to the business of building up the Philippines, to the welfare of all concerned.[15]

The most effusive statement of the case for annexation came from Albert Beveridge, who, like Lodge and Roosevelt, would be remembered as both a politician and a historian. At the turn of the century, the Indiana senator was best known as an orator, the William Jennings Bryan of the G.O.P. Beveridge soared above the Senate floor at the climax of the Philippine debate. He recited the standard argument regarding the necessity for expanded markets: Manila would serve as

[14] Henry Cabot Lodge, "England, Venezuela, and the Monroe Doctrine," *North American Review*, June 1895; idem, "Our Blundering Foreign Policy," *Forum*, March 1895.

[15] *Congressional Record*, Feb. 7, 1899, 1533.

the commercial gateway to China. Strategically, the islands constituted the "Gibraltar of the Pacific"; in American hands the archipel-
ago would secure America's Pacific shore against attack from any
quarter.

But a full understanding of the Philippine question, Beveridge declared, required a proper understanding of America's obligation to
the world. The question was deeper than any question of party politics, deeper than any question of mere foreign policy. "It is elemental.
It is racial. God has not been preparing the English-speaking and
Teutonic peoples for a thousand years for nothing but vain and idle
self-contemplation and self-admiration." By no means! "He has
made us the master organizers of the world to establish system where
chaos reigns. He has given us the spirit of progress to overwhelm the
forces of reaction throughout the earth. He has made us adepts in
government that we may administer government among savage and
senile peoples." Americans must recognize how fully the human race
depended on them, and on Providence acting through them. "Were it
not for a force such as this the world would relapse into barbarism
and night. . . . This is the divine mission of America, and it holds for
us all the profit, all the glory, all the happiness possible to man. We
are trustees of the world's progress, guardians of its righteous
peace."[16]

V

At a moment of progressivist optimism regarding the ability of enlightened government to improve the condition of human society, the
anti-annexationists found themselves fighting uphill in trying to persuade readers and listeners that American efforts to regenerate the
Filipinos not only would fail but would backfire and damage the
United States. The annexationists, on the other hand, enjoyed the
double advantage of delivering a message Americans liked to hear
and of capitalizing on the momentum developed during the recent
splendid (to use the adjective employed by John Hay, whose irony
was lost in most translations) war with Spain. Americans, as always,
were happy to believe they were engaged in the redemption of humanity. Further, the advocates of annexation could credibly contend
that the crusade to free Cuba led logically to the effort to uplift the

[16] *Congressional Record*, Jan. 19, 1900, 704–11.

Filipinos. That acquiring the Philippines would serve American commercial and strategic interests simply made the bargain the more attractive. For all these reasons, a ratifying majority of the Senate accepted the vindicationists' argument and awarded America its first overseas colonies.

Brooks Adams, ever seeking the deeper meaning behind events, attempted to place the Spanish war and its denouement in historical context. His ruminations took shape in two books: *America's Economic Supremacy* and *The New Empire*. Both works displayed the determined determinism of *The Law of Civilization and Decay*, and despite the seemingly upbeat tone of the titles, each evoked much of the gloom of that earlier work.

"Could we regard the Spanish War as calmly as if it were a thing of the past," Adams wrote in *America's Economic Supremacy*, "we should doubtless perceive that it formed a link in a long chain of events which, when complete, would represent one of those memorable revolutions wherein civilizations pass from an old to a new condition of equilibrium. The last such revolution ended at Waterloo; the one now at hand promises to be equally momentous." Waterloo to Adams signified the migration of economic predominance – and the military power that in the modern world accompanied it – from the European continent to Britain. In the mid-eighteenth century, Britain, France and Germany had been roughly equal in industrial production. By the second decade of the nineteenth century, Britain outproduced the two major continental powers combined. But economic evolution had continued, indeed at a faster pace than before. During the following fifty years, the United States overtook all three, with the result that on the eve of the late war, American mills produced nearly 10 million tons of pig iron, to 9 million for Britain, 7 million for Germany, and less than 3 million for France.

In the face of these statistics, which Adams buttressed with many more telling a similar story, the passing of economic world power across the Atlantic appeared indisputable. In fact, so dependent had the British become on trade with the United States that Britain might be described as "a fortified outpost of the Anglo-Saxon race, overlooking the eastern continent and resting upon America." Yet the prize didn't come free. As Britain had discovered, managing an empire required constant vigilance and effort. "The United States thus stands face to face with the gravest conjecture that can confront a people. She must protect the outlets of her trade, or run the risk of suffocation." In Europe, American hegemony was challenged by the same coalition that had threatened the British, to which coalition the British themselves might conceivably be added one day.

But the principal danger lay in the Far East, where collapsing China was producing an irresistible vacuum. "Already America has been drawn into war over the dismemberment of one dying civilization," Adams wrote. "And it cannot escape the conflict which must be waged over the carcass of another. Even now the hostile forces are converging on the shores of the Yellow Sea: the English and Germans to the south; Russia at Port Arthur, covering Peking; while Japan hungers for Korea, the key to the great inlet." The Philippines, now American, appeared "a predestined base for the United States in a conflict which probably is as inevitable as that with Spain." Though Americans might attempt to avoid this climactic battle, their efforts would fail. "It is in vain that men talk of keeping free of entanglements. Nature is omnipotent; and nations must float with the tide. Whither the exchanges flow, they must follow; and they will follow as long as their vitality endures. . . . These great catastrophes escape human control."

Adams suggested that an alliance with Britain could diminish the dangers America faced. An "Anglo-Saxon coalition," he said, would "alter profoundly the equilibrium of the world." Yet the United States mustn't count too heavily on the British, whose civilization showed definite signs of terminal decay. "The British, as a nation, are wasteful and profuse" – a fact evidenced by Britain's large and growing trade deficit. The consequences of British profligacy extended far beyond Britain itself. "Few unprejudiced observers have ever doubted that much of the financial stringency which prostrated Argentina, Australia, and America between 1890 and 1897 originated in the withdrawal of English capital." More recently, Britain had demonstrated its advancing decrepitude on the battlefield in South Africa, where "inertia and feebleness" characterized its campaigns.

Adams laid great emphasis on the outflow of British capital from the United States during the 1890s. He considered the financial panic of 1893, triggered by large withdrawals of British funds, the seminal event of the decade. (That the panic of 1893 nearly ruined the Adams family and almost forced Brooks to take a regular job doubtless figured, if perhaps not consciously, in his estimate of the gravity of the event.) Even the Spanish war was insignificant compared to "the catastrophe of 1893." But the catastrophe turned out to be more Europe's than America's, for the shock of 1893 provoked American producers to seek foreign markets for their goods. "In the end we succeeded in creating an enormous balance of trade in our favor, but in so doing we shook the civilization of the Eastern continent to its centre. As a result of our high fortune Europe is steadily sinking into economic inferiority."

Adams argued a neomercantilist line on trade. International commerce, he contended, inevitably created winners and losers. "Necessarily, as America gains in momentum Europe relatively loses. The mines of the precious metals failed her long ago, copper followed, and now iron and coal have reached a price which threatens to hamper competition. Under such conditions the people of Europe stand at bay, since ruin, more or less complete and immediate, menaces them if they fail to provide themselves with new resources as cheap and abundant as those of America."

From the wreckage of Europe, Adams saw one country rising, although he deemed Russia as much an Asian power as a European. For most of the nineteenth century, Britain had occupied itself circumscribing Russian ambitions. "From Waterloo down to 1899 Great Britain acted as a sort of balance wheel to human society. She operated as the containing force of civilization." (Both Adams's idea and his language would be appropriated by latter-day containers of Russia half a century hence.) The South African war signaled the end of that era. "The United Kingdom promises to be unequal to assume heavier burdens than those she now bears. Having failed to display either the military or the financial energy anticipated of her, by herself, her friends, or her enemies, England has stood aside, and as she has effaced herself Russia has dilated." Russian power had flowed into Persia and Korea; evidence suggested impending movement against China.

Americans commonly misjudged Russia, Adams said, by seeing in the Russians' eastward expansion the mirror of their own drive west. Americans expected the Russians' frontier experience to have produced traits of national character similar to their own. This view had little connection to reality. The two countries inhabited different historical eras, with the Russians opposing great age to America's youth. "Russia is venerable, even judged by Asiatic standards." The czar traced his divine right of rule to the emperors of Byzantium, and centuries before America was a gleam in the greedy eyes of conquis-

tadors and pirate-princes, Kiev claimed the riches of the trade with
the East.

Russia labored under significant burdens. The country was inhabited by "an archaic race: that is to say, by people who move more
slowly, and therefore more wastefully, than their Western contemporaries." (Adams didn't explain the "therefore" in this sentence,
which seemed to contradict his criticism of the also profligate, but
faster-moving, British.) The Russians, moreover, while patient and
tenacious, were "ignorant, uninventive, indolent, and improvident."
All the same, Russia's enormous natural resources and its strategic
geographic location made it a formidable rival for the century to
come. "Russia must play a leading part in the future of Asia." Should
the Russians somehow reshape themselves in the image of the efficient nations of the West, eliminating the feudal vestiges that retarded
their development, their influence would increase the more. "What a
social revolution in Russia would portend transcends human fore-
sight, but probably its effects would be felt throughout the world."

The Russians wouldn't take Asia without a contest. While the British were fading, Germany and Japan stood ready to do battle for the
spoils of China. The Russians' major competitor, however, would be
the United States. "Our geographical position," Adams said, "our
wealth, and our energy preeminently fit us to enter upon the development of eastern Asia, and to reduce it to a part of our economic
system." American wishes would have little weight in the matter.
"The laws of nature are immutable. Money will flow where it earns
most return, and investments once made are always protected." Welcome the idea or not, Americans were about to be swept into the
maelstrom, into the contest on which would hinge the economic supremacy of the next century. Adams concluded: "There can be no
escape."[17]

While Adams devoted *America's Economic Supremacy* to setting
out the facts of the current situation, he used *The New Empire* to
provide the theoretical framework. The latter book was as ambitious
as *The Law of Civilization and Decay*, but the argument was better
organized and easier to follow. To his previous amalgam of physics,
biology, and economics, he now added geography. "All my observa-

---

[17] Brooks Adams, *America's Economic Supremacy* (New York, 1900), 1–10, 19–25,
149–50, 162, 195–203, 218–22.

tions," he wrote, "lead me to the conclusion that geographical conditions have exercised a great, possibly a preponderating, influence over man's destiny." The key to empire lay in control of trade routes and the products that traveled over them. From prehistory, humans had engaged in commercial exchange. In the earliest days, metal constituted the principal item of traffic, and areas favored with workable metal deposits held an advantage over other territories. The rise of the Egyptian empire, Adams contended, owed chiefly to Egypt's control of the copper mines of Arabia and the gold and iron of Nubia. As civilization developed and commerce broadened, other centers of commerce emerged. Nineveh came to power along the caravan route from Bactria to the Mediterranean, while Persia arose on the silk road to Cathay.

History turned on trade, Adams explained. One civilization supplanted another as it seized – by force, cunning or industry – control of a greater portion of the available commerce of a region. Lust not for Helen but for access to the Black Sea had triggered the Trojan war. Rome fell as a result of a lack of exports. Moscow replaced Kiev when the purchases of Constantinople declined and those of the Hanse increased. The process of transformation never ceased, for wealth bred sloth and attracted competition. "Prosperity has always borne within itself the seeds of its own decay."

Until the end of the fifteenth century, the center of gravity of commerce approximated the center of mass of the Eurasian-African tricontinent. But with the discovery of the New World and the ocean routes to the Indies, advantage passed to the states with Atlantic exposure. Spain, Portugal, France, Holland, and England became the principal competitors in the race to fill the niche opened by the voyages of exploration. The Iberians first took the lead; the Dutch pressed close behind. By the start of the eighteenth century, Britain and France had surged ahead. When Britain defeated France in the long series of wars ending in 1815, the British definitively grasped the guiding lever of world trade and began expanding their economic empire to globe-girdling proportions.

Yet the wheel never ceased turning. As the Far East had once excited the cupidity of Westerners, so it was doing again. The foreign devils fought to master the markets of China, and their noisy presence had awakened hibernating Japan. China continued in decline, unable to defend itself – which tempted the exploiters still more – but the Japanese read the Western invasion as a warning to change or die. Modernizing in the age of steam and electricity, Japan accomplished in a generation what had required centuries in the West. As in Britain before, Japan's energy exceeded the territory the country occupied. As had Britain, Japan began extending its reach across the water. And just as the center of commerce and civilization had proceeded from the heartland of Eurasia to the Atlantic shore, so it would continue advancing west. "Each man can ponder the history of the last fifty years," Adams wrote, "and judge for himself whether the facts show that Great Britain apparently lies in the wake, and Japan in the path, of the advancing cyclone." Adams had no doubt they did.

Where did this leave America? At present, at the center of things. "The vortex of the cyclone is near New York," Adams wrote. "No such activity prevails elsewhere; nowhere are undertakings so gigantic, nowhere is administration so perfect; nowhere are such masses of capital centralized in single hands." As before, Adams deemed the process historically ineluctable, the work of forces beyond the capacity of mere individuals to control. "As the United States becomes an imperial market, she stretches out along the trade routes which lead from foreign countries to her heart, as every empire has stretched out from the days of Sargon to our own." The West Indies drifted toward America, as Mexico already had. A Panama canal would fasten Central America to the system. Americans were expanding into China, checking the advance of Germany and Russia in the process. Europe was being penetrated. "Great Britain especially is gradually assuming the position of a dependency, which must rely on us as the base from which she draws her food in peace, and without which she could not stand in war." Should the processes of the previous half century persist, as they doubtless would, the United States would soon control an empire outweighing all others combined. "The whole world will pay her tribute. Commerce will flow to her both from east and west."

Yet Americans mustn't think history would stop for them any more than for others. On the contrary, America's moment would probably pass more quickly than those of its predecessors. "Society is moving with intense velocity, and masses are gathering bulk with proportionate rapidity." The present equilibrium, coming after a period of economic disruption, was "delicate and unstable." "If so apparently slight a cause as a fall in prices for a decade has sufficed to propel the seat of empire across the Atlantic, an equally slight derangement of the administrative functions of the United States might force it to cross the Pacific."

As the whirlwind passed overhead, it couldn't but create strains within the country. "Under any circumstances an organism so gigantic as the American Union must generate friction." The friction had already developed between farm and city, between labor and capital, between borrower and lender. Any increase in the friction could destroy America's economic preeminence. "America holds its tenure of prosperity only on condition that she can undersell her rivals, and she cannot do so if her administrative machinery generates friction unduly." Adams saw little hope of resolving the problem; consequently he expected the center of economic gravity to continue migrating west.

Regardless of future prospects, America had no alternative to joining the fray. "Americans in former generations led a simple agricultural life. Possibly such a life was happier than ours. Very probably keen competition is not a blessing." But the old life had vanished. "We cannot alter our environment. Nature has cast the United States into the vortex of the fiercest struggle which the world has ever known. She has become the heart of the economic system of the age, and she must maintain her supremacy by wit and by force, or share the fate of the discarded."[18]

VI

The significance of Adams's theories didn't consist in their ability to persuade the dubious among his contemporaries. Most persons of intellectual and political stature considered him an eccentric, even a crank. And without the personal contacts he enjoyed through family and friends, his work almost certainly wouldn't have received the middling attention it did.

But Adams's ideas had two redeeming and highly relevant characteristics. First, by accounting for the undeniable economic impetus behind American imperialism in terms that transcended the class struggle, they offered an attractive and plausible alternative to the socialist notions of Marx and his up-and-coming Russian disciple Lenin. A reader of Adams could accept Marx's economic perspective

[18] Brooks Adams, *The New Empire* (New York, 1902), iii, xxxiii-xxxiv, 86, 208–11.

on the past without buying into the German theorist's class-revolutionary predictions for the future. For American imperialists, a thoroughly unrevolutionary class in a most unrevolutionary country, Adams's conservative radicalism held great appeal.

The second characteristic followed from the first. Just as Marx did for a century of socialist revolutionaries, Adams provided American imperialists with the cloak of inevitability. By treating American expansion as a continuation of trends reaching far into mists of prehistory, and, even more strikingly, by explaining the evolution of human societies as an expression of immutable laws of physics, Adams raised imperialism beyond the level of individual responsibility. With Adams in hand, proponents of imperialism could go their grasping way unbothered by pesky worries of right and wrong. What had morality to do with matters as impervious to human intervention as the laws of thermodynamics? Imperialists like Beveridge and Lodge and Mahan and Roosevelt might not have seriously questioned the rectitude of their actions in advocating American expansion, although the egregiousness of comments such as those Beveridge spouted over the Philippines betrayed at least a bit of protesting too much. Yet the opponents of imperialism demonstrated that there existed a strong strain of doubt as to whether imperialism would benefit either the United States or the territories imperialized. To those inclined to imperialism but unsure of its rightness, Adams furnished the reassurance of destiny. The reassurance came whether or not one accepted his dismal predictions regarding the future. For this reason, Adams's approach served the vindicationist purpose of Roosevelt and the other imperialists, however much they might dispute the tone and many of the specifics of his argument.

VII

Adams's theories gained additional attractiveness when events of the first decade of the twentieth century confirmed some particulars of his predictions. Several months before the outbreak of the Russo-Japanese War he reiterated that the Asian coast was the likely battleground between the imperialists. The Japanese looked to Asia for resources and markets, as did Russia, Germany, and Britain. For the United States, "Asia is the only certain base from whence we can draw raw material." Adams asserted that the great-power competition, while directed fundamentally at economic goals, would lead to military conflict. "There is but one way in which the possession of prizes of this nature can be determined, and that is by force."[19]

Although the United States avoided involvement in the fighting, Roosevelt's diplomatic intervention suggested that the next time it wouldn't. The prospect deepened Adams's pessimism, and he returned to his earlier theme of the decay of civilizations. In a 1910 essay, he defined civilization as "tantamount to centralization." Centralized life, he explained, was relatively costly on account of its complexity. "It is an economic axiom that, other things being equal, the cost of administration increases faster than the increase of the human mass to be administered." For this reason, unless a society enhanced its productive capacities at an ever accelerating rate, "a centralizing community must perish from inanition if it cannot live by plunder." Such a fate had overtaken the Romans, who first plundered, then perished.

The United States thus far had avoided the plunder-or-perish syndrome by unleashing the forces of science and technology. Yet in doing so it had run across the channel of social evolution onto the opposite shoal. Americans had learned how to produce but not how to turn production to useful ends. "We are abundantly inventive and can create wealth, but we cannot control the energy which we liberate." Economic competition, the prerequisite of America's industrial growth, had spawned its opposite, monopoly, which Adams took to be the epitome of centralization in the economic sphere. Monopoly begat turmoil, in the form of labor strikes and political agitation for regulation of the economy. Adams saw little hope for amelioration, given the applicable laws of science and civilization. "Monopoly is a natural phenomenon, as inexorable as the steam, the electricity, and the explosives which have created it under the guidance of the scientific mind. To attack monopoly is to attack the vital principle of our civilization. We may destroy monopoly, but with it we shall destroy civilization itself."[20]

Unfortunately, letting monopoly be monopoly afforded no solution, for monopoly appeared bent on self-destruction. Looking back over several hundred years of the history of the English-speaking peoples, Adams noted that social convulsions occurred about every

---

[19] Brooks Adams, "Economic Conditions for Future Defense," *Atlantic Monthly*, November 1903.
[20] Brooks Adams, "A Problem in Civilization," *Atlantic Monthly*, July 1910.

third generation. England's civil war and Glorious Revolution of the seventeenth century were followed by the imperial crisis and American revolution of the eighteenth, which in turn were followed by the American civil war of the nineteenth. In each case, the transition to a new level of social and political development required a violent rupturing of old forms. The third generation since Sumter had now reached maturity, Adams argued (apparently the generations of Adams's era turned over more rapidly than those of previous centuries, perhaps in accord with the accelerating pace of life generally). America was ripe for another rupture. Nor did it bode well for the peace of the world as a whole that domestic revolutions in countries of great importance to the international order often produced foreign wars. The American revolution had sparked a conflict among Britain, France, and Spain, while the French revolution had led to a quarter century of fighting that consumed nearly all of Europe and spread across the Atlantic. A new American revolution or civil war might well produce worse – in the industrial era, much worse.[21]

The fact that war began in Europe in 1914 before the crisis in America came to a head didn't fit Adams's model, but neither did it dispel his pessimism. On the contrary, it appeared to demonstrate that the influence of monopoly capitalism was more widespread and pernicious than he had thought. And the American reaction to the war showed that the decay in American society went deeper than he had known. Adams suspected that economic forces would drive the United States into the war, notwithstanding President Wilson's declaration of neutrality. Americans should prepare for the day. But he doubted they would, for Americans as a group refused to recognize that their government had any claim on their energies. In the name of democracy, they rejected mandatory military service and all else that limited their individual freedom. They elevated private self-interest so far above public interest that the latter disappeared entirely, producing the same irresponsibility in the political field that monopoly had produced in the realm of economics.

Writing at the beginning of 1916, Adams didn't profess to know who would win the war. Yet America already appeared a loser. Any country that couldn't command the loyalty and obedience of its inhabitants in time of danger – as the present time patently was – would not long prosper. "The hour cannot be far distant when some

[21] Brooks Adams, *The Theory of Social Revolutions* (New York, 1913).

superior because more cohesive and intelligent organism, such as nature has decreed shall always lie in wait for its victim, shall spring upon us and rend us as the strong have always rent those wretched because feeble creatures who are cursed with an aborted development."[22]

[22] Brooks Adams, "The American Democratic Ideal," *Yale Review*, January 1916.

3

Walter Lippmann and a New Republic *for a New Era*

I

Never a majority mood, Brooks Adams's pessimism was more out of place than ever during Woodrow Wilson's first term. The progressives who elected Wilson in 1912, as well as many of those who voted for Roosevelt, were not anti-determinists. They believed, for example, that the conditions in which individuals grew up and found themselves as adults strongly influenced their behavior – hence their emphasis on settlement work, child labor laws, minimum wages, and the like, which would improve society by fostering the improvement of individuals. But the progressives' determinism fell far short of what Adams had in mind when he described the emergence and decay of civilizations. Because it did, and because it allowed a large role for efforts at social betterment, its adherents found Adams's morbidness foreign.

The imperialism that had set Adams thinking about his grand themes likewise appeared out of place, at least as it applied to America. The war in the Philippines had demonstrated to Americans that holding an empire cost more than acquiring one, and they experienced no difficulty resisting the temptation to enlarge theirs. Besides, empire had always been more a Republican than a Democratic enthusiasm, and as American voters' enthusiasm for Republicans waned – evidenced most conspicuously in the Democratic landslide of 1910 – so did the country's attachment to empire. In nominating Wilson in 1912, the Democrats stood him on an explicitly anti-imperialist platform. The Democrats declared themselves "against a policy of imperialism and colonial exploitation" and condemned the experiment in imperialism as an "inexcusable blunder which has involved us in

47

enormous expense, brought us weakness instead of strength, and laid our nation open to the charge of abandonment of the fundamental doctrine of self-government."[1]

Voters might have been excused for expecting an exemplarist foreign policy from such a party and candidate; in fact, Wilson turned out to be no less a vindicator than Roosevelt. The Democratic president had scarcely warmed – many would have said chilled – the White House with his presence when he pointedly refused to recognize a new government in Mexico on grounds that it had seized power by violent means unbecoming to the western hemisphere. "We hold," he declared, "as I am sure all thoughtful leaders of republican governments everywhere hold, that just government always rests upon the consent of the governed, and that there can be no freedom without order based upon law and upon the public conscience and approval. We shall look to make these principles the basis of mutual intercourse, respect, and helpfulness between our sister republics and ourselves." Several months later, he stated his position more directly: "I am going to teach the South American republics to elect good men" (Wilson was a professor of politics, not geography).[2]

When diplomatic pressure proved insufficiently instructive, the president backed admonition with force. Exaggerating a run-in between drunken American sailors and Mexican authorities in Tampico to the level of a major crisis, he ordered the occupation of the port city of Vera Cruz. The attendant battle killed a score of Americans and hundreds of Mexicans, and it enmeshed the United States in the internal affairs of Mexico. By the spring of 1916, many thousands of American soldiers were roaming the mountains and arroyos of northern Mexico, searching for Pancho Villa and, indirectly, for a government in Mexico City that Wilson could embrace. They found neither, instead engaging Mexican troops in hostilities and escalating the affair nearly to the point of regular war. Only another, bigger conflict – the one in Europe – saved the situation. Wilson appreciated the likelihood of American involvement in the European war and the inadvisability of a simultaneous fight with Mexico. Muttering disgustedly,

---

[1] Arthur M. Schlesinger, Jr., ed., *History of American Presidential Elections* (New York, 1971), 2176.

[2] Robert H. Ferrell, *American Diplomacy: The Twentieth Century* (New York, 1988 ed.,), 94–5.

he accepted the regime the Mexicans, by their own methods, chose for themselves.

Wilson retreated from vindicationism in Mexico only after the opportunity arose for a more sweeping imposition of American values on the world. For two-and-a-half years, the president had contended that the United States was above the quarrel rending Europe; now he chose to take the country into the war. In doing so, he aimed not simply to defend American neutral rights or to avenge American losses to German submarines. He proclaimed nothing less than a crusade to make the world "safe for democracy."

In this endeavor, Wilson received the overwhelming support of American progressives. Systemicist by nature, the progressives looked for comprehensive solutions to the problem of international turmoil. Wilson once told Walter Lippmann that effecting reform was like painting a fence post: "If you want to preserve a fence post, you have to keep painting it white. You can't just paint it once and leave it forever. It will rot away." Wilson's passion for painting led him – and Lippmann and other progressives – to advocate a new approach to international affairs. Rejecting the traditional anarchic model, in which each nation was a law to itself and the strong preyed on the weak, the Wilsonians promoted a league of nations that would act as an incipient world government, policing the planet, restraining wrongdoers, and defending the helpless. Having applied their reforming notions to America's cities, then to the states, and most recently to the nation as a whole, the progressives now intended to go global.[3]

II

Harvard College around 1910 produced a constellation of luminaries that lit the American landscape for half a century. Budding journalist John Reed sharpened his pen writing for campus publications, as did fellow scribblers Heywood Broun and Hans von Kaltenborn. T. S. Eliot tried out for the track squad and failed, but his verses' feet showed more promise than his own. Bronson Cutting commenced a political career that wouldn't end until he represented New Mexico in the United States Senate. Van Wyck Brooks began probing for the

[3] Walter LaFeber, *The American Age: United States Foreign Policy at Home and Abroad since 1750* (New York, 1989), 261.

literary roots of American culture, spading the soil that produced *The Flowering of New England* et seq. Conrad Aiken vacillated between poetry and reporting, as he did for much of his life.

But the light shone soonest and brightest from Walter Lippmann. The precocious only child of a well-to-do family of assimilated German Jews, Lippmann entered Harvard intending to capture the place by charm of personality and force of intellect. He did. He early demonstrated his skill at cultivating distinguished older men, at reminding them of themselves in younger days; by this means, he quickly won the attention and respect of William James, George Santayana, and other campus notables. Lippmann adopted a fashionable socialism, after the manner of British Fabians George Bernard Shaw, H. G. Wells, and Beatrice and Sidney Webb. He organized debates and gave speeches. Although as a Jew he remained outside the clubs that traditionally staffed the *Crimson*, he gained a reputation writing articles for the *Harvard Illustrated* and the *Monthly*. His work and his friendships led to contacts with nationally known figures in journalism, including Lincoln Steffens, who convinced Lippmann to turn his talents to examining the condition of American society.

Steffens, then at *Everybody's* magazine, judged common sense and an open mind more necessary to effective reporting than experience or training. "Give me an intelligent college-educated man for a year," he bet his editors, "and I'll make a good journalist out of him." The editors obliged, hiring Lippmann as Steffens's assistant. The veteran muckraker had undertaken to expose big business in the manner he had already applied to city government, and he set Lippmann to work digging through prospectuses and annual reports, interviewing New York insiders and Kansas City outsiders, and analyzing the interlocking directorate of power in the corporate and political worlds. The experience proved invaluable for Lippmann, not simply for the education but for the network he began to fashion. People returned the calls of Lincoln Steffens's man, and Lippmann met influential progressives from all over the country. The time with Steffens also honed Lippmann's skill at ingratiating. "You often asked me whether the year had been worthwhile," he said when Steffens declared the experiment a success and dismissed his protege.

Lord, if I could tell you and make you believe it. You'd know then why "Everybody who knows you loves you." You gave me yourself and then you ask me whether it has been worthwhile. For that I can't write down my thanks. I shall have to live them. Whenever I understand a man and like him, instead of hating him, it'll be your work. You've got into my blood, I think, and there'll be a little less bile in the world as a result. ... You gave me a chance to start – you know what that means to a fellow who has an indifferent world staring him in the face.[4]

Lippmann contributed articles to assorted leftist and mainstream journals while he pondered how to return the gaze of that indifferent world. During the summer of 1912, he retired to the Maine woods in the company of Albert Kuttner, a friend who specialized in Freud, and committed his thoughts to paper. By autumn, he was back in New York with manuscript in hand; the following spring, *A Preface to Politics* appeared.

Full of the idealism of youth, Lippmann therein castigated what he called the "routineer," the creature of political habit who accepted the status quo from lack of imagination or energy to change it. Routineers, he contended, rather than evil persons, constituted the primary obstacle to reform. William Howard Taft, the Republican president and candidate during the campaign under way when Lippmann wrote the book, typified the routineer mentality. Other Republican regulars were more lackluster still. Lippmann said of Henry Cabot Lodge: "We know that probably his deepest sincerity is an attempt to reproduce the atmosphere of the Senate a hundred years ago. The manners of Mr. Lodge have that immobility which comes from too much gazing at bad statues of dead statesmen."

Theodore Roosevelt, whose impatience with the Republican party had led to his breakaway candidacy, struck Lippmann as the opposite of the routineer, as the innovator who shattered idols and enlarged the realm of the possible. Roosevelt, Lippmann said, during his presidency had effected "the greatest release of political invention in a generation." It was precisely for this that the established powers deemed him so dangerous.

As for the third candidate, Lippmann withheld judgment. "Woodrow Wilson brought to public life an exceedingly flexible mind. Many of us when he first emerged rejoiced at the clean and athletic quality of his thinking. But even he under the stress of a campaign slackened

[4] Ronald Steel, *Walter Lippmann and the American Century* (Boston, 1980), 35–9.

into commonplace reiteration, accepting a futile and intellectually dishonest platform, closing his eyes to facts, misrepresenting his opponents, abandoning, in short, the very qualities which distinguished him." In the knowing voice expected of twenty-three-year-old authors of first books, Lippmann explained, "It is understandable. When a National Committee puts a megaphone to a man's mouth and tells him to yell, it is difficult for him to hear anything."

Lippmann said much more in this book, but its lasting impact lay less in its substance than in its tone. In certain respects, *A Preface to Politics* was the typical tract of iconoclastic inexperience, and in denouncing the routineers Lippmann recapitulated the argument youth has always made against age. But Lippmann spoke with unusual grace and clarity, and if his use of the first person plural at times seemed excessive – "We cling to constitutions. . . . We trudge in the treadmill. . . . We emulate the mule" – it also told like-thinking readers that here was an eloquently kindred soul.[5]

Lippmann joined prolificacy to eloquence, producing *Drift and Mastery* just several months later. His second book was an attempt, as he phrased it, "to diagnose the current unrest." Building on portions of *Preface* and on his conversations with Albert Kuttner in Maine, he applied to American society the currently voguish theories of Freud, who had only recently returned to Vienna following a triumphal march through intellectually fashionable American circles. As he had before, Lippmann dichotomized society: The routineers were recast as those persons satisfied to "drift" in channels of least resistance, at the mercy of their own and the culture's collective unconscious; the innovators appeared as those who insisted on "mastery," the imposition of conscious intention on individual and group actions. In the latter category, Lippmann included most conspicuously the advocates of scientific solutions to community problems. He enunciated a view characteristic of progressives when he linked the scientific method to political reform. "Democracy in politics is the twin-brother of scientific thinking. They had to come together. As absolutism falls, science rises. It *is* self-government. For when the impulse which overthrows kings and priests and unquestioned creeds becomes self-conscious we call it science." (How closely Lippmann read Brooks Adams is unclear, but the language and some of the imagery are suggestive.) Because science continually questioned its

---

[5] Walter Lippmann, *A Preface to Politics* (New York, 1913), 6, 24, 33, 55.

own premises, it fostered the attitude required to penetrate the taboos and mythology surrounding entrenched social practices and institutions. Because it was rigorous, it was liberating. "The scientific spirit is the discipline of democracy, the escape from drift, the outlook of a free man."[6]

III

"We're starting a weekly here next fall – a weekly of ideas – with a paid up capital – God save us – of $200,000," Lippmann wrote to Van Wyck Brooks early in 1914. "The age of miracles, sir, has just begun." Lippmann explained that the magazine in question would follow the *Saturday Review* in form, while in substance it would be "American, but sophisticated and critical." Nonpartisan and nonideological, it would nonetheless be "socialistic in direction." "If there is any word to cover our ideal, I suppose it is humanist."[7]

A few months before, Lippmann had received an invitation to join the editorial staff of the journal he described to Brooks. The start-up money came from Willard and Dorothy Straight, respectively a dollar-diplomat under Taft and a Standard Oil heiress. Despite their conservative circumstances, the Straights liked the idea of promoting responsible reform, and when Herbert Croly, whose ideas and writing they admired, complained of a lack of a regular venue, Dorothy Straight asked, "Why don't you get out a weekly yourself, Herbert?" By the time the conversation ended, she had pledged support for four years of publication.[8]

Croly, though not far into his forties, was something of a patriarch among progressive thinkers. His 1909 book, *The Promise of American Life*, became a bible to the generation that thrilled when Theodore Roosevelt, himself a convert to Croly's philosophy, announced his stand at Armageddon in the service of the Lord. Croly's book marked a turn in the progressive movement – a turn Woodrow Wilson initially missed – away from its populist roots and toward in-

[6] Walter Lippmann, *Drift and Mastery: An Attempt to Diagnose the Current Unrest* (New York, 1914), 275–6.

[7] John Morton Blum, ed., *Public Philosopher: Selected Letters of Walter Lippmann* (New York, 1985), 16–7.

[8] Charles Forcey, *The Crossroads of Liberalism: Croly, Weyl, Lippmann, and the Progressive Era, 1900–1925* (New York, 1961), 173–5.

creasing reliance on scientific management of society. Croly sought
to span the traditional divide between Jeffersonian individualism and
Hamiltonian centralism by harnessing the governmental power of the
latter to the democratic purposes of the former. The combination had
a natural appeal to Roosevelt, whose only complaint about power
was that he never had enough. It also touched the elitist chord in
progressive thought that espoused democracy while wondering
whether the *demos* possessed sufficient wisdom to know what was in
the country's best interest. Education might remedy the deficiency
over time, but meanwhile reformers should take a shortcut across the
field of bureaucratic power.

Though the bulk of Croly's hefty book covered domestic matters,
he found room for an analysis of how his ideas applied to America's
foreign relations. Much as he had in the domestic realm, Croly held
that modern circumstances had altered crucially the conditions in
which American attitudes regarding the world had originally taken
shape. "The isolation which has meant so much to the United States,
and still means so much, cannot persist in its present form," he declared. Americans must recognize that the national interest required
an active promotion of American values abroad. "The United States
must by every practical means encourage the spread of democratic
methods and ideas." What Croly advocated, in essence, was a policy
designed to make the world safe for democracy. He applauded Roosevelt's efforts "to introduce a little order into the affairs of the tur-
bulent Central American republics," and he argued that Americans
must be prepared to take similar action across the Atlantic. "There is
no shibboleth that patriotic Americans should fight more tenaciously
and more fiercely than of America for the Americans, and Europe for
the Europeans." Such a conception may have served at the time President Monroe announced his doctrine (which Croly misdated to
1825); but it served no longer, and if Americans held unthinkingly to
it they would contribute decisively to America's "democratic degen-
eracy." For democracy to flourish in the New World, it must flourish
in the Old World as well. This required not merely America's good
example but America's active involvement.[9]

Croly's progressive vindicationism was slightly ahead of its time.
Progressives as a group wouldn't start thinking seriously about con-

---

[9] Herbert Croly, *The Promise of American Life* (New York, 1909, 1911), 292–3,
   311–3, 383.

structing an international system for peace for half a decade yet, until the present uneasy peace definitively broke down. Even at the beginning of 1914, when Croly brought Lippmann aboard the *New Republic*, foreign affairs continued to occupy a secondary place in progressive thought, behind efforts to secure congressional approval of the Clayton antitrust bill and establish a federal trade commission.

The August advent of war, which caught Lippmann in England lining up contributors to the new journal, immediately thrust international relations to the center of attention of thinking Americans. Lippmann was stunned by the collapse of the European order. "It all came so incredibly fast," he told a friend, describing the days surrounding the outbreak of fighting. "On Thursday in Ostende we were sunning ourselves on the beach; on Friday I was wandering around Fifteenth Century Bruges; on Saturday in Brussels people were weeping in the streets." Lippmann crossed the Channel amid hundreds of warships heading for the North Sea, then endured two suspenseful days waiting to see if the British parliament would declare war. "The most peaceful people you met were praying for war, praying that England should not stand aside while Belgium was annexed and France crushed." At this stage, Lippmann could see no good emerging from the conflict. "If Germany wins, the whole world will have to arm against her – the U.S. included, for Germany quite seriously intends to dominate the world. If Germany loses, Russia alone wins, and every country in Europe will arm for a struggle in which Asia is the stake."[10]

This attitude informed the thinking of the *New Republic* from the start – which was to say, from November 7, 1914. The journal deliberately adopted a stance of what editors Croly, Lippmann, and Walter Weyl thought of as pragmatic engagement in public affairs. The initial editorial prescribed an end to what the editors called "the self-complacent isolation" of the American people. The war in Europe had demonstrated the bankruptcy of the "combination of a crude colonialism with a crude nationalism" that had characterized, and often still did, the attitude of many in both Europe and America toward the world. The editors didn't endorse American intervention at this early date, but they contended that neither could the United States remain indifferent to the outcome of the struggle. "No matter who is victorious, the United States will be indirectly compromised

---

[10] Blum, *Public Philosopher*, 19–20.

by the treaty of peace. If the treaty is one which makes for international stability and justice, this country will have an interest in maintaining it. If the treaty is one which makes militarism even more ominously threatening, this country will have an interest in seeking a better substitute."[11]

The *New Republic* initially expressed impatience at the "timid neutrality" of the Wilson adminstration, aligning itself instead with the robust realism of Roosevelt. "Of all Americans commenting on the war," the editors said, "his judgment is the ripest." Almost alone, the former president confronted the vital question of the hour: "How is it possible to create the beginnings of international order out of the nations of this world? Not out of a world of pacifists, not out of a world of Quakers, but out of this world, which contains only a small minority of pacifists and Quakers. For it is peace on earth that men need, not peace in heaven, and unless you build from the brutalities of earth, you step out into empty space."

Lippmann, Croly, and Weyl, following Roosevelt, asserted the necessity of restoring respect to treaty obligations. This required backing paper pledges with force. "Treaties will never acquire sanctity until nations are ready to seal them with their blood," the editors predicted, adding, "It is our business to make no treaties which we are not ready to maintain with all our resources, for every scrap of paper" – the ironic reference was to the German foreign minister's already notorious dismissal of the treaty ostensibly guaranteeing Belgian neutrality – "is like a forged check, an assault on our credit in the world." Besides the Belgian treaty, the Germans were trampling other pacts, including Hague conventions that the United States had vowed to uphold. The editors stopped short of declaring this a casus belli for the United States, but they admonished American leaders to register objection. "Had we protested against the assault on international morality when Belgium was invaded, our faith in public law would have been made somewhat real." Americans had to take chances for international order and peace; had the United States stood by the principles of the Hague, "ruthlessness would have received the severest jolt it ever imagined." The editors didn't explain *how* American diplomatic protests would have jolted Germany more

[11] Untitled editorial and "The End of American Isolation," *New Republic*, Nov. 7, 1914.

severely than war with Britain, France, and Russia had, but they thought it would have.[12]

With most observers, the editors of the *New Republic* at first expected a brief war; only slowly, as the battle front sank in the mire and the carnage continued, did the true nature of the conflict become apparent. At the end of 1914, Lippmann reflected on the costs of the war, especially as they touched the valuation of human life. "Life is cheap," he wrote, at the same time remarking that some lives seemed to be cheaper than others, depending on who was fixing the prices. General Joffre had said France wouldn't waste the lives of its young men in pointless assaults, which roused suspicions across the Channel that the British would be left with the burden of the fighting. The British, for their part, evidently conceived of the Russians as an inexhaustible horde to be thrown against the German guns. Americans, though not directly involved, likewise applied a differential calculus, Lippmann said, tallying England's dead more carefully than Austria's, and Canada's more carefully than England's.

Lippmann attributed the differentiation by Americans to something beyond the cultural affinities America shared with the other English-speaking countries. He thought it characteristic of democracies to value life highly. "That is why democracies tend to be peaceful," Lippmann asserted, echoing, without crediting, Tocqueville among others. "In them the importance of each person has been enlarged, and the greater the equality, the less able are small groups to use their fellows as brute instruments. Democracies are compelled to look toward peaceful adjustments because the cost of war is too tremendous for them."

In this fact, Lippmann argued, lay the link between the two principal issues currently challenging Americans: domestic reform and world peace. As long as life remained cheap, countries would find war easy to wage. Americans couldn't readily raise the value of life in Austria-Hungary or Russia, but they could promote its appreciation in the United States, thereby setting an example for the rest of the world. "Here in America life is extraordinarily cheap," Lippmann declared. (What he really meant was that *some* life in America was cheap; either that or he was contradicting his assertion that democracies valued life highly.) He declared that there was no task so dull

[12] "Timid Neutrality, *New Republic*, Nov. 14, 1914.

or degrading that one couldn't find people to do it. "You can hire a man to walk up and down the avenue carrying a sign which advertises a quack dentist. You can hire rows of men for the back line of the chorus, just standing them there to fill up space. You can hire a man to sit next to the chauffeur; he is called a footman and his purpose is to make the owner of the car a bit more comfortable and a great deal more magnificent."

That such was the case in America, the most enlightened of the great powers, explained much about the present world conflict. "It is still hardly questioned that men should die to protect concessions, to collect debts, to hold markets, to glorify their king, to avenge imaginary insults. . . . We have not yet made life dignified and valuable in itself, we have not yet made it a sufficient treasury of good things, have not infused it with the riches which men will not wantonly waste." Investment in people, worthwhile in itself, would also serve the broader cause of peace, for societies wouldn't lightly squander that in which they had placed their resources. "Just so far as we can induce the state to sink money and attention in human beings, by just so much do we insure ourselves against idle destruction."[13]

When the war outlasted the forecasts of nearly all concerned, and the opposing sides settled in for a protracted struggle, the United States found itself caught between the contending parties – in particular, between the surface naval blockade Britain and France had imposed on Germany, and the submarine cordon Germany had thrown up around Britain and France. The *New Republic* denounced both sides for their violations of neutral rights. But in a scathing editorial of March 1915, the journal took the British especially to task for London's recently adopted policy of search and seizure of vessels suspected of trading with the enemy. "The German threat to innocent neutral commerce with England was wanton, but it was incidental. The English threat to innocent neutral commerce with Germany is polite and benevolent in form, but in substance it is deadly." The British couldn't hide behind the rationalization that their policy spared the innocent, as they said the German policy did not, for while German submarines did indeed take a toll of the crews of merchant vessels, the Allied blockade had the objective of starving an entire nation, of which women and children would be the first to succumb.[14]

---

[13] Walter Lippmann, "Life is Cheap," *New Republic*, Dec. 19, 1914.
[14] "The Other Cheek," *New Republic*, March 16, 1915.

For all the *New Republic*'s complaints, the British correctly guessed that their search-and-seize policy, while illegal under international convention, wouldn't produce the abhorrence Germany's use of submarines generated. In May 1915, when a German U-boat sank the British liner *Lusitania*, killing, among many others, more than one hundred Americans, the furor in the United States over the deadly deed drowned out complaints regarding Britain's continuing blockade. The *New Republic*, priding itself on calm rationality, resisted getting swept away by the tide of emotion, but it applauded the indignation as forcing contrition upon Germany. Shortly after Berlin stepped back and offered assurances against another such tragic incident, the magazine's editors explained that the German government was frightened. "Public opinion has at last spoken a language that the German bureaucracy understands."

For the *New Republic*, as for a large segment of the American populace, the *Lusitania* sinking started the moral and psychological scales tipping irreversibly in favor of the Allies. Despite the magazine's earlier criticism of the British blockade as being worse than Germany's U-boat policy, the shock of the mass murder compelled the editors to reconsider. Berlin became a greater threat – now and in the future – than the editors had realized. "We have a fair chance of living amicably with the fellow countrymen of the majority of the Lusitania victims, but we cannot live amicably with the nation who so deliberately and remorselessly condemned them to death."[15]

This being the case, the United States must prepare for war. The editors weren't quite ready to throw America's lot in with the Allies, but their arms were cocked. Americans had to take responsibility for the maintenance of world order. "Our traditional isolation is no longer justified either by physical conditions or by national ideals." Isolation required self-sufficiency. In a breathtaking overstatement, the editors explained that the United States wasn't much more self-sufficient than Belgium. From this dubious assertion followed their policy recommendation for their country: "It must eventually seek friends and even allies among the European nations, and it will have to share with them the work of European reorganization." And it might have to share more than mere work. "Before that work is

---

[15] "Dealing with Germany," *New Republic*, May 15, 1915; "Germany's Real Offense," *New Republic*, May 22, 1915.

finished the blood of American citizens may be mixed with that of their Canadian neighbors on the soil of Flanders."[16]

IV

The mixing would be gainful only if it yielded a lasting peace. Lippmann and his co-editors, along with other American liberals, looked to the creation of an international body designed to prevent a recurrence of war once this conflict ended. As early as March 1915, the *New Republic* described what it called a "League of Peace," attributing the original idea to Thomas Paine, who on the eve of the Napoleonic wars had proposed an antiwar pact among the United States, Britain, and France. The thought had surfaced intermittently since then, and was now widely current in Britain and America. Lippmann et al. endorsed the league as "a dream capable of an early translation into fact."

The editors stopped well short, however, of approving just any league of nations. Their primary reservation involved the possibility of the league's degenerating into a great-power condominium to preserve the international status quo. Germany must be defeated in the present war, but after the fighting ceased the Germans must be reintegrated into international affairs. "A League of the Satisfied might appeal to London and Paris and Petrograd. But Berlin will ask, 'What hope does it offer to me that when my population is still denser, my industry still more expansive, my need for markets and fields of exploitation, for my capital even more clamant than it is today, your League of Peace will provide me with an outlet? You bar the future, and you call it peace.' "[17]

Two months later, the journal gave further guarded support to a league of nations. A league would encounter no end of difficulties determining the scope of its activities, the editors granted. Did the nationalist aspirations of India rise to the level of international concern? If the league answered no, how could it expect to enlist the support of the colonial peoples of the world? If it answered yes, how would it retain the support of Britain? Should the opinions of all nations count equally? If Venezuela wielded as much power in the league as the United States, why should America join? If not, why

[16] "Not Our War," *New Republic*, June 15, 1915.
[17] "A League of Peace," *New Republic*, March 20, 1915.

should Venezuela? Who would settle differences of opinion between league members? Who would oversee enforcement of decisions? What would prevent the league from lapsing into the unworkable semi-sovereignty of the American government under the Articles of Confederation – or, for that matter, into the fratricide of the American civil war?

These objections led the editors to conclude that a league of nations would justify its existence only as a first step toward a more comprehensive, more powerful organization. "There is no stopping short at a league to prevent war. Such a league would either grow to a world federalism, or it would break up in civil war." Yet such an observation constituted not an objection to a league but the strongest possible argument for it. "It is the first step towards a closer world organization, and once that step is taken, the world will have to choose between taking some of the next steps and returning to the anarchy of sovereign nationalities." The vast implications of the league were what gave it significance. "Its real service to mankind may well be that it will establish the first rallying point of a world citizenship."[18]

Lippmann, Croly, and Weyl developed this idea further following the April 1916 torpedoing of the French *Sussex*. They printed an open letter to Wilson advocating that the president employ the renewed outrage over German war tactics to bring American influence decisively to bear internationally. The letter amounted to a call for the most sweeping form of American vindicationism. The *Sussex* crisis, the editors said, offered "an unparalleled opportunity for constructive leadership." The United States might simply declare war on Germany; yet if it did so without explicitly enunciating its goals, it would soon find its energies diverted to the less-than-noble purposes of the Allies. "We shall have begun for the purpose of vindicating our right to travel at sea, but we shall end by fighting to change the political control of the Near East. And when it is all over we shall not have the slightest idea whether we have attained the object for which we fought."

That object must be nothing less than a grand system of international security in which the vital interests of the least powerful received protection equal to that afforded the strongest, and in which the United States played a central enforcing part. The editors attrib-

[18] "A League of Peace," *New Republic*, June 26, 1915.

uted the failure of American policy heretofore and the more general
failure of the policies of the neutral countries to the fact that each
neutral had objected merely to violations of its own specific interests.
"The true principle is to uphold the law whether your rights are
violated or not. Only when all nations are ready to act in behalf of
the general rule will that rule come to have any binding force. A
common defense of rights is the only way individual rights can be
maintained."

What did this mean? "It means that we no longer intend to be
neutral between the violator and his victim. We have learned from
this war that one attack on law is followed by another, and that if
lawbreaking is permitted at one point the anarchy infects every one."
From now on, the United States must not be neutral; it must be
prepared to use its moral power, its economic resources and its military force against aggressors. How would aggressors be identified?
"The aggressor is the nation that will not submit its quarrel to international inquiry, that will not suspend action until the world has had
a chance to pass judgment upon it, or that pursues its quarrel after
the world has decided against it."

Ignoring the myriad difficulties such a definition of aggression
raised – beginning with the problems of deciding which countries
constituted "the world" and of determining how these countries
might "pass judgment" – the editors applied their criteria to the present instance. Washington should inform Berlin that it would not simply break diplomatic relations but would also aid the Allies until
Germany agreed to evacuate Belgium, France, and Serbia, to indem-
nify Belgium for injuries inflicted, and to submit future disputes to
international inquiry.

The editors didn't say so, but such demands had absolutely no
chance of winning German acceptance; for this reason, their rather
detailed description of what the United States would do if Germany
accepted – they suggested guaranteeing Belgium's future security, for
starters – meant nothing. In their open letter to Wilson, the editors
seemed to adopt the position that the statement of intent was the
thing that counted. If the president merely made the statement, he
would accomplish great good. "You will have turned this crisis to
the service of mankind. You will have done more than any one else
has ever done to put a sanction behind the law of nations. You will
have transformed what may be a meaningless rupture into a significant event." The worst outcome that could result from such a state-

ment was that the United States would have to resort to traditional instruments of diplomacy (evidently including war, although they refrained from saying so). The best? "You will have established the precedent that an injury to one is an injury to all; you will have put the power of the United States behind nations like Belgium which are the wards of mankind and can exist only in a world where international law is respected. You will have pledged this country to the principle that only in a world where Belgium is safe can the United States be safe."[19]

V

While the editors of the *New Republic* were forging their collective position on collective security and collateral questions, Lippmann honed his individual thinking. To Lippmann, as to Croly, the management of foreign relations constituted a crucial test for American democracy: Success in one would facilitate success in the other. In Lippmann's case, again as in Croly's, the connection was sometimes a bit strained, reflecting perhaps the liberal's discomfort at entering a realm often dominated by illiberal characters: European imperialists, benighted colonials, and American jingoes. The strain was clearly evident in Lippmann's *The Stakes of Diplomacy*, initially published in 1915, revised at the beginning of 1917, and containing the most comprehensive statement of his thoughts on international relations during the decade of World War I.

Lippmann began by asserting that American diplomacy as currently practiced had little connection to democratic principles. The absence of democratic control, he said, originated in "popular gullibility" and the "sloth of liberalism." Because the people at large were unsophisticated in foreign affairs, and because those who might offer them judicious guidance had abandoned the field, diplomacy largely remained in the hands of the enemies of democracy. To a considerable degree, Lippmann said, the European war had paralyzed American liberals. "We are less flexible in our thinking, at once more dogmatic and more capricious. . . . We have identified our opinions with our safety; whoever attacks them attacks us. . . . With the grimness of war to weigh us down and panic to make us uncertain, we are more heavy-footed than ever." A measure of the paralysis was the

<hr />

[19] "An Appeal to the President," *New Republic*, April 22, 1916.

liberals' flight from the concrete and the particular. "We have taken refuge in abstractions like Nationality, Race, Culture. They are easier to think about than men. They introduce that simplicity into the mind which it longs for so ardently."

On this account, and because conditions of crisis tended to undermine the institutions of democracy, the American government answered to the American people in foreign affairs only in the most superficial way. The *Lusitania* sinking had demonstrated that one man, the president, possessed the power of war and peace for the country as a whole. "Had Mr. Wilson wanted war with Germany," Lippmann asserted, "he could have had it. We were in his hands, and no amount of elections, or constitutional reservations about the right of Congress to declare war, can alter the fact that the real war-making power in the United States is the President." Neither public opinion nor received practice served to restrain the executive. Voters rarely inquired of a candidate's views on international questions. In Wilson's case in 1912, world issues "probably did not influence two hundred votes." As to received practice: "Traditional American policy is so vague that the administration may subscribe to it and still do pretty much whatever it pleases." To date, Wilson's actions had in fact accorded with both popular sentiment and custom, but the accordance was accidental. "Had he belonged to that powerful group in this country who would like to fight on the side of the Allies, he could have used the Lusitania incident to make war inevitable. Nothing would have been easier than to dramatize the issue, to close the door of negotiation, to inflame the press by publishing the whispered rumors about many of the undoubted provocations which German diplomacy has offered us." Liberals and others who valued democracy needed to come to terms with a fundamental truth: "On the issue of our national existence we are not a self-governing people."

The problem transcended the particular constitutional arrangements Americans had made among the branches of their government and between government and the people. These arrangements contributed to the irresponsibility of the president, but the lack of control also reflected the peculiar and characteristic nature of foreign, as opposed to domestic, affairs. In domestic life individuals could deal with each other as individuals. To be sure, modern existence diminished the role of individuals in favor of corporations, labor unions, and other conglomerates; but even so, the individual remained the basic unit of social interaction. In foreign affairs, on the other hand, the nation served as the fundamental unit. One hundred million Americans were "the United States"; sixty-five million Germans were "Germany." The government of each country presumed to represent the thinking and desires of its people. But this was impossible. "A whole people can no more think in unison than it can make love in unison." Confronting this impossibility, diplomats – of democratic countries as well as nondemocratic – took refuge in an elitism that denied any significant role for the untutored masses in the intricacies of international relations. Appreciating the same impossibility, the people tended to accept their exclusion from the diplomatic process. "It was a recognition of this that made the most democratic among us prefer 'trusting the President' to summoning Congress in the Lusitania crisis. We believed he could do for us what we wanted done better than we could tell him what we wanted done."

Yet the problem ran deeper even than politics considered generically. Its roots lay in the crevices of the human psyche. As soon as one nation began dealing with another nation, the fear of the outsider emerged. "The sense of an enemy makes us huddle together for defense and offense." The threat from outside overrode differences that developed in times of peace. "It almost obliterates personality, and throws us back into a herd with animal loves and animal hates." And the herd closed around its leader. The instinct acted as strongly in democrats as in royalists, in Americans as in Germans and English. "When we become 'one man,' we become so in the same sense that Germany personifies itself in the Emperor, or England in the Crown." In this regard, the American president might as well have been an absolute monarch.

Lippmann's thoughts on the psychological element in international affairs led him to the conclusion that most wars resulted, in the final reckoning, from conflicts regarding prestige. Small disputes over trade, fisheries, or frontiers metastasized into contests engaging national pride. "Just as a man will fight a lawsuit at tremendous cost for a trivial sum, so nations will risk war to score a diplomatic victory." In a comment he would essentially repeat half a century later, when he turned against Lyndon Johnson's Vietnam policy, Lippmann wrote, "They feel that defeat on one point will exhibit weakness and carry in its train defeat on other points."

Perceived threats to prestige, Lippmann continued, arose most frequently in those parts of the planet not fully integrated into the world political system. Individuals from one country – France, for example

– attempted to do business with certain indigenous peoples of Africa. The lack of legal and administrative infrastructure such as courts and law-enforcement agencies tempted French merchants to appeal to Paris for help. British competitors, fearing the closure of potential markets, petitioned London for help of their own. Soon a Fashoda developed, with the whole affair enveloped in national pride. Multiplied several times, and with the addition of various other countries, the result was the present war.

Lippmann still wasn't quite convinced that the situation in Europe demanded American belligerence. But he believed that America must take a more active part in global affairs if war were not to recur. "The interrelation of peoples has gone so far that to advocate international laissez-faire now is to speak a counsel of despair." No matter how the current struggle turned out, the problem of the periphery would remain. Therefore the chief task of world diplomacy – and of American diplomacy – was "the organization of virgin territory and backward peoples."

If the problem were left to the powers individually, another war would surely result. Any solution required collective action. Lippmann recommended permanent versions of the 1885 Berlin conference, which had apportioned West Africa among the European contenders. He had no difficulty with the notion of the advanced states dictating for the undeveloped regions of the earth; he saw no feasible alternative. But he thought the ad hoc and temporary character of past conferences, which he likened to international legislatures, rendered them dangerously deficient in the matter of enforcement. "These legislatures have had one great fault. They met, they passed laws, they adjourned, and left the enforcement of their mandate to the conscience of the individual powers. The legislature was international, but the executive was merely national." Lippmann wouldn't go so far as to delegate elaborate enforcement authority upon the permanent conferences; the world wasn't ready for that. But by remaining in session, the conferences would act as courts of first appeal for troubles that emerged in carrying out their mandates, and as such they would help defuse crises that might otherwise lead to war. His scheme, he said, provided "not a panacea but a method and the beginnings of a technique" for diminishing international tension. "It is internationalism, not spread thin as a Parliament of Man, but sharply limited to those areas of friction where internationalism is most obviously needed."

Lippmann recognized that even this narrow-gauge internationalism would require the support of more than the usual crowd of ar-
bitrationists and other one-world idealists. "No government," he
said, "has any chance of survival unless it serves the interests of powerful economic groups." The problem therefore reduced to transfer-
ring the loyalty of the various merchants, concessionaires, and financiers from their competing national governments to his framework of
standing conferences. "If they support it, there is a chance of its
success. If they fight it, failure is certain." Lippmann recommended
persuading the separate governments – he didn't specify how – to
inform their citizens and subjects that when they entered backward
regions, they must look for protection not to their national governments but to the agents of the appropriate international tribunal.
Lippmann didn't draw the analogy, but his reasoning was similar to
that of Alexander Hamilton in arguing for federal assumption of state
debts: The powerful economic classes would thus have a financial
stake in the success of the central administration. Lippmann foresaw
the eventual development of "international states" – what later
would be called mandates and trusteeships. "To set up international
states in certain territories," he contended, "is to construct the only
possible substitute for imperialism."

Beyond the pacifying effect his project would have on world affairs, Lippmann predicted that it would yield benefits for American
democracy at home. By ensuring the orderly opening up of the undeveloped regions, the proto-world government would encourage
participation by a broader cross-section of American society than
now took part. The larger the proportion involved, the greater interest the public as a whole would have regarding relations with other
countries. "By increasing the number of people concerned in diplomacy," he forecast, "publicity, criticism and discussion must follow.
From them education. The realities of diplomacy which are hidden
today under a cloud of ambiguous phrases and primitive emotion
will be revealed." The business of the diplomat would become the
business of the country as a whole. The people, quickened to the
impact of international affairs on their daily lives, would reclaim
much of the control of foreign policy they had relinquished to the
experts.

The positive effects would spill back over into the international
realm. The democratization of diplomacy, under conditions of informed popular opinion, would diminish the effect of emotional ap-

peals to nationalism. "There would be less need of sovereignty, less need of rigid military frontiers, less need of docile, uncritical patriotism, and consequently a vast increase of human cooperation."[20]

VI

In refining his views on foreign affairs, Lippmann benefited from the proximity of Herbert Croly, but he gained more from conversations with his other fellow editor, Walter Weyl. Weyl had made a name for himself among progressives with his 1912 *The New Democracy*, which argued for a democracy that went beyond politics to reshape economic relations among the classes in the United States. Largely on the strength of this book, Weyl received his invitation from Herbert Croly to join the *New Republic*. Lippmann judged Weyl the most acute thinker among the progressives on economic matters.

At the beginning of 1917, Weyl published *American World Policies*, which applied his economic theories to international affairs. With the Englishman John Hobson, the Russian Lenin, Brooks Adams, and a variety of others, Weyl perceived the modern struggle among nations as the manifestation of a certain stage of the capitalist international order. In Weyl's thinking, the fundamental development of recent decades had been "the integration of the world," defined as the technological emergence of the possibility of a single global market for natural resources, agricultural commodities, manufactures, and investment funds. Yet the competition a world market entailed held little appeal for large firms in the capitalist countries. These firms demanded protection from their respective governments. At home, protection took the form of tariffs; abroad, it resulted in the establishment of colonies and spheres of influence. If the world had included only one colonizing power, or if one omniscient individual could somehow have directed the entire process of colonization, the extension of the influence of the industrialized nations over the backward portions of the globe might have taken place without undue friction. In the real world, the powers had jostled roughly in the grabbing. This had led, in the present instance, to war.

Conceiving economic matters to lie at the heart of international conflict, Weyl proposed economic solutions. As a start, he recom-

---

[20] Walter Lippmann, *The Stakes of Diplomacy* (New York, 1915, 1917), x-xi, 8–10, 15–37, 81, 88–90, 124–5, 131–5, 155–8, 194–5, 203–4.

mended a reordering of priorities within the United States. To the degree the American economy depended on foreign trade and investment, it would remain forever hostage to the actions of the worst-behaved members of the world community. In order to lessen this vulnerability – and in the bargain ameliorate domestic ills – Americans should endeavor to develop the American economy more fully by raising wages and employment and guaranteeing a fairer distribution of wealth. Attempts in this direction could make use of the instinctive inclinations of the masses. "The demand of the workman for higher wages, shorter hours and better conditions is, whether the wage-earner knows it or not, a demand for international peace." Progressive income taxes, the regulation of railroads, and the conservation of natural resources all served the interests of peace. "In short the entire democratic struggle against the narrow concentration of wealth, by increasing the demand for capital within the country, tends to preserve us from a meddlesome, domineering, dangerous imperialism."[21]

VII

By linking domestic reform to international peace, Weyl and Lippmann revealed a principal trait of progressive thinking. Two decades later, this trait would underpin the exemplarist advocacy of Charles Beard; now it tended in a vindicationist direction. It was helped along by the actions of Germany, which in January 1917 announced a campaign of unrestricted submarine warfare. The *New Republic* responded that American belligerency was now all but certain. "No one who read the German note has any right to doubt that Germany means to go as far as she dares to, that she can be stopped only by a show of force. The only course of action now is to assume that there will be war, and to make it as evident as possible to Germany that it will be effective war."

Prudently for a group with no personal experience of war, the *New Republic* trio paid more attention to war aims than to war methods. Germany's denial of American navigation rights had triggered the current crisis, but the editors deemed it a mistake to fight for trading rights alone. "If the United States enters the war on any such flimsy basis as that, it will fight a sterile war, and peace will

---

[21] Walter Weyl, *American World Policies* (New York, 1917), 75, 188–9.

leave us without the least assurance that we have accomplished anything." The traditional system of maritime rights was obsolete, and
in any event the British had sinned against the system as frequently,
if perhaps not as mortally, as the Germans. Nor could the blood of
the victims of German submarine attacks be used as a primary argument against the Germans. "No American lives would have been lost
had we acquiesced in Germany's policy as we have in Britain's."

What, then, would America be fighting for? "We are becoming the
open ally of Britain and France because at the beginning of the war
we decided that they were fighting in the main for the kind of world
in which we wished to live." America could easily accommodate an
Allied victory, for the Allies represented values embraced not only in
America but in the broader Atlantic community. "On the two shores
of the Atlantic Ocean there has grown up a profound web of interest
which joins together the western world. Britain, France, Italy, even
Spain, Belgium, Holland, the Scandinavian nations, and Pan-America
are in the main one community in their deepest needs and their deepest desires." The Germans, or at least those who controlled Germany's government, did not belong to this community, and by
violating the ocean that held it together, they threatened its existence.
"A victory on the high seas would be a triumph of that class which
aims to make Germany the leader of the East against the West, the
leader ultimately of a German-Russian-Japanese coalition against the
Atlantic world."

This last was a strange comment to make at a time when Russia
and Japan were arrayed *against* Germany, but such trifles didn't dent
the self-confidence of Lippmann, Croly, and Weyl. They looked to
the end of the war as the ultimate justification for all arguments,
however dubious in the interim. They believed that American intervention was the price of postwar credibility and of an effective league
of nations. "By showing that we are ready now, as well as in the
theoretical future, to defend the western world, the cornerstone of
federation would be laid." By joining the war, even on the side of
reactionary nations like Russia and Japan, the United States would
provide a vital service to world liberalism. At present, the Allies relied
heavily on the Russians and Japanese, who would expect repayment
when the shooting stopped. America's decisive participation would
lessen this reliance and diminish the debt. "When the peace conference begins some time toward the end of 1917, as it most certainly
will, the final arbitrament between liberalism and reaction will be

made by the relative powers of each. If the liberal forces have the most strength left it is they who will decide the reorganization of the world."[22]

When German attacks on American shipping during March prompted Wilson to request a declaration of war, the *New Republic* registered effusive support. The editors particularly applauded the president's call for a crusade to save the world for democracy. "Only a statesman who will be called great could have made America's intervention mean so much to the generous forces of the world, could have lifted the inevitable horror of war into a deed so full of meaning. Other men have led nations to war to increase their glory, their wealth, their prestige. No other statesman has ever so clearly identified the glory of his country with the peace and liberty of the world."

The recent overthrow of the Russian czar caused the editors to silently drop their argument about American participation being necessary to balance the forces of reaction in the Allied camp. Fashioning fact into virtue, the editors announced that the revolution in Russia demonstrated the global appeal of the principles for which the Allies were fighting. "The cause of the Allies is now unmistakably the cause of liberalism and the hope of an enduring peace. Democracy is infectious – the entrance of the Russian and American democracies is sure to be a stimulus to democrats everywhere." Besides being a bit hasty to denominate Russia a democracy, Lippmann, Croly, and Weyl got carried away with what the recent events in Russia and the Atlantic portended. "It is now as certain as anything human can be that the war which started as a clash of empires in the Balkans will dissolve into democratic revolution the world over."[23]

VIII

Until the United States entered the war, the parasol of progressivism had sheltered a diverse array of individuals and groups espousing a variety of philosophies. Wilsonian New Freedomites coexisted with Rooseveltian New Nationalists, radicals with liberals, socialists with capitalist tinkerers. Although the coexistence was often uncomfortable, rarely did it become unbearable.

It became precisely that after April 1917. Wilson himself recog-

[22] "America's Part in the War" and "The Defense of the Atlantic World," *New Republic*, Feb. 10, 1917.
[23] "The Great Decision," *New Republic*, Apr. 7, 1917.

nized the strain belligerency would place on the progressive coalition.
As early as 1914, the president had predicted, "Every reform we have
won will be lost if we go into this war." He was mistaken, but at
least partly because he delayed intervention long enough for his reforms to sink roots. All the same, when the war did come to America,
it provoked a psychic about-face – from the cool rationalism of reform to the throbbing nationalism of blood struggle. Philosopher
John Dewey called the transition from neutrality to war an "immense
moral wrench."[24]

Wrench or not, most liberals – including Dewey – managed the
transition. Some justified support of the war on grounds of simple
patriotism. Some followed Wilson's lead and backed the war as a
means of regenerating the world, of applying the principles of progressivism on a planetary scale. Some calculated that on the side of
war lay influence: The ruling party had become the war party, and
influencing the war party required embracing the war. Lippmann and
his fellows at the *New Republic* fit all these categories, though they
admitted to the second more readily than to the first and third.

Radicals of sundry stripes, being less sensitive than liberals to the
requirements of relevance, had greater difficulty supporting the war.
Pacifists opposed this war as they opposed all wars. Socialists, having
previously denounced the conflict as a quarrel among capitalists that
oughtn't involve ordinary men and women, saw no reason to change
their minds simply because American capitalists had entered the fray.
Groups farther to the left and beyond the penumbra of progressivism,
such as the syndicalist Industrial Workers of the World, actively agitated against the war as a further manifestion of the insatiable appe-
tite of world imperialism.

A few radicals did manage the leap onto the bandwagon of belligerence. Economist Thorstein Veblen, the acerbic critic of capitalism
and other institutions cherished by the ruling groups in America,
stunned most of his small band of supporters by joining the war
effort, after a fashion. Yet only after a fashion, for so ambivalent –
or perhaps merely confusing – was his attitude that at the same time
that the Wilson administration's Committee on Public Information
was promoting Veblen's 1915 *Imperial Germany and the Industrial
Revolution* as an especially sound assessment of the international

---

[24] David M. Kennedy, *Over Here: The First World War and American Society* (New
York, 1980), 11, 49.

situation, the Post Office was barring it from the mails as pro-German propaganda.

Of those on the left who didn't succumb to the sirens of war, Randolph Bourne delivered the most trenchant and biting criticism of those who did. Even more precocious than Lippmann, Bourne had won a national reputation for social and cultural commentary by the time he graduated from Columbia in 1913. He began writing for the *New Republic* the following year, but as Lippmann, Croly, and Weyl took their journal toward war, Bourne veered off onto the more challenging ground of the *Masses* and *Seven Arts*.

In the latter journal in the spring of 1917, Bourne blistered the liberals who, like the *New Republic* threesome, had betrayed what he considered the intellectual's calling. "To those of us who still retain an irreconcilable animus against war," he wrote, "it has been a bitter experience to see the unanimity with which the American intellectuals have thrown their support of the war-technique in the crisis in which America found herself." Had the intellectuals been coerced into conformity, Bourne might have forgiven them. But the undisguised eagerness with which they leaped to the ramparts was nothing short of disgusting. Some were even claiming credit for engineering American belligerence. "A war made deliberately by the intellectuals!" he sneered. It boggled the mind.

Bourne predicted that liberalism wouldn't survive the war. In joining the war party, the liberals aligned themselves with the foes of reform – with Wall Street and its minions, and with the rest of the ruling classes of the Atlantic seaboard. "They have assumed the leadership for war of those very classes whom the American democracy has been immemorially fighting. Only in a world where irony was dead could an intellectual class enter war at the head of such illiberal cohorts in the avowed cause of world-liberalism and world-democracy."

From the first, American liberals had taken the part of Britain, becoming "more loyalist than the King, more British even than Australia." Bourne went on: "We became an intellectual Hungary where thought was subject to an effective process of Magyarization. The reputable opinion of the American intellectuals became more and more either what could be read pleasantly in London, or what was written in an earnest effort to put Englishmen straight on their war-aims and war-technique." Now that America had joined forces with the Allies, all vestige of impartiality had vanished. The "older colonials" among the American intellectual community, those who had let their prejudices dictate their thought from the outset of the war, continued to do so. "The war has taught them nothing and will teach them nothing." For the rest, "herd-intellect" reigned.

Bourne dismissed the liberals' pretensions to idealism. "We go to war to save the world from subjugation!" So had the Germans. Americans were now no better. "The Jew often marvels that his race alone should have been chosen as the true people of the cosmic God. Are not our intellectuals equally fatuous when they tell us that our war of all wars is stainless and thrillingly achieving for good?"

Bourne was utterly unmoved by the arguments of supporters of a league of nations. He called such a league "a palpable apocalyptic myth, like the syndicalists' myth of the 'general strike.'" It was, he said, "not a rational programme so much as a glowing symbol for the purpose of focusing belief, of setting enthusiasm on fire for international order." Symbols had their uses, but this one represented chiefly a desire to give the contemporary status quo the patina of international law. League proposals currently receiving consideration contained no provisions for dynamic national growth or for international economic justice; consequently they would produce more wars rather than peace.

The American declaration of war wasn't two months old, yet already Bourne noted its stultifying effect on life in America. Those who had attacked orthodoxy on principle now dismissed freethinkers as irrelevant or worse. "It is only on the craft, in the stream, they say, that one has any chance of controlling the current forces for liberal purposes. If we obstruct, we surrender all power for influence. If we responsibly approve, we then retain our power for guiding. We will be listened to as responsible thinkers, while those who obstructed the coming of war have committed intellectual suicide and shall be cast into outer darkness." Bourne conceded half the argument. "It is true that they may guide, but if their stream leads to disaster and the frustration of national life, is their guiding any more than a preference whether they shall go over the right-hand or left-hand side of the precipice?" Bourne granted that intellectuals faced a terrible dilemma: "Either support what is going on, in which case you count for nothing because you are swallowed in the mass and great incalculable forces bear you on; or remain aloof, passively resistant, in which case you count for nothing because you are outside the machinery of reality."

Bourne took his stand on the outside. The outside, he contended, was where genuine liberals belonged. Those who joined the war effort forgot their priorities. "The real enemy is War rather than imperial Germany." The job of liberals was to keep this real enemy in mind – "to prevent this war of ours from passing into popular mythology as a holy crusade." At a moment when American thought was on the verge of congealing in support of militaristic solutions to international problems and of an illiberal world order, the task of the honest critic of society was "to divide, confuse, disturb, keep the intellectual waters constantly in motion to prevent any such ice from ever forming."[25]

IX

Bourne might have been speaking directly to Lippmann, if the two had still been speaking. Lippmann represented to Bourne and many other observers the epitome of the liberal-gone-to-war. Since the *New Republic* had endorsed Wilson for reelection the previous autumn, the president and his associates, particularly Edward House, had reciprocated the approval and cultivated Lippmann, who in turn cultivated the administration. The symbiosis proved productive for both sides. Lippmann helped Wilson get reelected; Wilson and House fed Lippmann inside information about American policy. Upon America's entry into the war, the administration followed the *New Republic*'s advice and eschewed reliance on volunteer soldiers, relying instead on conscription. This made Lippmann, hale and twenty-seven, a prime candidate. While he preferred conscription as policy, he had no desire that it be applied to him personally, and he turned to the White House for relief. "My father is dying and my mother is all alone in the world," he pleaded. "I am convinced that I can serve my bit much more effectively than as a private in the new armies." Whether or not the administration bought the line about Lippmann's father – who lived for another decade – Wilson's war secretary, Newton Baker, was happy to preserve the bright and well-connected young man from boot camp and the trenches by offering him a staff job in his own office.[26]

Lippmann's first few months in the administration brought little

---

[25] Randolph Bourne, "The War and the Intellectuals," *Seven Arts*, June 1917.
[26] Steel, *Lippmann*, 116–7.

of earth-shaking importance his way. He provided Baker his impressions on the progress of the war, explaining why the peace conference he had so confidently predicted for year's end would have to be postponed. "The mistake of Allied diplomacy," Lippman wrote in August, "has been due to a failure to see that Prussian militarism which looks so dangerous to us looks to the German people like their best defense against a circle of enemies. They hold the handle of the spear which is pointed at us." Lippmann suggested to Edward House that the Wilson administration ease its harassment of domestic dissenters, although the expediential justification he offered would have appalled – but hardly surprised – Randolph Bourne. "So far as I am concerned I have no doctrinaire belief in free speech," Lippmann professed. "In the interest of war it is necessary to sacrifice some of it. But the point is that the method now being pursued is breaking down the liberal support of the war and is tending to divide the country's articulate opinion into fanatical jingoism and fanatical pacifism."[27]

Lippmann's advice neither cured the troubles of Allied diplomacy nor mitigated the crackdown on dissent, but it did convince Baker and House that Lippmann was capable of more-responsible duties. In September, House approached him with a presidential plan for a secret commission to examine options for a postwar settlement. House asked Lippmann to serve as general secretary.

The Inquiry, as the body became known when its existence became known, which it soon did, began work in New York in October. For several weeks, the historians, geographers, and other members couldn't figure out quite what they were expected to do. But after the Bolsheviks seized power in Russia in November and published the secret treaties that demonstrated the seamy side of the Allied war effort, word arrived from Washington to prepare a riposte. For three weeks, the group worked feverishly. At the end of December, Lippmann delivered to House a multipart proposal for postwar rectification of borders. Wilson merged the proposal with several general principles of his own, and the package became the famous Fourteen Points.

Wilson's points made a great impression when he announced them in January 1918, although, as with much the president did, they re-

---

[27] Blum, *Public Philosopher*, 69–71, 74–5.

verberated more strongly among people at large than with the governments that would have to implement them. Not long after the unveiling, Lippmann was dispatched to Europe to try to persuade the skeptics in London and Paris of the worth of Wilson's approach. At the same time, he served as a propagandist for the Allied cause, writing and distributing leaflets designed to dispirit German soldiers and cause them to desert.

Lippmann's efforts with the Allies proved less than compelling: When Berlin sued for an armistice on the basis of Wilson's program, the British and French demanded an outright surrender. Wilson then dispatched House to Europe to reinforce Lippmann. The two met in Paris, where House requested a briefing on the Fourteen Points. "You helped write these points," House explained. "Now you must give me a precise definition of each."[28]

House had better luck than Lippmann at getting the president's points across, and the Allies agreed to an armistice, subject to reservations on certain of Wilson's points. In actuality, though, the sudden flexibility of London and Paris had less to do with the arguments of House or Lippmann than with conditions on the ground in Germany: The kaiser's regime was reeling, and the Allies accurately calculated that once Berlin ceased fire, resuming would prove impossible. At that stage, they would press their demands on Berlin – and on Wilson.

The fighting done, Lippmann stayed on in Paris to observe the president's triumphant arrival. Yet while he still admired Wilson, he remained sufficiently objective, and enough of a reporter, to detect beneath the popular acclaim the iron resolve of the Allied governments. That Wilson apparently took the public applause at face value, and counted on employing it to soften the Allied demands, suggested that the president wasn't being entirely realistic.

Nor did it reassure Lippmann that Wilson no longer seemed to require his advice. Lippmann and his fellow liberal intellectuals had been useful while the war lasted, but now their usefulness was at an end, as the president demonstrated with each passing day. Perhaps Randolph Bourne had been right: Coopted by the war party, the liberals were to be discarded with the return of peace. Lippmann could console himself that Wilson wasn't listening to anyone else

[28] Steel, *Lippmann*, 149.

either, except maybe God. But this knowledge didn't allay his emerging doubts regarding the prospects for a lasting settlement.

Miffed as only a twenty-nine year old who has sipped inside influence can be, Lippmann left Paris in January 1919 and boarded ship for home.

4

When the Future Worked and the Trains Ran on Time: Lincoln Steffens

I

Walter Lippmann wasn't the only one disillusioned by the outcome of the war. The compromises Britain and France forced on Wilson at Paris repelled most American liberals – and many foreign ones, including John Maynard Keynes, who stomped out of the negotiations and tore off his scathing *Economic Consequences of the Peace*. The conservative opposition in America to even Wilson's attenuated treaty, combined with the president's refusal to budge the extra couple of inches that might have made the pact acceptable to the Senate, delivered the *coup de grace* to liberal hopes for a noble and lasting peace.

Not since before the Spanish-American War had the exemplarists held the advantage in American thinking on foreign affairs; now, with vindicationism clearly a bust, they began to reclaim lost ground. The first signs of the exemplarist revival took the form of retrospective assaults on Wilson's conduct of the war. Harry Elmer Barnes rejected the comforting notion that Germany bore primary responsibility for the conflict. Calling the war "the greatest crime against humanity and decency" since man's descent from the apes, Barnes identified the principal culprits as the leaders of France and Russia, with the British being accessories. As for the United States, he denied the causal role of German submarine warfare – which he characterized as "legitimate retaliation against the British violations of international law" – in triggering American entry. According to Barnes, Wilson's avowed neutrality had been a sham for many months prior to his request for a war declaration. "Mr. Wilson had decided to intervene as soon as he could swing the American people to this view

more than a year before January, 1917." Why? Partly out of solicitude for American business and financial interests, which were "very
strongly pro-Entente and pressed hard for intervention on the side of
the Allies." Partly from the spur of inflammatory articles in American
news media, which were "under the sway of the Entente propaganda." Partly as a result of the pro-British intrigues of Walter Hines
Page, the American ambassador in London, "whose maladministra-
tion of his duties was a chief obstacle to American impartiality in
dealing with the belligerent nations after 1914." The consequences
of intervention had been an "unmitigated disaster" for the United
States and the world. The expectation of American entry, which
proved all too accurate, had discouraged the British from meaningful
efforts to seek the negotiated settlement that Germany by 1916 was
prepared to accept. Millions died unnecessarily as a result. In America, the war had killed the reform spirit – killed, indeed, most positive
aspects of American public life. Barnes concluded his angry accounting: "We have been played for a bunch of suckers."[1]

C. Hartley Grattan was mad too. Explaining *Why We Fought*,
Grattan joined Barnes in blaming British propaganda, although he
thought Paris's purveyors of half-truths contributed as well. At bottom, however, were issues of economics. "The World War is on all
fours with every other war in having an economic foundation." Diplomacy, propaganda, statements of war aims, and the like were
"mere secondary structures reared on the foundation of money and
trade." This explained why, in Grattan's view, Wilson's professed
neutrality between Britain and Germany quickly proved to be an idle
dream. "That it was ever more than that, political realists may presume to doubt."[2]

Yet even as Americans generally rejected war as an instrument for
human betterment, some still held a candle for that stepchild of war,
revolution. The Russian revolution gave heart to American socialists,
and in Lenin's utopianism of the left they spied the possibility that
eventual good might come of the irrepressible conflict among the
capitalists. The fascist revolution in Italy followed less directly from
the war than the Russian revolution, and, on its face, Mussolini's
utopianism of the right contradicted nearly everything American rad-

[1] Harry Elmer Barnes, *The Genesis of the World War* (New York, 1926, 1927,
1929), xiii, 646–50.
[2] C. Hartley Grattan, *Why We Fought* (New York, 1929), 127, 182.

icals and liberals stood for. But at a more primitive level, the two movements ran parallel, for each demonstrated a disbelief in the ability of ordinary people to improve their lot without firm guidance from above. A substantial cadre of American public thinkers, convinced by the war (and by the Republican restoration the war helped produce) that democratic liberalism was dead, perceived in the methods of communism and fascism an unexpected avenue to reform.

As a result, there developed in the United States a school of authoritarian apologetics. Among the principal apologists, Lincoln Steffens stood out. Steffens romanticized the Russian revolution, lionizing Lenin and endorsing the Bolsheviks' accomplishment with one of the most durable and misleading pronouncements in the modern history of American political thought. Yet Steffens's partiality to communism had less to do with Marxist ideology than with Leninist technique, for when he met Mussolini, the fascist leader swept the American journalist right off his feet.

II

Steffens's road to Russia followed the path of another of his Harvard proteges. John Reed was personally close to Walter Lippmann at Cambridge, but their politics differed as much as their temperaments. Reed revealed the nature of the difference in a verse dedicated to his friend.

Lippmann – calm, inscrutable,
Thinking and writing clearly, soundly, well;
All snarls of falseness swiftly piercing through,
His keen mind leaps like lightning to the True. . . .
Our all unchallenged Chief! But one
Who builds a world, and leaves out all the fun –
Who dreams a pageant, gorgeous, infinite,
And then leaves all the color out of it –
Who wants to make the human race, and me,
March to a geometric Q.E.D.[3]

Reed encountered Steffens about the same time Lippmann did, with similar consequences. "More than any one man Lincoln Steffens

---

[3] Granville Hicks, *John Reed: The Making of a Revolutionary* (New York, 1936), 80.

has influenced my mind," Reed wrote later. "I met him first while I was at Harvard, where he came loving youth, full of understanding, with the breath of the world clinging to him. I was afraid of him then – afraid of his wisdom, his seriousness. . . . Being with Steffens is to me like flashes of clear light; it is as if I see him, and myself, and the world with new eyes. I tell him what I see and think, and it comes back to me beautiful, full of meaning. He does not judge or advise – he simply makes everything clear."[4]

Upon Reed's graduation, Steffens arranged a journalism job for him, on condition that he use the job as "a springboard from which to dive into life." What Reed dove into was revolution – first the Mexican revolution, which he covered while riding admiringly beside Pancho Villa, and then the Russian revolution. In Petrograd, Reed was utterly smitten by the drama of the struggle attending the birth of the Soviet state. He threw objectivity to the winds of October, embracing the Bolsheviks and their coup with the zeal of instant infatuation. In his breathless account of the affair, published as *Ten Days That Shook the World*, he described the solidarity that welled up within him and his fellow revolutionaries at the critical moment of Lenin's triumph: "Suddenly, by common impulse, we found ourselves on our feet, mumbling together into the smooth, lifting unison of the Internationale."[5]

Steffens would share Reed's sympathy with the Soviet regime, if not the full measure of Reed's infatuation. Meanwhile he shared a bit of advice. Reed had run into trouble on account of some allegedly seditious scribblings in the *Masses*; federal agents arrested him as soon as he landed in America on his return from Russia. They also confiscated the notes from which he planned to write his love letter to Lenin. Steffens suggested that Reed contact Lippmann for help. Reed thanked Steffens for the advice, but refused, having by now given Lippmann up for lost. "I wouldn't ask Walter L. for anything for the whole world," he insisted.[6]

The prosecution's case against Reed stumbled and collapsed, although not from want of assistance from Reed. Amid an incipient

---

[4] Justin Kaplan, *Lincoln Steffens* (New York, 1974), 169.

[5] David C. Duke, *John Reed* (Boston, 1987), 8; John Reed, *Ten Days That Shook the World* (New York, 1919, 1967), 130.

[6] Ronald Steel, *Walter Lippmann and the American Century* (Boston, 1980), 138.

anti-communist panic, he waved a Red flag in front of the bull of public opinion by accepting Trotsky's offer of a job as Soviet consul-general in the United States. He had some reservations about taking the job – but they weren't of the obvious divided-loyalty sort. Instead he feared that his new position might compel him to compromise his revolutionary scruples regarding personal relations. "When I am consul I suppose I shall have to marry people," he told a friend. "I hate the marriage ceremony. I shall simply say to them, 'Proletarians of the world, unite!' " In the event, Washington spared his conscience by refusing to accredit him.[7]

Even without Lippmann's help, Reed eventually retrieved his notebooks and wrote *Ten Days* in about thrice that long. The book didn't do much world-shaking upon publication, although a decade-and-a-half later it served as a weapon in the leftist wars of the Depression. (It would serve a similar purpose during the 1960s, and a quite different one during the 1980s, when it supplied verisimilitude to the portrait of Reed in the Hollywood feature *Reds* – a film that needed all the verisimilitude it could get.) After having been ignited by the revolutionary flame, Reed found socialist politics in America tepid, and he returned to the Soviet Union in 1919. It was a bad time for a visit: The civil war made life precarious and – in Reed's case – short. He contracted typhus and died in October 1920. The Bolsheviks, grateful for his propaganda work, buried him in the Kremlin wall.

III

If Reed's red meteor burned out early, Lincoln Steffens's less intense light lasted longer. Steffens initially established his progressive credentials in cahoots with Theodore Roosevelt, whom Steffens met when the two collaborated with reformer Jacob Riis to expose the corruption of the New York police bureau. "It was just as if we three were the police board, T.R., Riis, and I," Steffens exaggerated later. Steffens's exposés of city government, initially appearing in *McClure's* magazine and gathered in 1904 into book form as *The Shame of the Cities*, won Steffens a national reputation, and when he left *McClure's* for the *American Magazine*, some of the country's most influential muckrakers, including Ida Tarbell and Ray Stannard

---

[7] Hicks, *Reed*, 295.

Baker, joined him to push the latter journal to the forefront of progressive investigative reporting.[8]

But Steffens's free-lance temperament resisted the obligations of regular employment, and he left the *American* before long. An inheritance and a knack for picking stocks afforded him a comfortable living, which he supplemented with articles and part-time work on the editorial board of *Everybody's Magazine*. Invited to Boston to examine municipal corruption there, Steffens befriended President Charles Eliot of Harvard. It was through Eliot that Steffens came into contact with Lippmann and Reed. After the untimely death of his wife and the winding up of his Boston venture, Steffens briefly joined Mabel Dodge's circle in New York (where Reed already had the inside track to that fashionable radical's salon and, subsequently, her boudoir). In 1914, as Wilson embroiled the United States in the Mexican revolution, Steffens decided to follow Reed south and investigate the situation for himself.

Steffens was less impressed with Pancho Villa than Reed had been. He dismissed the guerrilla leader as an "illiterate, unscrupulous unrevolutionary bandit" and sided with Venustiano Carranza, the chief of the constitutionalist forces. Carranza took Steffens into his confidence, explaining why his government couldn't make peace on terms acceptable to President Wilson. "What you don't understand, I think," Carranza said, "is that this is an economic, not a political revolution. You keep asking us to establish peace first, then set up a constitutional government, and then enact our reforms." That was how the *norteamericanos* had accomplished their revolution, such as it was. But that was not the Mexican way. "We want to establish an economic democracy and then we will have a political democracy."[9]

Steffens didn't stick around long enough to learn that ordinary Mexicans weren't going to get a lot of either form of democracy, despite Carranza's ultimate victory; before then, he was off to Russia to cover the newest front in the wars of the world revolution. Steffens almost beat Lenin to the Finland Station. Immediately upon hearing of the overthrow of the czar, he booked passage for Petrograd. He arrived during the spring of 1917 – spring by the calendar, if not by the Russian weather, and spring most definitely by the mood of the Russian people. He described May Day in Petrograd for the readers

[8] Lincoln Steffens, *The Autobiography of Lincoln Steffens*, (New York, 1931), 258.
[9] Kaplan, *Steffens*, 212–13.

of *Everybody's*: "I went all over that city, all day long, and it was a day to remember. It was sunny, cold, very, very cold, for the ice had not run out of the Neva – and that's the sign of spring at Petrograd. But it was sunshine, physically and spiritually. The Russian people were glad, warm, kind."

The people were also organized. Skeptical informants and enemies of the revolution, as well as his experience of Mexico and his understanding of historical precedents, had led Steffens to expect social chaos, or at least widespread turmoil. He found nothing of the kind. "We were told we mustn't go out that day," he wrote, referring to May 1. "And that, the night before, we must lay in a store of food. We did this last. Everybody did. And that was necessary, for no worker worked in Petrograd on May first." Yet the demonstrations – celebrations, rather – were peaceful and orderly, without being any the less spontaneous. "Everyone knew where he was to go, where to march, where to speak or listen, as he wished. And anybody and everybody spoke; and all said what each thought. The notes sounded were happy – hope and faith and brotherhood."

Steffens couldn't get over the hopefulness and confidence the revolution was engendering daily.

I saw two processions meet on the bank of the Neva. One was of jolly Russians: men, women, girls and boys, soldiers and workers; the other of Tartars, Mongols and Chinamen, workers who did the dirty work of the city – street-cleaning, sewers, draining. These were shy, abashed, not sure. The two processions cheered each other; then, moved a bit, they halted to sing the revolutionary song together; and then, at a moment I felt – everybody seemed to get the full import of it – the two or three races rushed together, and embraced, and wept. A moment, and they recovered their dignity, and marched on their way. But the Mongols were not shy any longer; they looked a bit astonished at one another, but their step was sure.

Steffens acknowledged that the revolution wasn't accomplished entirely without violence. "There were mobs; and military motor-trucks and armored cars, full of armed workmen and wild girls and angry soldiers, shot here and there, like bullets, and there were clashes between contending crowds." But the foreign press made far too much of the violence. "I think you get a wrong impression of such things, because we reporters, naturally, pick out to report only incidents, and there were enough street battles on May fourth and

fifth to give, if described, a sense of great violence and disorder."
This impression wasn't accurate. "There must have been thousands
of meetings and hundreds of parades that day, with at least a million
people deeply moved and partly armed; and there were but three
'bloody incidents,' and seven killed and wounded. That was the
news."

Steffens found the restraint of the people astonishing. He described
the culmination of a clash between strikers and the police.

The strikers won, armed and unarmed, and all turned upon the police,
who retreated to cellars and roofs, but armed there with rifles and machine guns, fought. They fought like rats. The police shot into crowds
that didn't see the police till the police attacked them – for revenge,
apparently; in despairing hate.

And the mobs, the brutal Russian democracy, what did the dreaded
people do? Sometimes they caught and killed the police. Not often. Once
they fought and some of the crowd died to get a squad of police in a
fighting police-station, and they killed them all, and burned the station;
but that was because they found the basement full of "food for sale": a
Russian police graft. The police wouldn't let the shopkeepers sell to the
people, except on tickets, but they, the police, stored up big stocks and
sold to the rich who paid them graft prices. For that, the mob, in sudden
fury, killed. And sometimes they killed because in a battle between a
roof full of police and a street full of people, many people were shot
down.

But this wasn't typical. All witnesses agree that the typical thing was
for the people to fight up under a building that harbored an attacking
squad of policemen; go up, under fire, to the roof, fight well and take
the police, and bring them down to the street. There always some voices
clamored for blood. But always also some voice said: "Niet, niet. That's
what the Government did. We mustn't do any of the things the Government does. We must take the prisoners to the Duma and let them be
tried."

And this was done.

Steffens judged it significant that the first act of the revolutionary
government had been to abolish capital punishment. Quoting Kerensky that "if we must govern by force and fear, I will not govern in
Russia," Steffens ascribed the popular desire for justice and peace to
the teachings of Tolstoy and Jesus, which had "sunk deep into the
Russians."

The people's insistence on fair play, even in the heat of revolution,
manifested itself in an insistence on hearing all points of view. De-

bates – over the direction of the revolution, over the constitution of the revolutionary government, over the continuation of the war, over everything – never ceased. "The speakers were passionate; so was the crowd," Steffens said of one afternoon session that brought denunciations of secret treaties and calls for a war solely for justice, decency, and a better future. Feelings ran high and deep. "They said they were willing to fight for all this right there in the square at that moment, and you felt they were. There was a psychology about it; it gripped one, carried one along with it." Not everyone shared the sentiment, though. "Right in the midst of it, at the height of the feeling, after a good speaker had expressed that crowd to its satisfaction, a little clerklike dandy got up and began in a rasping voice to speak against this view. There was a murmur of anger, and I thought the moment had come: there certainly would have been trouble in some countries I know. Not in Russia. That hot mob turned upon that murmur: 'Niet,' a dozen voices said. 'Silence! We must hear him out, too. Everybody can say all that he thinks.' "

In a comment that would acquire irony after Lenin's coup, Steffens noted that tolerance of minority opinions extended to the radical fringe of the revolutionary party as well as in the opposite direction. "There was a moment when Lenin, the veteran radical who came home through Germany, was most unpopular both with the Provisional Government and the people; they said he was jeopardizing the Revolution; but the Soldiers and Workmen wouldn't forbid his meetings, and the people kept a small crowd before his house, to see that he was protected and heard." Yet even those who disagreed with Lenin defended his motives. Steffens inquired whether any substance informed the charge that Lenin was on Germany's payroll. "Certainly not," responded a man who had been denouncing Lenin's notions of revolution. "Lenin is as sincere as any of us. Only he is arrogant and risks the cause just to stick to his own theory."

What did the future promise for this bold experiment in participatory politics? Having come to Russia expecting to find anarchy and violence, and having discovered something entirely different, Steffens placed no limit on what the Russians might accomplish.

What I saw was – Order; no government and no disorder. What I heard was – Justice; no law, but all men full of respect for all men. And what I came to feel there was that I was one of a great, strong, young people in a state of exaltation; lifted by ideals far, far above anything I had ever believed the human animal capable of in the mass. That was the key to my understanding of the Russian Revolution.

It may not last – this state of mind. It had lasted from the start of the Revolution to the time I got there; it lasted during the five weeks I was in Petrograd. . . . It lasted – I found it all through Russia and Siberia on my way home. Men and women everywhere were rising above themselves to work out with humility and confidence, with passion, but with caution, their common – the nation's, a people's – job.

"It can't last," the foreigners there said, "it simply can't." And nobody says it can. I don't. I think I saw the beginning of the descent to earth just before I quit Petrograd. I heard some parlor Socialists, society folk and foreign investors discussing ways and means to split the Revolutionary Government: break off the Jews from the Gentiles, the soldiers from the working men, and set the peasants against both.

But this I can say: "Some of us who lived with the Russians in their joy will never again lose our belief in the possibilities of human nature in the mob; of man in the mass."[10]

IV

Steffens's enthusiasm for "man in the mass" survived the second stage of the Russian revolution, the ascent of the Bolsheviks chronicled by Reed. If anything, Steffens's almost mystical attachment to the Russian people as a millennial force in human history increased with the overthrow of the bourgeois provisional government of Kerensky and the establishment of the dictatorship of the proletariat. Writing at the end of 1918, a year after the Bolsheviks' seizure of power, Steffens summarized the course of the revolution. "In a line, one burning, enlightening line: 'The Millennium first; then the Messiah.' Thus the Russian prophecy. Hence the Russian revolution. The revolution in Russia is to establish the Kingdom of Heaven here on earth, now; in order that Christ may come soon; and, coming, reign forever. Forever and ever, everywhere. Not over Russia alone. The revolution in Russia is not the Russian revolution. It is 'The Revolution.' "[11]

Steffens's radicalism was of a peculiar sort. It shifted over time from the moderate reformism of his *Shame of the Cities* days to the Stalinism of his last years, but it followed no consistent track in between. It visited both Christian millenarian socialism and continental

---

[10] Lincoln Steffens, "What Free Russia Asks of Her Allies," *Everybody's Magazine*, August 1917.
[11] "Christian" (Steffens), "The Rumor in Russia," *Nation*, Dec. 21, 1918.

fascism – occasionally both at once. In his 1926 *Moses in Red*, Steffens described Jesus as simultaneously a leader of communists and a Galilean version of Tom Johnson, the reform mayor of Cleveland. Steffens saw Moses as the model for Lenin and Mussolini. He judged the divine destruction of Egypt's eldest sons the original "red terror" and he remarked that "in revolutions, in wars and in all such disorganizing, fear-spreading crises in human affairs, nations tend to return to the first, the simplest, and perhaps the best form of government: a dictatorship."[12]

To a certain degree, Steffens's inconstancy indicated an inability to settle down – a problem that vexed his personal life as well as his politics. To a greater degree, it reflected a conviction that an honest intellectual must remain a skeptic. As he explained to a friend, it was the job of the intellectual "to doubt." Steffens didn't always succeed. His critics, especially during the 1930s, found him shockingly credulous. But at least he recognized the pitfalls of excessive commitment, which was more than some of the critics did.[13]

During the decade of the Russian revolution, Steffens was in his Christian socialist phase. John Reed dedicated a poem to him, in which the hero Sangar, "the Mad Recreant Knight of the West," attempted to ward off a Hun invasion with the words of the Gospel. His message unavailing, Sangar fell at the hand of his own son, who rejected Sangar's appeal to conscience and insisted on meeting iron with iron. At this point Sangar went to his reward.

Oh, there was joy in Heaven when Sangar came.
Sweet Mary wept, and bathed and bound his wounds,
And God the Father healed him of despair,
And Jesus gripped his hand, and laughed and laughed . . .

The poem ended on this ambiguous note, which suggested the ambivalence Reed and other proponents of a standard, secular radicalism felt toward Steffens's mystical version.[14]

Idiosyncratic though it was, Steffens's approach to the Russian revolution afforded him a certain perspective denied thorough-going secularists. Despite the Bolsheviks' official antipathy to religion, Stef-

---

[12] Lincoln Steffens, *Moses in Red: The Revolt of Israel as a Typical Revolution* (Philadelphia, 1926), 13–14, 35–6, 82.
[13] Christopher Lasch, *The New Radicalism in America* (New York, 1967 ed.), 278.
[14] John Reed, *Sangar* (Riverside, Conn., 1913).

fens had no doubt that the popular enthusiasm for the revolution owed much to the pervasive religious sensibilities of the Russian people. In an article in the *Nation* that appeared just before Christmas 1918, under the byline "Christian," after John Bunyan's pilgrim, Steffens described "The Rumor in Russia":

Russia is alive with it. There is where I heard it first, this new, old, good tidings of great joy. The mighty mobs of the meek of Petrograd were passing it along like a lighted candle through the darkness of the dawn of their revolution.

"The great, white Christ is coming," they whispered. And they whispered lest Herod should hear: the Czar or their own lesser leaders, the small Messiahs, who would not believe and might mock them, denying the resurrection of their ancient faith and putting their new-born hope to death.

For this saying was no new saying to them of the mob. They were recalling the hoary prophecy Tolstoi heard and reported: that he was coming out of the North. But they believed it, those simple peasants, soldiers, sailors, and working men and women; verily. They accepted literally the word they were handing on, like a tiny light, along the trenches, across the battle lines, into the cities, towns, villages, and back again out over Siberia and all the Russias, whence it came, this burning word. And there was light in the Word; in the mere word. The lowly Russians believed, and they believe, that they are making ready a perfect people, prepared for the coming of the Lord.

The Russian people's simplicity was both their weakness and their strength. "All witnesses testify – some in scorn, others in pity, a few in awe – that under the yoke of the generations of their servitude the Russian people became as little children." Like little children, they were kept from the truth. Like little children, they learned to believe the lies they were told, of their stupidity and inferiority and incompetence. They heard voices in their darkness. Most of the voices repeated the lies.

But two voices were different. "Only two of all the many strange cries which broke the solid silence of the centuries of their darkness – only two said to those children of light that there was light; that there was hope ahead, in the darkness of despair, for them."

One of the voices belonged to the priest, who sermonized that Christ had come and lived and died and would come again. The returned Christ would lead them from their present darkness into the light of the Kingdom of Heaven – but only if they followed the teachings of His holy church.

The second voice sounded from beyond the pale of respectability. "This other voice that they heard was of one crying in the wilderness: the propagandist of the revolution." This messenger unsettled the priests and the powers, calling them Pharisees and Sadducees and offspring of vipers and warning them to flee the wrath to come.

At first the people didn't know how to respond to the two voices. "It was hard for the dark, untutored, drunken Russian mujik, kept dark and kept drunk, to hold apart the discordant notes of the two voices he heard battling for his soul in the silence of his fearful, weary stupor." It was more than hard; it was impossible. "His need was for both of them, so he took them both, as children do; he seized what he needed of those two songs and he joined them very simply together into one song."

And the song said: "Christ is coming, as the priest says. And as the revolutionist says, Heaven is coming also; and first. But neither will come until there are wars and the rumors of wars, and we, the people, have raised up the Revolution which is to prepare His way."

The great European war and the tribulations it produced convinced the Russian people that the time was at hand. They made their revolution, believing that in doing so that they were hastening the day of Christ's coming. The nations of the earth did not understand. "The world marvelled and was wroth, not comprehending; not apprehending that this was the first good news that the Russian race had ever heard; that this was the first good thing that had ever happened that was good for them; that this was the good tidings which was to bring in the golden rule of love for all the children of God."

But the Russians had understood, and they set about creating heaven on earth. Though they had accomplished much, much remained to do. "Not all the people had been perfected; not all the preparations had been made; the crooked ways had not all been straightened." Yet they had begun the task, and they wouldn't cease till they had finished.[15]

V

Lenin doubtless didn't have time to read Steffens's depiction of the revolution. If he had, he certainly would have been amused to see himself cast as John the Baptist. Still, the Bolshevik leader recognized the value of favorable, if eccentric, coverage in the American press,

---

[15] Lincoln Steffens, "Rumor in Russia."

and when Steffens returned to Russia at the beginning of 1919, Lenin honored him with an audience.

Steffens traveled in company with William Bullitt, a special envoy from President Wilson to the Bolshevik government. While covering the Paris peace conference, Steffens had suggested to Edward House an effort to determine the Bolsheviks' intentions toward the West and to reassure them of the good will of the Allies. House picked Bullitt, a journalist-turned-bureaucrat like Walter Lippmann, though one with far tonier social connections. Bullitt, impressed by Steffens's reporting of the Russian revolution, asked him to come along as political observer and liaison.

The Bullitt mission proved a failure, oversold by Bullitt, who thought he could negotiate an end to the Russian civil war, and undervalued by the Allied leaders, who were busy making the German pips squeak and in any event wanted to overthrow rather than reassure the Bolsheviks; to this latter purpose, they were backing the Bolsheviks' White opponents in the civil war Bullitt and Steffens wanted to end. Consequently, the Bullitt mission was doomed from the start, although Bullitt didn't realize it until he returned to Paris and got brushed off by Lloyd George, Clemenceau, and even Wilson.

Bullitt was incensed, and left Paris in a rage. He returned to the United States, where he did his best to subvert Wilson's plan for a settlement. He acted as a star witness before Henry Cabot Lodge's Senate foreign relations committee, which quickly published his indictment of Wilson's capitulation to the British and French. Bullitt's testimony was also published commercially, accompanied by a report Steffens wrote about the Russian trip.

Steffens's report was written with the purpose of dashing any vindicationist notions that the United States could – or should – attempt to reverse the recent events in Russia. The revolution was a fact, and a good thing too. By this time, Steffens's reply to friend and expatriate artist Jo Davidson, who asked where he had been lately – "I have been over into the future, and it works" – was well started on the path to immortality. Steffens's published report put the same sentiment in drier though not materially different terms. "Russia has reached a state of equilibrium," he wrote. "I think the revolution there is ended; that it has run its course. There will be changes. There may be advances; there will certainly be reactions, but these will be regular, I think; political and economic, but parliamentary. A new center of gravity seems to have been found." With the tearing down of the old regime completed, the building up of the new now commenced – in a most unrevolutionary fashion, Steffens said. "We saw this everywhere. And we saw order, and though we inquired for them, we heard of no disorders." Prohibition was universal. Robberies had fallen below levels normal in the West. Prostitution had disappeared. Sabotage was nonexistent. Even loafing on the job had all but vanished. "Russia has settled down to work."[16]

Steffens didn't deny the deficiencies of the Bolshevik system. "It is full of faults and difficulties; clumsy, and in its final development it is not democratic." It had committed excesses, not least because Lenin was an autocrat – "farther removed from the people than the Tsar was."

Even so, the government suited the Russians. "The Soviet Government sprouted and grew out of the habits, the psychology, and the condition of the Russian people. It fitted them. They understand it. They find they can work it and they like it." The secret of its appeal was that it represented the Russian people more accurately than any government ever had. "In Russia all legislators, all, are young or new. It is as if we should elect in the United States a brand-new set of men to all offices, from the lowest county to the highest federal position." Chosen during a time when the people were taking power into their own hands, the officials remained of necessity close to their origins. "The new leaders of the local soviets of Russia were, and they still are, of the people, really. That is one reason why their autocratic dictatorship is acceptable."

In this report, Steffens no longer spoke of the revolution in Christian-mystical language. Such an interpretation didn't suit his forum. Neither did it fit the present situation in Russia. Steffens was forced to admit that the Russian people had indefinitely postponed the Second Coming, perhaps canceled it altogether. Describing the single-mindedness with which the people had smashed every vestige of the imperial government and the prerevolutionary regime, he wrote, "They pulled down the Tsar and his officers; they abolished the courts, which had been used to oppress them; they closed shops, stopped business generally, and especially all competitive and speculative business; and they took over all the great industries, monopolies, concessions, and natural resources. This was their purpose. This is their religion."

If the Soviet system fell short of American democratic ideals, that

---

[16] Kaplan, *Steffens*, 250; Steffens report, Apr. 2, 1919, in *The Bullitt Mission to Russia* (New York, 1919).

shortfall simply indicated different priorities. Steffens remembered what Carranza had told him, and he heard the message again in Russia. "Not political democracy, as with us," Steffens said to his American audience. "Economic democracy is the idea; democracy in the shop, factory, business." If the transition to the desired end entailed suffering and privation, an accurate accounting would debit the regime that had rendered the wrecking of the old order necessary. "The revolution didn't do it. The Tsar's Government had rotted it. The war broke down the worn-out machinery of it; the revolution has merely scrapped it finally."

The Russian people accepted the cost of constructing a new order because all shared the burden equally, or soon would. Steffens described a three-tiered system of rationing designed to diminish inequality. The first tier included soldiers, workers in war industries, government officials, teachers, and other persons filling demanding and top-priority jobs. Members of this group were allotted one-and-a-half pounds of bread per day. The second tier comprised all other workers. They could buy three-quarters of a pound per day. The last group consisted of those who did no work – "the leisure class." Individuals in this category could purchase no more than one-quarter pound per day. The government knew that such persons would turn to the black market, but the high prices charged there would force them to spend down the savings they had squirreled away. When their hoards ran out, they would have to find jobs and make themselves useful.

Steffens noted that the ration rules didn't exempt even Lenin. "Lenin eats, like everybody else – only one meal a day – soup, fish, bread, and tea. He has to save out of that a bit for breakfast and another bit for supper. The people, the peasants, send him more, but he puts it in the common mess."

The system didn't lack compassion. Children received the best food: milk, eggs, meat, fruit. Children's rations took no notice of class, for the revolutionaries did not hold children responsible for the sins of their fathers. Nor did the system entirely lack amenities. Artists were considered essential workers, and their activities were sponsored by the government and patronized by the masses, rather than merely the rich. Children visited museums, theater, and opera with their classmates.

The solicitude for the children demonstrated not only humanitarianism but the sense of the Russian people that they were actively creating a better future. "The kids represent the future," one person committed to the revolution – an American, significantly – told Steffens. "Our generation is to have only the labor, the joy, and the misery of the struggle. We will get none of the material benefits of the new system, and we will probably never all understand and like it. But the children – it is for them and their children that we are fighting."

What did the Bolsheviks want from the world at large? At some point they would wish to share their revolution with other countries. At present, however, they recognized that they had their hands full completing the revolution in Russia. "They want to spread it all over the world, but only as it works." When Steffens had pointed out to the Bolshevik leaders that their propaganda suggested a more forceful attitude toward international revolution, they responded, "We are through with the old propaganda of argument. All we ask now is to be allowed to prove by the examples of things well done here in Russia, that the new system is good." Each country must make its own revolution in its own way. To impose revolution on another country was "not scientific, not democratic, not socialistic."

The Bolsheviks desired peace; but if the West would not allow them the peace and respect they required to perfect their revolution, they would defend themselves. "You must not treat us as a conquered nation," they said. "We are not conquered. We are prepared to join in a revolutionary, civil war all over all of Europe and the world, if this good thing has to be done in the bad way of force."

Via Steffens and Bullitt, the Bolsheviks issued their appeal and their warning to the nations gathered at Paris. "They are practical men," Steffens said. "They are all idealists, but they are idealists sobered by the responsibility of power. Sentiment has passed out of them into work – hard work." Steffens believed they were sincere in proposing a revolution in one country. He also believed they were sincere in threatening world revolution should the governments of the world leave them no alternative. "If I am any judge of character," Steffens concluded, "Lenin and his commissaires will stand by their offer to us until Paris has answered."[17]

VI

In fact, Steffens was *not* any judge of character, as events would prove, if they hadn't already. He may have understood the politics of

---

[17] Steffens report.

Kansas City and Cleveland, but postwar Russia wasn't like those comfortably middle-of-the-American-road locales. The origins of Russia's revolution lay deep in the Russian past – far deeper than Steffens (or Reed or anyone else) could dig in a couple of months of visits. Yet Steffens's assessment of Russia was less important for what it said about Lenin and his associates than what it said about Steffens and *his* crowd. The fact that at this time one of the pioneers of American progressivism could interpret the rise of communism in Russia as a hopeful new stage in the development of democracy spoke volumes about the discouragement of America liberals during the decade after the Great War. In 1917 they had gone to war to teach the world about democracy; now they were reduced to taking lessons in the subject from a Russian dictator. Vindicationism was truly dead; on Steffens's evidence, even exemplarism was ailing.

Some of the former progressives, again with Steffens in the lead, took lessons as well from an Italian dictator. Steffens landed in Italy partly by design, partly by accident. After his and Bullitt's rebuff by Wilson and the Allies at Paris, the two men went their separate but loosely parallel ways. Bullitt spent the 1920s emptying his spleen on Wilson and all that the Democratic president stood for. In a novel entitled *It's Not Done*, he blasted Wilson as "a middle-class Southerner with a colossal vocabulary and an even more colossal inferiority complex." (He didn't spend the *entire* decade denouncing Wilson: He also squeezed in a few moments to woo and win Louise Bryant, the widow of John Reed – which may have given the poet of the revolution a certain posthumous satisfaction, although, considering the blueness of Bullitt's blood, the red Reed might have been appalled.) Bullitt looked up Sigmund Freud, and the two collaborated on a curious politico-psychobiography of Wilson. By the time they finished, Bullitt was having second thoughts. He held off publishing until three decades later, by which time Freud's heirs were having second thoughts of their own. The manuscript found its way to the printer only in 1966, the year before Bullitt died.[18]

Steffens was less vitriolic by nature than Bullitt, but he was just

[18] William C. Bullitt, *It's Not Done* (New York, 1926), 264; Sigmund Freud and William C. Bullitt, *Thomas Woodrow Wilson* (Boston, 1966); Will Brownell and Richard N. Billings, *So Close to Greatness: A Biography of William C. Bullitt* (New York, 1987), 322–3.

about as disillusioned with life in America, and like Bullitt (and numerous other American writers and artists) he took up residence in Europe during the 1920s. He returned to Russia in 1923 but stayed only a short while, his travel plans complicated by visa problems as well as troubles of the heart. While pondering the future of a long-standing but desultory relationship with a woman in America, he fell in love in France with a woman thirty years his junior. Eventually he fathered a child, an accomplishment he had thought impossible, by the younger woman, Ella Winter, whom he proceeded to marry. Bullitt and Bryant hosted the wedding breakfast in Paris. The newlyweds leased a house in San Remo, partly for the view of the Mediterranean, partly for the view of the Maritime Alps, and partly for the view of that new feature on the Italian landscape, Benito Mussolini.

During the 1920s, Mussolini captured the imagination of a broad variety of observers. Winston Churchill and George Bernard Shaw discerned much to applaud in his revivification of Italian life. American business leaders liked his emphasis on efficiency, not to mention his concern for the health of capitalism. An editor of *Nation's Business*, the journal of the American Chamber of Commerce, depicted Mussolini's methods as "essentially those of successful business." The *Wall Street Journal* admired the Italian strongman's spurning of "word-froth" in favor of action. Journalist John Gunther meanwhile lauded Mussolini as "the only modern ruler who can genuinely be termed an intellectual." Another reporter, Edward Price Bell, praised Mussolini's "luminous and powerful intellect."

The man who eventually became Mussolini's most notorious American partisan, the poet and would-be economist Ezra Pound, considered the Duce the intellectual superior to anything the Anglo-Saxon system could produce. Pound wrote a friend, "I personally think extremely well of Mussolini. If one compares him to American presidents (the last three) or British premiers, etc. – in fact one can not without insulting him." Pound dedicated his forty-first canto to Mussolini.

"Ma questo"
said the Boss, "è divertente."
catching the point before the aesthetes had got there;
Having drained off the muck by Vada
From the marshes, by Circeo, where no one else would have drained it.
Waited 2000 years, ate grain from the marshes;

Water supply for ten million, another one million "vani"
that is room for people to live in.[19]

VII

Lincoln Steffens was hardly less enamored of Mussolini than was
Pound. In what Steffens called "the truest chapter" of his 1931 autobiography, he described the impact of the Italian leader's arrival on
the international scene.

Benito Mussolini came like thunder on the right. It was just as if the
Author of all things had looked down upon this little planet of His, and
seeing the physical, mental, moral confusion here, said to Himself, "How
can I, in a flash, clear up these poor humans? I haven't much time for so
small a ball of mud, but I must somehow help them to change their
minds and catch up with the changes I am making." And "I know," He
said; "I will have a political thunderstorm, big enough for all men to
notice and not too big for them to comprehend, and through it I will
shoot a blazing thunderbolt that will strike down all their foolish old
principles, burn up their dead ideas, and separate the new light I am
creating from the darkness men have made." And so He formed Mussolini out of a rib of Italy.[20]

In a 1927 article for *Survey*, whose title "Stop, Look, Listen!"
captured the urgency Steffens ascribed to the lesson Mussolini taught,
he sketched the Italian dictator as "a great man, much greater than
his many, wild, Italian eulogists say." Steffens continued, "Mussolini
is bold, physically and spiritually. He is the wilful man of action,
direct, swift, sure and wise, very wise." Mussolini had achieved
power, Steffens explained, by virtue of the fact that at Italy's moment
of despair, he was the only person who saw what needed doing and
possessed the will to do it.

"Go home," he said to his parliament in one crisis. "You are afraid. You
couldn't do in a year what has to be done. One brave man can do it in
a week. Go to your cafes and watch. By Wednesday of next week you
will see that I have done it."
    And because he was right – because they were afraid, they took that
insult, they dispersed, and by Tuesday the job was done; the crisis
passed.

[19] John P. Diggins, *Mussolini and Fascism: The View from America* (Princeton, N.J.,
    1972), 60; John Tytell, *Ezra Pound* (New York, 1987), 203, 229–30.
[20] Steffens, *Autobiography*, 813.

Mussolini's gift was his ability to perceive his place in history. "He believes in history. The man is as powerful as an elemental force, and he feels it. History told him that he was historically due; he and Lenin; fascism or bolshevism. . . . He is the personification of self-conscious history." Steffens hypothesized American parallels. "Imagine Theodore Roosevelt as aware in action of his place in the history of the United States and you will have Benito Mussolini in Italy. Or think of President Wilson the historian, thinking in Paris not of what was right and what wrong, not of the wise and the beautiful, but asking: What do the histories I have read and written say has always been done at this stage of such crises as these?"

Steffens deemed the Wilson analogy particularly instructive, since it spoke directly to the failure of American liberalism to shape the peace. Citing a conference of European powers at Lausanne that Mussolini had broken up when he failed to get satisfaction, leaving the powers to follow him meekly to Genoa, Steffens said Wilson should have acted similarly at Paris. When Lloyd George and Clemenceau refused a realistic settlement, the president should have walked out. "The peacemakers would have gone to Washington to make the Peace of Versailles if Wilson had gone home. The historian President might have won his fight if he had known history, current and past, as well – as practically – as Mussolini knows it."[21]

Like most of Mussolini's American admirers, Steffens found the Duce's technique more congenial than his objectives. The technique was what allowed Steffens to extol Mussolini at the same time that he applauded Lenin. "Mussolini took the method, the spirit, the stuff, of Bolshevism and used it to go – right. The method! Was that what the divine Dictator meant us to see – that there was a method, good either way?" Steffens was willing to give God and Mussolini the benefit of the doubt.

Mussolini's method allowed him to cut through the form-worship that paralyzed liberals. He took to heart the lesson of the Russian revolution. "Mussolini saw with his sharp, fearless mind that there was democracy for six months of the revolution, that it was ineffective and that, in the crisis of the mob-failure, Russia went to a dictatorship. He drew the conclusion that in every great crisis in every country there is a vacant throne and that the bravest, strongest man can leap into that throne, seize power and hold it, exactly as Lenin did."

[21] Lincoln Steffens, "Stop, Look, Listen!" *Survey*, March 1, 1927.

Mussolini disdained mere intellectuals, those who could talk and write but couldn't act. He threw aside the salon revolutionists to exercise the power of which they merely theorized. His masterful brilliance left Steffens stunned. "He seized power, not only the leadership but the throne, which he filled to overflowing. He let the king stand, aside, but he suppressed him and his ministers, and the parliament, and liberty, democracy, and aristocracy; he commanded the army, the navy, the police; he occupied the ministries – all by force, by the threat of the force of his personality, his decision, his activity, by the fear of his power to throw his small, organized minority of armed youth into violent action." Steffens was in awe. "It was a spectacle, so swift, so quiet, so tense but orderly; amazing; so easy – for the right man at the right psychological moment."

Mussolini's intuition penetrated the surface of events to a deeper psychological reality. "He knew something we did not know. Put it this way: Mussolini knew something which we did not know that we knew." Steffens asked the prodigy how he recognized that the time had come for action. "You were not elected," Steffens reminded Mussolini. "You did not seek election. You just jumped into the throne; you seized it and power." What made him think he could get away with such highhandedness?

His answer showed that he understood my question and me, that I was a liberal with preconceived liberal principles and the liberal's inquisitiveness about the way to do – whatever you want to do. His fierce face expressed contempt for me and my kind and our dead logic.

"You're a correspondent?" I nodded. "Yes," he mocked, and he asked and answered: "You saw the war? Yes. And the peace? Yes. And the revolution in Russia? Yes.

"Well," he sneered, "did you learn anything?"

God's question to man, that! Could we, could I, learn from experience, from history, from events, he meant, as he could and did? Or did I stick to my principles, theories in the face of the plain facts? My muttered reply was that yes, I had learned some things.

"Some things!" he exclaimed. "Some?" he bored. "Listen. Do you think now any of the things you thought before you saw the war, the peace, and the revolution?"

What a question! Did I? I did till Mussolini shot that searching question into me.

Mussolini's question, and more pointedly his actions, forced Steffens to reconsider his own position. Mussolini certainly had reconsidered his. "He, an ex-socialist of the left, almost an anarchist, had watched, had watched the war, as a soldier, to see how you get obedience unto death out of the people; he had watched the peace as a red to see what the war was about; he had watched Russia, as a leader seeking a way to do – whatever you want to do." He had learned from all this, and he had learned "because, no mere intellectual, he could change his mind, deep down, to the depths where it would change his acts, his every impulse."

Americans, Steffens argued, and American intellectuals especially, must follow Mussolini's example. "I – and my kind, the intellectuals – must learn to do that, else we'll never lead." The intellectuals' problem was their reverence for ideas, which got in the way of action. "We know too much," Steffens said. "The better educated we are, the harder we believe in axioms." Steffens had once interviewed Einstein, and had asked the physicist how he made his great discoveries. By challenging axioms, Einstein replied. Mussolini, Steffens contended, was accomplishing a similar feat in the field of politics. "Mussolini was challenging axioms, which brain-bound me, which spiked Europe to the past. As bold as Einstein, Mussolini, the willful man of action, saw by looking – at Russia, for example – that the people there in power were distracted by conflicting counsel and helpless. They wanted to follow, not to lead; to be governed, not to govern themselves."

Lenin had perceived the Russian people's need to follow and had made himself their leader; Mussolini had done the same in Italy. The success of both owed to their ability to put knowledge to work. "These new, revolutionary leaders read history, and not as the scholars do, for love of a growing body of knowledge, not even as scientists seeking the laws that govern events, but as men of action, reading a record of human experimentation to find out what can be done and how."

In this lay the lesson for Americans. Mussolini and Lenin were taking their countries in opposite directions: one to the right, the other to the left. "But never mind that," Steffens said. "The method is what we lack and need." What was the method, precisely? How had Mussolini and Lenin accomplished their revolutions? "They had both abandoned the democratic method and were using a dictatorship supported by a very small, instructed, disciplined, armed minority of rebellious but really romantic, obedient youth."

Had Mussolini suppressed the liberties of the Italian people? Indeed he had. "Mussolini abolished free speech, free thought, free assembly, a free press." But so had leaders in many other countries, including the United States, during emergencies. "Don't we always abolish liberty when we are afraid or in trouble? Isn't liberty a psychological matter? Isn't it something that depends, not upon laws and constitutions, but upon our state of mind? Isn't liberty a measure of our sense of security and nothing else?" Only countries that felt secure could afford the luxury of personal liberty. Mussolini was striving to give Italy security, by taking the burdens of governing upon himself and leaving the people to their own affairs. Steffens explained: "When Mussolini said that they, the people, might stop governing and go to work – he would do it all – it was almost as if all Italy sighed and said, 'Amen.' And the people did go back to work, and they worked as they had not worked before."

Observing Mussolini, after Lenin, caused Steffens to question still further the premises of democracy. What did the recent history of Europe show? "It shows that no real progress is being made by the old, approved ways of liberalism, political democracy, and representative parliaments." Only Italy and Russia, the two countries that had abandoned democracy, could claim social advance. What did this imply? "Is democracy a false theory? It may be an end, but is democracy the way to democracy?" At one time, progressives in the United States had prescribed more democracy as the cure for the ills of democracy. The medication, whether taken as direct election of senators, the franchise for women, the short ballot, or the initiative and referendum and recall, had left the patient nearly as debilitated as ever.

Mussolini proposed another treatment, one that appeared to be working in Italy. "It was a bracing sight to see the young black shirts walk through the streets, into an inn, or down the aisle of a railroad train, heads up, shoulders back, in command of the world." Steffens didn't deny the overbearing, even cruel, nature of fascism. "They were insolent. Youth is hard. The Fascists abused their power over their neighbors; they murdered, tortured, in some places." But Italians, for the most part, accepted the excesses as the cost of restoring Italy to respectability as a first-rate power. Speaking as an expatriate living above the sea on the Italian Riviera, but speaking even more as a citizen of an America observing Europe from afar, Steffens declared, "We on our hill must be as patient as the Italians in Italy. We must not judge and, like the correspondents and foreigners, say that because we believed in free speech, a free press, in liberty, democracy, justice, we will have none of Mussolini. Liberty, justice, etc., may be only our illusions."[22]

VIII

Steffens's gushing over Mussolini indicated a sorely enervated exemplarism. Not a decade earlier, American liberals had taken up arms to defend democracy abroad; now they – or Steffens, at any rate – wouldn't even take up words or pen. Democracy might suit Americans, but it wasn't for Americans to presume to tell Italians or Russians or anyone else that it would work for them. Freedom was merely a state of mind, and one state was as good as another. If America still had a lesson to teach, it was only the lesson of tolerance – even for the intolerant.

Not all American observers were so enamored of Mussolini. Newsman George Seldes, writing in *Harper's* in 1927, denounced the Italian leader for his stifling of the press, a violent campaign Seldes labeled "journalistic terrorism." Mussolini proceeded to stifle Seldes, in Italy at any rate, by expelling him from the country; Seldes retaliated with a book-length attack entitled *Sawdust Caesar*.[23]

Ernest Hemingway looked equally askance at Mussolini. During the early 1920s, Hemingway paid his bills and gathered material for his fiction as a stringer for the Toronto *Daily Star*. In 1922 he reported on the Genoa diplomatic conference, which brought a delegation from the Soviet motherland of socialism to the Italian fatherland of fascism. Rome had ordered fifteen hundred crack troops to Genoa to guarantee order among local Communists upon the arrival of the Bolsheviks. "This is a far-sighted move," Hemingway explained to his readers, "for the Italian government remembers the hundreds of fatal clashes between the fascisti and the Reds in the past two years, and is anxious that there should be as little civil war as possible while the conference is in progress." Hemingway went on:

There is no doubt but that the Reds of Genoa – and they are about one-third of the population – when they see the Russian Reds, will be moved

---

[22] Ibid.; Steffens, *Autobiography*, 813–24.
[23] George Seldes, "The Truth of Fascist Censorship," *Harper's*, November 1927; idem, *Sawdust Caesar: The Untold History of Mussolini and Fascism* (New York, 1935).

to tears, cheers, gesticulations, offers of wines, liqueurs, bad cigars, parades, vivas, proclamations to one another and the wide world and other kindred Italian symptoms of enthusiasm. There will also be kissings on both cheeks, gatherings in cafes, toasts to Lenin, shouts for Trotsky, attempts by three and four highly illuminated Reds to form a parade at intervals of two and three minutes, enormous quantities of chianti drunk and general shouts of "Death to the Fascisti!"

This is the way all Italian Red outbreaks start. Closing the cafes usually stops them. Uninspired by the vinous products of their native land, the Italian communist cannot keep his enthusiasm up to the demonstration point for any length of time. The cafes close, the "Vivas" grow softer and less enthusiastic, the paraders put it off until another day and the Reds who reached the highest pitch of patriotism too soon roll under the tables of the cafes and sleep until the bar-tender opens up in the morning.

Some of the Reds going home in a gentle glow chalk up on a wall in straggling letters, VIVA LENIN! VIVA TROTSKY! and the political crisis is over, unless of course they meet some fascisti.

In that event, things turned out differently. "The fascisti are a brood of dragon's teeth that were sown in 1920 when it looked as though Italy might go bolshevik," Hemingway wrote. Mostly veterans of the war, they had assumed the task of protecting the government against subversion. "In short, they are counter-revolutionists, and in 1920 they crushed the Red uprising with bombs, machine guns, knives and the liberal use of kerosene cans to set the Red meeting places afire, and heavy iron-bound clubs to hammer the Reds over the head when they came out." The fascisti enjoyed the protection of the government during the 1920 emergency, but having tasted power and lawlessness they had become nearly as great a threat to the public order as the Communists ever were.

The fascisti make no distinction between socialists, communists, republicans or members of co-operative societies. They are all Reds and dangerous. So the fascisti hear of the Reds meeting, put on their long, black, tasseled caps, strap on their trench knives, load up with bombs and ammunition at the fascio and march toward the Red meeting singing the fascist hymn, "Youth." The fascisti are young, tough, ardent, intensely patriotic, generally good looking with the youthful beauty of the southern races, and firmly convinced that they are in the right. They have an abundance of the valor and intolerance of youth.

Marching down the street, the fascisti, marching as a platoon, come on three of the Reds chalking a manifesto on one of the high walls of the narrow street. Four of the young men in the black fezzes seize the Reds and in the scuffle one of the fascisti gets stabbed. They kill the three prisoners and spread out in three and fours through the streets looking for Reds.

A sobered Red snipes a fascisto from an upper window. The fascisti burn down the house.[24]

At the beginning of 1923, Hemingway met the number-one fascisto. Mussolini headed the Italian delegation to a second Lausanne conference. He compared unfavorably, in Hemingway's opinion, with the other leaders at the conference. "Mussolini is the biggest bluff in Europe," Hemingway wrote.

If Mussolini would have me taken out and shot tomorrow morning I would still regard him as a bluff. The shooting would be a bluff.

Get hold of a good photo of Signor Mussolini some time and study it. You will see the weakness in his mouth which forces him to scowl the famous Mussolini scowl that is imitated by every 19 year old Fascisto in Italy. Study his past record. Study the coalition that Fascismo is between capital and labor and consider the history of past coalitions. Study his genius for clothing small ideas in big words. Study his propensity for dueling. Really brave men do not have to fight duels, and many cowards duel constantly to make themselves believe they are brave. And then look at his black shirt and his white spats. There is something wrong, even histrionically, with a man who wears white spats with a black shirt.

Hemingway went on to describe Mussolini trying to impress his audience at the conference. The Italian leader had announced a press briefing.

Everybody came. We all crowded into the room. Mussolini sat at his desk reading a book. His face was contorted into the famous frown. He was registering Dictator. Being an ex-newspaper man himself he knew how many readers would be reached by the accounts the men in the room would write of the interview he was about to give. And he remained absorbed in his book. Mentally he was already reading the lines of the two thousand papers served by the two hundred correspondents. "As we entered the room the Black Shirt Dictator did not look up from the book he was reading, so intense was his concentration, etc."

[24] Ernest Hemingway, "The Genoa Conference," *Toronto Daily Star*, April 13, 1922, in William White, ed., *By-Line: Ernest Hemingway: Selected Articles and Dispatches of Four Decades* (New York, 1967), 26–9.

I tiptoed over to see what the book was he was reading with such avid interest. It was a French-English dictionary–held upside down.

Later that day a group of Italian women visited Mussolini's hotel to deliver a bouquet of roses.

There were six women of the peasant class, wives of workmen living in Lausanne, and they stood outside the door waiting to do honor to Italy's new national hero who was their hero. Mussolini came out of the door in his frock coat, his gray trousers and his white spats. One of the women stepped forward and commenced her speech. Mussolini scowled at her, sneered, let his big-whited African eyes roll over the other five women and went back into the room. The unattractive peasant women in their Sunday clothes were left holding their roses. Mussolini had registered Dictator.

Half an hour later he met Clare Sheridan, who has smiled her way into many interviews, and had time for half an hour's talk with her.

Hemingway granted that news correspondents in Napoleon's time might have perceived similar traits in the French emperor. "The men who worked on the Giornale D'Italia in Caesar's day may have found the same discrepancies in Julius." Yet Hemingway was sure the two earlier leaders had more substance than Mussolini.

Hemingway conceded Mussolini's strengths, but grudgingly and with reservations regarding the future. "Mussolini isn't a fool, and he is a great organizer." He was a skillful gambler. Yet he was playing a hazardous game. "It is a very dangerous thing to organize the patriotism of a nation if you are not sincere." Perhaps Mussolini would win. Italians had given him their support, financial as well as moral. But success would come hard. "Once the Latin has sunk his money in a business he wants results and he is going to show Signor Mussolini that it is much easier to be the opposition to a government than to run the government yourself."[25]

IX

For all Hemingway's disdain, Mussolini produced sufficient results during the next several years to continue to satisfy the Italians – and many Americans. Lothrop Stoddard joined Lincoln Steffens in praise

[25] Ernest Hemingway, "Mussolini: Biggest Bluff in Europe," *Toronto Daily Star*, Jan. 27, 1923, ibid., 61–5.

for the Italian leader. Portraying fascism as "a thoroughgoing revolt against the sentimentality and phrase-worship of our age," and applauding fascism's emphasis on *gerarchia*, or hierarchy (applause that hardly surprised readers who knew Stoddard from his 1920 tract, *The Rising Tide of Color*, which warned that the superior white races might soon sink beneath a sea of brown and black), Stoddard predicted, "Fascist Italy may show the world some surprising results."[26]

Philosophers George Santayana and Irving Babbitt were similarly attracted to the hierarchical character of fascism. Santayana, a teacher of Reed's and Lippmann's at Harvard, had arrived in America from Spain during the era of Grant, and perhaps for that reason never got very enthusiastic about democracy. On the contrary, he espoused a Platonic, aristocratic form of government, to which Mussolini's fascism served as a fair approximation. Unlike most of Mussolini's American admirers, Santayana endorsed the Duce with his feet: He retired to Rome in 1925. Irving Babbitt was similarly unimpressed with democracy as currently practiced in America. An exponent of something called the "new humanism," an elitism that took pride in despising American mass culture, Babbitt contended that America and most Western countries needed "to substitute the doctrine of the right man for the doctrine of the rights of man." Italy had done so, with remarkable results. "Circumstances may arise when we esteem ourselves fortunate if we get the American equivalent of a Mussolini," Babbitt prophesied.[27]

X

Lincoln Steffens outlived half his illusions. By the mid-1930s, it was cognitively impossible to hold both fascist Italy and communist Russia in high regard. The ascent of Hitler complicated overlooking the brutality inherent in fascism, and the brutality in the Italian version grew more evident as Mussolini bid to out-Hitler the Nazi chief. It became undeniable when Mussolini attempted to recreate the Roman empire by savaging Ethiopia. The Abyssinian atrocities knocked the wind out of most of Mussolini's American apologists, although a few of the more resourceful managed to rationalize this minor matter

[26] Lothrop Stoddard, "Realism: The True Challenge of Fascism," *Harper's*, October 1927.
[27] Irving Babbitt, *Democracy and Leadership* (Boston, 1924, 1925), 246, 312.

away as they had rationalized others. Meanwhile, fascists and communists traded increasingly violent blows. Hitler attacked local communists physically and foreign communists rhetorically and diplomatically. Mussolini, now falling into Hitler's shadow, followed suit. The Kremlin-controlled Comintern gathered in Moscow in 1935 and issued a call for a popular front of antifascist groups against the madmen in Berlin and Rome. Stalin angled for an arrangement with the Western democracies to contain the Germans. When the Spanish civil war broke out in 1936, the fascists and communists rushed to the scene and went at each other in deadly earnest.

"The choice is between Fascism and Communism," Steffens admitted, with evident reluctance. Because he had first sighted the future in Russia, and because Stalin's sins remained more deniable than Hitler's and Mussolini's, Steffens chose communism. By this time, the American left was fracturing over the fascist question, over Trotsky, and over other sectarian issues. Though Steffens stayed clear of formal attachment to the Communist party, his defense of the Soviet Union dismayed some former associates. Max Eastman dubbed him "a pillar of the Stalinist church in America."[28]

Whether subsequent developments – the lifting of the veil on Stalin's crimes, or perhaps Moscow's 1939 *volte face* toward Berlin – would have caused Steffens to rethink his position is impossible to know. He died during the summer of 1936.

[28] Kaplan, *Steffens*, 313, 325.

5

Dr. Beard's Garden

I

If the alternatives to liberal democracy had appeared attractive during the 1920s, the attraction increased following the onset of the depression of the 1930s. The depression did more for communism than for fascism, in that the former spurned while the latter embraced the capitalism that appeared to be shattering itself on the shoals of history. American radicals thrived on the ruination Marx and Lenin had predicted. Lincoln Steffens greeted the depression with good cheer. "I am not a Communist," he assured a friend, before adding, "I merely think that the next order of society will be socialist and that the Communists will bring it in and lead it. . . . The Communists know that they can proceed (as the capitalists do) with a minority just as soon as capitalism busts." The Communist writer Michael Gold asserted hopefully that the depression marked "a great turning point in the consciousness of the American nation." Even a journal as close to the mainstream as the *New Republic* wondered "whether capitalism can survive as we know it, or must be at least modified greatly in the direction of a socialized order."[1]

Whether capitalism would survive, and if so how, obsessed American public thinkers during the 1930s. Some old-line liberals looked for a revival of the progressive movement. John Dewey judged that the basic issue confronting America remained essentially what it had been since the nineteenth century: Would the people of the United

[1] Steffens to Beverley Bowie, Nov. 19, 1932, *The Letters of Lincoln Steffens* (New York, 1938), 2:934; Richard H. Pells, *Radical Visions and American Dreams* (New York, 1973), 48–52.

States control the government, or would control continue to reside with the interests? Dewey called for "fundamental thinking and action along new lines." In characteristically progressive and pragmatic fashion, however, he eschewed revolution in favor of reform. Revolution might suit the Russians, but not Americans. "Russia is Russia, and the United States is the United States."[2]

John Chamberlain doubted that boring from within would yield the necessary improvements. Three years into the depression, Chamberlain bade *Farewell to Reform*. America had reached "the end of the Progressive trail," he declared, and if liberals persisted down the blind path they would provoke reaction. "Progressivism and Liberalism in this country are, at the moment, preparing the ground for American Fascism; they have been identified with the shopkeeper instincts of the common citizen, who is willing to make his trade with the 'big fellow' if he can retain a privilege or two."[3]

Journalist George Soule feared that Chamberlain was right. Soule contended that much of *The Coming American Revolution* had already happened. It had begun in the nineteenth century, as various groups recognized the need to gain political control over the economic forces industrialism had set in motion. Populism and progressivism were early manifestations of the revolution; the New Deal was the most recent. But the revolution wasn't complete: American capitalism remained largely a law unto itself. In Russia the Bolsheviks had carried the revolution farther, in a leftward direction; in Italy the Fascists had pushed it to the right. Of the two approaches, Soule thought fascism the more likely to gain adherents in America than communism. "Anyone can see with half an eye that many of the raw materials of Fascism are lying about within the United States," he said, listing mass unemployment, religious and racial prejudice, a tradition of violence and intolerance, belligerent nationalism, a growing criminal class, and demagogues like Huey Long. Fascism might not arrive today or tomorrow, but it was a real threat for next year or the year after.[4]

---

[2] Irving Howe and Louis Coser, *The American Communist Party* (Boston, 1957), 274; John Dewey, "The Need for a New Party," "Who Might Make a New Party," and "Policies for a New Party," *New Republic*, March 18–April 8, 1931.

[3] John Chamberlain, *Farewell to Reform: The Rise, Life and Decay of the Progressive Mind in America* (New York, 1932), 306–10.

[4] George Soule, *The Coming American Revolution* (New York, 1934), 293.

Edmund Wilson was more interested in the communist model than the fascist. In *Travels in Two Democracies* – these being the United States and the Soviet Union – Wilson avoided the oversell of Steffens and Reed. "Only idiots gush about Russia," he wrote. Only the willfully ignorant could deny the difficulty of life there. But precisely because of that difficulty, the Russians exuded an air of "extraordinary heroism." Wilson intended the "democracy" of his title ironically, with respect to both the United States, where nominal political democracy meant little to the economically dispossessed and the racially stigmatized, and the Soviet Union, where democracy didn't extend from the economic realm to the political. On the whole, the Russians got the better of Wilson's comparison. He acknowledged "the lack of democratic procedure, the suppression of political opposition, the constraint of the official terror" of the Stalinist system. At the same time, though, he held that Americans had no basis for boasting – and certainly not for acting on any such boasts – "till we shall be able to show them an American socialism which is free from the Russian defects."[5]

Franklin Roosevelt at first shared Wilson's exemplarist instincts, if not – definitely not – the radical conclusions Wilson drew from them. Roosevelt's approach to the depression rested on the premise that America's recovery would proceed independently of the economic condition of the balance of the planet. The president made his thinking clear in the context of a 1933 international economic conference at London, which he torpedoed by declaring in favor of a policy of every nation for itself.

No president in American history ever exhibited sharper political sensibilities than Roosevelt, and although his approach lacked economic credibility, it accurately reflected the desires of a majority of Americans. Never had the pendulum of American sentiment on foreign affairs swung so far away from active involvement as during the 1930s; vindicators were an endangered species through the entire decade. To the war-disillusionment of the 1920s was added the sour introspection brought on by the economic implosion of 1929 and after. When little and larger wars broke out in Asia and Europe, threatening to produce a repetition of the Great War, vindicators became rarer still.

Yet eventually they made a comeback in that most exclusive – but

[5] Edmund Wilson, *Travels in Two Democracies* (New York, 1936), 319–22.

most important – niche of the political environment: the White House. Roosevelt gradually grew convinced that the variety of evil currently abroad in the world would never yield to America's mere example; this evil went most seriously armed, and America's good had better go armed too if it hoped to survive. Before most Americans, Roosevelt saw a clash as nearly inevitable, and he worked, albeit with characteristic indirection, to prepare the country for the day.

Executive indirection was essential, on account of the continued popular aversion to foreign adventures. Much of this aversion was essentially emotional and not particularly deep-seated (as it would demonstrate by evaporating in three hours on a Sunday morning in December 1941). But adding intellectual substance to the emotion was some of the most carefully reasoned and articulated exemplarism in the history of American thought. The author of this exemplarism was Charles Beard.

II

It was slightly ironic that Beard became a spokesman for the majority mood in America, for by the 1930s he was well along on a career of contradicting conventional wisdom. Beard once told a student that there were three areas of human activity that might cause difficulties for a university professor: theology, sex, and politics. Beard said that a professor might demonstrate a taste for free thinking in one of these areas without running grave risk; unorthodoxy in two would cause trouble; flouting custom in all three would certainly result in dismissal. He said he had early decided to confine his radicalism to politics.[6]

But steering clear of creation and procreation didn't always leave him on safe ground. Born on an Indiana farm in 1874, Beard grew up in a prosperous family with Federalist-Whig-Republican inclinations. His grandfather had abetted escaped slaves; his father once provided lodging to an itinerant black preacher dangerously unwelcome elsewhere in the county. Young Beard attended a local Quaker academy, after which he joined his brother to publish a newspaper their father had purchased. In 1895 he matriculated at DePauw Uni-

---

[6] George S. Counts, "Charles Beard, the Public Man," in Howard K. Beale, ed., *Charles A. Beard: An Appraisal* (Lexington, Ky., 1954), 242–3.

versity. The next year he traveled to Chicago, where he took in the sights and the Democratic convention; although impressed by William Jennings Bryan and depressed by conditions in the stockyards and packinghouses, Beard wasn't quite ready to bolt the party of his forebears. When the Spanish-American War began, he volunteered.

But the army had too many bodies already and turned Beard down, which was just as well because before the fighting ceased Beard was doubting its moral justification. Freeing Cuba was one thing; seizing the Philippines was something else. The debate over annexation knocked the Republicanism out of Beard, ruining him for partisan regularity for life. "I left the G.O.P. on imperialism in 1900," he said decades later, "and have found no home anywhere since."[7]

Put off by American imperialism, Beard paradoxically fled to the motherland of modern imperialism. The paradox soon evaporated, however, for although he enrolled at Oxford, he found his studies at that bastion of the English establishment less engrossing than the populist agitations of Keir Hardie, Sidney Ball, and the founders of the Labour movement. Beard helped establish Ruskin Hall for the training of leaders of unions and cooperative societies. He lectured across England and Wales, educating the masses in the origins of their condition, and they him in its contemporary manifestations. During this period he published his first book, *The Industrial Revolution*, priced at a shilling and aimed at a popular audience. In this initial try, Beard demonstrated his ability to write books people would buy: The volume eventually went through ten printings.

If temperament had inclined Beard to activism, now activism reinforced his radical leanings. Graduate study at Columbia yielded a doctorate in 1904, a teaching position at Columbia the same year, and a book on English historians in 1906. In this work he displayed the economic orientation that would mark nearly all his writings. A single sentence summarized the book's orientation, and Beard's: "The general direction of the political movements and legislation in Great Britain during the last one hundred years has been determined by the interests and ideals of the three great economic classes: landlords, capitalists, and workingmen." Although trained and hired to teach European history, Beard gravitated toward current American affairs. He gained appointment as adjunct professor of politics in 1907; three

[7] Richard Hofstadter, *The Progressive Historians* (Chicago, 1968, 1979), 171.

years later he published a textbook, *American Government and Politics*, that went through ten editions during the next four decades.[8]

Genuine notoriety followed Beard's application of the ideas of the progressives and the techniques of the muckrakers to the founders of the American republic. His *Economic Interpretation of the Constitution*, which appeared the year Woodrow Wilson entered the White House, revealed Beard's penchant for making the work of the historian usable to contemporaries. By demonstrating – and sometimes exaggerating – the degree to which economic motivations influenced even the most revered generation in American history, Beard indicated the underlying class structure of American society.

In 1913 such views were provocative but hardly dangerous, and while they made their author's name, they didn't threaten his livelihood. The succeeding few years, however, produced a sharp right turn in America's political currents, with liberals like Lippmann going over to the establishment and the establishment going over there – to Europe. Yet the war deflected Beard scarcely at all, and the straightness of his path provoked some influential people. Beard supported American entry into the fighting in 1917, believing German militarism a genuine danger to American democracy, but he refused to accept that the war effort required the intellectual regimentation the Wilson administration demanded. He opposed attempts by the Columbia board of trustees to enforce patriotic thought and speech among the faculty; when the board dismissed a lecturer whose views on international affairs challenged prevailing opinions, Beard quit. That Beard himself had earlier opposed the man's hiring – on grounds of quality of work rather than politics – made his resignation the more dramatic. On his way out the door he expressed his disillusionment with Columbia in particular and American higher education generally. "I have been driven to the conclusion," he declared, "that the university is really under the control of a small and active group of trustees, who have no standing in the world of education, who are reactionary and visionless in politics, narrow and medieval in religion. . . . I cannot repress my astonishment that America, of all countries, has made the status of the professor lower than that of the manual laborer, who through his union has at least some voice in the terms and conditions of his employment."[9]

---

[8] Charles A. Beard, *An Introduction to the English Historians* (New York, 1906), 608.

[9] Counts, "Charles Beard," 244–45.

After departing Columbia, Beard joined John Dewey, James Harvey Robinson, and others in founding the New School for Social Research. During the 1920s he traveled widely in Europe and Asia. A long-time promoter of municipal reform, he also served in various capacities with the National Municipal League and as director of New York's Training School for Public Service. His activities in this area, combined with his travels, prompted the mayor of Tokyo to request his assistance in reorganizing city administration in the Japanese capital following the disastrous 1923 earthquake. In 1926 the American Political Science Association named him its president. The American Historical Association honored him similarly seven years later.

At the time the depression began, Beard was making a fair living from his writing and consulting activities. Curious at the troubles of farmers during the economy's dive, he purchased a farm in Connecticut to gain practical experience in the matter. He subsequently grew even more curious, because by his accounting he never profited less than two percent on investment even during the worst of times. He had less sympathy still for corporate capitalists. When the Missouri Pacific Railroad's bankers refused to pay debts owed stockholders – including Beard – he lobbied for and got a congressional investigation. He also got his money.

III

Because his early work in American history dealt with domestic politics, it was natural that when Beard turned to international affairs he should emphasize the connections between domestic policy and foreign policy. Then again, no one of even slightly radical opinions who lived through the decade of World War I in America could have missed the connections. The political link was unmistakable, as Beard learned at Columbia, and others, like John Reed, learned elsewhere. To Beard, the economic link was the more significant, since more fundamental. Yet unlike many on the left, Beard didn't believe that the economic influence in foreign affairs was necessarily pernicious. At the beginning of 1929 he stated in *Harper's*: "It is not wholly chimerical to conclude that international finance, a bit more enlightened by the experience of the past twenty years, is perhaps the best hope for peace now on the horizon." Writing while American Owen Young was meeting in Paris with representatives of the European powers to reschedule payments of war debts and reparations, Beard rejected the Leninist line that capitalism inevitably bred imperialism, and imperialism war. On the contrary, he thought, the bankers could see better than anyone else the fragility of the financial system they had constructed, and pecuniary self-interest, if not higher motives, would require them to preserve it from undue jolting.[10]

The stock crash and the onset of the depression didn't immediately change his opinion, although once the international defaulting began in earnest he had to reconsider and partially recant. The defaulting and the related raising of tariff barriers reinforced his conviction of the inseparability of foreign and domestic affairs. In a 1931 article he proposed a five-year plan for American economic recovery. After describing remedies required in the domestic arena he wrote, "Now we come to foreign affairs, which, strictly speaking, is a department of industry and marketing." Interestingly, in light of his later hostility toward Franklin Roosevelt, Beard advocated a policy of economic nationalism that resembled the approach the Democratic president initially followed. The rift between Beard and Roosevelt emerged only when the latter began going internationalist.

Throughout the 1930s, Beard contended that the United States could do more for world peace by reforming itself at home than by pursuing activist policies abroad. In terms that echoed Walter Weyl two decades earlier, he argued that efforts to develop the American domestic economy would pay a double dividend: once for America and again for the world. Americans would benefit from prosperity that didn't depend on uncertain conditions abroad, while the world would be blessed by the example of a great power that didn't need to manipulate and bully other nations to ensure its welfare.

International tension, Beard believed, resulted largely from competition among the powers for markets. Much of this competition, certainly as it pertained to the United States, was unnecessary, because the American market, if properly developed, could absorb essentially all that American farms and factories could produce. If it would only rationalize America's domestic economy, the nation could render most exports superfluous. "The feverish and irrational methods of unloading and dumping goods on foreign countries will be reduced to a minimum, if not discontinued entirely," he said. He added dryly, "The industrial countries of the world cannot live by taking in each other's washing."

Beard's argument frayed on this point, demonstrating more wish-

[10] Charles A. Beard, "Prospects for Peace," *Harper's*, February 1929.

fulness than rigor. Perhaps America *could* successfully pursue an autarkic policy, although it never had in the past. But other industrial powers – Britain, France, Germany, Japan, Italy – could not. Less blessed in natural resources than the United States, they had to take in each other's washing and plenty besides.

Even had Beard accepted this point, he doubtless would have rejoined that such was the other countries' problem, not America's. Nor would it have altered his larger argument. He refused to accept that American foreign policy ought to be driven by the interests of investors and international merchants. The United States should adhere to the Kellogg pact outlawing war, he said; it should join the World Court; it should cooperate with the League of Nations in noncoercive economic matters; it should support cancellation of European debts on condition that the Europeans reduce their military forces to a level required for internal police action (all this from someone commonly labeled an isolationist!). But the American government should abandon what Beard described as "the Coolidge theorem that the army and navy of the United States must be big enough to protect any American citizen who wants to make ten per cent on the bonds of Weissnichtwo or sell corn flakes, shoe horns, and collar buttons to the inhabitants of the world willy-nilly." A wise Washington would define American security clearly and conservatively. "For the policy of dominating the world, American diplomacy will substitute that of strict and adequate national defense – defense of the land and people of the United States."[11]

As the economic slump deepened and precipitated political turmoil throughout Europe and Asia, Beard emphasized more strongly than ever "the profound truth that domestic and foreign politics are parts of the same thing." A few months after Hitler took power in Germany, Beard noted how the German leader was conjuring up alien specters to consolidate his rule. "In crushing German democracy, seizing the loot of office for his followers, and persecuting the Jew, Hitler needed an excuse, justification and apology. The excuse was created. It struck at two groups of opponents, the Jews and the Communists, by linking them and portraying them as the enemies of the dear Fatherland."[12]

In 1934 Beard elaborated his thinking on the connection between

---

[11] Charles A. Beard, "A 'Five-Year Plan' for America," *Forum*, July 1931.
[12] Charles A. Beard, "Lenin and Economic Evolution," *New Republic*, May 17, 1933, and "Spooks – Made in Germany," *New Republic*, Dec. 6, 1933.

domestic and foreign affairs in a two-volume treatise, *The Open Door at Home*. This work extended his earlier admonition that the American government and people might most effectively ensure recovery in the United States and peace abroad by developing America's internal market. To Beard, the depression fundamentally represented a "crisis in modern thought." Bankers had *thought* their foreign loans were good; business executives had *thought* their plant expansions and improvements were prudent; farmers had *thought* markets would appear for the additional acres they brought under cultivation; government spokesmen and the elite of the country had *thought* America had achieved a plateau of permanent prosperity. Developments since 1929 had shown the bankruptcy of all this thinking. What the times required was a new mode of thought, one comprising a unified concept of domestic and foreign policy.

Tracing world history during the past forty years, Beard identified armed conflict as an inherent aspect of the international system as currently constituted. "The World War did not come as a deus ex machina to disrupt the system," he wrote. "It was one of the fruits of the system. It had been shortly preceded by the Spanish-American war, the Boer war, the Russo-Japanese war, the Italo-Turkish war, and the Balkan wars – all of which were entangled in commercial and territorial policies, rivalries, and ambitions." To assume that conflicts of this sort would not recur was "dangerous and dubious" and reflected thinking "based on a delusion."

Beard particularly challenged the contention that prosperity required a large overseas commerce and active participation in world affairs. As he had done in his *Economic Interpretation of the Constitution*, where he investigated who stood to gain from a strong central government, Beard asked *whose* prosperity demanded an activist foreign policy. "When the formula appears: 'The American standard of life depends upon foreign trade, and international collaboration can secure that trade for the United States,' the first appropriate operation is to enquire: Who are engaged in reiterating this assertion?" Beard answered his own inquiry. "Exporting and importing merchants, and their associates in the intellectual elite, reiterate it, individually and collectively, for reasons not difficult to fathom. Exporting bankers gravitate to that side. So do industrialists who manufacture extensively for the export market. One-crop farmers with a surplus to sell in foreign markets show a tendency in that direction."

Beard considered the advocates of interventionist and internationalist policies neither less self-interested nor more farsighted than such other groups as the proponents of protection, who at least admitted to their personal stake in the matter. Even those internationalists sincerely concerned for the public welfare, Beard asserted, failed to recognize the anachronism implicit in their arguments. The internationalism of Cobden and Bright might have matched the needs of an industrializing England in the nineteenth century, but it did not apply to an already industrialized America in the twentieth, as the current depression demonstrated. "It has failed, and must fail, to provide measures for bringing great technology into full use, assuring a high and continuous standard of living, and guaranteeing national security." Internationalism was finished and could not be restored. "The knot cannot be untied. It must be cut."

The sword of Alexander, in this case, was a new conception of national interest, what Beard dubbed "the nationalism of the commonweal." This conception rejected the primacy of *homo economicus*, resting instead on an idea that predated Adam Smith and the Manchesterians: that "man did not exist for the sake of production but production for the sake of man." In simplest form it asserted: "The supreme interest of the United States is the creation and maintenance of a high standard of life for all its people and ways of industry conducive to the promotion of individual and social virtues *within the framework of national security*."

In Beard's thinking, the heart of the issue lay in the stressed six words. He granted that a policy of economic internationalism might yield a marginally higher standard of living, measured in dollar terms. But it risked the peace of the nation by delivering American prosperity as hostage to the absurdities and outrages of an unruly world. On second thought, Beard wondered whether it might not render America poorer by requiring the expenditure of exorbitant and increasing amounts on armies and navies. His alternative policy of an "open door at home" – of developing American domestic resources and markets to the full, in preference to a dangerous and ultimately unavailing chase for foreign markets – promised a variety of benefits.

By domestic control over all foreign trade, by the relaxation of the capitalistic pressure of the United States on world markets in standardized manufactures and commercial investments, by concentrating national energies on the development of national resources and the efficient distribution of wealth at home, by deliberately withdrawing from the rivalries of imperialist nations, the United States would take its official nose out of a thousand affairs of no vital concern to the people of the United

States, would draw back its defense lines upon zones that can be defended with the greatest probability of victory in case of war, and would thus have a minimum dependence on the "strategic products" indispensable to war. And by multiplying many fold its outlays for scientific research in analytic and synthetic chemistry, it could steadily decrease its dependence on world markets for the essentials indispensable to our material civilization in times of peace.

The cycle would reinforce itself. As America grew more independent, pressure for war and for preparations for war would diminish. When war preparations diverted fewer resources, the country would become more self-sufficient. The key, Beard said, was to find the optimal combination of security and prosperity. "National interest involves stability and standard of life deliberately adjusted to each other in a long time perspective."[13]

IV

The world grew only more dangerous as the depression decade continued. Japan stole Manchuria; Hitler reoccupied the Rhineland and rearmed Germany; Mussolini ravaged Ethiopia; Franco crushed the Spanish republic. Each event elicited debate between exemplarists and vindicators, with exemplarists like Beard generally having the better of the argument. The world war had knocked the wind out of the vindicators, and though the Spanish civil war, to cite the most conspicuous instance, energized American radicals to a new level of vindicationism – in some cases personal, as members of the anti-fascist Abraham Lincoln battalion; in other cases literary, as defenders of Stalin, the only national leader willing to take a stand against Franco, Hitler, and the other fascists – on the whole the events of the mid-1930s left the vindicators gasping for air.

An admirer of Charles Beard asked him in old age how long it would take him to tell all he had learned in a lifetime of study. Beard thought the question over a moment and said about a week. After further reflection he guessed he could do it in a day. The conversation drifted to other matters. Beard interrupted to reduce his estimate again, to half an hour. Finally, still later, he said, "I can tell you all I have learned in a lifetime of study in just three laws. And here they

[13] Charles A. Beard with G. H. E. Smith, *The Open Door at Home: A Trial Philosophy of National Interest* (New York: 1934), 2, 127, 132–5, 147, 210–1, 273–4.

are. First, whom the gods would destroy they first make mad. Second, the mills of the gods grind slowly, yet they grind exceedingly small. Third, the bee fertilizes the flower that it robs." Several days after this, Beard encountered his questioner again. He said he wanted to add a fourth law: "When it gets dark enough you can see the stars."[14]

By 1936 the stars were out, or at least Beard thought he saw them. With darkness descending on three continents, the correct course for America seemed to him more obvious than ever. Wisdom required steering clear of the madness of the militarists and keeping America out of wars that had nothing to do with abiding American interests. Prudence demanded seeking a return to prosperity by means independent of a world evidently bent on self-destruction.

Yet if Beard's view of human history was simple enough to summarize in four laws, it wasn't simplistic. The popular isolationism that powered the Nye committee hearings and the neutrality legislation of this period was largely a reflexive phenomenon – a knee-jerk reaction to unacceptable developments overseas. Beard's interpretation of events wasn't reflexive but reflective. Where the emotional isolationists turned away from intervention and left the matter at that, Beard rejected intervention but described a carefully considered alternative policy.

Shortly after the Nye committee began posing Beardian *cui bono* questions about American entry into the world war, Beard cautioned against thinking that blame could be placed on a conspiracy of industrialists and financiers and their political collaborators. In a small book called *The Devil Theory of War*, he exploded the theory of the title. "War is not the work of a demon," he declared. Neither was it the result of the selfish actions of a small group or something that should catch anyone by surprise. "War is not made by a deus ex machina, but comes out of ideas, interests and activities cherished and followed in the preceding months and years of peace. . . . It is our very own work, for which we prepare, wittingly or not, in ways of peace."[15]

Yet Beard recognized the pervasive influence of capitalists, even in a Democratic administration. He supported neutrality legislation as a way of insulating popular government from the pressure of those

---

[14] Counts, "Charles Beard," 251–2.
[15] Charles A. Beard, *The Devil Theory of War: An Inquiry into the Nature of History and the Possibility of Keeping Out of War* (New York, 1936), 28–9.

who would manipulate the nation to their own narrow ends. "Neutrality, wide and mandatory, displays caution," he wrote. "This prevents the President and the State Department from taking on the burden of separating the good from the evil, and making commitments likely to involve the country in war . . . . It keeps the power to make war in Congress, where it belongs under the Constitution, and of right."

Beard didn't subscribe to the extravagant claim of the neutralists that American neutrality would cast a pacific influence across the Atlantic. "No one can tell in advance just what effect such a policy might have on European affairs. Will it encourage Hitler to launch his war? Or will it drive the European powers to more concerted efforts to keep the peace?" Beard declined to predict. Regardless, Europe's troubles were not for America to resolve. "We tried once to right European wrongs, to make the world safe for democracy. Even in the rosiest view the experiment was not a great success. Mandatory neutrality may be no better, for aught anyone actually knows. But we nearly burnt our house down with one experiment; so it seems not wholly irrational to try another line." Americans must keep the basic issue straight. "It is not: Shall we love Europe?, or, Was Europe a success? It is: How can this country avoid war?"[16]

Beard harbored no illusions about the thugs of Europe. Examining Hitler's Germany in *Foreign Affairs*, he cited *Mein Kampf* as the blueprint for current and future German policies. "It is quoted freely and reverently by all the writers of the new order," he explained. "No other book approaches in authority this sacred text." Beard anticipated, in general if not in deadly detail, what the future held for Jews in the Nazi reich. "Jews are condemned in language unprintable. They are to be driven to the Ghetto or out of Germany." Most important from the perspective of the United States, the Germans were bent on war. "Turned in upon themselves, nourishing deep resentments, and lashed to fury by a militant system of education, the German people are conditioned for that day when Hitler, his technicians, and the army, are ready and are reasonably sure of the prospects of success in a sudden and devastating attack, East or West." To think otherwise was to cling to a "delusion."[17]

This made it all the more imperative that Americans define their

---

[16] Charles A. Beard, "Heat and Light on Neutrality," *New Republic*, Feb. 12, 1936.
[17] Charles A. Beard, "Education under the Nazis," *Foreign Affairs*, April 1936.

interests accurately and realistically. Beard doubted that Roosevelt would provide the requisite leadership in the matter. Beard had initially expressed guarded approval for what he called "fragments of a new conception of national interest" put forward by the president, which appeared to center on the idea that "by domestic planning and control the American economic machine may be kept running at a high tempo supplying the intra-national market, without relying primarily upon foreign outlets for 'surpluses' of goods and capital." Yet even from the first he faulted Roosevelt's refusal to follow the logic of the economic nationalist position into the larger field of noneconomic affairs. "Enormous funds were allotted to naval construction," Beard complained, and these for no good reason. The administration acted as though it intended a thoroughgoing policy of machtpolitik "despite the repudiation of the assumptions respecting foreign trade upon which it rested."[18]

Eventually Beard would develop a fixation regarding Roosevelt; for the moment he merely watched the president with suspicion. By the beginning of 1935 he had come to believe that Roosevelt had little intention of seriously reforming even the domestic framework of American policy. "The party of wealth and talents survived the Jeffersonian revolution, and the Jacksonian revolution. If it has not lost its talents" – and Beard didn't think it had – "it will survive the Roosevelt revolution." Beard saw a close connection between the staying power of the moneyed classes and danger for America abroad. Should the New Deal fail and the depression deepen, Roosevelt would find foreign adventurism enormously tempting. Observing that the president had just approved "the biggest navy program in the history of the country in peace time," Beard continued: "If there is anything in American traditions and practices to guide us, it is that a wider spread of economic calamity will culminate in a foreign war, rather than in a drastic reorganization of the domestic economy. . . . It is well known, except to innocence, that it is a favorite device of statesmen to attempt the adjustment of domestic dissensions by resort to diplomatic fulminations, war scares, and war itself."

Although Beard was not quite prepared to charge Roosevelt with unadulterated cynicism, he was getting close. The administration was

[18] Charles A. Beard with G. H. E. Smith, *The Idea of National Interest: An Analytical Study in American Foreign Policy* (New York, 1934), 552–3.

muttering about Japan, and Beard expected the complaints to increase to a point where action was nearly inevitable. "There will be an 'incident,' a 'provocation.' Incidents and provocations are an almost daily occurrence. Any government can quickly magnify one of them into a 'just cause for war.'" Seven years before Pearl Harbor, Beard intoned, "The Jeffersonian party gave the nation the War of 1812, the Mexican War, and its participation in the World War. The Pacific War awaits."[19]

Roosevelt's reelection did nothing to improve Beard's mood. Asked by the *Nation* what he expected of a second term, Beard replied, "I have no way of knowing whether President Roosevelt will go to the right or the left. . . . What will he do in case of another European war or of another crash in business? Does he know himself?"[20]

As a measure of control upon the unpredictable president, Beard supported an extension of American neutrality laws. He advocated drastic limitations on loans and weapons sales to any belligerents. As before, he didn't expect American neutrality to redeem what he called "a mad world." But beyond keeping Americans out of other peoples' wars, neutrality would be in the best American tradition of setting a standard for other countries to emulate. "If we preserve a little bit of sanity ourselves amid madness, we may at least set the world an example."[21]

The first several months of Roosevelt's second term afforded Beard hope that the darkness was lifting a bit. Writing on "The Future of Democracy in America," he allowed himself the belief that such a future existed. Gains by workers in the automobile, steel, and coal industries indicated improvement in the condition of the less powerful in America; farm and housing legislation demonstrated national concern for those fallen behind in the race for material success. Americans were showing their fundamental common sense. "In domestic affairs they are renewing the progressive tradition that runs as far back as Thomas Paine's *Rights of Man* and *Agrarian Justice*."

In international matters, Americans were eschewing foreign entanglements. "With much twisting and turning, the American people are renewing the Washington tradition and repudiating both the Kipling-

---

[19] Charles A. Beard, "National Politics and War," *Scribner's*, February 1935.
[20] Charles A. Beard, "What I Expect of Roosevelt," *Nation*, Nov. 14, 1936.
[21] Charles A. Beard, "How to Stay Out of War," *Forum*, February 1937.

esque imperialism of Theodore Roosevelt and the universal philanthropy of Woodrow Wilson." They refused to be gulled by the pitch-
men of either reaction or radicalism. "They fear and suspect the
internationalism of finance-capitalism almost as much as they dislike
its counterpart – the international Bolshevism of Leon Trotsky."
Beard expressed cautious optimism regarding "the slowly maturing
judgment of the majority in the United States," evidenced by Americans' "firm resolve not to be duped by another deluge of propaganda
– right, left, or centre."[22]

Events of the next few months tested this resolve, as well as
Beard's optimism. In October 1937 Roosevelt replied to renewed Japanese aggression in China with a suggestion of a "quarantine" of
aggressors. Beard thought the recent downturn in the economy had
as much to do with the president's recommendation as the events in
Asia. "The Roosevelt administration, bewildered and baffled by the
economic impasse at home, is employing sentimental coverages for
excursions abroad." Beard believed that the democratic countries
might have sentiment on their side in dealing with aggression, but
little morality. "The great democratic powers want peace and the
possession of all they have gathered up in the way of empire by
methods not entirely different from those recently employed, let us
say, by Italy in Ethiopia." The British and French enjoyed scant
standing for criticizing the actions of Japan and Germany. "Does
anyone conversant with British history really believe that the operations of the British government since 1914, let us say, have been
controlled by some conception of democracy, as distinguished from
British interests in the Mediterranean, Africa and elsewhere? Or the
operations of the French government?" The Europeans were tardy in
showing concern for the rise of fascism. "What did these governments do for democracy in Germany between 1919 and 1933? And
what has the British government done in Spain?" Beard doubted that
a quarantine would accomplish any good. "War is not always – if
ever – the fruit of rational calculation, and I find in history no justification whatever for assuming as truth that Italy, Germany and
Japan would surrender unconditionally to a grand quarantine
if the quarantine could be arranged. On the contrary, I suspect that
they would strike back – first at the places in which the British

[22] Charles A. Beard, "The Future of Democracy in the United States," *Political Quarterly*, October-December 1937.

Empire is most vulnerable, and that then the big fire would begin to rage."

Beard reiterated his exemplarist theme that the United States must concentrate on setting its own affairs in order. "It is easy to get into a great moral passion over the distant Chinese. It costs nothing much now, though it may cost the blood of countless American boys. It involves no conflict with greedy interests in our own midst. It sounds well on Sunday." But China's troubles were not America's, which had sufficient troubles itself. "Anybody who feels hot with morals and is affected with delicate sensibilities can find enough to do at home, considering the misery of the 10,000,000 unemployed, the tramps, the beggars, the sharecroppers, tenants and field hands right here at our door."[23]

Although Roosevelt backed away from the interventionism his quarantine speech seemed to portend, Beard still feared the worst. "We're blundering into war," he wrote in the *American Mercury* at the beginning of 1938. The basis of the blundering, he said, was the oft-repeated but rarely examined assertion that the United States could not avoid international responsibilities. At the level the debate generally assumed, this was a tautology, an "empty truism." The important questions remained unanswered.

What responsibilities? To help France, Britain, and Russia police the world? To take part in suppressing all disturbers of world peace, everywhere? To give the world's poverty-stricken people economic goods sufficient to satisfy them? To see that the present distribution of territory and resources is altered only by 'negotiation' in a manner to bring justice to all? What justice? Who are to be the judges of the justice or equity?

Responsibilities to whom? To the peoples of the fifty-odd nations possessing independence? To the peoples of the British, French, Belgian, Dutch, Portuguese, and Italian dependencies? To the Negroes of British South Africa? To Nationalists in India? To the natives of Zululand as well as the natives of Ethiopia?

And how much responsibility? Responsibility equivalent to the full economic and military power of the United States? To the uttermost limits of physical and moral capacity? Responsibility equal to the ability of the upper and lower income groups in the United States to pay the bills?

Besides, what about the responsibilities of the Europeans? "What are they doing to bring peace, security, prosperity, a fair distribution of

[23] Charles A. Beard, "A Reply to Mr. Browder," *New Republic*, Feb. 2, 1938.

the world's goods, and stability in Europe? What are they doing to brighten up the corner where they are?"

Beard judged European diplomacy to be an exercise in greed and cynicism, or at best something that had scant to do with the United States. Of Italy's complaints against France, he summarized, "Italy demands more loot." Did Americans want to enter this den of multiple iniquities? "Should the United States pour out blood and treasure to help France hold Tunisia or Djibouti, or even Corsica?" As for the British, they seemed intent on fomenting a fight between Germany and the Soviet Union. Such an objective might be worthwhile. It might not. But in neither case should the United States get mixed up in the affair.

The Europeans, Beard argued, hoped to con the United States into doing what they could do readily enough themselves. "If the countries of Europe that are directly and immediately involved in preventing German and Italian domination are primarily or even fundamentally interested in that operation they can call the bluff and stop the peril within forty-eight hours. They can establish solidarity, if that is their real and secret wish. They have the men, the materials, the money, and the power."

Exemplarists like Beard inevitably faced allegations of condoning the crimes of the fascists. Beard countered by reiterating his loathing for the "barbaric, indecent, cruel, and inhuman" conduct of Berlin, Rome, and Tokyo. But barbarism, indecency, and inhumanity were not a fascist monopoly, nor were they within the province of America to remedy. For the United States to step in where those on the front line stepped back was "quixotic beyond anything Cervantes ever imagined." Further, the expressions of horror and calls to colors defeated their professed ends. "Far from checkmating the egomaniacs of Berlin, Rome, and Tokyo, this tongue-lashing merely inflates their importance, gratifies their egotism, flatters their vanity, swells their self-importance, and evokes retaliations."

Logic and interest combined to dictate a policy of distance. "The United States should and can stay out of the next war in Europe and the wars that follow the next war. Let this be known in advance, and the powers of Europe themselves will take it upon themselves to stop German and Italian aggression. They will not be able to shirk their own responsibilities and in a pinch shift an enormous burden to the shoulders of the American people."[24]

[24] Charles A. Beard, "We're Blundering into War," *American Mercury*, April 1939.

Beard laid increasing emphasis on this last point following Hitler's seizure of Czechoslovakia and Italy's invasion of Albania. So long as the other Europeans thought they might persuade the United States to come to their rescue, as they had a generation before, they would refuse to act. "If the British government think that they can get anything out of the United States they will doubtless engage in more shilly-shally, and this is no time to encourage them." Congress was then debating revision of the neutrality laws. To weaken the legislation, Beard contended, would simply encourage the Europeans in their feckless ways. To stand firm would signal that America expected the Europeans to defend their interests themselves. He repeated: "The European powers whose immediate business is to stop Hitler and Mussolini dead in their tracks should get down to their business, without expecting to muddle around and then fall back on the United States."[25]

V

The German invasion of Poland in September 1939 infused unprecedented urgency into the debate regarding the appropriate American response to developments overseas. American internationalists, to date organized most effectively, or at least most vocally, in the League of Nations Association, took the invasion and the Anglo-French war declaration that followed as confirmation of the views they had expounded for years. "The tragedy of the moment is grim justification for the ideals of the League of Nations," an association spokesman declared. William Allen White, the Midwestern editor who had risen to prominence in the 1890s by telling America what the matter with Kansas was, and who since had graduated to explaining the matter with the world, headed a group called the Non-Partisan Committee for Peace Through Revision of the Neutrality Act. This organization brought the weight of several hundred business leaders, college and university professors, writers, and clergy to bear upon Congress; with Hitler's help they persuaded the legislature to repeal the arms embargo of the current neutrality law.[26]

The following spring, as German panzers ripped through the Low

[25] Charles A. Beard, "America and the Next War," *New Republic*, June 14, 1939.
[26] Robert A. Divine, *Second Chance: The Triumph of Internationalism in America During World War II* (New York, 1967), 29–30.

Countries and France and threatened to bring the war to a sudden end, White and Clark Eichelberger, the director of the League of Nations Association, sponsored a new organization, the Committee to Defend America by Aiding the Allies. The name of the committee by itself indicated that the arguments of Beard and other noninterventionists hadn't failed of all effect. Where Walter Lippmann and the interventionists of Wilson's era had gone to war to redeem the world, the interventionists of Franklin Roosevelt's time spoke in much narrower terms of American defense. And for the moment they did not even speak in terms of military participation in the war. The interventionists explained that the point of their efforts was to keep the United States out of the war by keeping the Allies in. To this end they promoted an active program of American assistance to the antifascist forces.

By the time France fell, a majority of Americans accepted this portion of the interventionist program. A July 1940 poll taken by *Fortune* magazine found two-thirds of its respondents supporting American aid to Britain and the other countries fighting the fascists. The White House received petitions with nearly two million signatures advocating aid, and letters and telegrams poured into the offices of senators and representatives. White's and Eichelberger's committee ran advertisements in major papers depicting the fascist aggression and warning, "First Europe . . . then America," and asserting "Between Us and Hitler Stands the *British* Fleet!" The interventionists gained great favorable publicity from General John Pershing, who from Faneuil Hall in Boston told the British that American help was coming, or would be if right and reason counted in the question. "So long as Britain stands the danger may be kept at a distance," Pershing asserted. "Therefore, while organizing and equipping ourselves it is sound sense to do all that we can to keep Britain supplied with the food, arms and munitions of which she must have a continuous supply if that outer bulwark of democracy is not to crumble. If we do that, the last sacrifices may not be demanded of us."[27]

With an election looming – one to break precedent and make history – Roosevelt had resisted excessive alignment with the interventionists. But as the wind shifted, the veteran sailor trimmed accordingly, leaving few in doubt as to where his sympathies lay. Consequently, when the president opened his third term with a re-

[27] Walter Johnson, *The Battle Against Isolation* (Chicago, 1944), 94–100.

quest for an unexampled program of government aid to the Allies, disarmingly called Lend-Lease, few who had been paying attention could credibly claim surprise.

The events of 1939–41 remade the landscape of American political thought, even as they transformed the terrain of European politics. The Molotov-Ribbentrop pact had confounded the Popular Front cadres of American Stalinism, forcing even the ever-optimistic communist *New Masses* to concede that there might be some "difficulties with the intellectuals" in the near future. The left in the lurch scattered across the spectrum of American politics, with some commencing the ideological long march that would carry them to the conservatism of the 1950s and the neoconservatism of the 1970s and 1980s. The Trotskyist James Burnham renounced Marxism without yet espousing capitalism; the future, Burnham argued in *The Managerial Revolution*, lay with a new technocratic elite owing allegiance to neither labor nor capital. Max Eastman asked, *Marxism: Is It Science?* He replied equivocally and went on to shock leftists and intellectuals generally by reaching out to the masses of *Reader's Digest*. Sidney Hook, writing on *Reason, Social Myths, and Democracy*, pronounced the Soviet experiment a failure. The Soviets had industrialized, Hook declared, but their industrialization simply mimicked the pattern of the capitalist West rather than revealing any identifiably socialist theme.[28]

Thinkers and writers of the American mainstream, which had never diverged much from the Gulf Stream, flowing along the East Coast and out toward England and the Continent, took France's fall and Britain's danger as a challenge to the civilization they cherished. Walter Lippmann told his fellows of the Harvard class of 1910, at their thirtieth reunion, "We here in America may soon be the last stronghold of our civilization – the isolated and beleaguered citadel of law and of liberty, of mercy and of charity, of justice among men and of love and of good will." With "organized mechanized evil" loose in the world, Lippmann said, the path before America was plain. "We shall turn from the soft vices in which a civilization de-

---

[28] Pells, *Radical Visions*, 348; John P. Diggins, *Up from Communism: Conservative Odysseys in American Intellectual History* (New York, 1975), 203; James Burnham, *The Managerial Revolution: What Is Happening in the World* (New York, 1941); Max Eastman, *Marxism: Is It Science?* (New York, 1940); Sidney Hook, *Reason, Social Myths, and Democracy* (New York, 1940).

cays. We shall return to the stern virtues by which a civilization is made. We shall do this because at long last we know that we must, because finally we begin to see that the hard way is the only enduring way." Henry Luce, in an editorial in *Life* that christened the subsequently abbreviated, but later renewed, "American Century," proclaimed that the United States now possessed the opportunity to rectify its error of 1919, when it had passed up "a golden opportunity" to assume the leadership of humanity. This time Americans must not flinch; they must "accept whole-heartedly our duty and our opportunity as the most powerful and vital nation in the world."[29]

A few voices still held out for holding out. Harry Elmer Barnes, writing for the newsletter *Uncensored*, which served as a forum for refugees from the increasingly interventionist *New Republic*, characterized the war in Europe as "fundamentally a clash between totalitarian aggression and democratic dry-rot." C. Hartley Grattan reminded readers that American intervention in World War I had been "a stupendous disaster." Grattan saw no evidence indicating better fortune this time. Robert Hutchins of the University of Chicago pointed out that if Germany had Poland and France on its conscience, the British and French had half of Asia and Africa on theirs.[30]

VI

The shifting of the political ground didn't exactly leave Beard lonely, but it did place him and the dwindling number of noninterventionist intellectuals in curious company. The isolationist camp included the right-wing populists Gerald L. K. Smith and Father Charles Coughlin, who didn't hide their fascist sympathies; the aviator Charles Lindbergh, who, having examined Hitler's Luftwaffe and grossly overrated its strength, deemed the Nazis irresistible; the publisher William Randolph Hearst, who despised Roosevelt and instinctively opposed anything the president supported; the Republican senator Gerald Nye, who saw the new war as confirmation of his conclusions about the old one; and the odd collection of anti-Semites, business-

---

[29] Lippmann speech, June 18, 1940, in Clinton Rossiter and James Lare, eds., *The Essential Lippmann: A Political Philosophy for Liberal Democracy* (New York, 1963), 534–8; Henry R. Luce, "The American Century," *Life*, Feb. 17, 1941.

[30] Manfred Jonas, *Isolationism in America, 1935–1941* (Ithaca, N.Y., 1966), 230–1; C. Hartley Grattan, *The Deadly Parallel* (New York, 1940), 11–12.

men, student draft-resisters, Midwestern xenophobes, anti-British Irish-Americans, pro-Axis German-Americans and Italian-Americans, and convinced pacificists, who gathered under the banner of the America First Committee.

Uncomfortable or not, Beard held to the position he had maintained for most of the previous decade. In a pamphlet called *Giddy Minds and Foreign Quarrels*, he asked, "Does anyone in this country really know what is going on in Europe, behind the headlines, underneath the diplomatic documents?" A generation earlier, Americans had been asked to save Europe and democracy. "They nobly responded. Before they got through they heard about the secret treaties by which the Allies divided the loot. They saw the Treaty of Versailles which distributed the spoils and made an impossible 'peace.' What did they get out of the adventure? Wounds and deaths. The contempt of former associates – until the Americans were needed again in another war for democracy." What would be the outcome of this fresh crusade? Suppose Hitler and Mussolini should fall; what would follow? "A Victorian democracy, a communistic revolution, or a general disintegration?" Beard couldn't say with anything approaching certainty, and he defied anyone else to try. He remained convinced that the Roosevelt administration was looking abroad to avoid confronting continuing problems at home. He took his title from Shakespeare's deathbed scene in which Henry IV counsels his heir "to busy giddy minds with foreign quarrels . . . lest rest and lying still might make them look too near unto my state." More emphatically than ever, Beard rejected the argument that the United States must assume a world-pacifying role. "America is not to be Rome or Britain," he declared. "It is to be America."[31]

In 1940 Beard produced his most thorough rebuttal of the case for American intervention in the war. Examining a century-and-a-half of American foreign policy, he identified three strains of thinking on the subject. The first was "continental Americanism," which he described as the predominant mode for the first hundred years of the republic's existence. During this period Americans had concentrated their energies on securing territorial control of half of North America and political preponderance over much of the western hemisphere. Americans largely rejected involvement in the affairs of Europe and Asia,

[31] Charles A. Beard, *Giddy Minds and Foreign Quarrels: An Estimate of American Foreign Policy* (New York, 1939), 7, 59, 85–7.

heeding the wise counsel of men like Thomas Paine, who said, "Europe is too thickly planted with kingdoms to be long at peace," and a Swedish minister at London who cautioned John Quincy Adams, "Sir, I take it for granted that you have enough sense to see us in Europe cut each other's throats with philosophical tranquillity."

The second era, the age of "imperialism," commenced during the 1890s. The spokesman for the period – the tempter in the garden, as it were – was A. T. Mahan, whom Beard characterized as "the most successful propagandist ever produced in the United States." For all his success at propaganda, Mahan knew nothing of history. "He had no training whatever in historical research, the scrutiny and authentication of documents, or the philosophy of historical composition. In all this he was a veritable ignoramus. He took such old works as suited his preconceived purposes, tore passages and fragments out of their context, and pieced his notes together in such a fashion as to represent his own image of life, economy, sea power, greed, and war." Joining Mahan were Theodore Roosevelt, who practiced "no occupation at all except politics"; Henry Cabot Lodge, an aspiring historian who to his death was "inordinately proud of what he regarded as his ability to turn a classical sentence"; and Albert Beveridge, the "boy orator" of Indiana politics and the mouthpiece of the imperialist movement. Interestingly, in light of his earlier work, Beard laid little responsibility for the change of America's course upon business interests, whom he described as "followers rather than leaders in the revolution of foreign policy." The Mahan-Roosevelt-Lodge-Beveridge faction, with the assistance of John Hay and a few others, had created a tremendous uproar for their "large policy." Their fine phrases and appeals to national vanity had succeeded in entangling the country in numerous quarrels in Asia and Europe, and won – or stole – for America an empire.

At the same time, the imperialists built the foundation for the third stage of American foreign policy: "the internationalism which sets *world* peace as the fundamental objective." The internationalist movement in America, Beard said, had begun at the turn of the century under the guise of the Carnegie Endowment and the guidance of intellectuals like Columbia's Nicholas Murray Butler. It achieved greatest influence during the presidency of Wilson, when "the skepticism that had been encountered in the early days of agitation was now submerged in the sublime optimism of approaching triumph." The Senate's rejection of the League of Nations dealt the internationalists a setback, but not a deathblow. Their efforts contributed materially to the negotiation and approval of the Kellogg pact; at present they were regaining lost ground.

For all the energy they displayed and the victories they claimed, Beard said, neither the imperialists nor the internationalists had ever won a democratic mandate. "Twice in American history," he declared, "the governing elite had turned the American nation away from its continental center of gravity into world adventures. . . . First in 1898; second in 1917. But each time the main body of the American people had resisted the propulsion, had found the delusions in the false promises, and had returned to the continental orbit." Yet the adventurers refused to accept the verdict of the American people. Even now they demanded American involvement in the affairs of Europe and Asia, and what they couldn't get openly they would acquire by artifice. Noting that decisions in American foreign policy rested with a small group of individuals clustered around the White House, Beard wrote, "It is well within the truth to say that the lives, liberties, and properties of countless millions are today within the keeping of ten men. In this respect, democracies may differ little from dictatorships." When peace balanced on a knife-edge, "two or three men, even one man, may make decisions, magnify incidents, and create situations in which the nominal power of popular legislatures to declare war becomes an empty form and the power of the press futile."

For this reason, Americans must be more vigilant than ever. And more than ever must those not already swept away by the propaganda of the internationalists and the imperialists return to the policies that had guided America for most of its history. Continentalism had served Americans well in the past; it would serve them well in the present and the future.[32]

In earlier years, Beard had provoked his share of criticism, but not an inordinate amount for a writer on controversial themes whose books sold envy-provokingly well. (Lifetime sales figures for Beard's works ran past ten million.) But the earlier attacks were nothing compared to the torrent of vituperation that now poured down upon him. Beard's critics painted him as a downright danger to democracy. Shortly after the publication of *Giddy Minds*, a group of faculty from

[32] Charles A. Beard, *A Foreign Policy for America* (New York, 1940), 3–4, 9, 12–19, 39, 44–50, 67–72, 87, 101, 149–50.

several prominent universities coauthored a letter to the *New York Times* expressing their dismay that such a "vigorous fighter for law, justice and good faith" had taken to "cynically sneering at the attempts of our government to uphold somehow the sanctity of international law" and seemed "so coldly indifferent to brutal international aggressions and outlawry." Journalist-historian Walter Millis, whose view of the past was scarcely less skeptical than Beard's, found him distressingly fuzzy on how to bring the lessons he adduced from history to bear on the difficulties of the day. "Dr. Beard makes almost no effort to apply 'continentalism' to the actual problems of the actual situation now confronting us." Millis added that Beard's evident animus toward those he labeled imperialists and internationalists had led him into the errors of the "devil theory" he himself had cautioned against a few years before.[33]

Max Lerner found much to praise in the vigor of Beard's exposition. "He achieves the effects of a fierce polemicist by the methods of a detached historian," Lerner wrote. But Lerner, like Millis, questioned the relevance of Beard's history. Beard didn't appreciate the singularity of the fascist revolution, and for this reason his polemics fell short. "I began his book wanting very much to be convinced; I finished it unpersuaded." Historian Allan Nevins declared, "The book has some good history in it, but it also has a great deal of very bad and misleading history." Yet it wasn't really the history that exercised Nevins so much as the lack of present-mindedness. Beard simply did not address the crucial issues of the hour – an hour when the democratic world was fighting for its very life. "Men are dying under bombs and machine guns to save part of it," Nevins said. "They speak the language we speak; they hold our faith. But Mr. Beard turns away." Reinhold Niebuhr likewise castigated Beard's insensitivity to the suffering of those holding out against fascism, although he praised Beard's candor. "It is to Mr. Beard's credit," Niebuhr wrote, "that he does not obscure the moral indifferentism which his policy involves."[34]

In questioning the relevance of Beard's historical analysis to the

[33] Beale, "Beard's Historical Writings," in Beale et al., *Beard*, 262; *New York Times*, Nov. 12, 1939; Warren I. Cohen, *The American Revisionists* (Chicago, 1967), 217; Walter Millis in *New York Herald Tribune Books*, May 19, 1940.

[34] Max Lerner in *New Republic*, June 3, 1940; Allan Nevins in *New York Times*, May 26, 1940; Reinhold Niebuhr in *Nation*, May 25, 1940.

current war, the critics definitely hit the weak spot of his argument. Nevins might differ with Beard on matters of historical interpretation, but the differences, and most of the interpretation, were beside the point. Whether or not Tom Paine spoke common sense or George Washington wisdom, the founders had almost nothing to say to American leaders in 1940. The world had never seen anything like Hitler's Germany: an industrial nation mobilized for war, motivated by a malignant creed and hypnotized by a deranged despot. Beard rarely considered, and never in any systematic fashion, what the industrial revolution had done to increase the vulnerability of the United States to foreign aggression – as by a Germany that had defeated Britain and captured the British fleet. With an uncertain grasp of strategic matters, he assumed that America's twin moats remained nearly as wide as they had been during the nineteenth century. He spoke of "cultivating the American garden," of decreasing American dependence on foreign commerce and investment outlets. But he offered few and unconvincing specifics as to what this would do to the American standard of living, and he was consistently vague on how it might be accomplished. He forwarded no suggestions for persuading – coercing, rather – those who didn't accept his little-America view to curtail their overseas activities.

But what was most infuriating of all about Beard was what Niebuhr accurately identified as his "moral indifferentism." How could he stand by – "turn away," in Nevins's phrase – while the goons of the world worked their evil will on the helpless and weak? Some recent converts to internationalism might have agreed with Beard's earlier contention that the British and French were ducking their duty in hopes the United States would rescue them from Hitler; Beard was right that London and Paris could have done more in their own defense. But that error lay in the past. What counted now was stopping the monster before he devoured the rest of Europe.

Beard's rebuttal seemed lame while London burned. He remarked the dismal record of the Europeans in the colonies they controlled. Had Hitler done worse in France, he asked, than the French in Indochina, or in Belgium than the Belgians in the Congo, or in the Netherlands than the Dutch in the East Indies? How did the three-month old battle for Britain compare with two centuries of British oppression in India? In each case, Beard suggested, those currently suffering Germany's wrath were only reaping what they had sown.

Again Beard was correct, but again he was missing the point, which was the present danger to Europe, and the rest of humanity, from German aggression. Besides, as some of Beard's critics argued, if he thought the British or the French mistreated their colonial subjects, what did he think Hitler would do if Germany ever got control over India or Indochina?

Likewise, Beard's argument from historical incapacity – that America had attempted to right the world's wrongs before and failed – was unpersuasive. He spent little time explaining *why* American efforts had failed; he simply noted the past failure and extrapolated to the future. Circumstances had changed, and America's present leaders might learn from the mistakes of their predecessors. To be sure, on this point the argument of Beard's critics was, in one sense, weaker than his, for they didn't even have history on their side. But the interventionists – at least the moral interventionists like Niebuhr – weren't really insisting so much that America would *succeed* in saving Europe as that America must *try*. Obviously, they would win few converts predicting failure; but the times cried out for action, whether successful or not.

While Beard's skin was thick, he wasn't totally impervious to criticism. As events overseas continued to move in an ominous direction, he yielded ground, albeit slowly. At the beginning of 1941 he traveled to Washington to testify before the Senate foreign relations committee, then considering Roosevelt's Lend-Lease bill. Beard conceded he had been wrong about the ability of the Europeans to stop Hitler unaided. He had granted too much weight to the experience of World War I. Yet he hadn't been alone in his error. "Who among us in September 1939, for instance, could foresee that the French nation, which had stood like a wall for four cruel years, would collapse like a house of cards in four cruel months?" Nor did he reject the notion of aid to Britain, now thoroughly beset. "There is no question here of sympathy for Britain; this nation is almost unanimous in its sympathy. There is no question here of aid to Britain; the nation is agreed on that." But Beard remained as suspicious of Roosevelt as ever. He argued that in light of the sweeping powers the administration's measure would grant the president, the bill was misnamed. Instead of "An act to promote the defense of the United States," the title should read,

All provisions of law and the Constitution to the contrary notwithstanding, an Act to place all the wealth and all the men and women of the United States at the free disposal of the President, to permit him to transfer or carry goods to any foreign government he may be pleased to designate, anywhere in the world, to authorize him to wage undeclared wars for anybody, anywhere in the world, until the affairs of the world are ordered to suit his policies, and for any other purpose he may have in mind now or at any time in the future, which may be remotely related to the contingencies contemplated in the title of this Act.

Beard warned of what the administration's measure would lead to. "It is a bill for waging undeclared war. We should entertain no delusions on this point." He faulted the reasoning of the president and of the resolution's supporters. They claimed Lend-Lease was designed to support American interests in a war for democracy. Beard demurred: "My code of honor may be antiquated, but under it I am bound to say that if this is our war for democracy and if foreign soldiers are now fighting and dying for the defense of the United States, then it is shameful for us to be buying peace with gold, when we should be offering our bodies as living sacrifices."

Had the committee considered the war aims of the countries the administration wanted to assist? "Does Congress intend to guarantee the present extent, economic resources, and economic methods of the British Empire forever to the Government of Great Britain by placing the unlimited resources of the United States forever at the disposal of the British Government?" How long would Washington back the opponents of Germany and Germany's accomplices? "Until the French Republic is restored? Until the integrity of its empire is assured? Until all the lands overrun by Hitler are once more vested with full sovereignty? Until Russia has returned to Poland and Finland the territories wrested from them? Until democracy is established in Greece?" For how long was the Roosevelt administration committing the United States to the Chiang Kai-shek regime in China? "Until Japan is expelled from the continent? Until Chinese Communists are finally suppressed?"

Suppose the crusade in Europe succeeded and Hitler were destroyed. Was America prepared to deal with the chaos a world war would almost certainly set loose? "After Europe has been turned into flaming shambles, with revolutions exploding left and right, will this Congress be able to supply the men, money, and talents necessary to reestablish and maintain order and security there?"[35]

Beard lost the argument. Roosevelt got his bill and the broad sweep of powers it implied. Beard made himself more unpopular than

[35] U.S. Senate, 77th Congress, 1st session, *To Promote the Defense of the United States: Hearings Before the Committee on Foreign Relations . . . February 4 to February 10, 1941* (Washington, 1941), 307–12.

ever by his persistent nay-saying. But some of his objections proved prophetic, some soon. Within six months Roosevelt had indeed launched an undeclared war in the Atlantic. By then too he had committed the United States to the defense of the British empire – or so Winston Churchill interpreted the Atlantic Charter, and Roosevelt declined to correct the prime minister in any language the inveterate imperialist would have understood. Beard's forecasts of troubles with Russia over Poland, of American involvement in civil wars in Greece and China, and of a long-term American role in stabilizing postwar Europe were likewise prescient.

Yet the major flaw in Beard's case continued to be his failure to provide a credible alternative. In no small degree Beard lost the debate over intervention on grounds that were as much emotional as intellectual. The world was crashing down. Action entailed risks, but so did inaction. With destiny in the balance, doing something appealed more than doing nothing.

VII

The Japanese clinched the argument for the Roosevelt administration. Most likely, American and German ships couldn't have continued shooting at each other in the Atlantic forever without one side provoking the other to outright war; but until Pearl Harbor, Roosevelt remained sufficiently unsure of support for war to refrain from asking for a declaration.

The Japanese attack and Berlin's follow-up war declaration left the noninterventionists no place to stand. Nonintervention was now out of the question. Internationalism, or what at the moment passed for internationalism, carried all before it. Even the party of Versailles-wrecker Henry Cabot Lodge embraced the cause: Between his successively unsuccessful runs for the presidency, Republican candidate Wendell Willkie pronounced for "one world," the title of his 1943 bestseller.[36]

With nearly everyone else, Beard supported the war, although his lateness and lack of enthusiasm continued to throw a shadow across his reputation. In 1943 he published *The Republic*, an analysis of American government in the form of a Platonic dialogue on the federal constitution between Professor Beard and various questioners.

[36] Wendell Willkie, *One World* (New York, 1943), 197–8, 202, 205–6.

One character, obviously reflecting Beard's views, asserted that the government should "give up all idea of regulating the affairs of the world at large" and should concentrate on providing "adequate and complete protection to our interests lying within the continental limits of the United States." The book's Beard, amplifying this theme, warned against excessive ambition in the executive branch, especially during wartime. The president's war powers, Professor Beard said, were "the unexplored and dark continent of American government."[37]

Beard's persistent unenthusiasm for the war, even while Americans were dying, left him increasingly isolated. Approaching seventy and ignored by many of those who didn't vilify him, he sometimes wondered whether he had anything left to contribute to public discussion. "What in God's name," he asked a friend, "can be said now that will not soon be silly – made silly by events over which we have no more influence than a gnat? Sixty-nine years of it are too many!" From his Connecticut farm, he wrote to historian Merle Curti, "I am overwhelmed and moved to retire to a cave in Bull Mountain nearby, which I own in all its majesty." Beard asked Curti, by way of response to a critic: "What is back of the savage attack on me? I do not know for sure but suspect that it is due to the fact that I refuse to take the world-saving business at face value and think that Churchill and Stalin are less concerned with world saving than with saving the British empire and building a new and bigger Russian empire." He concluded, slightly more hopefully: "However, history to come will pass judgment on them and me!"[38]

Beard decided to help history along. As the war proceeded, he gathered material to demonstrate the accuracy of his arguments during the 1930s, and although he recognized that a revisionist account of the conflict's origins might be a bit much while the outcome still hung in the balance, he was ready to publish shortly after the war ended.

To the title of his 1946 *American Foreign Policy in the Making, 1932–1940,* Beard appended the subtitle, *A Study in Responsibilities.* At the time of publication, Munich brooded over American thinking

---

[37] Charles A. Beard, *The Republic: Conversations on Fundamentals* (New York, 1943), 91–2, 103.

[38] Ellen Nore, "Charles A. Beard: An Intellectual Biography," Ph.D. dissertation in history (Stanford University, 1980), 489–92.

on world affairs. Internationalists held that if the United States had
acted sooner – many blamers, especially those enamored of the
United Nations, set culpability at the date of American rejection of
the Versailles treaty and the League of Nations – the second great
war need never have occurred. Beard rejected this thesis. The United
States, he said, was not responsible for the tragic events of the late
1930s and 1940s. Neither the American senators who voted against
the Versailles treaty nor the American people who shied away from
international entanglements could reasonably be charged with a
"great betrayal," as the historian Thomas Bailey had just framed the
indictment. Beard found it nearly incomprehensible – except that the
contention fit their current world-redeeming agenda – that the internationalists could attempt to pin blame for the war on the United
States, when the war was so patently the work of the aggressors
abroad: Germany, Italy, and Japan.[39]

Beard's 1946 book wasn't one of his better efforts. Of course the
Germans, Italians, and Japanese had started the war; the question
was what the United States might have done to divert them or to
mitigate the consequences of their aggression for America and the
world. Beard addressed this question more directly in what he called
the sequel to the 1946 book, published in 1948. The opening sentence of *President Roosevelt and the Coming of the War* indicated
plainly what Beard was up to. The last chapter of the earlier book
had dealt with the election campaign of 1940, focusing on Roosevelt's pledge not to send American boys to fight foreign wars. Volume
two began: "President Roosevelt entered the year 1941 carrying
moral responsibility for his covenants with the American people to
keep this nation out of war – so to conduct foreign affairs as to avoid
war." The reader was hardly surprised to learn that Roosevelt, in
Beard's interpretation, had failed to live up to this responsibility.

Beard traced the actions of the administration in the months prior
to Pearl Harbor, through what he deemed the misleading represen-
tations of Lend-Lease, the unacknowledged commitment by the president at the Newfoundland conference to prevent a British defeat, the
undeclared war in the Atlantic against Germany, and the half-hearted
negotiations with Japan that immediately preceded the attack on Hawaii. Beard didn't exactly blame Roosevelt for Pearl Harbor – al-

[39] Charles A. Beard, *American Foreign Policy in the Making, 1932–1940: A Study in
Responsibilities* (New Haven, Conn., 1946).

though on another occasion he penned a dust-jacket endorsement of one of the first of the back-door-to-war accounts: George Morgenstern's *Pearl Harbor: The Story of the Secret War*. Nor did Beard charge the president with responsibility for what the war led to – although in this book he couldn't resist the reminder that "out of the war came the triumph of another totalitarian regime no less despotic and ruthless than Hitler's system, namely, Russia, possessing more than twice the population of prewar Germany, endowed with immense natural resources, astride Europe and Asia, employing bands of Quislings as terroristic in methods as any Hitler ever assembled, and insistently effectuating a political and economic ideology equally inimical to the democracy, liberties, and institutions of the United States."

To Beard, the whole matter turned on the fundamental issue of democratic control. He asserted – accurately, as some Roosevelt defenders would gradually admit – that the president had acted during the year before American entry into the war in a fashion that made him essentially unaccountable to the American people. Through his entire career, and certainly from the time he wrote his *Economic Interpretation of the Constitution*, Beard had rebelled at the notion that American leaders, in the name of the American people, might pursue objectives hidden from the people's view. To some degree, the problem came with the territory of representative government: Voters could never exercise complete control over their delegates. But the problem was especially acute in foreign affairs, where the executive branch operated with singular freedom. It became still more acute the greater the extent of American involvement with the world. Beard decried the idea, which he attributed to American internationalists, "that the President is serving the United States and mankind when he emits grand programs for imposing international morality on recalcitrant nations by American power." Such programs, Beard objected, served neither the United States nor mankind. If the American people appeared to support them, this simply indicated that the executive had added to its arsenal of foreign-policy weapons the ability to manipulate American public opinion.

Even while he criticized, Beard recognized that his was the view of a diminishing minority. "At this point in its history," he declared morosely, "the American Republic has arrived at the theory that the President of the United States possesses limitless authority publicly to misrepresent and secretly to control foreign policy, foreign affairs, and the war power." Recalling the prophecy of James Madison that the supreme test of American statesmanship would come in the mid-twentieth century, Beard concluded, "The test is here, now – with no divinity hedging our Republic against Caesar."[40]

Beard remained in opposition to the end. As he watched the Cold War develop, he grew more convinced than ever of the uncontrollable and anti-democratic nature of a world-embracing American foreign policy. In 1948 he prepared a statement for the Senate armed services committee, then debating the issue of universal military training. Seventy-three and ailing, Beard was unable to address the committee in person, so friend and fellow skeptic Charles Tansill read the statement for him. Beard opposed compulsory training on grounds that it would grant the president still greater power to entangle the country in international affairs and would diminish still further the capacity of the people to control the executive's actions. "In its insinuating and insidious course, it would serve the cause of those leaders in military and civil life who exalt the executive above the legislative and are now claiming that the President has a right to make war at his own discretion, without any declaration of hostilities by the Congress."[41]

Beard died several months later, too soon to see President Truman – at his own discretion and without declaration of hostilities by Congress – take the country to war in Korea.

[40] Charles A. Beard, *President Roosevelt and the Coming of the War, 1941: A Study in Appearances and Reality* (New Haven, Conn., 1948), 3, 577, 598.
[41] U.S. Senate, 80th Congress, 2nd session, *Universal Military Training: Hearings before the Committee on Armed Services . . . March 17 to April 3, 1948* (Washington, 1948), 1053.

6

Kennan, Morgenthau, and the Sources of Superpower Conduct

I

Months after Beard's death, the Senate commenced consideration of a treaty that killed the continentalism he spent the 1930s advocating. A few irreconcilables joined Robert Taft in pronouncing the Atlantic alliance a snare, a delusion, and a repudiation of tested tradition, but a solid majority of Americans – and two-thirds of the Senate – refused to risk a withdrawal from international affairs like that which, they believed, had played a significant part in producing World War II. The twentieth century reached the halfway mark with the United States for the first time formally pledged to defend territory it didn't own.

A variety of factors contributed to America's embrace of what became within a few years a policy of global vindicationism. The most obvious and frequently cited was the failure of appeasement during the 1930s. Had the democracies called Hitler's bluff at Munich, the conventional wisdom contended, either he would have backed down or the Germans would have toppled him, or both. In any case, the late world war wouldn't have happened. Whatever the historical accuracy of this line of reasoning, and whether or not what might have worked against Hitler was required against Stalin and later Mao, the no-more-Munichs line provided the principal justification for Americans' redefinition of their country's foreign policy.

At a deeper level, the argument for global activism amounted to little more than an elaboration of the case the vindicators had been making for sixteen decades. With evil abroad in the world, the United States could not simply cultivate its own garden. Americans must assume an energetic role in opposing aggressors and other disturbers of the peace. Americans owed the world – and themselves, now more clearly and firmly a part of the world than ever – their best effort to save it.

II

Both the exemplarists and the vindicators had, at various times, been burdened with being branded "idealist," a label often applied as a derisive synonym for utopian. The idealism of the exemplarists was said to consist in thinking evil abroad would succumb to the American example; the idealism of the vindicators in thinking it would yield to the modest and intermittent efforts even American activists usually contended would suffice. Each party rebutted the idealist charge – a serious allegation among a people that, however moralistic, has historically prided itself on pragmatism – by throwing the charge back in the face of the other side, and by claiming a higher realism. The higher realism of the exemplarists was the assertion that people have to save themselves; of the vindicators that they needed help to do so. After Munich, the Holocaust, and Hiroshima, being called an idealist was more damning than ever, and virtually all those aspiring to influence in the debate over foreign policy took pains to cast their arguments in terms of the coldest-eyed realism.

George Kennan's blue eyes weren't cold by nature. Career foreign service officers often begin professional life as idealists – the pay is poor, and if you just want to see the world, the navy moves you around faster – but unlike certain intellectuals and other foreign-policy kibitzers, they rarely retain their idealism for long. Whatever hopes for the moral uplifting of humanity they start out with, the professionals typically lose most of their idealism on the lower rungs of the career ladder. Like police detectives, they constantly encounter the seamier side of life – for the diplomats, the international life of states. They recognize that however noble the professions of governments, a more or less shrewd but invariably calculated assessment of self-interest nearly always motivates the actions of the players in the game of nations.

George Kennan had particular reason for believing that steel-edged interest, rather than necessarily more-nebulous ideals, motivated the actions of governments. After prep school in Wisconsin and college at Princeton, he joined the foreign service in 1926. In his case, he had already tried the navy, or a civilian approximation thereto, and been unimpressed; of his decision to try the foreign service, he could offer no compelling reason, only that he wanted to get out of Milwaukee, didn't know what else to do, and had liked international relations in college. Regarding his landing in the foreign service, he later mused, "Some guardian angel must have stood over me at that point."[1]

Kennan apprenticed under Robert Kelley, the director of the State Department's Eastern Europe division and the individual who served as the godfather of American Cold War policy. Kelley was dynamic and forceful, an instinctive bureaucratic empire-builder and a fervent anticommunist. He selected a cadre of young, talented, and impressionable officers to receive special training in Russian and Soviet studies. Under his direction, Loy Henderson, an inveterate hardliner later instrumental in formulating the Truman doctrine and other anticommunist initiatives; Charles Bohlen, ambassador to Moscow in the 1950s and a staunch advocate of containment; Bertel Kuniholm, a Kremlin-skeptic whose voiced suspicions of Stalin during World War II ran him afoul of those in Washington who valued smooth relations with America's socialist ally; and Kennan developed views that dominated American foreign policy for a generation. In Washington, while preparing briefs for continued American nonrecognition of the Bolshevik regime; in Latvia, peering across the border at the Kremlin's collectivization campaign and other efforts to force the pace of modernization; and especially in Moscow after recognition in 1933, observing at first hand the evil flowering of the Stalinist system, Kennan and his cohort arrived at the conviction that appeals to idealism would be utterly wasted on the Kremlin. The Soviets intended global conquest. As Loy Henderson asserted from Moscow in 1936, after consulting with Kennnan, Bohlen, and Kuniholm, the establishment of a "Union of World Soviet Socialist Republics" was "the ultimate objective of Soviet foreign policy." Against the Kremlin's expansionism, only force would prevail.[2]

Kennan received further lessons in the realities of power politics in Prague, where he joined the American embassy in 1938 at just the time Hitler was lying to Chamberlain and Daladier about the minor extent of his territorial aims. Another transfer took him to Berlin in the month when Germany and the Soviet Union partitioned Poland

[1] George F. Kennan, *Memoirs* (Boston, 1967–72), 1:17.
[2] H. W. Brands, *Inside the Cold War: Loy Henderson and the Rise of the American Empire, 1918–1961* (New York, 1991), 75.

and the world war began. Through the first half of 1941 he observed the Germans and Russians smashing up and grinding down their neighbors. In June 1941 he watched Hitler doublecross Stalin and send the Wehrmacht toward Moscow. Internment for six months after the German declaration of war against the United States in December 1941 did nothing to elevate his opinion of the near-term prospects of a peaceable kingdom.

Following posting to Portugal and Britain, Kennan returned to Moscow in July 1944 as Ambassador W. Averell Harriman's regional expert. He found the Soviets as ruthless and cynical as ever. Russian efforts, he declared, especially in the crucial realm of Eastern Europe, had one goal above all: power. "The form this power takes, the methods by which it is achieved: these are secondary considerations," he explained. "It is a matter of indifference to Moscow whether a given area is 'communistic' or not. All things being equal, Moscow might prefer to see it communized, although even that is debatable. But the main thing is that it should be amenable to Moscow influence, and if possible to Moscow authority." Kennan predicted that the Kremlin would demonstrate flexibility in pursuing its overriding objective. It would tamper with frontiers here, establish informal connections there, forge alliances somewhere else. The West mustn't be deceived by appearances. "It is not a question of boundaries or of constitutions or of formal independence. It is a question of real power relationships, more often than not carefully masked or concealed. As such – and in no other way – should it be judged."[3]

Writing to Charles Bohlen, Kennan warned that upon the end of the present conflict, the anti-fascist glue holding the United States and the Soviet Union together would dissolve, and Americans and Soviets would find themselves once more at odds. He described a "basic conflict" between "the interests of Atlantic sea-power, which demand the preservation of vigorous and independent political life on the European peninsula," and "the interests of the jealous Eurasian land power, which must always seek to extend itself to the west and will never find a place, short of the Atlantic Ocean, where it can from its own standpoint safely stop." By this time – the month before the Yalta conference of February 1945 – the Red Army had seized most of Eastern Europe and part of the Balkans. Kennan realized that the seizure couldn't have been prevented, but he criticized the Roosevelt

---

[3] Kennan memo of September 1944, reproduced in Kennan, *Memoirs*, 1:521–2.

administration for failing to receive something in return. The administration, beguiled by the chimera of a postwar partnership with Moscow, had let the Kremlin get away with a major land grab. "The sum total of our wisdom for the peace settlement in eastern and southeastern Europe has been to deliver the territory up without a murmur to the mercies of an uncertain and mistrustful Russia and to offer our sponsorship, in the form of a blank check, for whatever catastrophe might ensue." Far better if Washington had admitted forthrightly that a spheres-of-influence peace was the only genuine option and had acquired for itself the largest possible sphere. "That would have been the best thing we could do for ourselves and for our friends in Europe, and the most honest approach we could have made for the Russians."

Kennan declared the United Nations, to which many Americans looked with great hope, worthless as an instrument for ensuring peace. The League of Nations had failed because it could not command the support of the great powers; Kennan saw no reason to think its progeny would do better. Americans would gravely err if they went about the world "with our heads in the clouds of Wilsonian idealism and universalistic conceptions of world collaboration." Indeed, at this critical moment in history, a misplaced idealism would be irresponsibly counterproductive. "If we insist on staking the whole future of Europe," he said, "on the assumption of a community of aims with Russia for which there is no real evidence except in our own wishful thinking, then we run the risk of losing even that bare minimum of security which would be assured to us by the maintenance of humane, stable and cooperative forms of human society on the immediate European shores of the Atlantic."[4]

Had Kennan continued simply to warn his colleagues in the State Department of the inefficacy of idealism in moderating Soviet behavior, he would never have become a symbol of American Cold War policy. To be sure, Kennan wrote more gracefully than most of his associates in the foreign-policy establishment, and his ability to draw evidence from Russian history and Russian literature to support his arguments about the actions of the current Kremlin leadership made his briefs perhaps more convincing than those of others. (Occasionally his extraneous evidence simply confused matters. Trying to ex-

---

[4] Kennan to Bohlen, Jan. 26, 1945, in David Allan Mayers, *George Kennan and the Dilemmas of U.S. Foreign Policy* (New York, 1988), 95–6.

plain the Moscow purge trials during the 1930s, Kennan remarked that "the Russian mind, as Dostoevski has shown, knows no moderation; and it sometimes carries truth and falsehood to such infinite extremes that they eventually meet in space, like parallel lines, and it is no longer possible to distinguish between them.") Yet what Kennan was saying differed little from what the career Russianists and East Europeanists had been saying for twenty years.[5]

By the beginning of 1946, however, events had begun to play into the hands of the advocates of a stern stance against the Soviets. Just as Kennan and the others had predicted, the end of the war revealed the rift that continued to divide the United States from the Soviet Union. In September 1945 the foreign ministers of the antifascist allies met in London to arrange a peace settlement with Germany. The conference collapsed amid mutual bickering and recriminations. A second try in December produced few more substantive results. In January 1946 the Soviets refused to evacuate troops from Iran according to what the Americans and British considered a commitment to do so. The refusal, combined with Moscow's encouragement of separatist tendencies among Iranian Azerbaijanis, provoked the first crisis of the developing superpower standoff. In February 1946 Stalin announced the fundamental incompatibility of capitalism and socialism. The two camps, he claimed, could not cohabit the earth; one would triumph, the other disappear. In March 1946 Winston Churchill declared the existence of an "iron curtain" in Europe separating the Russian-dominated zone of repression from the free world of the democracies to the west.

At this juncture, Kennan delivered his views regarding the appropriate response of the West to Soviet actions. In an eight-thousand word telegram – "neatly divided," he explained afterward, "like an eighteenth-century Protestant sermon into five separate parts" – he dealt with the background and salient characteristics of the Russians' postwar outlook, the manifestations of this outlook in the Kremlin's official and unacknowledged foreign policy, and the implications of outlook and policy for the United States. Kennan described Moscow's perspective on world affairs as the result of influences both historical and ideological. In the former category he identified a "traditional and instinctive Russian sense of insecurity," born of the ex-

---

[5] Kennan memo, Feb. 13, 1937, *Foreign Relations of the United States 1933–1939: The Soviet Union* (Washington, 1952), 362–9.

periences of an agricultural people trying to make a living on an exposed plain in the neighborhood of fierce marauding nomads. More recently Russia had been attacked by the better organized and more technologically advanced societies to the west. A hard history had produced in Russia's leaders a distinctive approach to relations with bordering states: "They have learned to seek security only in patient but deadly struggle for the total destruction of rival power, never in compacts or compromises with it." The advent of Marxism as Russia's governing ideology had reinforced Moscow's no-quarter approach. Defining itself as the workers' state, the Soviet Union transformed its internal class struggle into an international struggle, and its leaders believed that just as the conflict between proletarians and capitalists would end with the destruction of the capitalists, so the battle between the Soviet Union and its imperialist rivals would culminate in the ruin of those rivals.[6]

In pursuit of their objective of national security, obtained through progressive advances into adjacent territory, Soviet leaders would conduct a two-track foreign policy. One track would comprise public pronouncements and acknowledged initiatives. "The Russians will participate in international organizations" – the United Nations, for example – "where they see an opportunity of extending Soviet power or of inhibiting or diluting the power of others." They would seek agreements with strategically placed neighbors like Turkey and Iran to increase Russian access to important bodies of water. They would play on disaffection toward the West, especially in colonial areas, to increase Soviet influence in Asia and Africa.

The second track of Soviet diplomacy would involve the activities of foreign Communist parties and groups not officially connected to the Kremlin. Communists in the Western nations would engage in efforts "to disrupt national self-confidence, to hamstring measures of national defense, to increase social and industrial unrest, to stimulate all forms of disunity." People with economic, racial, or other griev- ances would be encouraged to wage a violent struggle against the status quo. "Poor will be set against rich, black against white, young against old, newcomers against established residents." Soviet opera- tives would agitate in colonial areas for the expulsion of Western influence. "On this level, no holds will be barred. Mistakes and weak-

---

[6] Kennan, *Memoirs*, 1:293.

nesses of Western colonial administration will be mercilessly exposed and exploited. Liberal opinion in Western countries will be mobilized to weaken colonial policies. Resentment among dependent peoples will be stimulated." Even more than in the case of official policy, Soviet efforts on the covert level would be "negative and destructive in character, designed to tear down sources of strength beyond the reach of Soviet control."

How should the United States respond? First, Kennan said, American leaders must forget about reaching any accommodation with the Kremlin of the sort taken for granted among the democratic countries of the West. "We have here a political force committed fanatically to the belief that with the U.S. there can be no permanent modus vivendi." The Soviet Union was incapable of compromise. Its leadership was "impervious to the logic of reason." At the same time, the Kremlin was "highly sensitive to the logic of force." Convinced of the inevitability of their ultimate victory, the Soviets could, and usually did, withdraw in the face of superior power. "If the adversary has sufficient force and makes clear his readiness to use it, he rarely has to do so." The Soviets considered time their ally; the West must prove them wrong. In the struggle that lay ahead, the United States and like-minded countries must be as patient as Russia. American leaders must prepare the American public for a drawn-out contest. The struggle had developed over centuries, at least on the Russian side. It might be resolved over decades, but not sooner.[7]

III

Kennan's telegram arrived in Washington at an opportune moment. Stalin's speech had announced the Kremlin's attitude toward the West, while Churchill's had staked out that of conservatives in the West toward the Russians. Where the United States government would align itself remained unclear. Liberals like Commerce Secretary Henry Wallace urged continued cooperation with Moscow, and although Harry Truman recognized the importance of the New Deal (and war-weary) constituency Wallace represented, the president grew increasingly impatient with the Kremlin's truculence. Kennan's

[7] Kennan to Byrnes, Feb. 22, 1946, *Foreign Relations 1946* (Washington, 1969), 6: 696–709.

telegram, circulating in the upper echelons of the American policy-making establishment, provided intellectual pull to the position Truman was gravitating toward already.

Moscow's meddling in Iran, its stubbornness regarding the role of Germany in a peace settlement, and its pressure on Turkey for joint control of the outlet from the Black Sea facilitated Truman's gravitation. Communist military successes in the Greek civil war contributed to American worries, as did Communist political gains in France and Italy. A Washington primed to think the worst of Moscow found it easy to interpret each of these actions, as well as the Red Army's deepening entrenchment in Eastern Europe, as evidence of grand expansionist designs.

In the summer of 1947 Kennan, now director of the State Department's policy planning staff, drew the strands of Washington's suspicions into what amounted to an American manifesto for the postwar world. In an article in *Foreign Affairs*, Kennan drew heavily on his long telegram, and although he signed the article "X," his authorship soon became known. Interestingly, in this version Kennan alluded little to the prerevolutionary period of Russian history, focusing instead on the modern ideological basis of Soviet expansionism. Perhaps Kennan had rethought his previous position; more likely he was sharpening the argument to give it greater bite. The spring of 1947 had witnessed the unveiling of the Truman doctrine and the Marshall plan. Congressional members and American taxpayers, who had to fund these initiatives, didn't want to hear about the Mongols and the troubles of Kievan Rus; they were interested in Communists.

In any event, Kennan characterized Soviet leaders as preoccupied by the principles of Marxism and Leninism. "Ideology . . . " he wrote, "taught them that the outside world was hostile and that it was their duty eventually to overthrow the political forces beyond their borders." In the three decades since the Russian revolution, the Kremlin had spent most of its energy consolidating the rule of the Communist party at home and defending the country against external enemies. But the original ideological imperative survived. The Soviet government was fully committed to Marxism, subscribing to a belief in "the innate antagonism between capitalism and Socialism." Likewise it remained Leninist, insisting on "the infallibility of the Kremlin" and the "iron discipline of the Communist Party."

Moscow's ideological orientation rendered Soviet leaders at once easier and more difficult to deal with than leaders of traditional great powers. They were easier because they believed in the certainty of their success and felt no compulsion to hurry the wheel of history. Opposed by superior force, they would retreat and seek another path to their goal. They were more difficult to deal with in that they did not accept the legitimacy of their opponents' aspirations. Any accommodation, therefore, was nothing more than a truce. Temporary setbacks they would accept with equanimity; defeat they would never acknowledge.

This analysis led Kennan to his prescription for American policy. The main element of the American approach, he declared, must be "a long-term, patient but firm and vigilant containment of Russian expansive tendencies." Hard-line speeches and political posturing would serve no purpose. In fact, by threatening Soviet prestige and provoking responses in kind, they could readily backfire. (Kennan's readers might have wondered why, if the Soviets were as convinced of their ultimate success as Kennan indicated, they would feel obliged to react to the fulminations of the capitalists. Here Kennan's esthetic aversion to loud and blustery talk may have been influencing his advice.) The crucial elements of American policy must be flexibility and steadfastness. Flexibility was required in order that America and the West be able to pursue a policy consisting of "the adroit and vigilant application of counter-force at a series of constantly shifting geographical and political points, corresponding to the shifts and maneuvers of Soviet policy." Steadfastness was necessary that the West persevere as long as the Russians did. Moscow would press outward; Washington must respond with "a policy of firm containment, designed to confront the Russians with unalterable counter-force at every point where they show signs of encroaching upon the interests of a peaceful and stable world." The Soviets looked forward to "a duel of infinite duration." Americans could do no less.

Yet Kennan contended that the struggle would not in fact continue forever. The Truman administration had allowed the publication of Kennan's article in the belief that it would encourage Congress to fund the Marshall plan and related measures. Kennan would hardly convince many legislators if he said the struggle – and presumably the appropriations it would require – would have no end. Thus he concluded on a relatively optimistic note. After the trials of the previous thirty years, he asserted, the Soviet Union was "physically and spiritually tired." The Soviet people were "disillusioned, skeptical and no longer as accessible as they once were to the magical attraction which Soviet power still radiates to its followers abroad." Soviet economic development, while impressive in some sectors, had been "precariously spotty and uneven." Stalin was mortal, and Russia's Communists hadn't demonstrated the ability to manage a smooth succession. For these reasons, Kennan suggested, the Soviet Union was considerably less robust than it appeared to outsiders. "Who can say with assurance that the strong light still cast by the Kremlin on the dissatisfied peoples of the Western world is not the powerful afterglow of a constellation which is in actuality on the wane?" This couldn't be proved, nor disproved. "But the possibility remains (and in the opinion of this writer it is a strong one) that Soviet power, like the capitalist world of its conception, bears within it the seeds of its own decay, and that the sprouting of these seeds is well advanced."

Consequently Kennan asserted that if the West could find the physical and moral resources "to contain Soviet power over a period of ten to fifteen years," the threat Moscow posed would diminish and perhaps disappear. In the meantime, even as American leaders resisted Soviet advances, the United States could demonstrate the superiority of democratic ways and thereby hasten communism's decline. Kennan went so far as to deem the current confrontation an occasion for rejoicing. The thoughtful observer of Russian-American relations, he said, would find no cause for complaint in the Kremlin's challenge to American society. "He will rather experience a certain gratitude to a Providence which, by providing the American people with this implacable challenge, has made their entire security as a nation dependent on their pulling themselves together and accepting the responsibilities of moral and political leadership that history plainly intended them to bear."[8]

IV

Kennan's article made his career. No other foreign service officer ever created such an impression among the literate public. None ever captured a policy in a single word. Kennan later disowned his offspring, claiming that "containment" had been corrupted shortly after birth by those intent on treating the Soviet Union as principally a military problem. Yet to some degree Kennan should have blamed himself,

[8] X (Kennan), "The Sources of Soviet Conduct," *Foreign Affairs*, July 1947.

for phrases like "unalterable counter-force," written not two years after the end of World War II and in the context of civil wars and armed insurgencies in the Balkans, China, and Southeast Asia, certainly lent themselves to a military interpretation.

Kennan's article provoked controversy at once. The most trenchant and influential of Kennan's critics was Walter Lippmann. Unrecovered from his disillusionment with Wilson, the mature Lippmann rejected any such sweeping internationalism as he had embraced as a young man. In a series of syndicated columns gathered under a title – *The Cold War* – that was already becoming synonymous with the developing conflict between the United States and the Soviet Union, Lippmann attacked Kennan's semi-authoritative statement of Truman administration policy. Ironically, Lippmann may have assisted in Washington's adoption of the containment concept. In his preface, Lippmann noted that when the identity of Mr. X became known, the administration did not distance itself from the containment piece. "After that Mr. X's article was no longer just one more report on the Soviet regime and what to do about it. It was an event, announcing that the Department of State had made up its mind, and was prepared to disclose to the world at large, and of course also to the Kremlin, the estimates, the calculations, and the conclusions on which the Department was basing its plans." The readership of *Foreign Affairs*, while influential, has never been wide – certainly not as wide as Lippmann's; by focusing on Kennan's article as being "of primary importance" in the shaping of American foreign policy, Lippmann introduced containment to a broader audience than it yet had achieved, and he attached the idea more firmly to the Truman administration than it had been attached before.

Lippmann criticized Kennan at the levels both of objectives and of methods. He rightly asserted that containment stood or fell on the accuracy of Kennan's prediction that communism, or at least the version practiced and promoted by the Kremlin, bore "within itself the seeds of its own decay." Lippmann considered this prediction, which Kennan conceded couldn't be proved, little more than wishful thinking. Besides, even if one granted that in ten or fifteen years the Soviet empire would begin to crumble from within, it was unlikely that the American people would be able to maintain the requisite pressure for that long. "Americans would themselves probably be frustrated by Mr. X's policy long before the Russians were."

Lippmann predicted that in containing the Soviet Union, the

United States would be forced to rely on proxies. This would put America at the mercy of a motley array of regimes, factions, and tribes. "They will act for their own reasons, and on their own judgment, presenting us with accomplished facts that we did not intend, and with crises for which we are unready." Identifying what would become the crux of America's Cold War dilemma, Lippmann contended, "We shall have either to disown our puppets, which would be tantamount to appeasement and defeat and the loss of face, or must support them at an incalculable cost on an unintended, unforeseen and perhaps undesirable issue."[9]

V

Kennan considered himself a realist in proposing containment; Lippmann considered *himself* a realist in opposing it. This contradiction made plain in a Cold War context what had always been true: that realism, like idealism, lay in the eye of the beholder.

Hans Morgenthau spent most of his career trying to clear up the confusion – with indifferent success. Late in life, Morgenthau, a German-born political scientist at the University of Chicago, recalled that his first memories of politics involved the Balkan wars of the years just before 1914; in light of the direction his career subsequently took, it was significant that those memories were of a region traditionally one of the fulcrums of the European balance of power. Morgenthau studied philosophy at the University of Frankfurt for a short while during the early 1920s, but, put off by aridities of the epistemologists, turned to Munich and law. Liking law little better than epistemology, he spent much of his time attending lectures on history. One course, covering nineteenth-century Germany, especially captured his attention. "For the first time," he remembered afterward, "I felt the impact of a coherent system of thought, primarily a distillation of Bismarck's *Realpolitik*, that appeared to support my isolated and impressionistic judgments on contemporary issues of foreign policy."

A decision to specialize in international law was complicated only by a gradual realization that international law was nearly oxymoronic. Nations being laws unto themselves, international law lacked

[9] Walter Lippmann, *The Cold War: A Study in U.S. Foreign Policy* (New York, 1947), 9–11, 20, 23.

most of the attributes of law within states. It partook more of the constant struggle of politics. "I now discovered that the main source of its weakness stems from the intrusion of international politics. From that discovery there was but one step to the conclusion that what really mattered in relations among nations was not international law but international politics."[10]

Having found his calling, Morgenthau had only to decide where to practice it. Germany during the 1930s wasn't the place, especially for a sharp-minded Jew determined to speak his mind. So he relocated to the United States, arriving in 1937. Not long after landing, he took a post at Chicago, where he remained for the next three decades. During that period he enjoyed a reputation as the leading exponent of the "realist" school of international relations.

In his 1946 book *Scientific Man vs. Power Politics*, Morgenthau identified a number of themes that would inform all of his work. He attempted to explain the late failure of liberalism to recognize in time the onslaught of fascism. The problem, he argued, resulted from a basic misreading of the central issues of human existence, dating to the Enlightenment enthroning of rationalism as the model of intellectual endeavor. Rationalism had misunderstood the nature of man, the nature of the social world, and the nature of reason itself. "It does not see that man's nature has three dimensions: biological, rational, and spiritual. By neglecting the biological impulses and spiritual aspirations of man, it misconstrues the function reason fulfils within the whole of human existence." Rationalism distorted the problem of ethics, especially in the political field, and it perverted the natural sciences into an instrument of social salvation for which they were ill suited.

The flawed rationalism of the eighteenth century had given birth to the equally flawed liberalism of the nineteenth, which compounded rationalism's errors by assuming that the interests of the rising bourgeoisie – in market economics, in free trade across borders, in minimal government interference in social activities, in diplomacy and negotiation as feasible alternatives to war – had universal validity. So influential was the rationalist-liberal model that it was adopted even by those who had little use for the results the liberals strove for. Of

[10] Hans J. Morgenthau, "Fragment of an Intellectual Autobiography: 1904–1932," in Kenneth Thompson and Robert J. Myers, ed., *A Tribute to Hans Morgenthau* (Washington, 1977), 1–9.

imperial Germany, Morgenthau wrote, "The foreign policy of Wilhelm II simply exchanged the frock coat of the liberal merchant for the mummeries of monarchical romanticism and the rational language of Manchester liberalism for the Wagnerian bombast of a decadent divine-rights philosophy."

The new century and the world war it soon produced brought no relief from liberalism's mistakes. On the contrary, Woodrow Wilson's call for a war to save democracy was "the expression of an eschatological hope deeply embedded in the very foundations of liberal foreign policy." Versailles and the League of Nations entrenched liberalism in the framework of international affairs. Presupposing an underlying rationality that united both victors and vanquished, and assuming that international relations were merely an extension of relations among individuals and that violence was anachronistic, leaders of the liberal democracies rendered themselves vulnerable to those who put the methods of liberalism to antiliberal uses. Again speaking of Germany, this time Hitler's, Morgenthau asserted, "The liberal statesmen of western Europe were intellectually and morally unable to resist German expansion as long as it appeared to be justified – as in the cases of Austria and the Sudetenland – by the holy principles of national unification." To a large extent, the liberals had only themselves to blame for the emergence of fascism, which was the predictable outcome of a hundred years of liberal misconceptions. "In a sense it is, like all real revolutions, but the receiver of the bankrupt age that preceded it."

Although fascism by 1946 was dead, the liberal errors that had allowed it to flourish remained as dangerous as ever. If the world were to be spared another cataclysm, intellectuals and political leaders in the West must recognize the importance of irrational human passions and reexamine the premises of their approach to international affairs. This reexamination must start with the recognition that power politics was rooted in the lust for power which was common to all men, and consequently was inseparable from political life itself. From this recognition could arise a new, higher, rationalism. "In order to eliminate from the political sphere not power politics – which is beyond the ability of any political philosophy or system – but the destructiveness of power politics, rational faculties are needed which are different from, and superior to, the reason of the scientific age."

Practitioners of the new rationalism would recognize that ideology, which in most cases was the old scientific rationalism writ deep, played a minor role in international relations. The long-term continuity in the foreign policies of the major European states demonstrated how little ideology had to do with the broad shape of international affairs. "The fundamental foreign policies of the Great Powers have survived all changes in the form of government and in domestic policies." France, Britain, and Russia during the last two centuries were cases in point. Morgenthau explained why this was so: "Continuity in foreign affairs is not a matter of choice but a necessity; for it derives from geography, national character, tradition, and the actual distribution of power, factors which no government is able to control but which it can neglect only at the risk of failure."

Americans weren't exempt from this rule. Unfortunately American leaders were acting as though they were, much as they had in Wilson's day. Morgenthau was unimpressed by Truman's response to recent developments in Greece and Turkey. "Our concern for democracy in the Balkans . . . " he wrote, "is but another instance of the liberal disposition to fight for abstract slogans rather than for political interests."

Morgenthau asserted that interests, not ideals, and stability, not democracy, should be the objectives of American foreign policy. In an imperfect and often irrational world, an insistence on perfect, rational solutions could only be counterproductive. "Man cannot hope to be good but must be content with being not too evil." Expanding on this theme, Morgenthau argued, "There is no escape from the evil of power, regardless of what one does. Whenever we act with reference to our fellow men, we must sin." Inaction was no solution. "We must still sin when we refuse to act, for the refusal to be involved in the evil of action carries with it the breach of the obligation to do one's duty." Intellectuals bore the burden of duty and guilt fully as much as those who decided policy and issued orders. "No ivory tower is remote enough to offer protection against the guilt in which the actor and the bystander, the oppressor and the oppressed, the murderer and his victim are inextricably enmeshed."

The recognition that political ethics was "the ethics of doing evil" was the key to understanding the real world of international affairs. "It is only the awareness of the tragic presence of evil in all political action which at least enables man to choose the lesser evil and to be as good as he can in an evil world." No scientific theory, no rationalistic model, could resolve the inevitable conflict between politics, the domain of power, and ethics, the realm of right. Morality con-

sisted in facing this fact squarely. "We have no choice between power
and the common good. To act successfully, that is according to the
rules of the political art, is political wisdom. To know with despair
that the political act is inevitably evil, and to act nevertheless, is
moral courage. To choose among several expedient actions the least
evil one is moral judgment." In the combination of political wisdom,
moral courage, and moral judgment, man reconciled his political nature with his moral destiny. "That this conciliation is nothing more
than a *modus vivendi*, uneasy, precarious, and even paradoxical, can
disappoint only those who prefer to gloss over and to distort the
tragic contradictions of human existence with the soothing logic of a
specious concord." Morgenthau quoted Goethe's advice for dealing
with this basic issue: "While trying to improve evils in men and circumstances which cannot be improved, one loses time and makes
things worse; instead, one ought to accept the evils, as it were, as raw
materials and then seek to counterbalance them."[11]

VI

The necessity of choice, the willingness to live with partial and precarious solutions, the acceptance of evil as inevitable and as the raw
material for action – these principles formed the foundation of the
realist philosophy with which Morgenthau became identified. What
liberal idealists derided as cynically manipulative, Morgenthau defended as the most ethical – indeed the only ethical – approach to a
world of intractable evil. The liberals had had their opportunity.
They had failed because they misunderstood the nature of the world.
Their failure had exacted the horrendous consequences of the recent
war, of the Holocaust, of the shattering of Western civilization. Regardless of the nobility of their intentions, the liberals had done enormous evil.

Morgenthau continued his assault on liberal idealism in a book
that became the bible of the Cold War realists. The opening words
of *Politics Among Nations* put the realist case succinctly.

International politics, like all politics, is a struggle for power. Whatever
the ultimate aims of international politics, power is always the immedi-

---

[11] Hans J. Morgenthau, *Scientific Man vs. Power Politics* (Chicago, 1946), 5–10, 52–
4, 59–60, 70–2, 201–3, 218.

ate aim. Statesmen and peoples may ultimately seek freedom, security, prosperity, or power itself. They may define their goals in terms of a religious, philosophic, economic, or social ideal. They may hope that this ideal will materialize through its own inner force, through divine intervention, or through the natural development of human affairs. But whenever they strive to realize their goal by means of international politics, they do so by striving for power.

As in his earlier work, Morgenthau rooted the struggle for power not in the historical accidents of particular circumstances among countries but in the essential nature of human beings. The desire to dominate, he said, was "a constitutive element of all human associations, from the family through fraternal and professional associations and local political organizations to the state." Morgenthau read in the contest between in-laws and spouses a foreshadowing of the challenge to status-quo powers by have-not nations; other personal and social relationships at every level demonstrated that the contest was ubiquitous and never-ending. "Social clubs, fraternities, faculties, and business organizations are scenes of continuous struggles for power between groups which either want to keep what power they already have or desire to attain greater power." Disputes between labor and management, between litigants at court, between political pressure groups and parties, between branches of government – all were manifestations of the struggle for power.

Morgenthau didn't deny a role for what he called "the ideological element" in international relations, but he considered it principally a means for explaining and justifying the quest for dominance. "While all politics is necessarily pursuit of power, ideologies render involvement in that contest for power psychologically and morally acceptable to the actors and their audience." This wasn't to say ideology was something extrinsic to politics. On the contrary: "It is the very nature of politics to compel the actor on the political scene to use ideologies in order to disguise the immediate goal of his action" – which goal, of course, was power. Nor, perhaps in the interest of public honesty, could ideologies lightly be discarded. "The nation which would dispense with ideologies and frankly state that it wants power and will, therefore, oppose similar aspirations of other nations, would at once find itself at a great, perhaps decisive, disadvantage in the struggle for power." The other nations, unused to such candor, would unite in opposition to the unabashed dominion-seeker. Of equal importance, the people of the country in question, accustomed to calls for sacrifice in the service of ideals higher than a propagation of power, would hesitate or stumble in their efforts on behalf of the homeland. "A government whose foreign policy appeals to the intellectual convictions and moral valuations of its own people has gained an incalculable advantage over an opponent who has not succeeded in choosing goals which have such appeal or in making the chosen goals appear to have it."

If the nations of the world insatiably sought power, why was the world not constantly convulsed in war? This question led Morgenthau to one of the cardinal concepts of realist thought: the idea of the balance of power. The idea was sometimes slippery. Morgenthau used the term in at least three different ways, as signifying variously any current distribution of power among a group of nations, a particular form of distribution in which power was divided in approximately equal measure among competing coalitions, and a policy designed to achieve such an equal distribution. The underlying principle was that relatively weak states could or did join forces to guard against aggression by the relatively strong.

To some degree, the balance of power was self-adjusting. When one state gained power relative to its rivals – potentially all other states – and threatened to disrupt the international system, the other states adjusted their coalitions and policies to offset the challenge. As Morgenthau put it, "The aspiration for power on the part of several nations, each trying either to maintain or to overthrow the status quo, leads of necessity to a constellation which is called the balance of power and to policies which aim at preserving it." In Morgenthau's view, the participants in international affairs had no genuine choice in the matter. It was the balance of power or nothing. Those who thought otherwise were simply wrong. "Here again we are confronted with the basic misconception which has impeded the understanding of international politics and has made us the prey of illusions. This misconception asserts that men have a choice between power politics and its necessary outgrowth, the balance of power, on the one hand, and a different, better kind of international relations, on the other." This was indeed a misconception. The balance of power, including the policies designed to preserve it, was "not only inevitable, but an essential stabilizing factor in a society of sovereign nations."

The inevitability of the balance of power followed from the unrelenting efforts of all nations to maximize their individual power.

Weak nations naturally banded together; in no other way could they defend themselves against the strong. Yet the inevitability of efforts to secure a balance didn't always confer success on those efforts. Here Morgenthau's multiple usages led to a certain confusion. Over time, the system adjusted itself, but in the short run, instability could occur. Countries might react tardily to changes in economic and political circumstances; they might miscalculate their rivals' power and their own. Their leaders might run risks prudence would reject.

Morgenthau didn't draw the analogy, but his model of a balance-seeking system of international relations worked much like Adam Smith's model of free-market economics. Smith's actors sought to maximize profits, Morgenthau's to maximize power. From the competitive pursuit of self-interest, each system produced something good for all: prosperity in Smith's version, stability in Morgenthau's. As Smith's model was liable to short-term bottlenecks and entrepreneurial misjudgments, while in the long run it sorted things out, so Morgenthau's tended to eventual equilibrium after possible temporary disruptions. And just as Smith's model, premised on the proven axiom that individuals could be counted on to seek their own advantage, resisted efforts at substantial modification, as by well-meaning socialist planners, so Morgenthau's defied the attempts of one-worlders and others who would similarly repeal the laws of human nature.

Yet where a disciple of Adam Smith might dismiss as inconsequential the short-run imperfections in the working of free markets, Morgenthau couldn't so readily overlook the failures of the balance of power. Smith's failures cost only money; failures in international relations produced wars and their attendant mass misery. Keynes's famous remark that in the long run we are all dead might, in the atomic age, apply equally to the short run if the international political system failed.

Accordingly Morgenthau, having demonstrated the tendency toward a balance of power and shown the protective function the balance served in international affairs, was compelled to concede the potential shortcomings of balance-of-power policies. He acknowledged the uncertainties involved in attempts to secure the balance, citing examples from Frederick the Great to Neville Chamberlain to demonstrate that things didn't always turn out as leaders of states anticipated. He noted that participants in power-balancing endeavors often didn't settle for a true balance: Never knowing just where the balance lay, they tended to err on the side of what seemed safety – namely, more power for themselves. This erring introduced elements of disequilibrium, which never disappeared as each state constantly adjusted to its perceptions of the others. In theory, this deficiency was no more fatal than the inclination of Adam Smith's actors to accumulate wealth at the expense of others. But because international political power was divided among a relatively small number of countries, each with the capacity to wreak considerable havoc on its neighbors, as opposed to the far more diffused influence of the large numbers of actors in a competitive economy, the errors of national leaders had much greater ill effects.

This deficiency of the international system was most pronounced, in Morgenthau's view, in a configuration with but two major participants. Unfortunately for the present generation, such was precisely the circumstance resulting from the recent world war. The United States and the Soviet Union eyed each other over the wreckage of Europe, their options limited by the lack of commensurately powerful partners. "They can advance and meet in what is likely to be combat, or they can retreat and allow the other side to advance into what to them is precious ground." There was no third route. "Those manifold and variegated maneuvers through which the masters of the balance of power tried either to stave off armed conflicts altogether or at least to make them brief and decisive yet limited in scope, the alliances and counteralliances, the shifting of alliances according to whence the greater threat or the better opportunity might come, the sidestepping and postponement of issues, the deflection of rivalries from the exposed frontyard into the colonial backyard – these are things of the past."

But the fundamental theme of international relations – the quest for power – hadn't changed, and the need for a framework to limit the violence of the unavoidable conflicts was more pressing than ever. Morgenthau in 1948 was less gloomy than he had been earlier; the world had survived three years of the atomic era, and the worst memories of the late war were dimming. Yet he was far from hopeful. Disarmament initiatives had gone nowhere. Even if they picked up momentum they would only mitigate, not remove, the consequences of a slip between the superpowers. The United Nations was becoming an arena for, rather than a solution to, the confrontation between East and West.

The logic of Morgenthau's entire argument impelled him to the conclusion that conflict among nations would end only when nations ended – when separate states were subsumed into a world state. "Reforms within the international society have failed and were bound to fail. What is needed, then, is a radical transformation of the existing international society of sovereign nations into a supranational community of individuals." On this point, Morgenthau concurred with many of the liberals he had attacked earlier. Yet where the liberal cast of mind anticipated the arrival of the world state in the foreseeable, or at least conceivable, future, Morgenthau continued pessimistic. "The world state," he declared, "is unattainable in our world."

Even so, individuals and countries might take action to change the world, to make the world state somewhat more attainable. This was the task facing diplomats in the modern age. The diplomats must determine when the objectives of one state were compatible with those of others, and when they were not. In cases of compatibility, they must attempt to expand the common ground; in cases of incompatibility, they must decide whether the interests at issue were vital. If not, they might be abandoned or modified. If so . . .

Morgenthau had no answer to this. Of two hypothetical countries in such a situation, he wrote, "Even provided that both sides pursue intelligent and peaceful policies, A and B are moving dangerously close to the brink of war."

Though Morgenthau had no answer, he did have advice. Diplomats could minimize the risk of war by observing several rules. First, diplomats must divest themselves of any crusading spirit. Morgenthau quoted William Graham Sumner: "If you want war, nourish a doctrine. Doctrines are the most frightful tyrants to which men ever are subject, because doctrines get inside of a man's own reason and betray him against himself." Second, foreign policy must be confined to the pursuit of national security and must be supported by sufficient political and military power to ensure that security. Third, diplomats must endeavor to examine circumstances from the point of view of other nations. Here Morgenthau cited Edmund Burke: "Nothing is so fatal to a nation as an extreme of self-partiality and the total want of consideration of what others will naturally hope for or fear." Fourth, diplomats must prepare to compromise on issues not vital to national security. Fifth, diplomats must shun legalism in favor of practicality. Substance mattered far more than symbol. To stand on principle for principle's sake was the mark of folly rather than wisdom. Again Morgenthau turned to Burke: "The question with me is not whether you have a right to render your people miserable, but whether it is not your interest to make them happy. It is not what a lawyer tells me I *may* do, but what humanity, reason and justice tell me I *ought* to do." Sixth, nations must avoid putting themselves in positions from which retreat entailed loss of prestige, and advance serious risk. History abounded with examples of countries that went to war to prevent a loss of face. Seventh, nations must never allow weak allies to make decisions for them. Failure to observe this rule often led to violation of the preceding one. Eighth and last, armed forces must serve foreign policy, never drive it. "The military mind knows how to operate between the absolutes of victory and defeat. It knows nothing of that patient, intricate, and subtle maneuvering of diplomacy whose main purpose is to avoid the absolutes of victory and defeat and to meet the other side on the middle ground of negotiation and compromise." A foreign policy given over to military preparations could lead only to war. Citing Sumner again: "What we prepare for is what we shall get."[12]

VII

The United States government prepared for the worst. In the spring of 1950, the Truman administration produced a policy paper depicting the communist threat in nearly apocalyptic terms. "The issues that we face are momentous," the authors of NSC-68 declared, "involving the fulfillment or destruction not only of this Republic but of civilization itself." The Soviet Union, unlike previous aspirants to world power, was animated by "a new fanatic faith, antithetical to our own." The result was "a basic conflict between the idea of freedom under a government of laws, and the idea of slavery under the grim oligarchy of the Kremlin." Formerly, aggression could be localized. No longer. "In the context of the present polarization of power a defeat of free institutions anywhere is a defeat everywhere." The United States did not seek a large role, but it couldn't avoid the responsibility events had thrust upon it. "Unwillingly our free society finds itself mortally challenged by the Soviet system. . . . The absence of order among nations is becoming less and less tolerable. This fact imposes on us, in our interests, the responsibility of world leadership.

[12] Hans J. Morgenthau, *Politics Among Nations: The Struggle for Power and Peace* (New York, 1948), 13, 17–18, 61–3, 125, 150–9, 284, 391–2, 419–21, 438–43.

It demands that we make the attempt, and accept the risks, inherent in it, to bring about order and justice by means consistent with the principles of freedom and democracy."[13]

NSC-68 was the handiwork primarily of Kennan's successor on the State Department's policy planning staff, Paul Nitze. Although the Cold War blueprint the paper articulated followed logically from the containment policy Kennan had sketched three years earlier, its simplism grated on his sensibilities and its call for what turned out to be a tripling of the American defense budget seemed to sacrifice the subtleties of diplomacy to the bluntness of the military. Kennan had already left the planning staff; now he decided to leave the State Department entirely, the better to continue his work of educating America to its obligations to itself and to the world. "If I am ever to do any good in this work," he noted in his diary, "having the courage of my convictions, it must be outside the walls of this institution."[14]

Shortly after departing Washington, Kennan accepted an invitation from Morgenthau's University of Chicago to deliver a series of lectures subsequently published as *American Diplomacy 1900–1950*. In the lectures and book, Kennan sought to explain the striking, indeed paradoxical, fact that while the United States was incomparably more powerful in 1950 than it had been at the beginning of the century, American security – "or what we took to be our security": an important difference he failed to clear up – had suffered "a tremendous decline."

The problem, Kennan argued, resided in the fundamental American approach to international affairs. Politically, American leaders, particularly presidents, paid too much attention to "the short-term trends of public opinion in the country" and to "the erratic and subjective nature of public reaction to foreign-policy questions." Kennan softened this traditional complaint of professional diplomats against meddling politicians by adding that over time public and politicians eventually understood what American interests required. But the world lived, especially in matters of foreign policy, in the short term, as Pearl Harbor had decisively demonstrated, and as nuclear weapons made plainer than ever. If the past possessed any predictive value, the United States faced trouble. "I think the record indicates

[13] NSC 68, Apr. 14, 1950, *Foreign Relations of the United States 1950* (Washington, 1977), 1:237–41.
[14] Kennan, *Memoirs*, 1:468.

that in the short term our public opinion, or what passes for public opinion in the thinking of official Washington" – another distinction Kennan declined to clarify – "can easily be led astray into areas of emotionalism and subjectivity which make it a poor and inadequate guide for national action." Not surprisingly, Kennan thought matters might be mitigated by handing more power to the professionals. He harbored little hope, however, that such an obvious solution would be implemented, and he feared that America was condemned to foreign policy fashioned by vote-seeking politicians and responsive chiefly to uninformed public opinion.

Kennan's complaint was precisely the opposite of Charles Beard's. Where Beard had decried the lack of democratic control over foreign policy, Kennan believed that the American people exercised too *much* influence in international affairs. To some degree, the difference in judgments of the two men reflected their different backgrounds and positions, with the outsider Beard naturally opposing the insider (until recently) Kennan. To some degree, it reflected different times. During the 1930s, Americans tried to ignore the rest of the world. Though they didn't always succeed, their efforts allowed the Roosevelt administration considerable autonomy in managing foreign affairs. During the early 1950s, the world intruded on all aspects of American life. American soldiers died in Korea; Soviet spies – many imagined but some real – frequented the front pages; the Soviets exploded nuclear bombs, threatening, for the first time, the physical destruction of the United States. Under the circumstances, it was scarcely surprising that officials of the Truman administration received more than their share of amateur advice on foreign affairs. Whether Beard would have appreciated the form popular interest in international relations took during the McCarthy era is uncertain; Kennan definitely did not.

Kennan brought another indictment against America's method of making foreign policy. This complaint originated in what he deemed a peculiarly American perspective on the world. "I see the most serious fault of our past policy formulation to lie in something that I might call the legalistic-moralistic approach to international problems. This approach runs like a red skein through our foreign policy of the last fifty years." Kennan's skein tied together the Open Door notes, the Hague conferences, Wilson's League of Nations, the Kellogg pact, and the United Nations – the connection being the conviction that "it should be possible to suppress the chaotic and dangerous aspirations of governments in the international field by the acceptance of some system of legal rules and restraints."

Kennan hypothesized on the genesis of this conviction, suggesting that it represented an attempt "to transpose the Anglo-Saxon concept of individual law into the international field." It probably stemmed as well from a national memory of the origins of the American political system – "from the recollection that we were able, through acceptance of a common institutional and juridical framework, to reduce to harmless dimensions the conflicts of interest and aspiration among the original thirteen colonies and to bring them all into an ordered and peaceful relationship with one another."

Even ignoring the fact – which Kennan did – that forging a permanent American union involved considerable coercion, eventually requiring one of the bloodiest wars to that date in Western history, the American belief in the efficacy of legal restraints neglected the profound differences between the American experience and the experiences of other peoples. Americans, Kennan argued, being fairly well satisfied with the condition of the world, placed peace and order at a premium. "To the American mind, it is implausible that people should have positive aspirations, and ones that they can regard as legitimate, more important to them than the peacefulness and orderliness of international life."

Kennan identified the most glaring evil consequences of the American world view. First, it rendered incomprehensible to most Americans the depth of international dissatisfaction with the status quo, and the extreme measures the dissatisfied were willing to employ to change things. "We tend to underestimate the violence of national maladjustments and discontents elsewhere in the world if we think that they would always appear to other people as less important than the preservation of the juridical tidiness of international life." Second, although the American perspective was superficially internationalist, it often worked in just the opposite direction. A legalistic approach required parties at dispute to have legal standing. Sovereign national governments automatically possessed such standing, even when the peoples they represented lacked most other characteristics of nationhood. For this reason, governments were loath to consent to anything that might threaten their sovereignty, including international organizations with greater power. Third, the American tendency to treat all governments as equals – an obvious but ill-considered extension of the one-person-one-vote principle of domestic democracy – displayed patent unrealism. Burma was not Britain, nor Czechoslovakia China. (Neither was Taiwan China, but Kennan didn't choose to press a sore spot.) Yet in the thinking of American legalists, they received comparable, if not entirely equal, treatment. Such thinking couldn't fail to obscure the true power relationships of the real world.

Fourth, the legalists' emphasis on national sovereignty handcuffed American leaders in dealing with countries like those of Eastern Europe, which had the legal attributes of sovereignty but were actually satellites of the Kremlin. The internal affairs of other nations were declared out of bounds. Thus while the American mode of thought was prepared to handle direct aggression, as in Korea, a communist takeover from within, as in Czechoslovakia, left the legalists at a loss. In drawing a line between internal and external affairs, the legalists created a further false distinction. Violence didn't respect borders. Many civil wars grew out of international conflicts; other civil wars grew *into* international conflicts.

Fifth, the legalistic approach placed sanctions in the hands of coalitions of nations. Coalitions were notorious for their inability to agree on much for long. As the joint military operations in Korea demonstrated, each member brought to the coalition its own agenda and priorities. Because the ultimate sanction was military action, and because only the great powers possessed sufficient military strength to make military action meaningful, the legalists' vision of international collective security ultimately relied on the cooperation of the great powers. Korea was the exception that proved the rule that cooperation would often be lacking when it was needed most. (Korea was also the exception that guaranteed the rule's persistence: by bringing the Soviets back to the Security Council.)

All this was damning enough, but Kennan withheld his sharpest criticism until last. Here his argument most closely resembled Morgenthau's. Kennan castigated what he called "the inevitable association of legalistic ideas with moralistic ones: the carrying-over into the affairs of states of the concepts of right and wrong, the assumption that state behavior is a fit subject for moral judgment." Kennan overspoke slightly on this point. The connection between legalism and moralism wasn't inevitable, even in America. Plenty of illegal actions are not generally deemed immoral, and much that many people consider immoral is not illegal. Yet Kennan's assertion still told – and echoed here not only Morgenthau but Tocqueville. "Whoever says there is a law must of course be indignant against the lawbreaker and feel a moral superiority to him. And when such indignation spills over into military contest, it knows no bounds short of the reduction of the lawbreaker to the point of complete submissiveness – namely unconditional surrender." This had a curious and ironic result. "The legalistic approach to world affairs, rooted as it unquestionably is in a desire to do away with war and violence, makes violence more enduring, more terrible, and more destructive to political stability than did the older motives of national interest. A war fought in the name of high moral principle finds no early end short of some form of total domination."

Writing against the background of conservative complaints at the Truman administration's unwillingness to unleash General MacArthur against the Chinese, Kennan declared that there existed "no more dangerous delusion" than the concept of total victory. Kennan doubted that the concept had ever made much sense. Militarily it might have, on occasion, but not politically, and wars were ultimately about politics. In any event, the development of atomic weapons rendered the notion especially wrongheaded.

Kennan concluded, in tones John Quincy Adams would have approved, with a call for "an attitude of detachment and soberness and readiness to reserve judgment." From the thrusting vindicationism of his X article, Kennan was retreating toward exemplarism, for the attitude he prescribed would dispose Americans to refrain from dictating solutions to the world's troubles. "It will mean that we will have the modesty to admit that our own national interest is all that we are really capable of knowing and understanding – and the courage to recognize that if our own purposes and undertakings here at home are decent ones, unsullied by arrogance or hostility toward other people or delusions of superiority, then the pursuit of our national interest can never fail to be conducive to a better world." Kennan understood that such advice wouldn't appeal to those enamored of American globalism. Some might find it narrow-minded and reactionary. Some would consider it unworthy of American ideals. "I cannot share these doubts," he said. "Whatever is realistic in concept, and founded in an endeavor to see both ourselves and others as we really are, cannot be illiberal."[15]

---

[15] George F. Kennan, *American Diplomacy 1900–1950* (Chicago, 1951), vii, 93–4, 97–103.

VIII

All sensitive observers of the world scene in the early 1950s found considerable cause for disquiet, and Kennan was nothing if not sensitive. The two superpowers were racing headlong into an era of thermonuclear weapons and long-range missiles. Already the United States was at war with China, Moscow's principal ally; it took little imagination to contrive scenarios by which this World War Two-and-a-Half would become World War III. And not surprisingly, Kennan felt a certain responsibility for the current state of affairs. He had provided the intellectual justification for much of current American policy. Claim as he might that he had been misunderstood – and indeed a large part of Kennan's subsequent career could be interpreted as an extended effort to clarify what he had *really* meant in his long telegram and X article – containment had become the touchstone of American Cold War policy. Containment dictated the war in Korea; containment justified the system of alliances that had begun with NATO and was rapidly extending around the globe; containment mandated rearming America with the newest and most powerful weapons. So completely had Kennan's concept changed the terrain of American thinking, in fact, that what had seemed ambitiously interventionist in 1946 was by the early 1950s being assailed as timid and insufficient. The 1952 elections featured Republican candidates castigating containment as defeatist and demanding the more forthright – and even more explicitly vindicationist – policy of "liberation."

These demands were typically couched in the kind of moralistic language that made Kennan cringe. It made Morgenthau cringe too, and in a successor series to the Chicago lectures Kennan gave, Morgenthau offered his own accounting for the moralism. He explained it in terms of the rationalistic philosophy he had attacked earlier. That philosophy rested on two basic assumptions, he said: that the struggle for international power was an accident of history, associated with non-democratic government and therefore destined to disappear with the triumph of democracy throughout the world; and that, in consequence, conflicts between democratic and non-democratic nations were not simply struggles for power but contests between good and evil, which could end only with the complete triumph of good, and with evil wiped off the face of the earth.

The problem of moralizing had grown with American power. Initially weak relative to its rivals, the United States in those early years of its existence had been forced to a realistic appraisal of the world and the possibilities for American action. But with increasing strength came an increasing temptation to remake the world in the American image; this temptation culminated in Wilson's disastrous crusade. "The very logic of his moral position – let us remember that consistency is the moralist's supreme virtue – drove him toward substituting for the concrete national interest of the United States the general postulate of a brave new world where the national interest of the United States, as that of all other nations, would disappear in a community of interests comprising mankind."

Morgenthau believed that the pursuit of American national interest – which he defined as assured predominance in the western hemisphere and a balance of power elsewhere – had acquired an undeservedly unsavory reputation. Entitling his lectures *In Defense of the National Interest*, he undertook to remedy the situation. "The fundamental error that has thwarted American foreign policy in thought and action is the antithesis of national interest and moral principles," he asserted. He modified his earlier contention that all choice in world affairs involved the chooser in sin and that morality consisted in choosing the least evil; but the essence of the argument remained. Although moralists sought the good, he said, they failed to achieve it. "A foreign policy guided by moral abstractions, without consideration of the national interest, is bound to fail; for it accepts a standard of action alien to the nature of the action itself." Morgenthau went further: He declared the moralistic influence not simply inefficacious but pernicious. Governments had as their overriding responsibility the defense of the interests of their people. "To ask, then, a nation to embark upon altruistic policies oblivious of the national interest" – policies bound to fail – "is really to ask something immoral." On the other hand, policymakers who kept national interest foremost in mind not only had the greatest chance of promoting the welfare of those they were charged with serving, but also contributed to world welfare. "In the absence of an integrated international society, the attainment of a modicum of order and the realization of a minimum of moral values are predicated upon the existence of national communities capable of preserving order and realizing moral values within the limits of their power."

Morgenthau took American reactions to the Soviet Union as a case in point. For the sake of discussion, he admitted three possibilities

regarding the causes of the Cold War. First, it was all a mistake:
False propaganda and inflated suspicion had manufactured unwarranted tension between the superpowers. Second, communism per se,
with its threat of world revolution and the overthrow of capitalism,
was at the heart of the conflict. Third, Soviet expansionism – contemporary Russian imperialism – was the source of the trouble. (Morgenthau was sufficiently orthodox not to include the possibilities that the
Cold War resulted from capitalism per se or from American imperialism.)

Morgenthau conceded that the three causes might in practice be
intermixed. Since 1917, each had contributed to American responses
to the Soviet Union. Yet he contended that at present only the third –
Russian imperialism – was a genuine problem. He posed a simple test
to doubters. Suppose Lenin and Trotsky had died in exile and the
czar still ruled in the Kremlin. "Does anybody believe that it would
be a matter of indifference for the United States to see the Russian
armies hardly more than a hundred miles from the Rhine?" Of course
not. Or, turning the question around: Would anyone fear communists in America if they weren't sworn disciples of Moscow and
therefore agents of Russian imperialism? Hardly. "Their importance
is that of treason, not of revolution."

Nevertheless the American people, beguiled by their unrelenting
moralism, treated the Cold War as if it were predominantly a problem of ideology, the consequence of the existence of communism.
"To American public opinion the conflict between the United States
and the Soviet Union appears first of all as a struggle between two
systems of political morality. . . . Good and evil are linked in mortal
combat, and the struggle can only end, as it is bound to end, with the
complete victory of the forces of good over the forces of evil." To be
sure, American leaders sometimes displayed greater insight. Morgenthau commended Dean Acheson for recent speeches stressing the primacy of Russian imperialism, of which, the secretary of state had
explained, communist revolutionary activities were an instrument.
Yet such perspicacity could hardly be said to characterize American
policy.

Morgenthau considered this discrepancy typical of the way the
United States managed its foreign affairs. With Kennan, Morgenthau
considered democracy generally deleterious to sound international
policy. "The kind of thinking required for the successful conduct of
foreign policy must at times be diametrically opposed to the kind of

considerations by which the masses of the people and their representatives are likely to be moved. The peculiar qualities of the statesman's mind are not always likely to find a favorable response in the
popular mind." The people must have their heroes and villains. Their
alternatives must be straightforward and distinct. But reality knew
few of either heroes or genuine villains, and life's options muddled
good with evil. A "tragic choice" therefore confronted the designers
of a democratic foreign policy. "They must either sacrifice what they
consider good policy upon the altar of public opinion, or by devious
means gain popular support for policies whose true nature they con-
ceal from the public."

The tragedy had already engulfed American policy. The Truman
administration – Acheson too often included – had succumbed to
opposition complaints and pandered to the unsophisticated and gul-
lible among the American public. "This is the disheartening tale of a
noble people" – after 200 pages of criticism, Morgenthau evidently
felt compelled to say *something* nice about his adopted compatriots –
"ignobly led." He concluded with an indictment of America's ignoble
leadership, and a prophecy.

You have deceived once: now you must deceive again, for to tell the
truth would be to admit having deceived. . . .

You have falsified the real issue between the United States and the
Soviet Union into a holy crusade to stamp out Bolshevism everywhere
on earth, for this seemed a good way of arousing the public; now you
must act as though you meant it. . . .

Your own shouts, mingled with the outcries of the opposition, have
befuddled your mind; now you wonder whether you are fighting Russian
imperialism or trying to obliterate Communism. . . .

Instead of leading public opinion on the steady course that reason
dictates, you will trail behind it on the zigzag path of passion and prejudice. . . .

You will become, in spite of your own better self, the voice not of
what is noble, wise, and strong in the nation, but of what is vulgar,
blind, and weak. . . .

The leader will then have become the demagogue; as the mouthpiece
of popular passion, you will at last have forsaken leadership altogether.

The message was getting rather melodramatic, but Morgenthau
persisted to the end. Admonishing those who would keep America
on the straight path, he perorated: "Remember always that it is not
only a political necessity but also a moral duty for a nation to follow

in its dealings with other nations but one guiding star, one standard for thought, one rule for action: THE NATIONAL INTEREST."[16]

IX

If Acheson sometimes disappointed Morgenthau, John Foster Dulles infuriated him. The Republican secretary of state, who wore his anticommunist ideology on his sleeve and conducted foreign policy by what Morgenthau characterized as "a series of hoaxes – sensational, confusing, and disquieting in the short run, but virtually meaningless in the long run," seemed to Morgenthau the epitome of the moralistic unrealism that vexed American foreign policy. Morgenthau challenged most aspects of Republican policy throughout the 1950s; on two issues, however, he thought the Republicans particularly misguided.[17]

The first was nuclear strategy. The budget-conscious Eisenhower entered office in January 1953 determined to reduce defense spending. During the next several months, the president directed a review of American weapons policy. At the end of the year, he authorized the Pentagon to place greater reliance than heretofore on nuclear weapons. This policy of the "New Look" allowed savings on conventional weapons, which were more expensive per unit of destruction than nuclear weapons.

The New Look initially lacked an intellectual foundation, being motivated by economic concerns rather than considerations of military need. In January 1954, Dulles attempted to remedy the deficiency. In one of the most provocative speeches of his china-rattling tenure, the secretary unveiled the doctrine of massive retaliation: a policy embodying a "basic decision" by the Eisenhower administration to "depend primarily upon a great capacity to retaliate, instantly, by means and at places of our choosing" to foreign acts of aggression.[18]

[16] Hans J. Morgenthau, *In Defense of the National Interest: A Critical Examination of American Foreign Policy* (New York, 1951), 11–2, 26, 33–8, 69, 76–8, 223–4, 242.

[17] Hans J. Morgenthau, "The Political and Military Strategy of the United States," *Bulletin of Atomic Scientists*, October 1954.

[18] John Foster Dulles, "The Evolution of Foreign Policy," *Department of State Bulletin*, Jan. 25, 1954.

Morgenthau judged massive retaliation foolish in the extreme. "The new policy," he wrote in the *New Republic*, "assumes that the threat to the U.S. will take the form of open military aggression to be prevented by the threat, or answered by the reality, of atomic retaliation." A threat of this nature might once have carried credibility, but the Soviet Union had been building atomic weapons for nearly half a decade. "It may seem trite, but in view of the somnambulistic quality of much official argumentation it is not superfluous, to point out that a policy of atomic retaliation is a sure deterrent only if the retaliatory power has a monopoly or at least a vast superiority in the retaliatory weapon. But what if the power to be retaliated against is in a position to retaliate against the retaliation or to make retaliation impossible by prevention?"

The logic of the administration's policy – though Morgenthau doubted that logic was the appropriate term – was that the threat of retaliation by the United States would prevent aggression analogous to that committed by Germany against Czechoslovakia in 1938 or by North Korea against South Korea in 1950. Morgenthau predicted an opposite effect. He cited a British advocate of massive retaliation, Air Marshal Sir John Cotesworth Slessor, who had written a script for a nuclear-era version of the Sudeten crisis. The first step, Slessor said, would be a confidential warning that any move toward the seizure of territory would bring a nuclear response. If this didn't suffice, the guarantor powers would broadcast the warning publicly. At the same time, they would move their bomber forces closer to the scene. Morgenthau replied to this depiction with sarcasm. "Splendid strategy for 1950," Morgenthau wrote, "but nothing short of absurd in 1954!" For what did Slessor expect the aggressor nation to do in the face of such a threat? "Once things have gone so far as the Air Marshall anticipates they might, the aggressor nation has only one choice: to start a war of atomic aggression against the threat of a war of atomic retaliation."

Although development of a defense against atomic attack might give plausibility to massive retaliation, Morgenthau noted that the Eisenhower administration had proposed nothing of the sort. Consequently the new policy simply heightened the danger to the American people. "The defenseless installations of a nation committed to a policy of atomic retaliation offer a temptation to an aggressor, which under certain circumstances might well nigh be irresistible, to make retaliation impossible through an atomic war of prevention."

Close examination revealed yet another flaw in the administration's reasoning. While Dulles might speak bravely in public about waging nuclear war, an actual decision for such a conflict was another matter. "No President would give an order to start an atomic war without much soul searching, hesitation and doubt. Yet a policy of atomic retaliation will prevent an atomic war rather than provoke it only if there is not the shadow of a doubt in the minds of friend and foe alike about what will happen in the case of local aggression."[19]

Morgenthau was wrong on this last point. Events of the next thirty-five years demonstrated that a reasonable expectation of retaliation, short of certainty, sufficed to keep the safety catches on the nuclear triggers. Even so, much of his criticism of massive retaliation *was* warranted, and as the Soviet nuclear arsenal grew during the 1950s, and with it the threat of a counter-retaliatory strike, the Eisenhower administration spoke less frequently and less loudly of using nuclear weapons to prevent peripheral aggression.

Morgenthau's second major bone of contention with the Republicans involved American policy toward Asia. As he explained in a four-part series in the *New Republic* in 1956, the Eisenhower administration displayed "an all-pervading deficiency of understanding" regarding the nature of the challenge American interests faced internationally. This deficiency, whose chief symptoms were ideological posturing and an insatiable desire for military alliances, was discernible in American relations with much of the world, but it was most noticeable with respect to Asia. "It is in Asia that the weakness of our thinking on foreign policy becomes fully apparent. For here both the extremes of philosophic generalities and local military preparations completely miss the point. The ideological cannonade, as it were, soars far above the advancing enemy, and military pacts, far from stopping him, actually help him to advance." The difficulty arose from American leaders' conflation of nationalism and communism. By treating America's competition with the Soviet Union primarily as an ideological crusade, rather than as a traditional struggle for power, Americans read far too much into the anti-Western tendencies of Asian nationalism. In doing so they left the field open to the communists, who adopted a less encompassing and more realistic – and hence more successful – approach. "Nowhere in Asia, with the

[19] Hans J. Morgenthau, "Will It Deter Aggression?" *New Republic*, Mar. 29, 1954.

exception of Japan, is the conflict between Communism and democracy relevant or even intelligible as a philosophic contest between tyranny and freedom, between the total state and the individual." Nowhere in Asia did the Soviet Union or China advance under the banner of Marxism, calling on the masses to assume the historic role that Marx had assigned them. Instead, communism was advancing by identifying itself with the concerns and grievances of different Asian groups, especially the concern about and grievance against Western imperialism.

Morgenthau argued for a realistic reassessment of American policy toward Asia. Washington should recognize the dangers of trying to impose its views on Asians. It must be willing to let Asians show the way in solving Asia's problems. "A passive policy of patient, watchful waiting goes against the grain of the American genius. Yet there is no escape from the necessity to learn how to tread cautiously the narrow path between the Scylla of failure and the Charybdis of universal destruction." American relations with Asia wouldn't improve until the United States adopted an approach that was "discreet rather than spectacular, restrained rather than indiscriminately active, cautious, pragmatic, and humble rather than confident in its superior principles and technical ability and not caring who knows it."[20]

X

Kennan concurred. Kennan didn't exactly disavow containment, but, observing the elephantiasis that afflicted his brainchild under the Republicans, he called for a rethinking of the concept. Americans, he remarked, tended to carry reasonable ideas to unreasonable conclusions, in the belief that the world could be made to conform to American desires if Americans tried hard enough. He lamented the "lack of flexibility in outlook," the "stubborn complacency about ourselves and our society," the "persistent demand for absolute solutions," and the "unwillingness to accept the normal long-term hazards and inconveniences of a great power" that characterized the American approach to international affairs. With Morgenthau, he advocated a strong dose of realism, a recognition that wisdom entailed an understanding that the important problems of humanity were never settled

---

[20] Hans J. Morgenthau, "The Immaturity of Our Asian Policy," *New Republic*, March 12, 19, 26 and April 16, 1956.

once for all. He asserted the necessity of freeing policy from "that peculiar form of American extremism which holds it possible that there should be such a thing as total security, and attaches overriding concern to the quest for it."[21]

Like Morgenthau, Kennan found the Republicans particularly culpable. In 1956 Kennan assessed the importance of Khrushchev's de-Stalinization campaign. Responding to Eisenhower administration suggestions that nothing had changed, that the Kremlin's "peace offensive" was simply a new tactic in the same old program of world conquest, Kennan wrote, "It is quite true that there has theoretically been no change of objective. But there *has* been a very significant change of method." Khrushchev and his associates had traded "the most nightmarish sort of modern totalitarianism" for "something resembling a traditional authoritarian state, oligarchically governed." Kennan queried, "What more do we want in three and a half years?" Meanwhile the ideological straitjacket into which Eisenhower and Dulles had stuffed American policy worked in Moscow's favor. "Is it not we who have rendered ourselves vulnerable to the peace campaign by the overmilitarization of our entire approach to world problems in these recent years? . . . Is it not we who have estranged the neutral world with our own self-centeredness? . . . Have we not played into Soviet hands by our overemphasis on military aid to the detriment of economic aid?"

Kennan reiterated, with greater emphasis than before, his belief that what Americans accomplished domestically would figure centrally in the success or failure of their foreign policy. "In the Soviet challenge," he declared, "there are two components, one composed of Soviet strength and another composed of our own weaknesses and deficiencies." The United States had focused almost exclusively on countering Soviet strength while it did next to nothing to remedy American weaknesses. This was an error, for the world would judge America not by the might of its armies but by the soundness and humaneness of its methods of social organization.[22]

Kennan wouldn't yet go so far in the exemplarist direction as Charles Beard had. Where Beard urged cultivating the American garden as an alternative to engagement abroad, Kennan perceived do-

---

[21] George F. Kennan, "The Illusion of Security," *Atlantic Monthly*, August 1954.
[22] George F. Kennan, "Overdue Changes in Our Foreign Policy," *Atlantic Monthly*, August 1956.

mestic reform as complementary to an internationalist policy. Yet when Kennan spoke, as he did in a 1954 Princeton lecture series, of the importance of cleaning up America's cities, controlling juvenile delinquency, combating crime, perfecting democracy, and generally demonstrating that modernization could be accomplished "without destroying the traditional values of a civilization and corrupting the inner vitality of its life," he spoke a language Beard would have had no difficulty understanding. Kennan had done more than any other person to define the policy that marked the zenith of American vindicationism, but he concluded the final lecture of the Princeton series with words that went to the heart of the exemplarist case. Describing the current inability of America to devise a coherent approach to international affairs, he asserted that Americans would never find such coherence so long as they sought it in relationships "external to our national life." Rather they must look within. They would discover coherence, and a fruitful foreign policy, only when they acknowledged "the obligation of each of us, as an individual, to his God and his faith; the obligation of all of us, as a political society, to our own national ideals." Only through those ideals could Americans reach out to "the wider human community of which we are in ever increasing measure a part."[23]

[23] George F. Kennan, *Realities of American Foreign Policy* (Princeton, N.J., 1954), 116–20.

7

Reinhold Niebuhr and the Foreign Policy of Original Sin

I

Kennan's invocation of God and faith, while hardly the hinge of his argument, suggested that the religious element in American thinking about the world, so noticeable in the nineteenth century, still lived. American anticommunists during the 1950s certainly made much of the "godless" character of the Soviet and Chinese regimes, and as Kennan and Morgenthau both noted, with more than a little dismay, American attitudes toward the world frequently betrayed the mentality of a religious crusade. As always, Americans tended to assume that God was on their side in matters of international affairs.

Yet the Manicheism of popular anticommunism hardly exhausted the range of religious thought on the appropriate role of the United States. Kennan and Morgenthau both probed the subtle question of whether the kind of morality religions prescribed for the private realm applied to relations among states. Because they approached the intersection of religion and foreign policy from the latter direction, though, the religious aspect of their analyses was intermittent and unsystematic.

Reinhold Niebuhr arrived at the crossing from the religious side. The son of a minister of the German Evangelical Synod, Reinhold – along with brother H. Richard, who also became a distinguished theologian – grew up in small-town Missouri. Reinhold took a master's degree at Yale Divinity School, then worked for a decade as pastor of a middle-class parish in Detroit before joining the faculty of the Union Theological Seminary in New York. He later commented that the conditions in the Detroit automobile factories, and especially the autocratic methods of Henry Ford, drove him to consider the limits of morality in social settings. One thing led to another – quickly enough in the modern age of autocracy, with dictatorships taking root on nearly every continent – and before long he was thinking and writing in terms that had global application.

II

Niebuhr's early reflections on the social constraints on morality gave rise to a 1932 book entitled *Moral Man and Immoral Society*. The dual thesis he stated simply: "that a sharp distinction must be drawn between the moral and social behavior of individuals and of social groups, national, racial, and economic; and that this distinction justifies and necessitates political policies which a purely individualistic ethic must always find embarrassing." Niebuhr explicitly distanced himself from moralistically minded progressives – he cited John Dewey as a prime example – who contended that social problems resulted principally from the failure of the social sciences to keep pace with technology, and who argued that time and tinkering would produce solutions. Such amelioristic optimism, Niebuhr declared, neglected the fundamental fact of "the brutal character of the behavior of all human collectives," and failed to understand that the basic elements of collective behavior "belong to the order of nature and can never be brought completely under the dominion of reason or conscience."

Consequently, an examination of ethics, the domain of conscience, necessarily became, when applied to groups, an investigation of politics, the arena of power. "All social cooperation on a larger scale than the most intimate social group requires a measure of coercion," Niebuhr wrote. The larger the scale, the greater the coercion. At the largest scale, that of international relations, coercion took the form of war. Niebuhr rejected the view of internationalists and others in America – a country whose political culture he described as "still pretty firmly enmeshed in the illusions and sentimentalities of the Age of Reason" – that war was an aberration, something that might be abolished by reforming the international system. On the contrary, he claimed, the very national sovereignty that made international politics possible rendered international conflict unavoidable. "The whole history of mankind bears testimony to the fact that the power which prevents anarchy in intra-group relations encourages anarchy in intergroup relations." Democracy was no solution, as the experience of the French after their revolution had demonstrated. Closer in time and distance was the counterexample of the Spanish-American War, an unconscionable case of aggression reflecting "the will-to-power of an adolescent nation and the frustrated impulses of pugnacity and martial ardor of the pitiful little 'men in the street.' " The persistence of war during all ages and across all types of human organization compelled any thinking person to conclude that society was in "a perpetual state of war." Peace was the anomaly, not war.

Niebuhr's examination of history and literature convinced him that states operated according to a different moral calculus than individuals. "The selfishness of nations is proverbial," he wrote, citing George Washington to the effect that governments must never be trusted beyond their interests, and a less famous figure, an otherwise undistinguished German diplomat, who declared, "No state has ever entered a treaty for any other reason than self interest. A statesman who has any other motive would deserve to be hung." Nations were as hypocritical and dishonest as they were selfish. Dishonesty resulted in part from the desire of individuals and classes controlling governments to turn those governments to their own purposes. But the root cause was more complex. "The dishonesty of nations is a necessity of political policy if the nation is to gain the full benefit of its double claim upon the loyalty and devotion of the individual, as his own special and unique community and as a community which embodies universal values and ideals. The two claims, the one touching the individual's emotions and the other appealing to his mind, are incompatible with each other, and can be resolved only through dishonesty."

Niebuhr again pointed to the Spanish-American War to document his argument. He described the conflict as providing "some of the most striking illustrations of the hypocrisy of governments." Members of the war party, he asserted, covered their expansionist designs with the cloak of humanitarianism. They captured the Philippines under the pretext of freeing Cuba. In pacifying the Filipinos, they employed strategies and devices they had condemned in the hands of the Spanish.

Niebuhr published this book before the public elaboration of the totalitarianisms of the 1930s. Thus it was with prescience – or so Niebuhr's followers could claim after the nature of Hitler's plan for perfecting European civilization became evident – that he warned that a belief in social perfectability, far from being an innocuous error of whiggish progressives, contained the capacity for untold evil. Insistence on perfecting society could produce "a sublime madness in the soul," which encouraged "terrible fanaticisms." Of this tendency, liberals and other social reformers must take account.[1]

Moral Man and Immoral Society brought Niebuhr notice as a thinker to contend with. Not all readers agreed with his message. A number of reviewers, especially among the clergy, thought he gave God insufficient credit for showing a way out of the ethical dilemma he described. Norman Thomas lamented the book's "defeatism." Yet as the immorality of world society grew increasingly evident in the years before and during World War II, Niebuhr's influence spread. His impact on Hans Morgenthau was obvious in Morgenthau's writings; George Kennan described Niebuhr as "the father of us all."[2]

Much of the power of Niebuhr's thought owed to his ability to distill an idea into a phrase, which he then used as the title of a book. No reader – or browser even – could mistake the thesis of *Moral Man and Immoral Society*. Niebuhr's 1944 work *The Children of Light and the Children of Darkness* required a bit more explanation, but here again the title summarized the argument. The children of light were those persons who sought to curb the excesses of individual and collective self-interest by restraints of higher law. The children of darkness were those who resisted such restraints. Niebuhr wrote at what he took to be a critical moment for democracy. The democracies – with a singular assist from the communists – were surviving the war, but just barely. Whether they would survive the peace remained an open question. If the previous decade offered any clues, the democratic nations might well lapse into the enervation that had made fascism seem so dynamic by contrast.

At one level, consequently, Niebuhr's presentation took the form of an intellectual and ethical justification for democracy. He judged the traditional justification – the argument from individual liberty – to have been rendered obsolescent by the economic and political transformations that had manifested themselves in the interwar depression. Describing democracy as a "bourgeois ideology," character-

[1] Reinhold Niebuhr, *Moral Man and Immoral Society: A Study in Ethics and Politics* (New York, 1932), xi-xx, xxv, 3, 16–19, 84, 95–6, 277.
[2] Norman Thomas in Richard Wightman Fox, *Reinhold Niebuhr* (New York, 1985), 142; George Kennan in Walter LaFeber, *America, Russia, and the Cold War, 1945– 1984* (New York, 1985), 63.

istic of the rise of the European middle class, he said, "Since bourgeois civilization, which came to birth in the sixteenth to eighteenth
centuries and reached its zenith in the nineteenth century, is now
obviously in grave peril, if not actually in *rigor mortis*, it must be
obvious that democracy, in so far as it is a middle-class ideology, also
faces its doom." Fortunately an alternative justification for democracy lay at hand. Democracy was more than libertarianism modified
to fit a crowded planet, Niebuhr argued. It was a social and political
philosophy that balanced the human desire for autonomy with the
human need for order. As he would during the Cold War, when
many on the American side would not, Niebuhr carefully distinguished between democracy and freedom. The former provided the
structure within which the latter could develop. As such, democracy
transcended the historical and economic circumstances in which it
had arisen. "Ideally, democracy is a permanently valid form of social
and political organization which does justice to two dimensions of
human existence: to man's spiritual stature and his social character;
to the uniqueness and variety of life, as well as to the common necessities of all men."

The justifiability of democracy, however, didn't guarantee its via-
bility. Democracy continually came under attack – as it was under
attack at the moment – from the cynical and self-seeking children of
darkness, who, as the Bible warned, were wiser in the ways of the
world than the children of light. Yet democracy might also fall at the
hands of the foolish children of light, who not only mistook the
strength and cleverness of the children of darkness, but also underestimated their own inclination to self-interest. The children of darkness played on this weakness. The democratic world had come close
to disaster not merely because it never believed that Nazism possessed
the demonic fury it avowed, but because the democrats refused –
until very late – to suppress their internal differences. "The children
of darkness meanwhile skilfully set nation against nation. They were
thereby enabled to despoil one nation after another, without every
civilized nation coming to the defence of each."

In preparing for the postwar period, thinkers and leaders in the
democratic states must bear in mind both the wiles of the children of
darkness and the folly and weakness of the children of light. For the
first time in history, a world community was plausible. Until the
present century, universalists – religious prophets primarily, but a few
secular types as well – had dreamed of a community comprising all

of humanity, but they had never possessed the requisite technology of transport and communication. Now the technology of communitarianism had arrived, and none too soon, considering the more-than-commensurate development of the technology of destruction. The liberal children of light, speaking the language of internationalism, sought the creation of the world community. But in their endeavors thus far they had not demonstrated a sufficient appreciation of the difficulties involved. "They all underestimated the power of particular and limited vitalities in human history. They failed to understand the persistence and power of the pride of nations or to comprehend the inertial force of traditional loyalties."

Niebuhr grouped the children of light into two categories, "one more naive and the other a little more sophisticated." Those in the former group dealt chiefly in ideas, expecting the world community to arrive on the wings of a new, broader definition of international law. "They think that we lack an international government only because no one has conceived a proper blueprint of it." These people, Niebuhr added, possessed "a touching faith in the power of a formula over the raw stuff of human history." The sophomores of the school of light acknowleged a role for power, recognizing the need for international sanctions to compel adherence to the mandates of international law. But this group overlooked the fundamental and necessary role of mutual interest in creating a community. "While a single sovereignty may be the final and indispensable instrument of a common community, it is not possible to achieve unity by the power of government alone. Government may be the head of the body, which without a single head could not be, or become, a single body; but it is not possible for a head to create a body." Nearly every extended community that had developed in the past – in particular, nearly every nation of the world – had exhibited a collective self-consciousness, based on some combination of cultural, religious, ethnic, and historical ties, in advance of becoming a state. No such ties yet bound together a nascent world community.

Americans, especially, fell into the error of thinking a world community could be summoned into existence by international legislative fiat. Misreading their own experience, believing that their nation had sprung fully formed from the brows of Madison and Hamilton and the other writers of the Constitution, they blithely attempted to frame constitutionalist solutions to current international problems. Their historical memories ignored such traumas as the Civil War, and their present efforts at legislating order and stability would be equally at variance with reality.

Yet while internationalism promised some difficulties, a return to isolationism guaranteed more. What Niebuhr called "this negative form of national egotism" was "incompatible with the ultimate necessities of the world community." Fortunately, isolationism no longer possessed its former appeal. The present war had seen to that. But isolationism would remain "a temptation for the great powers for some time to come." The winners of the war, lulled by "the illusory hope of security by their own power," would be particularly susceptible.

The course chosen by the great powers after the war would determine the fate of the world community project. To some extent, the Grand Alliance represented a center around which such a community might coalesce. In the interest of the common goal of victory, each ally consented to abridgments of its sovereignty. "But" – in what proved to be a massive understatement – "it is not certain that this potential center will be actualized after the war is over." Hitler held the alliance together; his demise might be that of the alliance as well. "No doubt there is a general appreciation among the great powers of the peril of international anarchy; and this appreciation may serve to preserve war-time accords. But since the fear of anarchy is less potent than the fear of a concrete foe, the general tendency will be for war-time accords to be weakened rather than strengthened."

Self-styled realists (Hans Morgenthau, for example) were advocating a settlement based on a balance of power among the victors; an arrangement of this sort, Niebuhr said, would be better than nothing, though not much. "Such a policy, which holds all factors in the world situation in the most perfect equipoise, can undoubtedly mitigate anarchy. A balance of power is in fact a kind of managed anarchy. But it is a system in which anarchy invariably overcomes the management in the end." The problem consisted in the fact that no participant in the balance scheme ever quite accepted its portion of power. "Every center of power will seek to improve its position; and every such effort will be regarded by the others as an attempt to disturb the equilibrium." Tension and conflict would inevitably ensue.

Morgenthau, of course, recognized this problem but did not think it disqualifying; Niebuhr disagreed, and he concluded that the balance-of-power realists had as little to offer toward lasting peace as the world-community idealists. "Pure idealists underestimate the perennial power of particular and parochial loyalties, operating as a counter force against the achievement of a wider community. But the realists are usually so impressed by the power of these perennial forces that they fail to recognize the novel and unique elements in a revolutionary world situation." Nor did the misjudgments stop there. "The idealists erroneously imagine that a new situation automatically generates the resources for the solution of its problem. The realists erroneously discount the destructive, as well as the creative, power of a revolutionary situation."

Although Niebuhr didn't do justice to either the more pragmatic of the idealists, who appreciated the enormous challenges any scheme of international law would face, or the more insightful of the realists, who understood that conditions of the postwar period would differ in significant ways from those that had obtained before, his overstatement of the two positions served the purpose of bracketing the territory in which an approach to a peace settlement would have to be sought. As for specific directions inside the territory, Niebuhr's comments served to remind readers that he was, after all, a theologian rather than a geopolitician. "Clearly it has become necessary for the children of light to borrow some of the wisdom of the children of darkness, and yet be careful not to borrow too much," he wrote vaguely. Even less helpfully: "The task of building a world community is man's final necessity and possibility, but also his final impossibility." The world community was simultaneously "the final possibility and impossibility of human life" and "the perpetual problem as well as the constant fulfillment of human hopes."

Who would square the circle and accomplish the impossible? No mortal, Niebuhr said. "The task of achieving it must be interpreted from the standpoint of a faith which understands the fragmentary and broken character of all historic achievements and yet has confidence in their meaning because it knows their completion to be in the hands of a Divine Power, whose resources are greater than those of men."[3]

III

Using God as a backstop – How many divisions did *He* have? – didn't seem quite fair to those attempting to design policy in the here and

---

[3] Reinhold Niebuhr, *The Children of Light and the Children of Darkness: A Vindication of Democracy and a Critique of its Traditional Defense* (New York, 1944), 2–3, 9–12, 161–7, 171–6, 187–90.

now. But Niebuhr's overriding sense of the futility of the human quest for lasting world peace bolstered, indeed contributed materially to the development of, the arguments of those like Morgenthau who held that morality lay in choosing the path of least evil. Niebuhr's rebuke to the realists in *The Children of Light and the Children of Darkness* amounted to little more than friendly urging to recognize what had changed in the world situation. By contrast, his critique of the idealists signified a flat denial that their vision of a world community would materialize this side of the Second Coming. If policy-makers had to choose – and policy-makers, unlike theologians, *do* have to choose – they would find more in Niebuhr to support a realist approach than an idealist one.

As the confrontation between the United States and the Soviet Union developed, Niebuhr continued to hammer the idealists, those he called "liberal perfectionists." In April 1949 he published "The Illusion of World Government" in *Foreign Affairs*, by this time a bastion of Cold War orthodoxy. Expanding his argument against the one-worlders, Niebuhr isolated the crux of the difficulty confronting the human race. "Our problem," he wrote, "is that technics have established a rudimentary world community but have not integrated it organically, morally or politically. They have created a community of mutual dependence, but not one of mutual trust and respect." Niebuhr had no expectation that the trust and respect necessary to a successful world government would develop soon, or ever.[4]

Niebuhr summarized what he deemed the fallacy of world government in two propositions. First, governments are not created by deliberate design but emerge organically from the communities they govern. Second, governments cannot generate the organic development they require. The world-government theorists, Niebuhr said, based their advocacy on the notion of the social contract, by which individuals living in a Hobbesian state of nature surrender aspects of their individual sovereignty to government in exchange for protection. Niebuhr denied that any government had ever originated by such means. "It must certainly be obvious by this time that the conception of a state of nature in which all men were at war with all, and of a subsequent social contract through which men established a power over themselves to avoid mutual annihilation, is a pure fiction." Community, he asserted, was coeval with individuals. Govern-

---

[4]   Reinhold Niebuhr, *Christianity and Power Politics* (New York, 1940), x; Reinhold Niebuhr, "The Illusion of World Government," *Foreign Affairs*, April 1949.

ments developed by gradually accreting power from communities rather than by being summoned from the void. That the world community necessary to sustain a world government did not exist was evident from the ongoing Cold War. Niebuhr doubted that such a community would form even if the Cold War ended. At the moment, Russian intransigence masked underlying dissension among the democratic countries. Should the Russians decide tomorrow to cooperate, world government might well founder the next day on differences in the camp of democracy.

Niebuhr thought his second point, that government could not generate community, a still greater obstacle to the one-worlders' plans. The enthusiasts of world government labored under a misconception about the nature of governmental authority, he said. Their social contract notions led them to believe that authority rested principally on government's monopoly of law and lawful force. This put things just backward. "The authority of government is not primarily the authority of law nor the authority of force, but the authority of the community itself. Laws are obeyed because the community accepts them as corresponding, on the whole, to its conceptions of justice." By definition, this statement held for democratic governments. But it generally characterized traditional, nondemocratic governments as well, as evidenced by the fact that even under monarchies and autocracies people distinguished between legitimate regimes, which embodied prevailing views of the proper relation of government to individuals, and tyrannical regimes, which did not. The very discrepancy between a tyrant's demands and individuals' perceptions of the ruler's due was what defined tyranny.

Niebuhr conceded that at certain times in the past governments had been imposed from without and eventually contributed to the development of a supporting community. The empires of Egypt, Babylon, and Persia swallowed surrounding groups that initially felt no allegiance to their imperial overlords, but with the passage of years the peripheral peoples came to identify with the metropolis. Such instances, however, demonstrated the essential role of "preponderant power" in the process – preponderant power being the capacity to enforce submission for a sufficiently long period for social and cultural ties to develop. An analogy in the present would require a major nation, presumably either the United States or the Soviet Union, to reduce the rest of humanity to submission in some final global struggle. Needless to say, such wasn't what the one-worlders had in mind.

Niebuhr didn't claim that the social fabric of a world community completely lacked threads. Cross-border economic transactions created an international community of interest among the parties involved. The fear of atomic annihilation brought peoples of different countries together. To an unmeasurable but not inconsequential degree, enlightened individuals in many countries were beginning to recognize their moral responsibility to those with whom they shared the planet, regardless of nationality.

But the threads were weak and thinly woven. The tariff wars of the 1930s demonstrated that economics could divide nations as easily as bring them together. The specter of a world-ending nuclear holocaust, while felt across borders and regions, was based not on a fear of destruction descending from space but on various countries' fears of one another. Definitions of moral responsibility differed enormously from one country to the next. Americans defined morality in terms of liberty, Russians in terms of equality. The different definitions lay at the heart of the ideological contest between the superpowers.

Yet Niebuhr – here writing for an audience of foreign-policy practitioners – held out some hope of progress in the direction of the world community he still deemed essential to lasting peace. He argued for humility in prosecuting the Cold War. "We would, I think, have a better chance of success in our struggle against a fanatical foe if we were less sure of our purity and virtue. The pride and self-righteousness of powerful nations are a greater hazard to their success in statecraft than the machinations of their foes." By granting the possibility of error in their approach to the world, Americans would better place themselves to convince the Russians of error in the Russian view. In the bargain, "we might also gradually establish a genuine sense of community with our foe, however small."[5]

Beyond his emphasis on the humanly impossible nature of the predicament facing the contemporary world – summarized by his statement to the general assembly of the World Council of Churches that "the final victory over man's disorder is God's and not ours" – Niebuhr's advocacy of humility was his principal continuing contribution to the debate on the Cold War. Of course, his advocacy of humility followed from his postulate of human impossibility, for if victory rested with God alone, then Washington (or Moscow or London or Paris or whoever) had better not get too cocky. Communism

---

[5] Niebuhr, "Illusion of World Government."

might be godless, but that didn't mean God had enlisted on democracy's side.[6]

On this point, Niebuhr again provided aid and comfort to the Cold War realists. The entire thrust of Morgenthau's (and others') balance-of-power argument was that the game of nations never ended. Victory was never more than partial and temporary: As soon as one nation edged a little ahead, the others joined forces to pull it back. In heaven, struggle might cease, but on earth there was always another round. To think otherwise was ahistorical, illogical, and hubristic – and, according to Niebuhr, perhaps even blasphemous.

Niebuhr held that liberals, in particular, needed to beware of the sin of prideful self-confidence. "Practically all schools of modern culture, whatever their differences, are united in their rejection of the Christian doctrine of original sin," he told an audience at Westminster College. Marxists, of course, discarded original sin, along with God, temptation, and the other paraphernalia of religious addiction. But Western liberals, enamored of the power of their new social sciences, also at least implicitly rejected original sin, believing that their intellectual paradigms, if accepted by those who wielded power, would sweep away the evils afflicting the human race. (Western conservatives evidently didn't qualify for consideration under Niebuhr's rubric of "schools of modern culture.")

Of the error of the Marxists in this matter, Niebuhr felt obliged to say little more, beyond a reminder that even as Stalin and the other heirs of Marx committed the most monstrous evils, they remained convinced of their innocence. "The powers of human self-deception are seemingly endless," he declared. "The communist tyrants may well legitimatize their cruelties not only to the conscience of their devotees but to their own by recourse to an official theory which proves their innocency 'by definition.' "

Yet Western liberals, and American liberals in particular, fell prey to the same temptation. "We are (according to our traditional theory) the most innocent nation on earth." What made this belief particularly ironic – Niebuhr delighted in irony, even more than in finding archaic variants ("innocency") of perfectly usable words – was that it derived in substantial measure from Calvinism, one of the most guilt-laden strains of Christianity. The Massachusetts Puritans, by

---

[6] Reinhold Niebuhr, "The Christian Witness in the Social and National Order," reprinted in *Christian Realism and Political Problems* (New York, 1953), 116.

separating themselves from their sinful homeland, had created a "new" England in the western hemisphere. As individuals they might still be sinful, but their new home was free of the taint that had driven them across the sea.

Feeding this conviction of "the innocency and virtue of the new nation" was what Niebuhr identified as the second (after New England Puritanism) fundamental religious-moral tradition in America: the deism of Virginia and Jefferson. The Jeffersonians, as heirs of the Enlightenment, thought that emigration from the blighted land of feudalism and class distinctions had sufficed to establish a society based on the principles of equality and freedom. In both cases, the Puritan and Jeffersonian, the physical and intellectual act of separation had produced a moral feeling of innocence. "Every nation has its own form of spiritual pride," Niebuhr asserted. "Our version is that our nation has turned its back upon the vices of Europe and made a new beginning."

The American illusion of innocence shaped the country's domestic politics, contributing, for instance, to a peculiar and unfounded reverence for agriculture as a uniquely honorable vocation. Yet the illusion of innocence produced its most marked effects in America's relations with the rest of the world. During the first century of the republic's existence, Americans had shunned involvement with the powers of Europe. In remaining aloof, Americans determined to preserve their innocence – while they seized half a continent from the indigenous inhabitants and anyone else who happened in the way. Even a war as patently imperialistic as the conflict with Spain could be rationalized as a manifestation of American concern for the welfare of the Cubans and, as an afterthought, of the Filipinos.

American involvement in World War I did nothing to diminish the feeling of innocence. On the contrary, the American president, while condemning the self-interested motives of the other belligerents, insisted that America fought to save the world for democracy. (Here Niebuhr remarked another irony, applicable not only to the United States: "Every nation is caught in the moral paradox of refusing to go to war unless it can be proved that the national interest is imperiled, and of continuing the war only by proving that something much more than the national interest is at stake." How, this being the case, nations frequently ceased fighting short of complete victory or utter annihilation, Niebuhr didn't reveal.) After World War I, when Americans rejected the peace treaty, they did so convinced that their redemptive mission had been corrupted by cynically crafty Old World-ers. The American unilateralists of the 1920s and isolationists of the 1930s extended the principle of innocence by a return to noninvolvement.

World War II and the events that followed destroyed forever the possibility of American separateness, Niebuhr said, but they only reinforced Americans' belief in their country's innocence. The war came to America unsought. Once engaged, Americans destroyed the principal locus of organized evil in the world. The aftermath of the fighting revealed a new malignancy; again Americans took arms in defense of right and virtue.

America's real history, of course, had always been more complicated than this mythology allowed, Niebuhr noted. Americans had never been the innocents they thought themselves to be. Now, possessing – and having used – atomic weapons, they were less innocent than ever. "Thus an 'innocent' nation finally arrives at the ironic climax of its history. It finds itself the custodian of the ultimate weapon which perfectly embodies and symbolizes the moral ambiguity of physical warfare." The United States could not forswear the bomb, because no nation had the moral right to deny itself an instrument that might be necessary for its survival. "Yet if we should use it, we shall cover ourselves with a terrible guilt. We might insure our survival in a world in which it might be better not to be alive." To this had America, and humanity, come. "The moral predicament in which all human striving is involved has been raised to a final pitch for a culture and for a nation which thought it an easy matter to distinguish between justice and injustice and believed itself to be peculiarly innocent."

Niebuhr stopped well short of positing a moral equivalence between communist and American leaders. "The whole world suffers from the pretensions of the communist oligarchs. Our pretensions are of a different order because they are not as consistently held. In any event, we have preserved a system of freedom in which they may be challenged."

Yet he warned against persons who deemed communism so malicious as to warrant the potential use of any and all weapons against it. Those holding such a view, Niebuhr said, "closely approach the communist ruthlessness." On the other hand, to renounce the use of atomic weapons might deliver the world to that very ruthlessness. "This is merely the old pacifist escape from the dilemma of war."

Between the two extremes, which admittedly sometimes crowded close together, Americans must tread carefully. "Otherwise either we will seek escape from responsibilities which involve unavoidable guilt, or we will be plunged into avoidable guilt by too great confidence in our virtue."[7]

IV

Niebuhr wasn't always so unhelpful to those seeking to draw the sharpest possible distinction between the United States and its Russian rival. In a 1953 essay he queried, "Why is communism so evil?" and he replied in terms guaranteed to satisfy the most rabid red-baiter. "We are bound to ask the question," he said, perhaps a little defensively, "because we are fated as a generation to live in the insecurity which this universal evil of communism creates for our world." Niebuhr dismissed the "timid spirits" who wondered whether American conservatives exaggerated the danger communism posed to democratic institutions and values. The conservatives did not exaggerate, he said; the danger was fully as great as depicted. If the conservatives erred, they did so by stressing the magnitude of the danger while failing to analyze sufficiently its nature.

A correct analysis was necessary, Niebuhr asserted, lest one fall into the mistake of those – he might have mentioned Morgenthau, but didn't – who argued that Moscow's actions reflected chiefly the maneuvers expected of an ordinary great power. Such a judgment, Niebuhr declared, obscured "the difference between the comparatively ordinate and normal lust for power of a great traditional nation and the noxious demonry of this world wide secular religion."

Interestingly, considering Niebuhr's personal calling, his complaint against communism derived hardly at all from its avowed atheism. His criticism rested instead on the – related, to be sure, but only indirectly – insistence of the communists on a monopoly of power. In every time and place, "disproportions of power" (Niebuhr didn't specify what *pro*portions of power were) gave rise to injustice. "But a system which gives some men absolute power over other men results in evils which are worse than injustice." Niebuhr rejected the

---

[7] Reinhold Niebuhr, "The Innocent Nation in an Innocent World," reprinted in *The Irony of American History* (New York, 1952).

argument that the totalitarianism of communist practice followed not from the original theoretical doctrines of Marx but from subsequent additions by Lenin and Stalin. Admittedly, Marx hadn't conceived of the highly organized power structure of modern communism. "But Marx did plan for the 'dictatorship of the proletariat'; and the progressive moral deterioration of such a dictatorship was inevitable rather than fortuitous." This latter was true for two reasons. First, Marx's conceptual division of society into the powerful and the powerless encouraged a practical monopoly by the former at the expense of the latter, which monopoly unavoidably degenerated into dictatorship by a faction, then by a few individuals, then by one. Second, Marx's supposition that economic power consisted solely in the *ownership* of property had led him to assume that abolition of ownership would end economic oppression; in fact, the communist oligarchs who merely *managed* property succeeded in oppressing workers as thoroughly as any capitalist.

Niebuhr's second reason for blaming Marx had a firmer basis than his first. With many other observers, he mistakenly took Stalin to be the model for all future communist rulers – even as Stalin's heirs were busy dismantling the recently deceased Georgian's system, attempting (for the most part successfully, as things turned out) to ensure that his most flagrant excesses weren't repeated.

Niebuhr's logic wobbled on another matter as well. He asserted that Marxist utopianism was the basis of the evils of communism, in that it provided "a moral facade for the most unscrupulous political policy, giving the communist oligarch the moral warrant to suppress and sacrifice immediate values in the historical process for the sake of reaching so ideal a goal." Niebuhr then suggested that the moral facade wasn't a facade at all, but a conviction sincerely held by Soviet leaders. "Such are the powers of human self-deception that, for all we know, they may still be believers who persuade themselves that they are doing what they do for noble ultimate ends. Stalin is reported to have rebuffed a journalist who compared him with Napoleon. Napoleon, he declared, had no good purpose as the goal for which his power was the means." Apparently unconvinced by either of these positions, moral facade or true belief, Niebuhr threw up his hands and asserted – or did he? – that what the masters of the Kremlin believed was irrelevant. "In one sense the presence or absence of cynicism among the oligarchs is beside the point. The important point is that the ruthless power operates behind a screen of pretended ideal ends, a situation which is both more dangerous and more evil than pure cynical defiance of moral ends."[8]

Niebuhr was wrong about the presence or absence of cynicism in the Kremlin being beside the point. It was very much the point, for it was the crux of the issue the United States confronted in the Cold War. Only if Soviet leaders were *not* cynics were they qualitatively different from history's myriad other empire-builders. If ideology didn't matter in Moscow, if the communists' ideal ends were merely "pretended," then the Soviet Union was simply another great power. In that case, American leaders should listen to Morgenthau, not Niebuhr.

V

Niebuhr's fretting about American liberals' hubris and their ignorance of original sin was timely, for by the early 1950s liberals dominated foreign policy. Or perhaps conservatives did: It was hard to tell. The fact of the matter was that recent events – especially Mao Zedong's victory in China, the Soviet acquisition of the atomic bomb, and the outbreak of the Korean war – had fostered a unique convergence in American thinking on foreign affairs. Americans were either all conservatives or all liberals: Whichever, they essentially agreed that the communist danger was real and immediate, and that America needed to take strong measures to repel it. In other words, they were all vindicators.

The liberal-conservative convergence prompted various reactions. Louis Hartz yawned, saying that Americans had always been all alike. American parties and movements had merely offered variations on a single underlying tradition, which Hartz labeled liberal, but more in the nineteenth-century European sense than the twentieth-century American. Daniel Bell disagreed on the historical point: Ideological differences had once existed. But no longer: America had reached the "end of ideology." Richard Hofstadter complained that what passed for contemporary conservatism was mere "pseudo-conservatism" – although it was unclear how sincerely he mourned the demise of the genuine article. Arthur Schlesinger Jr. positively celebrated the blurring of differences between left and right, for the

[8] Reinhold Niebuhr, "The Evil of the Communist Idea," *New Leader*, June 8, 1953.

emergence of a "vital center" conferred a singular legitimacy on America's vindicationist approach to the Cold War. There was no avoiding fate. "History has thrust a world destiny on the United States," Schlesinger wrote.[9]

Niebuhr agreed with Schlesinger about America's world destiny, and with Hartz and the others on the diminishing utility of labels. "American conservatism," he wrote in a 1953 volume, "is not conservative at all in the traditional sense; it is a part of the traditional liberal movement." One indication of this was its adherence to free-market economics; another – related – indication was its "blindness to ambitions and lusts among nations which are not contained within the economic motives which prevail in the business world." In consequence, American conservatives were seriously handicapped in relations with regimes inspired by such ambitions and lusts. Reaching for a European parallel, Niebuhr described American conservatism as akin to the approach of Neville Chamberlain and the other appeasers. "It is characteristic of the business mind," Niebuhr said, "that Chamberlain thought that Hitler had a price which reasonable men could meet, and that the typically bourgeois Dutch sought to make themselves safe against Hitler's will-to-power by a meticulous neutrality." (Niebuhr didn't indicate what feasible alternative the Netherlands had.)

Niebuhr wished for – without expecting – the development of a genuinely conservative party in the United States. America needed a corrective to what he saw as the Democrats' tendency to moralistic idealism. Despite their commitment to the Cold War, the Democrats still displayed a "too unqualified confidence in the power of abstract ideas amidst the complexities of international relations." The key was to strike a balance. "Our problem," he asserted, "both in foreign policy and in other affairs, is how to generate the wisdom of true conservatism without losing the humane virtues which the liberal movement developed."

The Eisenhower administration appeared unlikely to solve the

---

[9] Louis Hartz, *The Liberal Tradition in America: An Interpretation of American Political Thought Since the Revolution* (New York, 1955); Daniel Bell, *The End of Ideology: On the Exhaustion of Political Ideas in the Fifties* (New York, 1961); Richard Hofstadter, "The Pseudo-Conservative Revolt," in Daniel Bell, ed., *The New American Right* (New York, 1955); Arthur M. Schlesinger Jr., *The Vital Center: The Politics of Freedom* (Boston, 1949), 219.

problem. Eisenhower's background as soldier and statesman stood him well, but he and his handlers had made too many concessions to Republican conservatives – to those elements of the party that had criticized "any policy which was meant to meet the responsibilities of our power in the world."[10]

Eisenhower lived down to Niebuhr's expectations. At the beginning of 1955, while the administration aggravated a crisis in the Taiwan Strait by threatening to use nuclear weapons against China, Niebuhr analyzed what he labeled "American nationalism." Located chiefly in the right wing of the Republican party, the phenomenon combined in curious fashion the belligerence of McKinley-era imperialism with the suspicions of interwar isolationism. It focused on Asia, where it sought to reverse what it interpreted as the errors wrought by the Democrats, and it refused to accept that there might exist problems the United States could not remedy. General MacArthur embodied the views of the nationalists, both in his Asian orientation and in his inability to understand that the United States couldn't simply go out and win the Cold War as it had won earlier wars. MacArthur apparently believed that what Niebuhr described as "the inconclusiveness of history" was not an inevitable aspect of human fate but the consequence of a false and defeatist doctrine. "He is on this point the spokesman of those in our nation who are unable to comprehend why we had more control over our destiny in the days of our infancy than in the day of our maturity and seeming omnipotence."

Niebuhr thought the Asian emphasis of the nationalists especially striking. There, if anywhere, America operated at a disadvantage, in that Washington had chained itself to a "disintegrating colonialism" and a "decaying feudalism." What explained the nationalists' affinity for this hard road? Without putting the matter quite so bluntly, Niebuhr in effect attributed it to the fact that nationalism had become the last refuge of the isolationists. The nationalists disliked and disdained Europe. "It is the continent of our allies, who are tardy or recalcitrant about any given policy of ours." In Asia, by contrast, Americans exercised a freer – or at least less fettered by allies – hand.[11]

---

[10] Reinhold Niebuhr, "The Foreign Policy of American Conservatism and Liberalism," in *Christian Realism and Political Problems*, 55–67.

[11] Reinhold Niebuhr, "The Anatomy of American Nationalism," *New Leader*, Feb. 28, 1955.

On this point, Niebuhr neglected to note that the United States by 1955 had nearly as many allies in the Asia-Pacific region as in Europe, but his implication that the opinions of those allies counted for less in American policy-making was correct. To a far greater degree than in Europe, the United States could act unilaterally in Asia. Unilateralism, more than isolationism per se, was what the so-called isolationists desired.

Niebuhr expressed cautious relief that the president was resisting the worst of the importunities of the nationalist-isolationists and retained a "wholesome perspective" on the appropriate balance between Europe and Asia. At the same time, Niebuhr feared that the administration was falling victim to the other of the nationalists' fundamental follies: their overreliance on military measures. Niebuhr granted that "military action must frequently be the *ultima ratio* in a struggle with a foe," and he applauded the Truman administration's prompt use of military force in Korea. But the Republicans, he said, resorted indiscriminately to military force or its threat. Writing in the aftermath of the Geneva conference of 1954, the formation of SEATO, and the creation of a government for South Vietnam, Niebuhr asserted: "The contemporary situation in Vietnam should certainly instruct us on the limits of military power in the long cold war. For what we are witnessing is the revelation of the poverty of our cause in moral and political terms in a nation which we sought to save from Communist aggression by military defense." The difficulty the Saigon regime encountered in consolidating its authority over religious sects, war-lord gangs and other dissidents – while the United States pumped in military aid – demonstrated the inefficacy of military power when it lacked a moral and political base. "It is the fist of a hand; but the hand must be attached to an arm, and the arm to a body; and the body must be robust before the fist can be effective."

Yet despite the increasingly obvious limits on the usefulness of military power – Niebuhr included the fall of the Nationalists in China as supporting evidence – the Eisenhower administration seemed strangely enamored of militarism, especially in Asia. "We treat the Asian continent with its nationalistic and social upheavals as if it were possible to establish order out of chaos by the assertion of military might. We are preoccupied with our 'defense perimeter' in Asia and have little interest in the vast political complexities of the great continent except to express consistent contempt for the great uncommitted nation, India, though that nation's neutralism is not informed by the slightest degree of sympathy for communism."

The animus of the American government toward India – which Niebuhr considerably overstated – he deemed symptomatic of "our indifference toward the political complexities of a continent in ferment" and "our blindness to the hazards which our cause inevitably faces on that continent." Military force could not eliminate these hazards. If anything, it aggravated them. "Our preoccupation with military power and strategy places us in a false light in Asia, particularly since it creates a picture which seems to conform to the Communist slogans that identify 'militarism' and 'imperialism' with 'capitalism.'"

Niebuhr discerned two causes for America's counterproductive militarism. The first had its origins in human psychology, in the fact that "a serious predicament may persuade even a pacific man to rely upon his fists." The United States confronted a serious predicament in Asia, and the resort to force came naturally, if imprudently. The second source of American reliance on military power was the simple fact that America possessed more military power than any other country, and it possessed more of military power than of the other principal instruments and techniques of diplomacy. Niebuhr judged that the United States hadn't emerged from the adolescence of nationhood. "Our apprenticeship in the leadership of world affairs has been brief, and we have not had time to accustom ourselves to the acquisition, and to know the importance, of prestige as a source of power; or to learn patience with the endless complexities of loyalties and resentments of traditions and established forms of cohesion which govern the actions of nations."

Niebuhr warned that even if military power accomplished its narrow objective of forcing countries to bow to American desires, it might still backfire. "In collective, as well as individual, life the force which coerces the body but does not persuade the will can have only negative significance. It can prevent something which we abhor more than conflict, and it can enforce our will and purpose momentarily on a recalcitrant foe. But the loyalties and cohesions of the community are managed and transfigured not by force but by a wise statecraft." The United States deployed force aplenty; wisdom it had yet to demonstrate.[12]

The disparity Niebuhr saw between force and wisdom grew during the latter half of the 1950s. While America's stock of wisdom didn't

[12] Reinhold Niebuhr, "The Limits of Military Power," *New Leader*, May 30, 1955.

conspicuously increase, its supply of force expanded exponentially with the continued rapid development of the nation's nuclear arsenal. Much the same thing was occurring in the Soviet Union, although the stunning 1957 launch of the Russian Sputnik led many commentators in America to conclude that the Soviet store of wisdom – at least that portion related to science – had outstripped America's.

Niebuhr interpreted American surprise at the Russians' breakthrough as the consequence of two mistaken assumptions about the Soviets. "Russia is not a 'backward' country, except in living standards and political organization," he wrote. "Even the political tyranny is not backward; it is a novel form of harnessing utopian dreams to despotism." By focusing on lagging Soviet production of consumer goods and exaggerating the inefficiencies of the Soviet bureaucracy, Americans had lulled themselves into believing that America's ascendancy in technological matters was guaranteed. "We forgot that it required Japan less than half a century to transmute its economy from an agrarian to an industrial and technical pattern. We were wrong to assume that a technical culture, requiring so many centuries to germinate in the West, could not be transplanted in much shorter time."

Americans' second false conception touched more directly on the philosophical differences between the American and Soviet systems. "We were wrong in assuming that despotism excluded democracy in education, at least the democracy of freedom of opportunity. We should have known for a long time that the Russian young people had a passion for education." (Why Americans should have known this, Niebuhr didn't say.) He went on to assert that the Soviets had bested the United States on turf America once owned. Russia took the idea of free public education, pioneered in America, to a logical conclusion Americans couldn't bring themselves to accept. While government in the United States paid tuition for children in elementary and secondary schools, Moscow funded its brightest clear through postdoctoral study. Referring to higher education, Niebuhr argued, "We give everyone the right to acquire an education if the family budget and the resourcefulness of the youth are able to cope with our ever-higher educational costs. That is 'Jacksonian' democracy in practice. The Russian system is 'Jeffersonian' in insisting on an aristocracy of excellence."

Yet after complaining at the economic barriers to higher education in America, Niebuhr oddly proceeded to assert that too many Americans were attending college. The colleges were inundated with "students of little ability and less scholarly eagerness who prevent the real students from getting a good education." Unless the United States tightened entrance requirements to keep the unfit out, and loosened scholarship funds to get the able poor in, "the Russian advantage over us is likely to be permanent."

Niebuhr wondered whether the Sputnik experience, by revealing the degree to which Americans had wrapped themselves in a narcissistic consumer culture, indicated a passing of the American age. In language of the sort Brooks Adams used in *The Law of Civilization and Decay*, Niebuhr wrote, "We have in fact become so self-indulgent that one may raise the question whether our position vis-à-vis the Russians is not the old historic situation: the 'barbarians,' hardy and disciplined, are ready to defeat a civilization in which the very achievements of its technology have made for soft and indulgent living. . . . We are just as effete, and probably more vulgar, than the Byzantines when the Moslems took Constantinople. The Communists are just as strong, fanatic and disciplined as the hordes of Islam were."[13]

VI

Niebuhr pondered at greater length the question of the world-historic roles of communism and democracy in his single most sustained analysis of the fundamentals of international affairs, *The Struggle of Nations and Empires*. Published in 1959, the book reflected the proto-detente of the late Eisenhower period. Partly as a consequence, it was Niebuhr's least value-laden assessment of Soviet-American relations. No longer did he belabor the evilness of the Kremlin; for the most part, he placed the Soviet empire and the American empire on essentially equal moral footings, at least for the purposes of investigation.

Again echoing Brooks Adams, Niebuhr devoted much of the book to summarizing the experiences of the empires of the past, although he dealt more with their intellectual and political foundations than with their economic bases. He traversed the globe from the valley of the Yellow River across Persia and Mesopotamia to the Greek pen-

---

[13] Reinhold Niebuhr, "After Sputnik and Explorer," *Christianity and Crisis*, March 4, 1958.

insula and Italy, noting in the East the origins of state-centered politics, in the West the politics of individualism. He examined the impact of religions, especially the proselytizing creeds of Christianity and Islam, on the Roman and subsequent empires. He charted the rise of European nationalism and its effect on the imperial ambitions of the contenders for power in Europe and beyond. He identified in the French and Scottish enlightenments the intellectual underpinnings of American political thought. To German philosophers he ascribed the roots of modern Russian thinking on government and power.

Niebuhr perceived three impulses driving what he called "vital nations" – those containing the seeds of empire – to expansion. The first was the missionary impulse: "the desire to extend the fruits of a culture, whether conceived in religious, political or technical terms." (Niebuhr took care to distinguish his use of the term missionary from that applicable to real missionaries, who, he conceded, might play a role in political conversion but who at least tried for higher, religious objectives.) The missionary impulse had long been evident in American expansionism. For contemporary communists, Marxism and science served as a secular religion.

The second impulse was economic. The communists, Niebuhr asserted, exaggerated the importance of economics when they defined imperialism as the ultimate stage of capitalism. But the quest for natural resources, markets, and investment opportunities undeniably figured significantly in the imperialist activity of the capitalist countries of the West. Economics counted for less in the imperialist endeavors of the Soviets, who were largely self-sufficient in resources and lacked exportable products.

The third impulse was more difficult to characterize explicitly. Niebuhr settled for calling it "the expression of a national vitality and of the desire for power and glory, for the enhancement of the prestige of the imperial power." The politics of prestige had played a substantial role in the evolution of empires, and continued to figure in the calculations of their leaders. The Western drive for prestige was informed by, and gave rise to, explicit and implicit racism on the part of European and American imperialists; in the process, it engendered resentment that worked against the present further extension of the American empire in Asia and Africa. The communists sought to enlist this resentment in the service of the expansion of their own prestige and power.

Examining the ongoing competition between the United States and

the Soviet Union, Niebuhr remarked that the contest was partly ideological, with the Russians pursuing a more consistent line in this
regard than the Americans. Because Moscow deemed itself the head-
quarters of world revolution and the capital of socialism, it openly
claimed the right to intervene on behalf of the socialist revolution
anywhere. The American position was more haphazard, not least
because the American sphere contained nations – from social democracies in Western Europe to authoritarian dictatorships in the Middle
East and East Asia – that shared little ideologically except a declared
opposition to communism.

Yet while ideology made the competition between America and
Russia inevitable, economics made it possible. "The two nations with
power of imperial proportions," Niebuhr said, recalling Tocqueville
nearly a century-and-a-half earlier, "are in their positions because
they alone have the capacity to organize a great continental economy
which surpasses the economic resources of any other nation."

A striking irony of the competition between the two imperial systems was that the guiding philosophy of each denied the legitimacy
of empire. American anti-imperialism drew sustenance from the
American past. "The history of the birth of the nation in a revolutionary war against an imperial power gave us the anti-imperial animus; and the continental expanse of the nation made imperial ven-
tures, at least of the overt variety, unnecessary." (Surviving American
Indians might have disputed this latter point.) Soviet anti-imperialism
originated in Marx's attacks on capitalism. Lenin extended the critique, which persisted in the utopian vision of a world free of the
empire-inducing vice of private property.

Niebuhr found revealing the relationship of communist utopianism to Soviet imperialism. "The world," he argued, "is confronted
with what seems to be an entirely unique emergence in history: a
despotic and imperialist political system based upon rather implausible utopian illusions." But in reality, he explained, the utopian imperialism of the Kremlin wasn't new at all. It represented a reversion
to the enthusiasms of religious conquerors like Mohammed and secular zealots like the radicals of the French revolution. In this interpretation lay the key to understanding the connection between Marxism
and dictatorship. Religious utopians had long justified conversion by
the sword; secular utopians were no different. What Lenin practiced
he had learned from the likes of Cromwell.

Niebuhr judged the Cromwellian approach of the communists –

their need to resort to force to maintain power – to be "one of the elements of real promise in the present situation." Each time the Soviets used force, as in Hungary in 1956, the illusionary nature of their utopia grew more evident. The communist revolution was revealed as a fraud, an imposition from above rather than a transformation from below. The circle closed as greater force was required to prevent inspection of the fraud.

While the ideology of communist utopianism inclined the Soviet empire toward ever harsher – and eventually self-destructive, Niebuhr predicted – applications of force, the ideology of the American empire worked in the opposite direction. "Bourgeois democracy is rightly regarded in the West as the best form of government because it checks every center of power and grants no immunity to any form of prestige." Yet Western institutions were far from perfect, and Niebuhr questioned whether what worked for Americans would travel well to other parts of the world. Democracy had required centuries to evolve in the West, and Asia and Africa couldn't wait. The high American standard of living, which made democracy possible, was simply "beyond the dreams of avarice of the poor nations." As a result, both American democracy and American prosperity were irrelevant to current relations with Asia and Africa.

Niebuhr may or may not have been right about democracy's irrelevance – events of the next forty years delivered a mixed judgment – but he was quite wrong about the irrelevance of the American standard of living. A few educated and personally affluent Asian leaders – India's Nehru, for example – made a practice of dismissing America as a vulgar land of insufferable materialists, but for most of the underdeveloped world the relevance of the American model consisted almost entirely in its promise of prosperity. The only item of dispute involved the fastest method of achieving a similar prosperity. On this point, as Niebuhr noted without fully appreciating the significance of his insight, the Soviets benefited from their own recent poverty: Moscow could promote communism as offering the shortest path to a better – that is, wealthier – life.

Niebuhr cautioned Americans, as he had from his first writings, against the sin of pride. "As the leading exponents of an 'open society,' we introduce a stubborn insistence on our own kind of openness. . . . In consequence of this fanatic protagonism of a non-fanatic culture we are threatened with the alienation of the sympathies of the uncommitted nations." It was ironic, he said, that "the principles of liberal democracy, fashioned in a domestically pluralistic culture, should appear more inflexible, in a pluralistic global community, than the pretensions of a despotic culture which has distilled despotism from utopia."

Niebuhr also returned to his theme of the moral ambiguity and inconclusiveness of human existence. "It is man's ineluctable fate to work on tasks which he cannot complete in his brief span of years, to accept responsibilities the true ends of which he cannot fulfill, and to build communities which cannot realize the perfection of his visions." This was as true for American liberals as for Soviet or Chinese communists. Liberals, whom he here complimented only to the extent of placing them among "the lesser culprits of history," must, without losing heart or ceasing to strive, recognize the inevitable incompleteness of their endeavors. "Our best hope, both of a tolerable political harmony and of an inner peace, rests upon our ability to observe the limits of human freedom even while we responsibly exploit its creative possibilities."[14]

[14] Reinhold Niebuhr, *The Struggle of Nations and Empires: A Study of the Recurring Patterns and Problems of the Political Order in Relation to the Unique Problems of the Nuclear Age* (New York, 1959), 10–12, 202, 217, 234–5, 272, 295–9.

8

God Blinked but Herman Didn't

Niebuhr's conclusions about the ambiguity of human existence derived mostly from his beliefs regarding the nature of human beings
and their relationship to higher realities, especially God. These beliefs, clearly evident in *Moral Man and Immoral Society* and *The
Children of Light and the Children of Darkness*, reflected the technical civilization in which Niebuhr lived, yet they depended far more
on what Niebuhr conceived to be timeless truths than on the current
state of scientific knowledge.

Niebuhr's later writings placed greater emphasis on science and
technology, for the good reason that in 1945 the world changed forever. The invention of atomic weapons threatened humanity with
devastation on a scale unimagined before. The United States briefly
enjoyed a monopoly of the new instruments of destruction, but no
one who understood the physics involved expected the monopoly to
last more than a few years. It didn't. The Soviet Union joined the
atomic club in 1949, prompting the American government to seek a
new circle of exclusivity. The Soviets followed close behind, and by
the end of 1953 both Americans and Russians possessed hydrogen
weapons. The development of long-range missiles during the next
several years enhanced the danger still more, and conjured up the
prospect that each side would soon be able to obliterate the other
within minutes.

The nuclear menace added bite to Niebuhr's remarks about the
ambiguity and inconclusiveness of human activities, and implicitly
challenged the vindicationist consensus on which American policy
during the early Cold War rested. When people had labored toward

distant goals in the pre-nuclear era, they could console themselves with the knowledge that though they might not live to see their objectives realized, their children or grandchildren might. If the goals were beyond human grasp, each succeeding generation could at least approach a bit closer than the one before. The invention of nuclear weapons changed the situation entirely. Now there existed a real possibility that the whole human experiment would be canceled midway. In that event, not even future generations – because there wouldn't be any – would know how things turned out. Under the nuclear cloud, the meaning of human existence grew murkier than ever.

Ambiguity increased in a specialized sense as well. Almost from the first, individuals who devoted themselves to the study of nuclear strategy understood that devising effective physical defenses against the new weapons might prove impossible. Assuming continued tension between the superpowers, the only safeguard against enemy attack would be psychological – the threat of retaliation. But retaliation would probably provoke counterretaliation, with the likely end result being the annihilation of both sides. Consequently, the arsenals each country devoted great energy to building would be useful only if they were never used. To live, each country must prepare to commit suicide.

Much of Niebuhr's influence on American thinking about foreign affairs resulted from his amateur standing. His obvious inexpertness on the finer points of international relations occasionally led him into dubious generalizations, but his position as an outsider afforded him a perspective often inaccessible to insiders and specialists like Kennan and Morgenthau. Coming from a noted theologian, Niebuhr's message possessed a moral resonance it might not have had otherwise.

Amateurs and outsiders like Niebuhr brought certain insights to discussions of nuclear strategy, and in some instances their moral and political judgment contributed significantly to the debates the subject of nuclear war aroused. But because the subject was highly specialized, and because crucial decisions regarding use or nonuse of nuclear weapons hinged on interpretations of increasingly esoteric information, the debate spawned a class of experts who devoted large portions of their careers exclusively to it. The amateurs soon found themselves informationally outgunned.

Another aspect of the nuclear issue put off those unwilling to immerse themselves entirely. Niebuhr and Morgenthau spoke of the fundamental immorality of governmental actions, and of morality, such as it was, being the choice of the lesser evil; but when they had first enunciated these ideas, they had no conception of the magnitude of evil that governments would be able to accomplish by the 1960s. Looking war in the face during the age of chemical explosives was bad enough, but looking war in the face during the age of hydrogen bombs was another matter altogether. When the United States had embarked on its Cold War career of vindicationism, Americans had gauged the potential cost by the standard of World War II's destructiveness; during the next two decades, that cost took several quantum leaps upward. The escalation caused many Americans to ponder a career change for their country; it caused more than a few of the nuclear specialists to ponder a career change for themselves. Amateurs unwilling to steel themselves to the daily contemplation of the annihilation of the human race had an even more difficult time sticking with their nuclear studies.

Yet for all the horrendousness associated with nuclear weapons, there were a few people who seemed to revel in staring straight at this final Armageddon. Among those who did, Herman Kahn crowded to the front to ensure he got the best view.

II

But Kahn was a fairly late arrival on the scene. The first of the important nuclear intellectuals was Bernard Brodie. In *The Absolute Weapon*, published in 1946, Brodie moved beyond the reactive war-is-now-unthinkable attitude that typified discussions of atomic weapons immediately after Hiroshima and Nagasaki. He conceded that the art of war – and consequently the risks of an assertive foreign policy – had entered a new phase with the introduction of the atomic bomb, but he didn't believe that the transition released military strategists from trying to render this horrible weapon somewhat less horrible. Brodie proffered a list of postulates regarding warfare in the atomic age; from these he derived a corresponding list of conclusions. The most significant followed from the practical impossibility of defending against the new weapons; this conclusion also formed the fundamental insight of the atomic age. "Thus far the chief purpose of our military establishment has been to win wars," Brodie declared. "From now on its chief purpose must be to avert them. It can have almost no other useful purpose." This insight led in turn to the fundamental paradox of the age: that the very destructiveness of atomic weapons made them potentially decisive instruments of peace. Brodie advocated a variety of measures to ensure that any aggressor would face nearly certain retaliation; he predicted: "If such arrangements are made, the bomb cannot but prove in the net a powerful inhibition to aggression."[1]

Brodie anticipated events by more than a decade. Not until the late 1950s would the United States and the Soviet Union possess enough sufficiently daunting weapons and effective delivery systems to achieve the stalemate he described. In the meantime, American leaders attempted to parlay their nuclear advantage into significant strategic gains. The Truman administration failed, preventing neither the consolidation of communist control in Eastern Europe nor its expansion into East Asia. In the process, Truman and his associates discovered how difficult the art of atomic diplomacy was. The Eisenhower administration's chief contribution to the art was the doctrine of massive retaliation, announced by John Foster Dulles and denounced by Hans Morgenthau.

Massive retaliation was denounced in even greater detail, although with somewhat less scorn, by a young professor of government at Harvard named Henry Kissinger. Like Morgenthau a Jewish refugee from Hitler's Germany, Kissinger initially possessed no expertise in what was rapidly becoming a specialized field. He had connections, though. At the time when the Eisenhower administration was formulating the massive retaliation policy, the arch-establishment Council on Foreign Relations decided to invest in the new intellectual growth industry of nuclear strategy. The council gathered a panel of nearly three dozen soldiers, professional diplomats, scientists, and think-tank types to examine the issues involved in nuclear strategy. The panel engaged Kissinger as study director, and after many months of deliberation and discussion, the members charged Kissinger to write a book on the subject.

In essence, *Nuclear Weapons and Foreign Policy* represented an effort to take the massive out of massive retaliation. Kissinger saw two related, but distinct, problems with the all-or-nothing approach. The first was the obvious one: Few of the peripheral regions where

[1] Bernard Brodie, "War in the Atomic Age" and "Implications for Military Policy," both in Bernard Brodie, ed., *The Absolute Weapon: Atomic Power and World Order* (New York, 1946); quoted 75–6.

the Soviet Union would most likely test American resolve were worth the risk of an earth-shattering nuclear war. The second was more subtle: By putting all its eggs in a single nuclear basket, in the name of deterrence, the United States might actually *in*crease the danger of nuclear war. Deterrence required not merely the means of waging nuclear war, but the will to employ those means. Massive retaliation increased the means, but tended to paralyze the will. "No threat," Kissinger said, "is stronger than the belief of the opponent that it will in fact be used." Soviet leaders might soon conclude, if they hadn't already, that the United States would never use its most horrible weapons. If they did so conclude, they might engage in precisely the kind of provocative behavior that would trigger the holocaust. The only way out of this corner, Kissinger concluded, was to enhance the credibility of the American nuclear arsenal by improving its usability. Smaller, less destructive weapons would allow the United States to fight a limited nuclear war, thereby diminishing the risk of an unlimited one.[2]

Not everyone was persuaded by Kissinger's arguments. James King, reviewing Kissinger's book for the *New Republic*, thought the author had a weak grasp of military tactics, which weakness led him to overrate the difference between conventional war and limited nuclear war and vitiated his claims regarding the benefits of early resort to tactical nuclear weapons. Paul Nitze, lately of the State Department's policy planning staff and an individual whose long career encapsulated the policy of Cold War vindicationism, faulted Kissinger's strategic reasoning as "doubtful or at least unclear." William Kaufmann charged Kissinger with "wishful thinking" regarding the prospects for the deployment and use of tactical nuclear weapons. "To read Kissinger's chapters on limited warfare is to believe that the military equivalent of the stringless yo-yo is at hand," Kaufmann said. Thomas Schelling argued – with many others – that in a crisis situation, the only obvious firebreak short of all-out nuclear war was that between conventional weapons and nuclear weapons: Once either side crossed the firebreak, even to small, tactical nuclear weapons, there likely would be no halting short of the apocalypse. Bernard Brodie concurred, citing the unacceptable probability that "limited wars may develop explosively into total wars." Brodie held that humans were too emotional and unpredictable to sustain the kind of

[2] Henry A. Kissinger, *Nuclear Weapons and Foreign Policy* (New York, 1957), 133.

cool thinking limited nuclear war would require. For that matter, they might well be too unpredictable to make massive retaliation work either. Brodie did not quite predict that deterrence would fail, but he did express distrust of any doctrine or technological development, whether involving massive retaliation or limited war, that relied too much on human judgment, which was all too fallible. "The danger of total war is real," he declared. And nothing now on the horizon would alter that fact.[3]

III

The doubts Brodie voiced reverberated only faintly among the community of war planners. Perhaps because most forecasting in the field involved irrefutable claims – irrefutable short of nuclear war, that is, in which case survivors would have worries more pressing than figuring out who had guessed wrong – nuclear strategists often stated their views with boldness bordering on arrogance. This tendency increased with the development of intercontinental missiles during the late 1950s, which narrowed Armageddon's lead time to minutes and appeared to place a greater premium than ever on conceptual audacity.

For audacity, no one matched Herman Kahn. Kahn had worked at Rand Corporation with Brodie, but as the 1950s wound down he grew disenchanted with what he judged to be the intellectual stagnation of the place. Rand in turn thought Kahn had become fixated on the notion that a nuclear war would be survivable if the United States concentrated on constructing a suitable civil defense network, and if it revised its estimates of what constituted survivability. About the time he left Rand to set up the Hudson Institute in upstate New York, Kahn gathered into book form a series of lectures he had given to defense intellectuals around the country; the book explained that nuclear war was much like conventional war, provided one looked at it in the proper light.

[3] James King, "Limited Defense," *New Republic*, July 1, 1957, and idem, "Limited Annihilation," *New Republic*, July 15, 1957; Paul Nitze, "Limited Wars or Massive Retaliation?" *Reporter*, Sept. 5, 1957; William W. Kaufmann, "The Crisis in Military Affairs," *World Politics*, July 1958; Thomas C. Schelling, *The Strategy of Conflict* (Cambridge, Mass., 1960); Bernard Brodie, *Strategy in the Missile Age* (Princeton, N.J., 1959), 349, 397.

Kahn delighted to provoke. From its title, which called to mind Clausewitz's dictum that war was simply politics extended, to the nonexistent index, which rendered navigation through the disordered tome nearly impossible, *On Thermonuclear War* provoked. Reviewer James Newman, writing in *Scientific American*, said he first had thought that Kahn had composed a send-up of the defense establishment, a "hoax in bad taste." After discovering that Kahn was serious, Newman denounced the work as "thermonuclear pornography" and urged Kahn to change his first name to Genghis. Bernard Brodie disliked Kahn's use of the coinage "wargasm" to denote a reflexive all-out exchange. "So grim a subject does not exclude an appropriate kind of humor used very sparingly," Brodie instructed, "but levity is never legitimate."[4]

The essence of Kahn's message was that although a nuclear conflict would be disastrous, it need not terminate civilization. "A thermonuclear war is quite likely to be an unprecedented catastrophe for the defender," he granted. "Depending on the military course of events, it may or may not be an unprecedented catastrophe for the attacker, and for some neutrals as well. But an 'unprecedented' catastrophe can be a far cry from an 'unlimited' one." Kahn denounced as pernicious the work of novelist Neville Shute, whose "interesting but badly researched" *On the Beach* purported to describe the globally lethal poisoning of the atmosphere by a nuclear exchange. He decried as irresponsible the so-called Mainau declaration of fifty-two Nobel laureates that unless the great powers renounced war, humanity would "cease to exist." Exaggerations like these, Kahn asserted, served only to paralyze persons who might otherwise make concrete – literally, in some important cases – preparations to minimize the damage a general war would produce.

Preparing for war required, at the outset, recognition of the distinctions between different degrees of destruction. Kahn littered his pages with graphics lifted from the lecturer's sheaf of visual aids; among the more chilling was a chart labeled "Tragic but distinguishable postwar states," which counted seven steps on the staircase to annihilation. At the first step, 2 million Americans died and the country required 1 year to recuperate economically. At the second step, the figures grew to 5 million and 2 years. At the third, they were 10 million and 5 years. From there, the numbers successively doubled

---

[4] Gregg Herken, *Counsels of War* (New York, 1985), 206–7.

before reaching 160 million dead and 100 years for recovery at step seven. Kahn understood the temptation to declare the tallies academic beyond a certain threshold. But he said that American officials must resist the temptation. To hold the deaths to 20 million, for instance, rather than 40 million, would save 20 million lives. "The survivors will not dance in the streets or congratulate each other if there have been 20 million men, women, and children killed; yet it would have been a worthwhile achievement to limit casualties to this number." Kahn rejected most vigorously the oft-forwarded view that in the wake of a nuclear conflict the living would envy the dead. "Objective studies indicate" – sensitive readers would shudder at this phrase long before reaching the book's end – "that even though the amount of human tragedy would be greatly increased in the postwar world, the increase would not preclude normal and happy lives for the majority of survivors and their descendants."

For this reason, Kahn deemed it imperative to venture into the realm of what the tender-minded called the unthinkable. He began with a sally into an area many found particularly frightening: the genetic effects of radioactive fallout on future generations. In numerous tables he compared levels of radioactivity likely to follow wars of various intensities with levels encountered in peacetime by individuals in different occupations and places of residence. He discussed mutation rates in survivors' children, grandchildren, and great-grandchildren. His conclusions hardly exuded optimism: The excess deaths and debilitations he projected ran into the tens and hundreds of millions. But here, as throughout the book, he refused to let the grimness of his task deter him. Defense intellectuals had a particular obligation to enlighten the public on these matters, he said, precisely because the stakes were so high and because unreflective fear would make impossible the measures necessary to deal effectively with the dangers. Kahn related a personal experience to highlight the current degree of popular ignorance on the subject. At one of his lectures a woman rose and declared in an accusing voice, "I don't want to live in your world in which 1 per cent of the children are born defective." To which Kahn replied that it was not *his* world, and in any event 4 percent of newborns already arrived defective.

One of Kahn's most controversial calculations involved advice for food rationing in a postwar environment. On the thoroughly logical grounds that elderly people stood less chance than the young of developing cancer in response to radioactive exposure, since they had less time left to live, he advocated feeding individuals over forty-five the most highly contaminated food still fit – so to speak – for human consumption. As Kahn put the issue, "Most of these people would die of other causes before they got cancer." In addition, he recommended discouraging consumption of the least contaminated food by marketing it at a premium price. He suggested, for example, that a price difference of five cents per quart would suffice to direct consumers away from milk showing low levels of radioactive strontium to milk with readings ten times as high. He likewise recommended the purchase of large numbers of personal radiation meters so that after a war the truly radiation-sick could be separated from malingerers and hypochondriacs.

Critics would find Kahn's reasoning implausible and insensitive, if not downright ghoulish. Nor were they reassured by his arithmetic reminder that if the Russians wiped out a third of America's population by obliterating fifty of the country's biggest cities, two-thirds of the American people would remain. Further, because the United States doubled its economic production every fifteen or twenty years, it would rebound within a generation. The loss of sixty million persons "does not seem to be a total economic catastrophe," he asserted. "It may simply set the nation's productive capacity back a decade or two plus destroying many 'luxuries.'" Should the destruction take a much larger urban toll, leveling America's one hundred principal cities, there would still exist "more wealth in this country than there is in all of Russia today and more skills than were available to that country in the forties." Moreover, at present much of the industrial capacity outside the largest metropolitan areas was old, inefficient, and consequently under-utilized. Should the more efficient factories and mills vanish in a nuclear attack, these secondary producers might expand output readily.

The details of Kahn's argument, myriad though they were, mattered less than the overall perspective they revealed. "Few people differentiate between having 10 million dead, 50 million dead, or 100 million dead," he observed. This was not surprising – but it was still wrong. "It does not take much imagination to see that there is a difference between having a country which five or ten years later has a population of 150 million (or more) and a GNP of over 300 billion dollars and is strong and prosperous, and one which has only a few million scattered survivors grubbing out a miserable existence." Kahn declared that it was "absolutely essential" to take this long view if one were to think constructively about defense, deterrence, and national survival.

Regarding survival, Kahn called for a major program of civil defense. He recommended appropriating $100 million for those radiation meters, with special priority for individuals – farmers, construction crews, relief workers – whose duties would take them outdoors in a post-attack environment. He called for $150 million to identify, inventory, and provision existing structures for use as fallout shelters. He suggested setting aside an additional $75 million for research on innovative new designs for shelters to complement buildings already standing. Smaller sums would go to preparing evacuation plans, educating the public in techniques of survival, perfecting methods of decontamination, and undertaking other measures crucial to minimizing casualties and speeding recovery.

In what struck some readers as rationalism run amok, Kahn described a "War Damage Equalization Corporation," a government bureau charged with providing nuclear-war insurance. In advance of a war, the W.D.E.C. would collect premiums from individuals and businesses, with the rate schedule calculated to encourage clients to reduce their vulnerability to attack. After a war, the agency would compensate policy holders for losses suffered. Whether anyone would be willing to bet on the continued existence of the W.D.E.C. after a major conflict, Kahn couldn't say with confidence. Yet on this subject as on others related to the country's ability to carry on, he inclined to hopefulness.

Regarding defense and deterrence, Kahn saw these two issues as opposite sides of the same coin. He conceded the difficulty of defending against ballistic missiles, but for the near future the majority of the damage done the United States in a Soviet attack would be the work of bombers, against which defense *was* possible. Kahn didn't require perfection from an anti-bomber screen: Air defense would serve a vital purpose if it merely forced Soviet planners to factor an extra uncertainty measure into their equations. The outer line of defense, the radar stations in the far north, would provide time to set civil defense procedures in motion. Fighter planes and anti-aircraft missiles and batteries would save lives and property by diminishing the number of bombs delivered on target. They would afford more-nearly comprehensive protection against second and subsequent strikes.

By increasing the uncertainty surrounding a nuclear attack, active defense measures would contribute to deterrence, which remained the chief guarantor of American security. For all Kahn's analysis of what might happen should deterrence fail, and despite his relative cheerfulness regarding the possibility of America's surviving a nuclear war, he understood that the foremost task of defense intellectuals was to ensure that such a war never occur. Yet serious though the obligation, Kahn couldn't resist a certain impishness in elucidating the principles on which deterrence rested. To clarify thinking on the subject, he proposed three thought experiments, each built around the properties of a postulated invention.

Kahn's first postulated invention was the "Doomsday Machine," which had one function only: "to destroy all human life." How it accomplished this chore was immaterial, although the ever-helpful Kahn suggested "the creation of really large amounts of radioactivity or the causing of major climatic changes." He added that such a device might be constructed within ten years for a cost of not more than $100 billion. The essential characteristic was its automatic nature: Should the Soviets detonate more than some specified number of nuclear warheads upon the United States – five, perhaps, to allow for accidents – sensors connected to computers would trigger the machine, killing Khrushchev, the Politburo, and the rest of humanity (including all theretofore surviving Americans).

The "Doomsday-in-a-Hurry-Machine" improved on the basic model by including sophisticated computer programs allowing it to keep abreast of current international affairs. American programmers would inform the machine and the Soviets of what Washington desired the Kremlin to do and to refrain from doing in some crisis. The machine, on detecting noncompliance, would destroy the world.

The "Homicide Pact Machine," which was actually two machines for the price of one, wouldn't obliterate humanity entirely. It would merely guarantee the destruction of each superpower by the other. In this regard, it held attractions for those who disliked the idea of being wiped out by a contraption of their own government's making. "While intellectuals may not so distinguish," Kahn said, "the policy makers and practical men prefer being killed by the other side."

Kahn identified six characteristics of the ideal deterrent, listing them, naturally, in a table. It must be frightening, inexorable, persuasive, cheap, foolproof, and controllable. For the first five, the Doomsday, Doomsday-in-a-Hurry, and Homicide Pact machines beat anything currently or imminently on the market. They were as frightening as anyone could desire, inexorable and foolproof by definition, persuasive of all except the criminally insane, and cheap by comparison with other forms of deterrence. Unfortunately, they lacked control, and while they maximized the probability that deterrence would succeed, they raised the cost of failure so high as to render them unusable. In this sense, however, their deficiency was of degree rather than kind, leading Kahn to ask, "If it is not acceptable to risk the lives of the three billion inhabitants of the earth to protect ourselves from surprise attack, then how many people would we be willing to risk?"

Though this was the crucial question, it wasn't the only one involving use of Kahn's imagined devices. For example, in the event Moscow suspected the Americans of building a Doomsday machine, the Russians would certainly try for preemption. Doomsday-in-a-Hurry would create problems of interpretation: Who would determine noncompliance? Doomsday-in-a-Hurry also suffered from the credibility troubles of the real-life policy of massive retaliation. Would the programmers actually jeopardize their country's existence to prevent relatively minor provocation? Similar problems plagued the Homicide Pact machine, which, as Kahn pointed out, "has become extremely close to being consciously adopted as official U.S. policy."

Kahn had plenty more to say, often several times over. He reviewed the origins of recent wars, seeking to identify how deterrence historically had failed. Challenging conventional wisdom, he deemed it "most improbable" that Hitler would have backed down at Munich had the Western democracies stood fast. He made estimates of the likelihood of the development of almost unimaginably large bombs, as well as of the possibility of seeing a handheld "atomic six-shooter," with each bullet carrying the equivalent of ten tons of TNT. He drew a hypothetical past, sketching world wars that might have broken out during the 1950s had nuclear developments gone differently. Conceiving his role as that of intellectual agent-provocateur, he posed more questions than he answered.

Kahn's fundamental message was that if Americans desired deterrence to succeed they must prepare for its failure. And failure might well occur anyway, despite their best efforts. "Our almost complete reliance on deterrence working," he said, "is probably an example of frivolity or wishful thinking." In perhaps his bleakest analogy, he likened the predicament of the United States to that of inhabitants of regions prone to hurricanes. Americans could learn something important from these hardy, but not foolhardy, folk. "They do not bewail the money they spend on protection against hurricanes; it is simply a fact of life. They can, if they choose, move to another state or country where there are no hurricanes. Presumably they prefer living in the hurricane country and accepting the cost." Americans could move away from nuclear country by accommodating themselves to Soviet designs. But most didn't wish to do so, preferring to remain part of the Free World and take their chances. The possibility of preventing a nuclear storm was greater than of preventing hurricanes, but "even an imprudent person should be unwilling to place all bets on deterrence working, so long as there are reasonable ways to hedge the bet."[5]

IV

A foreign visitor who traveled widely around the United States before seeing Texas once described Dallas as just like the rest of the country, only more so. An analogous remark might have placed Kahn within the community of defense intellectuals. At the other end of the spectrum – occupying a position similar to San Francisco, perhaps – were those scientific specialists who questioned the entire nuclear enterprise. Some of the dissenters challenged the vindicationist premises on which America's nuclear policy currently rested; others accepted the premises – including, for example, that the United States would fight a nuclear war to prevent a Soviet takeover of Western Europe – but desired to reduce that policy's potential costs. Still others (and many of the same people as well) demanded a reduction in the costs the world incurred simply in consequence of the existence of the new weapons – costs that might have been called the overhead of Cold War vindicationism.

Albert Einstein probably enjoyed the greatest credibility of all the dissenters. As perhaps the most famous scientist on earth, and one with a peculiar responsibility for the theoretical breakthrough that made nuclear weapons possible, Einstein was particularly well-placed to ask whether this time science, or technology anyway, hadn't gone too far. He began registering his doubts almost before the echoes

---

[5] Herman Kahn, *On Thermonuclear War* (Princeton, N.J., 1960), 9–10, 20–1, 46, 67, 76–7, 91–2, 100–8, 116, 145–52, 401, 494, 562–8, 597–612, 626–40.

from Hiroshima had died away. In a 1946 piece in the *New York Times Magazine*, he remarked the irony that "the war which began with Germany using weapons of unprecedented frightfulness against women and children ended with the United States using a supreme weapon killing thousands at one blow." He warned that while Americans might consider themselves trustworthy custodians of atomic weapons, being honest and sober citizens of the world, enormous power held temptations. "A sober nation can become drunk with victory." The war was over, yet preparations for war continued. "We are still making bombs and the bombs are making hate and suspicion. We are keeping secrets and secrets breed distrust. I do not say we should now turn the secret of the bomb loose in the world, but are we ardently seeking a world in which there will be no need for bombs or secrets, a world in which science and men will be free?"[6]

Initially the problem of nuclear weapons appeared to hinge on the destruction they would cause if used in war, and the efforts of Einstein and the other dissenters focused on preventing such use. By the mid-1950s, however, when both superpowers were conducting sustained programs of atmospheric testing of fusion and fission devices, a new danger emerged. The tests produced vast clouds of radioactive fallout that blanketed the globe and affected nearly all living organisms. The size and seriousness of the effects, especially as they related to humans, elicited considerable controversy and led to demands for a halt to testing. Perhaps predictably, the most vocal of those calling for a test ban included individuals and groups unenamored, to say the least, of the utility of nuclear weapons as instruments of diplomacy and war. Arguments against testing frequently coincided with campaigns for nuclear disarmament.

In 1958 Linus Pauling, a Nobel laureate in biochemistry from the California Institute of Technology and subsequently a recipient of the Nobel peace prize, published *No More War!* The book contained the expected indictments of nuclear weapons as unusable and dangerous to the existence of civilization, but it also included charges that test-produced radiation was inflicting major injury upon the human species. Pauling noted the sharp environmental increase in radioactive strontium-90, a poison so potent that one teaspoon distributed evenly would kill everyone on earth. A single bomb such as that detonated

[6] Albert Einstein, "The Real Problem is in the Hearts of Men," *New York Times Magazine*, June 23, 1946.

by the United States on March 1, 1954, produced a thousand times this amount. "All over the world," he explained, "cows now eat grass containing strontium-90, and the strontium-90 is now present in the milk of all cows. Human beings eat vegetables and drink milk – all of the vegetables and all of the milk in the world now contain strontium-90. The human beings build some of the ingested strontium-90 into their bones, where it stays throughout the lifetime of the individuals." The effects of the strontium could only be estimated, but previous and current work with radioactivity provided guideposts. Pauling cited two studies, one indicating 8,000 excess deaths per year from leukemia, the other suggesting 2,000 excess deaths annually from bone cancer.

More alarming because more insidious were the effects of radioactive fallout on human genetic material. Pauling noted that although chemical poisons generally demonstrated a threshold below which they produced no ill effect, the human body appeared to have no such tolerance for radiation. Radiation involved subatomic particles that Pauling likened to "little bullets that shoot through the body," a single one of which could do harm. Human genes were most vulnerable, for scrambling or otherwise disrupting the code responsible for the development of subsequent generations nearly guaranteed offspring defective in one or more characteristics. As in the case of strontium-90, estimates regarding birth defects involved significant guesswork. Pauling placed the number of children seriously malformed as a result of nuclear testing at 15,000 per year. Putting this figure more concretely, he asserted that a March 1954 American bomb test had required "the sacrifice of 15,000 children."

Pauling thought American policy had been led astray by self-anointed realists who argued that morality must yield to efficacy in the struggle against communism. "I believe in morality, in justice, in humanitarianism," he declared, and he thought most Americans did too. He insisted that American policy must be fundamentally reoriented. The United States, as instigator of the arms race and possessor of the largest arsenal, had a special obligation to humanity. It should start meeting this obligation by halting testing, but it must go further. Pauling advocated American sponsorship of international peace studies, with funding comparable to what Washington was currently spending on war studies. Disarmament should follow, and measures to ensure peaceful adjudication of international disputes. "We must recognize now that the power to destroy the world by the use of nuclear weapons is a power that cannot be used – we cannot accept the idea of such monstrous immorality. The time has come for morality to take its proper place in the conduct of world affairs. . . . We must move towards a world governed by justice, by international law, and not by force."[7]

The complaints and warnings of Pauling, Einstein and the other antinuclear activists moved the defense community to counterattack. Edward Teller spoke loudest in favor of unfettered testing and weapons development, as he had for the previous fifteen years and would for the next thirty. Teller, more than anyone else, had been responsible for America's hydrogen bomb: He supplied both the political persistence necessary to persuade the Truman administration to underwrite the fusion project, and the technical insight required to bring a scientific possibility to reality. Against Pauling's pacifistic exemplarism, Teller opposed a militantly anti-Soviet vindicationism. The fact that the Russians had only recently crushed a pro-independence movement in Hungary, Teller's homeland, merely added to his conviction that the United States must maintain its nuclear lead at any cost, and must be prepared to exploit that lead to keep the Kremlin contained.

In *Our Nuclear Future*, written with Albert Latter of Rand Corporation, Teller rebutted Pauling's arguments. He contended, correctly, that evidence linking radioactive fallout to cancer and birth defects was merely circumstantial. He asserted, again correctly, that moving from sea level to Denver exposed a person to more additional radiation, in this case in the form of natural cosmic rays, than all the weapons-testing to date. A similar effect accompanied a move from a wood house to one made of ordinary brick, which contained trace radioactive elements. Taking the numbers that even the doomsayers put forward as testing's toll, and comparing these to the tens of millions who would naturally die of leukemia and bone cancer, Teller declared the excess statistically insignificant. On the question of genetic damage, he rejected Pauling's "little bullet" analogy as misleading, and suggested that a threshold below which radiation caused no harm did indeed exist. He held that some radiation-induced genetic mutations might even be beneficial, just as the mutations that had allowed evolution of the human race to its present level had been. In any event, whatever deleterious effect the mutations had on the race

[7] Linus Pauling, *No More War!* (New York, 1958), 73, 101–5, 208–9.

would be overwhelmed by the larger influence of other human activities, in the same way that an avalanche overwhelmed in minutes the decades' work of a glacier. (Pauling got the better of the battle of the analogies, pointing out that a bullet through a laggard alarm clock *might* improve its performance but more likely would stop it altogether. He also asked what were the chances that a typographical error would improve *Hamlet*.)

Teller postulated that nuclear testing would allow the development of "clean" bombs producing great blast and heat but little or no radiation. Inadvertently, however, he undermined this part of his argument by contending that the United States might also develop a cobalt bomb, which was just the opposite of a clean bomb, producing almost entirely radiation. When he sketched circumstances in which such a weapon might be used in what he called "a humane manner," he gave the impression he had never met a bomb he didn't like.

What clinched the argument, in Teller's view, was the existence of the Soviet nuclear stockpile. So long as the Russians had bombs, the United States needed more and better. Only by continued testing could America maintain its nuclear deterrent and thereby keep the peace. "The danger of the test," Teller wrote, "is nothing compared to the catastrophe that may occur if great numbers of these weapons should be used in an unrestricted nuclear war."[8]

V

With arguing scientists occupying the extremes of the nuclear debate, laypersons found ample room for entry. Among the informed laity, the one who reached the largest audience was probably Norman Cousins, the editor of *Saturday Review*. Cousins early convinced himself of the evils of nuclear testing, and in 1956 he traveled to Lambaréné in French Equatorial Africa to urge Dr. Albert Schweitzer to speak out against it. Schweitzer initially hesitated to enter such a politicized arena, but when the philosopher-humanitarian received the Nobel peace prize the following year, he decided to take the opportunity to describe the genetic damage from atmospheric testing as a potential "catastrophe" for the human race. Alone of the American press, *Saturday Review* reproduced the text of Schweitzer's mes-

---

[8] Edward Teller and Albert L. Latter, *Our Nuclear Future: Facts, Dangers and Opportunities* (New York, 1958), 85, 136.

sage, and Cousins commenced a campaign to end testing and to reduce American reliance on nuclear weapons.[9]

Cousins avoided the thicket of contention surrounding the un-
knowable long-term consequences of radioactive fallout. Instead he
attacked the strategy of deterrence that presumably necessitated testing. Cousins described American nuclear strategy and its Soviet counterpart as fundamentally flawed. The main deficiency of deterrence,
he said, was obvious. "It does not deter. The possession by the Soviet
Union of advanced nuclear weapons has not served as a deterrent to
the United States in matters involving our national interests. The U.S.
has not allowed fear of nuclear weapons to deter us from making
clear that we were prepared to fight with everything we had to keep
from being pushed out of Berlin. Nor has our own nuclear stockpile
prevented the Soviet Union from pressing its demand that we pull out
of Berlin."

Berlin was a bad example, in that the Kremlin in fact did not push
its demand for Western evacuation to the point of war. Perhaps
Cousins recognized this, for he moved quickly to another instance.
He pointed out that the years of America's atomic monopoly – 1945
to 1949 – had coincided with "the period of maximum Soviet aggression and intransigence." The communists had not refrained from cap-
turing Czechoslovakia, blockading Berlin, or conquering China.
Most tellingly, the American monopoly had done nothing to hinder
the Soviets in their efforts to break the monopoly. If anything, it had
increased their desire to match the Americans and had sped the arms
race. Cousins saw something similar, with the positions of the two
sides reversed, in the wake of the 1957 Sputnik launch. "The advent
of the Soviet sputnik, with its portents of long-range rockets carrying
nuclear bombs, did not cause the United States to ask for surrender
terms. What it did was to light fires of determination in the United
States to close the gap."

As a general rule, Cousins said, "one nation's deterrent becomes
the other nation's incentive." The consequences were dangerously
destabilizing. The American military had recently hatched some in-
credible schemes for offsetting the Russians' edge in rocketry. One
called for hundreds of American bombers to be constantly in the air,

[9] Robert A. Divine, *Blowing on the Wind: The Nuclear Test Ban Debate, 1954–1960* (New York, 1978), 122–3; Albert Schweitzer, "A Declaration of Conscience," *Saturday Review*, May 18, 1957.

loaded with nuclear bombs and circling just hours from targets on Soviet soil. The point was to guarantee survival of America's retaliatory force in the event of a Russian surprise attack, thereby deterring such an attack in the first place. Cousins contended that the implementation of such a strategy would simply cause Moscow to take "more extreme countermeasures." The Soviets might place hydrogen bombs in orbit, or they might put nuclear warheads on missiles aboard submarines that would prowl near American shores.

If the two sides escalated in this or similar manner, or even if they stood pat with the weapons they already owned, the world would face a continuing unacceptable risk of a war-triggering accident. Cousins cited the case of a French pilot who, frustrated at his government's unwillingness to adopt what he judged sufficiently strong measures against Algerian rebels, had taken matters into his own hands by picking out an Algerian village and bombing it. Cousins remarked that the man wasn't insane, just impatient and angry. Might there not be such persons in the air forces of the United States and the Soviet Union?

Cousins argued that nuclear weapons had rendered obsolete received notions of national security. Americans, Soviets, and the rest of humanity must think in broader terms than heretofore. "In the atomic age, no *national* security is possible. Either there is a workable *world* security system or there is nothing." Just as settlers in the American West had recognized that the only answer to the anarchy of unfettered individualism was the creation of the institutions of domestic government, so contemporary citizens of the world must recognize that the only answer to the anarchy of absolute national sovereignty was the creation of the institutions of international government.[10]

Some of these institutions already existed. The United Nations, though currently confounded by the obstructionism of the great powers, could serve as the basis for a stronger international authority. Cousins said "the central objective" of American foreign policy should be the bolstering of the United Nations, to the degree where small and large countries alike could look to the international body for security. Writing now in September 1961, when the Soviets had just taken the most recent Berlin set-to as the occasion for ending a

---

[10] Norman Cousins, "The Fallacy of the Deterrent," *Saturday Review*, April 16, 1960.

de facto Soviet-American moratorium on nuclear testing, Cousins contended that a strengthened United Nations would have been just the forum for dealing with the Berlin question. Even in its present condition, the United Nations should be America's court of first resort. The Kennedy administration ought to exhaust the resources of the United Nations before responding in kind to Moscow's nuclear-punctuated protest. "Inadequate and inconclusive though a debate on Berlin may be in the U.N., it is better than a specific and tangible eruption of nuclear power."

Besides, testing was essentially unnecessary, even granting the premises of the deterrence theorists. Cousins noted that President Kennedy himself had stated that America's existing arsenal of nuclear weapons was adequate to the country's needs. Building more was not merely superfluous but provocative. Recent Soviet actions were provocative, to be sure; yet certainly Washington possessed sufficient imagination to allow it to do other than merely react to Moscow's moves.

Moreover, Cousins argued, the resumption of atmospheric testing underscored the damage testing did to the global environment. While experts might debate the details of the damage, none could deny that it was serious. This fact placed a grave moral burden on testers. Cousins could scarcely put the matter in strong enough language. "Any nation that engages in atmospheric testing has in effect declared war on the human race," he wrote. "Atomic bombs are not 'tested.' They are used. Every time a nuclear bomb goes off people get hurt. Atomic fission converts the sky into an open sewer for radioactive garbage. The poison particles created by nuclear tests are carried by the winds over vast distances, falling out like rain on crops and reservoirs, infecting the whole process by which life is nourished and sustained."[11]

The arguments of Cousins, Pauling, and other anti-testers gradually took hold, though the purchase they obtained owed less to the world's grasp of the arguers' biological brief than to the tightening grip of fear many people felt regarding the danger of nuclear war. The October 1962 showdown between Washington and Moscow over Soviet missiles in Cuba jolted leaders on both sides of the superpower divide into accepting limits on testing as a step toward reduc-

---

[11] Norman Cousins, "Nuclear War: The Life-and-Death Questions," *Saturday Review*, Sept. 23, 1961.

ing the risk of another such close call. The two governments didn't go as far as their critics desired – to a complete ban on tests above and below ground – but in 1963 they agreed to halt testing in the atmosphere.

VI

When the editors of *Scientific American* refused to publish a Kahn article rebutting the harsh review of *On Thermonuclear War* by James Newman, Kahn authorized his children to burn Newman's four-volume tome, *The World of Mathematics*, over the kitchen sink, slowly, one page per day. He also expanded the article into a book entitled *Thinking About the Unthinkable*.[12]

Kahn devoted the first part of the book to a defense of his earlier work, beginning with an illustrative tale from Victorian Britain. In the late nineteenth century, he said, the vice of white slavery was rampant in the most morally conservative of European nations. Young English girls were kidnapped by the thousands and forced into prostitution, at a time when the countries of the European continent had all but abolished the evil practice. An important reason, Kahn explained, was that the prudishness of English society prevented honest discussion of the problem and rendered a solution inordinately difficult. Americans, Kahn asserted, demonstrated similar tendencies regarding nuclear war, and they risked analogous results. National security demanded confronting the issue. "Thermonuclear war may seem unthinkable, immoral, insane, hideous, or highly unlikely, but it is not impossible. To act intelligently we must learn as much as we can about the risks. We may thereby be able better to avoid nuclear war. We may even be able to avoid the crises that bring us to the brink of war."

Kahn judged the reluctance to rationally ponder the prospect of nuclear war a form of superstition. "It is based on nothing sounder than a supernatural fear of the magical power of words (to talk about cancer is to bring on cancer) or of actions (to build shelters is to create the need for their use). Many have this primitive belief that speaking of evil or preparing for evil creates evil." Arguments from the notion of self-fulfilling prophecies he deemed slightly more sophisticated but no less specious. He considered prophecies equally

---

[12] Herken, *Counsels of War*, 207.

likely to be self-defeating, as he exemplified with a story about a friend who was a chronic – and chronically convicted – embezzler. Why do you keep committing this crime?, Kahn asked. "I can't help it," the friend replied. "People trust me."

Stuffy readers might have found Kahn's anectodal evidence frivolous, however much in character they thought his association with con artists. But the idea of the self-defeating prophecy lay at the base of his approach to national security. Kahn displayed little patience for those who, considering nuclear weapons too lethal to use, proceeded to erect barriers to their use. Such persons, he believed, lacked either the intelligence to comprehend the strategy of deterrence or the honesty to act on their comprehension. No more than the next person did Kahn desire to witness a nuclear war, although the scientist in him would certainly have made use of the opportunity to ascertain the accuracy of his predictions. Yet successful deterrence rested on the ability and willingness of the United States to fight a nuclear war. Whatever inhibited the use of nuclear weapons, whether technological inadequacy, bureaucratic ineptitude, or psychological paralysis, weakened deterrence and endangered the United States. Unless American leaders and the American people were willing to accept this fact, they had better figure out some other strategy for national defense.

Thinking About the Unthinkable contained an elaboration of several of the ideas in Kahn's previous book, delivered in a better organized and more comprehensible fashion. He identified four methods by which nuclear war might come. Most likely was war by inadvertence. Vacuum cleaners broke, so why not fail-safe mechanisms on nuclear-tipped missiles? Flocks of geese and solar flares had been mistaken for bomber fleets before, so why not again? Tongue-in-cheek – one suspects – Kahn suggested that the Soviets didn't place much weight on such possibilities, because Marxist dialectic wouldn't brook a stuck switch materially diverting the course of history. On the other hand, the traditional Russian distrust of subordinates might diminish the danger of accidents by making Moscow's leaders cautious in delegating attack authority. At the moment, Kahn held, inadvertent war didn't pose a great danger. But as the first-strike capabilities of each side increased, each would be tempted to adopt a launch-on-warning policy or even to move preemptively during a crisis. In this area, Kahn conceded the validity of the notion of the self-fulfilling fear. Fearing war, one side would take defensive action, perhaps evacuating cities, leading the other side, interpreting evacuation as a precursor to attack, to fire the first salvo.

Related to accidental war and almost as worrisome was war by miscalculation. Kahn reminded that the superpowers used nuclear weapons all the time – as the implied sanction behind their diplomacy. Whenever the United States and the Soviet Union confronted each other on contentious issues such as Berlin, the possibility existed that one side would push the other into a position from which the threat of nuclear weapons offered the only exit. If confusion fouled communications, as it often must between two societies as different as America and Russia, one party or both might mistake the seriousness of the other, with tragic results.

War might also come as the result of a calculated decision by one of the nuclear powers that armed conflict was the least distasteful of available alternatives. Neither side, certainly, would deliberately choose an all-out thermonuclear exchange. But if the Russians and their allies, for whatever reason, attacked West Germany, the United States might well respond with tactical nuclear weapons. Russian leaders might accept the risk of such a response, recalling the devastation their country had survived during World War II. Kahn anticipated the counter-assertion that the Kremlin hadn't known when the world war began that twenty million Soviet citizens would die, by saying that even if Stalin had he probably would have accepted the cost, because the alternative was Nazi domination. Should the Russians fear Western domination in the future, they might make a similar decision. As for Americans, while many claimed that there was "no alternative to peace," almost none embraced the logical equivalent: "peace at any price." Until most did, war remained an option.

As a fourth possibility, Kahn described what he called "catalytic war." In this scenario, a regional quarrel spread and drew the superpowers into a general war. A world laced with alliances, as the present world was, increased the likelihood of such an outcome. World War I, Kahn argued, had been a catalytic war, with the dispute between Serbia and Austria catalyzing a much larger conflict among those countries' allies. During the 1950s, trouble between Taiwan and China had repeatedly threatened to escalate; it might do so again.

As in *On Thermonuclear War*, Kahn stressed the need for improvements in America's civil defense capabilities. He granted that neither fallout shelters nor evacuation plans would protect the majority of the nation's people from a surprise attack. With ballistic missiles now an important part of each superpower's arsenal, a war could start and finish and millions be killed all in the space of an hour or two. Kahn often encountered charges of heeding only the conclusions of his cold logic; his stock response was, "Would you prefer a warm, human error?" In this instance, he went out of his way to avoid making the case for civil defense as enhancing deterrence, which, by rendering the defended populace less vulnerable to counterattack, it surely did. Instead he argued from morality. "People are ends, not means. After all, our military forces exist to protect our people; not vice versa."

However unlikely one hoped nuclear war might be, the American government had the obligation to protect as many of its citizens as possible, on the chance that deterrence would fail. Kahn rejected the contention that an effective system of civil defense would promote recklessness on the part of American leaders. In the best of circumstances, American casualties in a major war would number in the millions. He again denounced those critics of civil defense who held that in the aftermath of a nuclear war the living would wish they were dead. He conceded that there would be serious problems of life in a post-attack environment, but he saw no evidence that life would not be worth living. "People have lived under far worse conditions than we in America are accustomed to today, not only throughout most of human history, but even in vast areas of the contemporary world. To argue that an effort to save people's lives is useless because life would be harsher in the postwar world is tantamount to saying that it is preferable for people's lives to be forfeit than for them to endure a lower standard of living or a lower standard of health." Kahn declared the very idea "preposterous."

Although this book was better organized than his previous one, *Thinking About the Unthinkable* included a number of observations Kahn could find room for only in a catch-all chapter he typically called "Some Strange Aids to Thought." Continuing the counterfactual history he had begun in *On Thermonuclear War*, he sketched a situation in which the Soviets in 1960 had deployed three hundred ballistic missiles to America's none. The United States, hoping to diminish the threat, dispersed its nuclear bombers to fifty bases around the country. Russian strategists, targeting each base with six missiles, urged Khrushchev to launch a preemptive strike. Kahn contended that despite the overwhelming Soviet advantage, the Kremlin would move cautiously. He scripted the parts of Khrushchev and a top Russian general:

G: So you can see that if you press these three hundred buttons there is a good chance of our getting away scot-free, a small chance of our suffering moderate damage, and no chance at all of our suffering as much damage as we suffered in World War II.

K: The Americans are on fifteen minute alert. If they have any spies or even if we have a defector we will be destroyed.

G: Don't worry. I have arranged to have a training count-down operation at noon every Saturday. All you have to do is pick up the telephone and give the order. You will be the only one who knows when the attack is going to take place.

K: I don't believe it. What if some Ukrainian who is still mad at me presses one of the buttons ahead of time just to get me in trouble? Or else some don't fire and leave five or six American bases untouched?

G: Don't worry. I know that some Ukrainians are still harboring unjustified grievances against you. There are no Ukrainians in this force. In addition to being specially selected for reliability, every officer is married and has children and we have told these officers that if they fire early not only will they be shot but their families will be severely punished. We can take this extraordinary measure without hurting morale because every officer realizes that this issue is of overriding importance.

K: I still don't like it. I can imagine what will happen. I will pick up the phone and say, "Fire!" The officer will reply, "What did you say?" I will repeat, "Fire!" He will say, "There seems to be a bad connection. I keep hearing the word 'Fire.' I will say, "If you don't fire I will have you boiled in oil." He will say, "I *heard* you that time. Don't fire! Thank you very much!"

Kahn concluded that even under his supposed conditions of overwhelming Soviet missile superiority, the Russians would require a leader "much more reckless, calculating, or desperate" than Khrushchev to launch an attack of the kind described.

Yet a different strategy, given the same premise of Soviet superiority, might prove more tempting. By airbursting bombs over American air bases, the Russians could avoid kicking up much fallout, and by using small warheads against those bases that were close to cities, they could minimize civilian American casualties. The American government presumably would find this approach less provocative than an all-out assault. The Russian attack wouldn't destroy America's entire retaliatory force, but Moscow would neutralize what remained with a warning that if the United States struck back at Soviet cities, the Soviet Union would take out America's population centers at a five-for-one exchange rate. Kahn obligingly drafted the ultimatum: "If you, for example, destroy Moscow, we will destroy New York, Washington, Los Angeles, Philadelphia and Chicago; if you destroy Leningrad, we will destroy Detroit, Pittsburgh, San Francisco, New Orleans and Miami."[13]

VII

Scenarios like this suffered from the fact that the Soviet superiority they posited was never anywhere close to realization, despite American fears during the late 1950s and early 1960s of a "missile gap" favoring the Russians. Yet whatever its demerits, *Thinking About the Unthinkable* indicated the growing sophistication – critics called it sophistry – of the defense intellectuals' approach to matters of military strategy. In the first days of the nuclear era, some observers had predicted an end to the strategic art. The huge new weapons, they suggested, would transform war into a mere test of technology, an exercise in mindless destructive force. Kahn and his colleagues proved the predictions of their own demise premature. As the weapons proliferated, so did the possibilities the strategists theorized about regarding the weapons' use. Whether the theories were any good, no one could say for certain. But neither could anyone show them to be bunk.

The proliferation of possibilities culminated, for the time being at least, in Kahn's 1965 book *On Escalation*. Raymond Aron once characterized Kahn's strength as the "exhaustive enumeration of hypotheses." In *On Escalation*, the great enumerator outdid himself. Popularizing the concept of "escalation," current for some time among the initiated, and currently being applied, after a fashion, in Vietnam, Kahn identified forty-four rungs on the ladder of escalation, from the stage of "ostensible crisis" to "insensate war." As in his previous works, he deemed it his duty to carry readers across the nuclear threshold. "Probably never in the history of the world has

13 Herman Kahn, *Thinking About the Unthinkable* (New York, 1962), 17–19, 28–9, 35, 39–51, 57–8, 83–8, 150–5.

there been so widespread a conviction that 'war is unthinkable' or 'impossible,' and so extensive a belief that a serious concern with the problems in fighting and surviving a war – as opposed to deterring it – is misguided and perhaps even immoral." So far this view hadn't gravely damaged American security. But if unchallenged, it might. And it wasn't being challenged. "The detailed requirements for the wartime use of capabilities, as reflected in the tactics to be chosen if war occurs, are not forcibly brought to anyone's attention. Decisions are made passively, perhaps by default or inattention, and are not fully understood; their consequences are neither necessarily fully grasped nor, indeed, very visible. Often these decisions are classified, which further decreases discussion of them, since, by and large, one does not know what they are." Kahn essayed to remedy this deficiency by a detailed and public analysis of what fighting a nuclear war involved.[14]

Kahn paraphrased Aron to formulate the central questions at issue in situations prone to escalation: Who influences whom, toward or away from what actions, by what threats or enticements, in the face of what counterthreats and counterenticements? And why do the participants succeed or fail? Kahn cited several examples from recent history to demonstrate that military superiority in any given circumstance scarcely assured dominance. In 1953, the United States could have forced the Chinese out of North Korea rather than accept a truce. In 1958, Washington could have intervened in Iraq to install a pro-Western successor to the overthrown Hashemites. In 1964, America possessed the capacity to destroy North Vietnam in response to attacks on South Vietnam. But in each of these instances, the American government chose not to employ its full military power, and accepted less-than-ideal results. Such cases demonstrated that understanding escalation, and non-escalation, required examining the full spectrum of human emotions, values and idiosyncracies.

If pressed, Kahn probably would have admitted that forty-four categories were not strictly necessary to understand escalation, but, beyond the purposes of analysis, he hoped to create a vocabulary for crisis management. He likened the situation to that confronting diplomats in the eighteenth and nineteenth centuries, who devised a careful set of phrases to convey the nuances of threat their govern-

---

[14] Raymond Aron quoted in introduction to Kahn, *Thinking About the Unthinkable*, 12.

ments intended. For a statesman to say that his government was "not uninterested" in a matter indicated a slight level of concern. With characteristic exactitude, Kahn set the probability of war in such circumstances at one in a hundred. If tension increased, the government became "interested," and the likelihood of war rose to one in twenty. When the government registered "concern," war would follow one time out of ten. "Vital interest" raised the hazard to one in four. A declaration that the government was "not responsible for the consequences" amounted to an ultimatum. Kahn noted that this ladder of communicative escalation had taken generations to develop, and even then it had occasionally failed, most spectacularly in 1914. The nuclear age needed an idiom specially suited to its peculiar risks. So far none had arisen, and until it did, fatal misunderstandings would be an ever present danger.

Kahn devoted some energy, although not much enthusiasm, to examining the issue of de-escalation. The simplest way down the ladder took the rungs in reverse order, yet Kahn thought few crises would end thus. The problem, and the reason for Kahn's lack of enthusiasm, was that de-escalation was devilishly unpredictable (not to mention that, being by definition anticlimactic, it provoked fewer shudders in readers). When countries climbed up the ladder, their fear of annihilation kept them from moving too fast and skipping many rungs. But once they decided they had had enough, they might back down a single step at a time or take several rungs at a leap. Kahn contended that this unpredictability made accurate communications all the more imperative. One side might desire to back away from the brink of war, or stop a war that had already started, and not be able to communicate that desire to the other. "Typically, in order to coordinate de-escalation moves by easing pressure, both sides must have a shared understanding of what is happening. They might not have a sufficient shared understanding if one side's paradigm of the world differed in important ways from the other's." Needless to say, the world paradigms of the two countries that counted most in nuclear affairs did differ in important ways.[15]

---

[15] Herman Kahn, *On Escalation: Metaphors and Scenarios* (New York, 1965), 134–8, 195–7, 206–7, 222, 231.

VIII

On Escalation marked Herman Kahn's last major effort in the field of nuclear strategy. He never lost his conviction that Americans needed to appreciate the full implications of their reliance on nuclear weapons to enforce what amounted to a policy of global vindication-ism, but even he ultimately found probing the possibility of global annihilation off-putting. Besides, protest though he might that he was merely pursuing the logic of deterrence to inescapable conclusions, much of his method (and most of his notoriety) relied on shock value. As with the third remake of a suspense movie, the shock wore off. In Kahn's case, the nuclear war he kept warning against never hap-pened, and by the late 1960s its chances of happening in the near term seemed to be diminishing. The world had lived with nuclear weapons for almost a generation since Hiroshima and Nagasaki, and hadn't again resorted to their use. The Cuban missile crisis had been hair-raising, but like many near-death experiences it had a chastening effect, leading to the partial test ban of 1963 and movement toward a nonproliferation treaty, which would be signed in 1968 and take effect in 1970. Perhaps most important for Americans, by the late 1960s the consequences of Cold War vindicationism that caused the greatest immediate distress involved not a future clash with the com-munists of Russia but a current one with the communists of Vietnam.

Kahn had no desire to spend his time studying messy little wars like Vietnam; where was the excitement in that? Anyway, it was unclear what effect his books and lectures to date had had on public policy or anything else. People read his books and got mad, but then they pretty much went back about their business. His most substan-tial recommendation – for improved civil defense – may have contrib-uted to the marginal improvements in that area made by the Kennedy administration, but the Cuban missile crisis contributed more. About the only thing he could definitely point to was the Doomsday Ma-chine, which, without becoming reality – as not even he would have wished – served as the crucial plot element in Stanley Kubrick's 1964 black comedy film *Dr. Strangelove, or How I Learned to Stop Wor-rying and Love the Bomb*. So Kahn decided to depart the field of nuclear studies for the sunnier realm of "futurology" – of forecasting what the world would look like decades hence in the increasingly likely absence of general nuclear war.

9

On Wisconsin:
Madison and Points Left

I

The messy little war in Vietnam dashed far more than Kahn's career in nuclear studies: It exploded the consensus on which American Cold War vindicationism rested. By the late 1960s, consensus thinking in the United States had been under assault for some time, and on many issues besides foreign affairs. The domestic problems of the 1960s were no greater, objectively speaking, than those of the 1950s, but to the myriad reformers and would-be revolutionaries of the later decade, that was hardly a recommendation. The turbulence of the 1960s was largely a generational matter: Where the survivors of the Great Depression and World War II appreciated the peace and prosperity of the 1950s, their children, knowing nothing *but* peace and prosperity, found their parents' world insufferably boring. Their parents' tolerance for imperfection they took for hypocrisy; their parents' desire for community, crushing conformism.

The revolt of the 1960s wasn't entirely generational, of course. America did have some real problems. Poverty persisted, as Michael Harrington documented in *The Other America*. Prejudice and discrimination continued to typify treatment of African-Americans, who were taking their fate into their own hands and demanding an end to segregation. Women, in certain respects, suffered discrimination almost as crippling as that confronting blacks.[1]

But many of the complaints of the decade focused on the inner life, on matters that earlier would have seemed trivial. Paul Goodman

---

[1] Michael Harrington, *The Other America: Poverty in the United States* (New York, 1962).

captured the feeling in *Growing Up Absurd* when he lamented the alienation and ennui that condemned the middle class to an existence of respectable banality. Herbert Marcuse, wedding Freud to Marx, carried Goodman's analysis further. The complacence of the middle class, Marcuse contended, represented not simply alienation but repression. Americans, beguiled by the baubles of modern capitalism, suffered from the false consciousness of the *One Dimensional Man*. They thought they were happy when in fact they had simply subordinated their instinctual yearnings to the needs of the technocratic order.[2]

Marcuse received reinforcement from an unlikely source. In January 1961, on the eve of his retirement, Dwight Eisenhower warned that a "military-industrial complex" was threatening American values. "This conjunction of an immense military establishment and a large arms industry is new in the American experience," the old general said. "The total influence – economic, political, even spiritual – is felt in every city, every statehouse, every office of the federal government." Eisenhower left the American people with an admonition: "In the councils of government, we must guard against the acquisition of unwarranted influence, whether sought or unsought, by the military-industrial complex. The potential for the disastrous rise of misplaced power exists and will persist."[3]

Eisenhower probably hadn't read C. Wright Mills' *The Power Elite*. The president's continuing interest in Columbia University, which he had headed while still a war hero but not yet president, didn't encompass the works of the motorcycle gang in the sociology department. But much of what Eisenhower said echoed Mills's description of the intimacy among politicians, generals, and scientists at the highest levels of the American system. The trend held particular dangers for the conduct of American foreign affairs. Describing the Cold War rise of the Pentagon, Mills wrote: "No area of decision has been more influenced by the warlords and by their military metaphysics than that of foreign policy and international relations. In these zones, the military ascendancy has coincided with other forces

---

[2] Paul Goodman, *Growing Up Absurd: Problems of Youth in the Organized Society* (New York, 1960); Herbert Marcuse, *One Dimensional Man: Studies in the Ideology of Advanced Industrial Society* (Boston, 1964).

[3] *Public Papers of the Presidents: Dwight D. Eisenhower, 1960–1961* (Washington, 1961), 1038–40.

that have been making for the downfall of civilian diplomacy as an art, and of the civilian diplomatic service as an organized group of competent people." Of Mills's "other forces," the most significant was the American tendency to define the contest with communism as a military struggle, a tendency both reflecting and exacerbating the broader militarization of American policy. "With the elite's acceptance of military definitions of world reality, the professional diplomat, as we have known him or as we might imagine him, has simply lost any voice in the higher circles." Further, as military leaders gained stature in the American decision-making process, their political and bureaucratic needs – for bigger budgets, newer weapons, and closer ties to the American corporate structure, which many generals and admirals hoped to join upon retirement from active service – increasingly set the boundaries of what was possible in foreign policy. What was *im*possible was genuine peace.[4]

II

Mills had arrived at Columbia by way of the University of Wisconsin. The Madison connection wasn't coincidental, for although Wisconsin didn't generate the leftist critique of American foreign policy unaided, as much as any single institution it was responsible for the radical challenge to Cold War vindicationism during the 1960s. Wisconsin radicalism ran back to the boat-rocking tradition of the La Follettes and the Farmer-Labor alliance. This tradition was what had drawn Mills north from Texas just before World War II. But its contemporary flowering, as it related to international affairs, owed primarily to the work of another and more recent import.

William Appleman Williams had studied at Wisconsin during the late 1940s, and after academic sojourns elsewhere, he returned to Madison to join the history faculty. His first book, *American-Russian Relations, 1781–1947*, made a minor name for its author in 1952 by its attack on containment as "intellectual sleepwalking," and on George Kennan and other American policy-makers as practitioners of a "sophistry of super-realism." The size of Williams's reputation grew slightly in 1959 when *The Tragedy of American Diplomacy* first

---

[4] C. Wright Mills, *The Power Elite* (New York, 1956, 1959), 205–6.

appeared. But the Cold War consensus remained solid as the Eisenhower decade wound down, and the book created little stir.[5]

The U-2 fiasco in 1960 cracked the consensus slightly by revealing the American president to be a liar and hinting that if he had misled the country on one issue he might have done so, and might continue to do so, on others. The Bay of Pigs botch in 1961 widened the crack, showing a bit more of the seamy underside of American Cold War policy. Meanwhile, as the American commitment to South Vietnam grew, skeptics began asking just where containment was taking the United States.

Williams published an expanded version of *The Tragedy of American Diplomacy* in 1962. He used the Bay of Pigs operation as an example of America's flawed approach to world affairs, and he prophesied a greater debacle in Southeast Asia or elsewhere should the United States not mend its containment ways. This time his message found a larger and more receptive audience. And as America's Vietnam venture intensified and then unraveled during the next several years, Williams's audience continued to grow. At the same time, a cadre of historians who studied with Williams at Wisconsin elaborated the arguments he propounded in *Tragedy*, creating a Wisconsin school of historical revisionism.

As befit a charter document, *Tragedy* read like a manifesto. Williams worked backward from the Bay of Pigs to depict American relations with Cuba as insidiously and consistently imperialistic. In April 1898, the United States had declared war on Spain for the ostensible purpose of liberating Cuba. Cuban independence, nominally speaking, had indeed resulted from the war, but American influence so pervaded the island's economy and political system as to render formal independence nearly meaningless. Williams acknowledged the benefits Cuba derived from association with the United States: The economy of the country modernized, certainly compared to the situation under Spain, and modernization brought tangible benefits to some segments of the Cuban people. Yet reality never lived up to the rhetoric of American promises. Democracy died at the hands of tyrants, strongmen valued by American leaders for their reliability rather than for any attachment to the rights of common Cubans. The Cuban economy, controlled by American sugar firms

[5] William Appleman Williams, *American-Russian Relations, 1781–1947* (New York, 1952), 258.

and their Cuban collaborators, developed unevenly, producing great wealth for the few and widespread misery for the many. Eventually the people rose against the imperialist system and overthrew it. They replaced the discredited Batista with the genuinely popular Castro, who announced his intention to establish the democracy Americans had pledged but never delivered. What was Washington's response? The White House unleashed the dogs of counterrevolution in a predictable but failed effort to restore the status quo.

The appeal of Williams's work – like that of Charles Beard, whom he admired enormously and for whom he felt a deep intellectual kinship – often consisted less in what he said than in the manner in which he said it. To Williams, as to Beard, the great failing of American diplomacy was its denial of the true and essential American vision. Not bitterness but profound sadness informed Williams's writing; he spoke, as Beard spoke, the language of disheartened idealism. He was convinced that America had greatness within her, and he believed that Americans might yet redeem their claim upon the admiration of the world if only they would recognize the error of their ways.

More than a work of scholarship, *Tragedy* was a call for America to return to the path of right. The Cuban situation, Williams said, "was not caused by purposeful malice, callous indifference, or ruthless and predatory exploitation." He added, "American leaders were not evil men. They did not conceive and execute some dreadful conspiracy. Nor were they treacherous hypocrites. They believed deeply in the ideals they proclaimed." Williams chose his title advisedly. "American diplomacy contained the fundamental elements of tragedy. It held within itself, that is to say, several contradictory truths. Those truths, if left to follow out their given logic without modification by men who understood that process and acted on their knowledge, would ultimately clash in a devastating upheaval and crisis."

Of the contradictory truths, Williams identified three as basic. The first was Americans' "warm, generous humanitarian impulse to help other people solve their problems." The second was the principle of self-determination, the notion that every society should enjoy the right to set its own internal objectives and to attempt to realize them by means it deemed appropriate. So far, so good. "These two ideas can be reconciled," Williams asserted. "Indeed, they complement each other to an extensive degree." But the third idea disrupted the harmony, for it held "that other people cannot *really* solve their problems and improve their lives unless they go about it in the same way as the United States." Williams didn't claim uniqueness for America in this self-centered regard; every people demonstrated a certain chauvinism. Yet the United States more than any other nation possessed the political, economic, and military power to impose its chauvinism on others, and in doing so it negated the high principles of its humanitarianism and its belief in self-determination.

Williams followed Beard closely in another respect. He noted a dangerous propensity in Americans to look abroad for solutions to their internal problems. Citing the long history of American efforts to promote foreign trade and investment opportunities, he described, disapprovingly, "the firm conviction, even dogmatic belief, that America's domestic well-being depends upon such sustained, ever-increasing overseas economic expansion." With Beard, Williams saw two pernicious effects in this externalizing tendency. "First, it leads to an indifference toward, or a neglect of, internal developments which are nevertheless of primary importance. And second, this strong tendency to externalize the sources or causes of good things leads naturally enough to an even greater inclination to explain the lack of the good life by blaming it on foreign individuals, groups, and nations." From the latter effect arose both McCarthyism and endless attempts to remake the world in America's image.

Although Williams discerned eighteenth-century origins for the American tendency to look abroad, he began his analysis in earnest with the 1890s. That decade of economic, social, and psychological crisis, he said, produced in spades the conflation of the internal and external that vexed American politics and foreign policy ever after. Under the influence of manufacturers, naval enthusiasts, and Social Darwinists, Americans came to view overseas expansion as essential to the survival of the American democratic experiment. Williams never approached the economic determinism of some later revisionists, and he didn't say that the maturing American economy *required* new markets and investment opportunities. Indeed, although he declined to address the issue as specifically as Beard did, his contentions regarding the mistaken externalization of American troubles indicated a belief that the economy did *not* require foreign expansion. In any event, Williams concentrated on perceptions. It sufficed for his purpose that the captains of industry *thought* expansion was vital to America's prosperity and growth, and that various other groups, for reasons of their own, joined the expansionist chorus.

Williams took the Open Door notes of the turn of the century as emblematic of American policy throughout the six decades following. The Open Door represented two faces of American dealings with the world: sincere solicitude for the welfare of downtrodden foreigners (in the original case, Chinese), and insistence that the foreigners' welfare be served in terms beneficial to American economic and political interests. Because the Open Door theme formed the centerpiece of his argument – in fact, it would provide the touchstone for much revisionist writing – Williams took pains to explain its significance. "It was neither a military strategy nor a traditional balance-of-power policy," he wrote. "It was conceived and designed to win the victories without the wars. In a truly perceptive and even noble sense, the makers of the Open Door Policy understood that war represented the failure of policy." Nobility aside, the Open Door approach also displayed extreme practicality. "It was derived from the proposition that America's overwhelming economic power would cast the economy and the politics of the poorer, weaker, underdeveloped countries in a pro-American mold." American leaders didn't expect competition among the great powers to cease. But they aimed to channel competition in a direction that was both relatively peaceful and advantageous to the United States. While Williams criticized the consequences of the Open Door approach, he didn't dispute the originality and power of the idea. In its way, he said, "it was the most impressive intellectual achievement in the area of public policy since the generation of the Founding Fathers."

Enunciated under McKinley, the Open Door policy matured under McKinley's successors. Williams asserted that beginning with Theodore Roosevelt the philosophy and practice of imperialism implicit in the Open Door notes became the central feature of American foreign policy. "American economic power gushed into some underdeveloped countries within a decade and into many others within a generation. It also seeped, then trickled, and finally flooded into the more developed nations and their colonies until, by 1939, America's economic expansion encompassed the globe."

Williams found Woodrow Wilson more intriguing than Theodore Roosevelt, because more complex. Wilson embodied in a way Roosevelt never could the artless combination of moralism and self-interest that characterized the Open Door. Williams quoted approvingly Raymond Robins's assessment of the Democratic president, judging the sentiment Robins's remark conveyed equally applicable to America as a whole. "Wilson was a great man but he had one basic fault," Robins said. "He was willing to do anything for people except get off their backs and let them live their own lives. He would never let go until they forced him to and then it was too late. He never seemed to understand there's a big difference between trying to save people and trying to help them. With luck you can help them – but they always save themselves."

Wilson had more in mind than saving people: He intended to make the world safe for American capitalism. Williams saw Wilson as a nineteenth-century liberal, pursuing the same sorts of policies Manchester had given the world, via London, three generations before Wilson's time. Williams followed British theorists of imperialism, notably Ronald Robinson and John Gallagher, in identifying imperialism as a phenomenon that transcended the bounds of formal empire and imperial preference. "For Wilson, as for his predecessors and successors," Williams said, "the Open Door Policy was America's version of the liberal policy of informal empire or free-trade imperialism." Wilson aimed to use American influence, by means of the League of Nations and otherwise, to order the world in such a way that competition could proceed in peace. "If this could be done, he was confident that American economic power could take care of the United States – and of the world."

Though the American Senate rejected Wilson's blueprint for international order, the defeat of the Versailles treaty, Williams said, represented a minor difference over tactics rather than a fundamental split on strategy. The Republicans who counted during the 1920s, especially Herbert Hoover, Charles Evans Hughes, and Henry Stimson, sought the same kind of liberal world capitalism Wilson had. They simply tolerated fewer political commitments than Wilson, and they recognized the counterproductive character of his moralizing, especially among the business classes that formed the base of Republican politics. In certain respects, they pushed the Open Door idea farther than Wilson had. The Republicans perceived an intimate connection between America's domestic health and the country's standing abroad, and they incorporated this perception into public policy. "Overseas expansion became an integral part of the domestic expansion of the system itself, rather than the interest or concern merely of certain segments of the system."

The administration of Franklin Roosevelt continued the process. Despite the prevailing isolationist atmosphere of the country, Roosevelt and his advisers pressed for greater access to foreign commercial and financial opportunities as a means of alleviating the depression. At times, the Democratic administration seemed to be pursuing a policy of narrow economic nationalism, but this appearance, Williams said, simply reflected modest disagreements regarding how best to achieve the expansion all desired. "The issue was never whether or not to continue America's overseas economic expansion, but rather the question of how it should be furthered." The key figure in the debates, for Williams (and for other revisionists), was Cordell Hull, who took tariff reduction and the opening of markets nearly to the point of obsession during his record-length term as secretary of state. In the thinking of Hull and others in the administration, the freeing of trade not only promised to shore up the international order but also held the key to an escape from America's domestic troubles. "Only healthy international trade," Hull declared, "will make possible a full and stable domestic economy."

Hull's influence and the attitude it reflected carried over into the years of World War II. To this stage in his analysis, Williams had broken no icons not already damaged by other critics. The empire-building aspects of the war of 1898 had drawn fire from before that conflict began; World War I took a little longer to revise, but by the mid-1920s C. Harley Grattan and Harry Elmer Barnes had roughed up Wilson and the crusade for democracy pretty badly, and Gerald Nye and the isolationists piled on during the 1930s. World War II, however, remained essentially untouched. While Franklin Roosevelt's opponents, including Charles Beard, faulted the president's handling of events leading to Pearl Harbor, almost no one disputed the necessity and fundamental righteousness of the fight against the fascists.

Williams stopped short of declaring that the war had been unnecessary. In light of the Japanese attack on American territory, and the subsequently revealed Nazi atrocities, such a charge would have placed him entirely beyond the bounds of respectable opinion. Nor, in actual fact, did he believe American participation in the war had been entirely unjustified. But he did question the high-mindedness with which Americans claimed to have fought and the purportedly selfless ends they pursued. He labeled the United States' part in the conflict "the war for the American frontier," and he asserted that the Open Door thinking that had driven American policy since the 1890s operated as powerfully as ever during the continuing crises of the late 1930s and 1940s. Quoting a remark by a consultant to the State

Department that "our economic frontiers are no longer coextensive with our territorial frontiers," Williams commented, "No one ever offered a more succinct description and interpretation of the single most important aspect of twentieth-century American diplomacy – either in general, or pertaining explicitly to the nation's involvement in World Wars I and II."

In support of this assertion, Williams added the testimony of no less an authority on capitalism than the editorial board of *Fortune* magazine. "The U.S. economy has never proved that it can operate without the periodic injection of new and real wealth," the editors had declared as Americans debated whether to jump into the fight against Germany and Japan. "The whole frontier saga, indeed, centered around this economic imperative." Although the nature of America's frontier had changed, the economic imperative remained much as before. To revive the still-depressed economy would require a tremendous expansion of foreign trade and investment. Secretary Hull's campaign for lower tariffs, *Fortune* said, marked "a step in the right direction," but to "open up real frontiers, under a general policy of raising the standard of living of other countries, we shall have to go much further." The magazine looked back as it looked forward. "The analogy between the domestic frontier in 1787, when the Constitution was formed, and the present international frontier is perhaps not an idle one. The early expansion of the U.S. was based upon firm political principles; and it may be that further expansion must be based upon equally firm – and equally revolutionary – international principles."

Williams, having defined World War II as a contest by which American leaders aimed to extend the principles of the Open Door to broad new reaches of the globe, found it easy to characterize the Cold War in similar terms. Without setting a halo atop Stalin's head, he accounted the United States chiefly responsible for the conflict that developed between the erstwhile allies. From 1944 to the present, he said, America had possessed "a vast preponderance of actual as well as potential power vis-à-vis the Soviet Union." The Soviets recognized this fact, if many of the American people did not, and consequently Moscow's actions were largely defensive responses to American pressure. As to the nature of this pressure: "The United States used or deployed its preponderance of power wholly within the assumptions and the tradition of the strategy of the Open Door Policy. The United States never formulated and offered the Soviet Union a settlement based on other, less grandiose, terms." Stalin, to whom an Open Door for capitalism and American-sponsored democracy appeared an intolerable challenge to Soviet security, naturally rejected Washington's take-it-or-leave-it approach, and the Cold War resulted.

Two new factors increased American attachment to the Open Door beyond pre-World War II levels. The first involved the nightmare of a return to the calamities of the 1930s. Dean Acheson forecast a probable grim future during testimony before a congressional committee in 1944. "It seems clear that we are in for a very bad time, so far as the economic and social position of the country is concerned," Acheson declared. "We cannot go through another ten years like the ten years at the end of the twenties and the beginning of the thirties" – a loyal Democrat, Acheson tried to push as much of the blame for the depression as possible on Hoover – "without having the most far-reaching consequences upon our economic and social system." Speaking of the foreign markets that Hull and the State Department were attempting to open to American penetration, Acheson said, "We need these markets for the output of the United States. . . . We cannot have full employment and prosperity in the United States without the foreign markets." Other Americans, Williams averred, amplified Acheson's arguments. Journalist Marquis Childs urged Americans to consult the work of Brooks Adams on the subject of economic competition; to facilitate the consulting, Childs republished some of Adams's work. He added that the author would have "to alter scarcely anything to relate his views to the world today." The *Wall Street Journal* supported the idea of an Adams revival, saying it was "high time to face the problem created by what Brooks Adams called 'America's vast and growing surplus.' "

The second new factor concerned the atomic bomb, which fostered what Williams called a "vision of omnipotence" in American leaders and rendered them unwilling to mitigate their demands. Williams suggested that the decision to use the bomb in 1945 turned on matters relating to Moscow as much as on the situation between America and Japan. "The United States dropped the bomb to end the war against Japan," he wrote, then switched to italics for emphasis: "*and thereby stop the Russians in Asia, and to give them sober pause in eastern Europe.*" Williams argued that if, as American leaders later contended, they saw the bomb chiefly as a device to save lives likely to be lost in an invasion of Japan, they might have delayed using the new weapon for several months until the invasion date drew closer (and the atomic arsenal included more bombs). But a fear that the Russians, pledged to declare war on Japan in August, would reap the spoils of victory at nearly no expense, caused Washington to press ahead. "The bomb had to be used quickly, and if necessary repeatedly, if the war was to be ended before the Russians honored their promise to attack within three months after Germany was defeated."

The Truman administration's atomic diplomacy didn't prevent the Russians from entering the Pacific war, but it did poison the atmosphere between the United States and the Soviet Union. At the same time, it demonstrated the quixotic nature of American foreign policy generally. The goal of the Open Door had possessed a certain validity when first enunciated. "The Open Door Policy had provided the strategy and tactics that enabled the United States to establish a new and persuasive empire during the era when the colonial empires of the eighteenth and nineteenth centuries were dying and being given the *coup de grâce* by the twentieth-century revolutions in economics and politics, in the relationship between the colored and the white peoples of the world, and of anticolonial nationalism." But the Open Door fell victim to its own accomplishments. By spreading the gospel of self-determination, Americans eventually rendered impossible the reshaping of the world in the American image. The peoples of the underdeveloped nations demanded true self-determination: the right to chart their destinies according to their own preferences and needs, not those pushed upon them by Washington.

Williams argued that a fundamental questioning of the premises of American policy was long overdue.

Isn't it time to stop defining trade as the control of markets for our surplus products and control of raw materials for our factories? Isn't it time to stop depending so narrowly – in our thinking as well as in our practice – upon an informal empire for our well-being and welfare?

Isn't it time to ask ourselves if we are really so unimaginative that we have to have a frontier in the form of an informal empire in order to have democracy and prosperity at home? Isn't it time to say that we can make American society function even better on the basis of equitable relationships with other people?

What Williams was advocating, in other words, was a shift from the vindicationism of the American empire to an exemplarism of true American democracy. In place of the Open Door for American exports, he called for "an open door for revolutions," a policy that, while inviting other countries to follow the American example, wouldn't force them to do so. He concluded that only in this way could the tragedy of American diplomacy be transcended in a creative, peaceful manner.[6]

III

In other works, Williams expanded on the themes of *The Tragedy of American Diplomacy*. His 1961 *Contours of American History* emphasized the influence from colonial days of economic factors, identifying in turn the ages of mercantilism, of laissez faire, and of corporate capitalism, the last persisting to the present. As before, he stressed the intimate connection between foreign and domestic policy. He acknowledged more explicitly his debt to Charles Beard, to whose name he added Herbert Hoover and Eugene Debs on a short – too short, in Williams's view – list of prophets who understood that American security, prosperity, and harmony did not require an American empire. In his 1969 *Roots of the Modern American Empire*, he responded to critics' charges that his attention to industrialists' late-nineteenth-century demands for foreign markets skewed his perspective on a period when the majority of American exports were still agricultural; he adduced masses of evidence that farmers were fully as anxious as the manufacturers to find fresh overseas outlets for their surpluses.

But *The Tragedy of American Diplomacy* was the work that inspired Williams's students and triggered the development of the Wisconsin school of historical revisionism. Walter LaFeber enlarged on Williams's treatment of the last four decades of the nineteenth century, calling the post-Sumter era "the crucial incubation period of the American overseas empire." LaFeber specifically examined the linkage between expansionism and the maturation of the American industrial economy. He granted that the United States had exploded onto the world scene only in 1898, but he contended that the powder train ran back to the Civil War. McKinley and Theodore Roosevelt

---

[6] William Appleman Williams, *The Tragedy of American Diplomacy* (New York, 1959, 1962), 2–3, 9–11, 49–50, 82–3, 91, 116, 169, 193–4, 199–200, 203, 208, 235–6, 254, 272, 299, 305–7.

continued work well begun by William Seward, William Evarts, and Frederick Frelinghuysen.[7]

Thomas McCormick, another Wisconsin product, applied Williams's Open Door concept to the region that had inspired the original: China. McCormick traced the development of American interest in the China market from the financial panic of 1893 through the early twentieth century. Like Williams and Beard, he detected domestic roots for American overseas expansion. The economic and social crises of the 1890s precipitated – "perhaps psychologically compelled," McCormick suggested – efforts to explain America's increasing troubles in terms that left the nation's self-image intact. Such efforts, McCormick wrote, "led almost inevitably down the corridor marked 'overproduction.'" The result was "concerted agreement on the necessity of a militant, broad-gauged expansion into the surplus absorbing markets of the world." Of these markets, China, long the object of American desire, and in the dying days of the Manchu dynasty more susceptible than ever to foreign penetration, appeared particularly tempting. The combination of need and opportunity caused Americans to try to export their domestic difficulties across the Pacific – "to define the China market as the solution to the closed frontier and the industrial glut at home."[8]

Lloyd Gardner, yet another Wisconsinite, brought the discussion closer to the present, and thereby gave it a sharper bite for current discussions of foreign affairs. Applying the Open Door paradigm to the administration of Franklin Roosevelt, Gardner described a steady pursuit of American economic interests, defined largely in terms of access to foreign markets, from the New Deal through World War II. Following Williams, Gardner identified Cordell Hull as the underappreciated but crucial figure in Democratic foreign policy. Hull, Gardner said, pressed assiduously for an updated Open Door policy of economic expansion, and generally, if quietly, won out. This policy led the Roosevelt administration to oppose Japan's efforts to claim an exclusive sphere in East Asia, led it to challenge the hegemony of Britain and France in the Middle East, and finally led it to confront

---

[7] Walter LaFeber, *The New Empire: An Interpretation of American Expansion, 1860–1898* (Ithaca, N.Y., 1963), vii.

[8] Thomas J. McCormick, *China Market: America's Quest for Informal Empire, 1893–1901* (Chicago, 1967), 30, 53.

the Soviet Union in central Europe. Gardner saw a direct connection between the diplomacy of the New Deal and the Cold War: "In Manchuria (before, during, and after the war), in the Middle East, in Latin America, in fact nearly everywhere, the United States wanted the Open Door Policy and an open world. Russia did not. And therein was the struggle which developed into Cold War."[9]

IV

The influence of the Wisconsinites soon spread beyond the circle of those who practiced or studied history at Madison. To some extent, their influence reflected the persuasiveness of their arguments, which in turn reflected, among other things, the gradual opening of previously classified records relating to American diplomacy in the 1940s. The heroic posture for American leaders became harder to maintain as researchers gained access to their closed-door discussions of the need for an open door abroad and related matters.

At least equally, however, the success of the revisionists testified to the growing disenchantment among intellectuals, students, and many others regarding the direction of contemporary American foreign policy. As the war in Vietnam turned sour, then disastrous, it became tempting, then irresistible, for historians and political scientists to read the errors of the present back into the past. Vietnam appeared the logical outcome of the policy of containment; if Vietnam was a bad idea, then containment must have been a bad idea too. And if containment, the cornerstone of American Cold War policy, had been misguided, then any number of other policies and decisions might have been flawed, or at least misrepresented, as well.

Gar Alperovitz went after what he judged a major misrepresentation from the very outset of the Cold War. Following up Williams's suggestion that the atomic bomb had stiffened American resolve not to compromise with the Russians at the end of World War II, Alperovitz accused the Truman administration of engaging in "atomic diplomacy" toward the Kremlin. With Williams, but supplying additional evidence, Alperovitz challenged the conventional justification that the atomic bomb had been necessary to save hundreds of thousands of American lives. He pointed out that Truman's top aides

[9] Lloyd C. Gardner, *Economic Aspects of New Deal Diplomacy* (Madison, Wis., 1964), 329.

didn't think military considerations required the use of the bomb. "Before the atomic bomb was dropped," Alperovitz stated, "each of the Joint Chiefs of Staff advised that it was highly likely that Japan could be forced to surrender 'unconditionally,' without use of the bomb and without an invasion." The real target of the bomb, Alperovitz argued, wasn't Hiroshima but Moscow. Truman intended the bomb for a diplomatic trump card against Stalin, a device to compel Soviet compliance with American wishes regarding the future of Europe and Asia. By contrast to Truman, the hero of Alperovitz's tale was Henry Stimson, to whom the author dedicated the book. After initially expressing enthusiasm that the bomb would prove a master card in America's foreign relations, the war secretary had changed his mind. He tried to persuade Truman to forget about employing the bomb as an instrument of power politics and to open talks with the Russians regarding international control of atomic energy. "If we fail to approach them now," Stimson told the president, "and merely continue to negotiate with them, having this weapon rather ostentatiously on our hip, their suspicions and their distrust of our purposes and motives will increase." To seek diplomatic advantage from America's atomic monopoly "would be by far the more dangerous course," perhaps leading to "an armament race of a rather desperate character."[10]

Gabriel Kolko didn't believe in heroes, or in villains either. Kolko took the Williams interpretation of American foreign policy and veered hard left toward traditional Marxism. Where Williams never completely decided whether blame for American imperialism lay with individuals or with the system – the overall thrust of his work suggested systemic imperatives, but his call for an open door for revolutions indicated that individuals could buck the system – Kolko explicitly indicted the system. Examining the origins of the Cold War, Kolko judged the distinguishing characteristic of American policy to be a consistent effort to implement the liberal-capitalist philosophy of America's ruling circles. Unlike many other revisionists, he saw little to choose between Roosevelt and Truman. The styles of the two presidents differed, but capitalists were capitalists. Before, during, and after World War II, American elected officials, in league with top business executives, insisted on expanded opportunities for American

---

[10] Gar Alperovitz, *Atomic Diplomacy: The Use of the Atomic Bomb and the American Confrontation with Soviet Power* (New York, 1965), 11, 233–8.

overseas trade and investment. In this insistence lay the roots of the
Cold War, whose sprouts were nourished by policies developed in
Washington during the world war. In this insistence also lay the roots
of American involvement in Vietnam. Southeast Asia's raw materials
weren't inconsiderable, but far more important was what Vietnam
represented for the world order as a whole. "The dominant interest
of the United States is in world economic stability," Kolko wrote,
"and anything that undermines that condition presents a danger to
its present hegemony." From Kolko's perspective, American intervention in Vietnam was "the inevitable cost of maintaining United States
imperial power." The stakes in Vietnam, he claimed, were global.
"Ultimately, the United States has fought in Vietnam with increasing
intensity to extend its hegemony over the world community and to
stop every form of revolutionary movement which refuses to accept
the predominant role of the United States in the direction of the
affairs of its nation or region."[11]

The question of necessity split the revisionist camp. Kolko spoke
for the revolutionary left in stating that American capitalism needed
empire for its continued existence. To end imperialism required junk-
ing the American system. Williams represented the reformist right
(within the spectrum of leftist thought) in suggesting that empire was
a tragic mistake. Clear minds and good hearts might yet save the
system from its excesses.

Ronald Steel sided with Williams on the necessity issue. Indeed,
Steel placed himself to Williams's right. Steel granted that the United
States possessed an empire, but like John Seeley, the British historian
who said that Britain had acquired its empire in "a fit of absence of
mind," Steel saw little premeditation in the matter. "The American
empire came into being by accident," Steel wrote in *Pax Americana*.
"Nobody planned our empire. In fact nobody even wanted it." As
empires went, the American version was fairly benevolent, with its
primary victims being not foreigners but Americans themselves. "We
have not exploited our empire. On the contrary, our empire has exploited us, making enormous drains on our resources and our energies." What accounted for the empire's origin and continued existence? In essence, a mistakenly vindicationist view of the world. "It

---

[11] Gabriel Kolko, *The Politics of War: The World and United States Foreign Policy,
1943–1945* (New York, 1968); idem, *The Roots of American Foreign Policy: An
Analysis of Power and Purpose* (Boston, 1969), 55, 85, 132.

was acquired because we believe we have a responsibility to defend nations everywhere against communism. This is not an imperial ambition, but it has led us to use imperial methods." With the other reformists, Steel thought a cure for the imperialist affliction would follow a correct reordering of priorities. Americans must cleave to the exemplarism that constituted their true calling. "It is now time for us to turn away from global fantasies and begin our perfection of the human race within our own frontiers. . . . America's worth to the world will be measured not by the solutions she seeks to impose on others, but by the degree to which she achieves her own ideals at home."[12]

Harry Magdoff would have none of this nonsense about empire being optional and misguided. The American empire, he asserted, was neither accidental nor dysfunctional. Investigating the economics of American foreign relations, Magdoff ascertained that imperialistic policies yielded substantial benefits to the sectors of the American political economy that exerted greatest influence on the shape of those policies. Exports and military spending fortified the complex of international manufacturers and arms merchants Magdoff called a "strategic center of the existing industrial structure." Foreign sales, though small as a percentage of total American production, provided a cushion of prosperity "by acting as a bulwark against the slippage of minor recessions into major depressions." In any event, Magdoff held, narrow cost-benefit accounting obscured more than it revealed. American leaders didn't ask whether intervention in a particular Latin American nation would pay for itself; instead they viewed such intervention in the context of American hegemony over the entire hemisphere. Washington didn't calculate what returns to expect from each application of the Open Door principle. "How much or how little an open door may be exploited at any given time is not the issue. The principle must be maintained." Only in such terms could the significance of Vietnam be appreciated. "The killing and destruction in Vietnam and the expenditure of vast sums of money are not balanced in the eyes of U.S. policy makers against profitable business opportunities in Vietnam; rather they are weighted according to the judgment of military and political leaders on what is necessary to control and influence Asia, and especially Southeast Asia, in order to keep the entire area within the imperialist system in general, and

[12] Ronald Steel, *Pax Americana* (New York, 1967), 15–8, 354.

within the United States sphere of influence in particular." Reformists like Williams and Steel deluded themselves, Magdoff summarized. "Imperialism is not a matter of choice for a capitalist society; it is the way of life of such a society."[13]

Richard Barnet disagreed, although the structuralist approach of Barnet's 1972 *Roots of War* showed the influence of Kolko and Magdoff, as well as of C. Wright Mills. Speaking from personal experience of the State and Defense departments, Barnet argued that the American penchant for international violence and coercion – evidenced, in Barnet's accounting, by the fact that since 1945 the United States had conducted major military campaigns or paramilitary covert operations in foreign countries at an average rate of one per eighteen months – resulted from the interplay of forces within the national-security bureaucracy, the corporate-capitalist economy, and the domestic political system. Vietnam, Barnet suggested, represented the most recent and egregious example of what he called the "bureaucratization of homicide." Barnet followed Beard, Williams, and others in delineating an intimate connection between foreign policy and domestic politics, yet for all his belief that war was "primarily the product of domestic social and economic institutions," he hadn't abandoned hope that things might change. The national-security establishment was discrediting itself in Vietnam. Even old Cold Warriors like Richard Nixon were conceding the limits of America's ability to shape the world to American order. To capture the moment, reform-minded Americans must insist on greater democratic control over the foreign-policy bureaucrats and recognize that an economy premised on never-ending expansion and the profligate use of imported raw materials such as oil inevitably led to Vietnams and other international disasters. "Until the majority of people who do not directly benefit from it come to see in concrete terms how they are being hurt by American foreign policy, they will continue to give uncritical support to expansionist policies wrapped in the flag and promoted through fear."[14]

[13] Harry Magdoff, *The Age of Imperialism: The Economics of U.S. Foreign Policy* (New York, 1966, 1969), 14–15, 20, 26, 189.
[14] Richard J. Barnet, *Roots of War* (New York, 1972), 5, 14, 48–49, 65, 109, 266–7, 337–41.

V

Among American public thinkers, the war in Vietnam had much the same effect as World War I a half-century earlier. Just as many Wilsonian liberals – Walter Lippmann, for instance – had followed their chief into the European war, so most of the Kennedy liberals followed Kennedy, and then Kennedy's heir Lyndon Johnson, into the war in Vietnam. Radical intellectuals criticized liberal intellectuals for betraying their calling during the 1960s, just as radicals had criticized liberals during the 1910s.

Noam Chomsky assumed the role of a latter-day Randolph Bourne. The M.I.T. linguist and social critic angrily denounced American participation in the war in Vietnam as "criminal insanity." But he reserved special vitriol for the war's intellectual supporters. Citing a Bourne diatribe against the cooption of the elite, Chomsky noted that the piece, written in the era of Wilson's New Freedom and bearing the title "Twilight of Idols," applied as well to Kennedy's New Frontier. "With the Vietnam war," he added, "twilight has turned to midnight." Chomsky assailed the social scientists who designed the "strategic hamlet" program of forced relocation of Vietnamese peasants. He condemned the international-relations experts who sold their intellectual objectivity for passing political influence. He singled out the "appalling" actions of Roger Hilsman of the Kennedy State Department, and dismissed as irrelevant Arthur Schlesinger Jr.'s recent tactical criticism of the Johnson administration's handling of the war. He suggested that the thinking that had led to Vietnam was of a piece with the thinking of Herman Kahn, whose "pseudoscientific posing" approached the "pathological" and whose *On Thermonuclear War* was "surely one of the emptiest works of our time."[15]

In certain respects, Chomsky's 1967 attack was a late hit. Much of the intellectual community, including many liberals, had abandoned the war effort by then. The abandonment was already in evidence during the summer of 1965 when the Johnson White House sponsored a "festival of the arts," designed to put a high-brow patina on the president's social reforms. To Johnson's dismay, the affair evoked protests from several of those invited. Poet Robert Lowell

---

[15] Noam Chomsky, *American Power and the New Mandarins* (New York, 1967, 1969), 6–7, 126, 249, 266, 311, 340.

publicly refused to attend on account of the administration's Vietnam policy. John Hersey arrived but read an excerpt from his *Hiroshima* that had obvious implications for the American bombing campaign against North Vietnam. Critic Dwight Macdonald circulated a petition censuring the president's policies – and nearly came to blows with actor and Vietnam hawk Charlton Heston, who threatened to smite Macdonald as he had once smitten, with the help of God and special effects, the pharoah's minions.[16]

Yet a sizable contingent of liberals continued to defend the war, if with less enthusiasm than previously. In January 1967 McGeorge Bundy – who, on Vietnam, was something of a Walter Lippmann to Chomsky's Randolph Bourne (except that Bundy was closer to Kennedy than Lippmann ever was to Wilson, and leaving aside that the real Lippmann was still alive) – addressed opponents of the Vietnam war in an article in *Foreign Affairs*. Having departed government the previous year, Bundy no longer spoke as one responsible for American policy in Vietnam. And he conceded part of the critics' case, regarding the difficulties that enmeshed the war. "Nothing about it is simple," he wrote, adding that both sides in the debate over the war could draw from "a great pile of evidence" in which there was plenty to support contradictory opinions. "The truth in Viet Nam is that there is both aggression from the North and civil conflict in the South, both corruption and self-sacrifice, both strong anti-Communist feeling and a weary lack of affection for much of the present anti-Communist leadership." The international ramifications were equally complex. "Viet Nam is indeed a test of Communist revolutionary doctrine, and what happens there will affect what happens elsewhere; but victory for Ho [Chi Minh] would not mean automatic communization of all Asia, and the defeat of aggression would not mean an end to the pervasive – if sometimes exaggerated – threat of China." For all the complications, however, the United States was on the right track. Absent previous decisions to support Saigon, South Vietnam almost certainly "would have been delivered to the tender care of Hanoi and the chances for peaceful progress in many Pacific nations would have been heavily reduced." The struggle had proved more difficult than anyone expected, but America must stay the course. "It is right to persevere." For the sake of South Vietnam, and, more importantly, for the credibility of American com-

---

[16] Melvin Small, *Johnson, Nixon, and the Doves* (New Brunswick, N.J., 1988), 52.

mitments across the globe, Americans must finish what they had started. "The true value of the United States as an ally and friend rests not on the language of treaties which always have escape clauses, and not on mechanical notions of cause and consequence, but rather upon the fact that this is a nation which sees things through and tries to see them straight."[17]

VI

If hard cases make bad law, they do no better shaping foreign policy. By now most supporters of the overall policy of containment recognized that Vietnam was an unfavorable ground on which to mount a philosophical defense of that policy. For this reason, and because the revisionist assault, while recently energized by Vietnam, in fact antedated and transcended the ongoing conflict in Southeast Asia, critics of the revisionists shifted the debate twenty years back in time.

Arthur Schlesinger had a variety of complaints about the revisionists' interpretation of the origins of the Cold War. He objected to their near-exclusive focus on American contributions to Cold War tensions, a focus that left untold the Soviet half of the story, which he considered by far the more revealing half. He charged the revisionists with ahistoricity: They watched the sluggish, slightly seedy Soviet Union of the 1960s trying to fend off allegations of rightist deviationism leveled by Peking and its partners along the revolutionary front, and acting much as traditional national states had always acted, and they assumed it was ever so. "The great omission of the revisionists – and also the fundamental explanation of the speed with which the Cold War escalated – lies precisely in the fact that the Soviet Union was *not* a traditional national state." Whatever the condition of the country after Khrushchev, Stalin's Russia was "a totalitarian state, endowed with an all-explanatory, all-consuming ideology, committed to the infallibility of government and party, still in a somewhat messianic mood, equating dissent with treason, and ruled by a dictator who, for all his quite extraordinary abilities, had his paranoid moments." By ignoring "the intransigence of Leninist ideology, the sinister dynamics of a totalitarian society and the madness of Stalin," the revisionists drew a distorted and therefore false picture of the period of the early Cold War. Schlesinger granted that American

[17] McGeorge Bundy, "The End of Either/Or," *Foreign Affairs*, January 1967.

leaders had made mistakes. But he had no doubt where responsibility for the breakdown of the Grand Alliance lay. "The most rational of American policies could hardly have averted the Cold War."[18]

Perhaps the sharpest, and indeed most acute, critic of the revisionists was Robert Tucker, a Morgenthavian professor of international relations at Johns Hopkins. Tucker appreciated the energy the revisionists brought to the study of American foreign policy, and he judged their work sufficiently significant to warrant a book-length reply, his 1971 *The Radical Left and American Foreign Policy.*

Though generally fair-minded, Tucker occasionally succumbed to the temptation of damning all the revisionists for the excesses of a few. He took Chomsky to task for declaring the United States "the most aggressive power in the world" and Carl Oglesby for describing America as "history's most violent nation." While Tucker conceded that these were "extreme views" even among the revisionists, he added, "They are nevertheless suggestive of the unrelentingly harsh judgment radical historiography as a whole passes on American diplomacy in this century." Suggestive such views may have been, but they were still extreme – although they became more characteristic, justifiably, following the Nixon administration's record-shattering Christmas bombing campaign against North Vietnam in 1972.

Tucker also lumped together radical idealists like Williams and radical realists like Kolko. Tucker clearly understood the differences between the two, and he recognized the hazards of oversimplification. Yet he thought the similarities sufficient to warrant broad-brush treatment. "Williams may find the history of American diplomacy tragic because we have denied our better self, whereas Kolko may find no tragedy in this history because we have no better self. Williams may take America's professed ideals seriously, though he believes we have constantly subverted them in practice, whereas Kolko may dismiss these ideals as no more than empty rhetoric." But in the end, this amounted to a distinction without a difference. "There is no marked disagreement between the two on the way we have behaved in the world or on what we must do in order to redeem ourselves."

Tucker taxed the revisionists with selectivity in adducing evidence. American officials gave lots of reasons for what they did. Why did Williams and the radicals choose to highlight only those supporting

---

[18] Arthur M. Schlesinger Jr., "Origins of the Cold War," *Foreign Affairs,* October 1967.

the case for economic motivation? What about the Truman doctrine, perhaps the single most significant statement of postwar American foreign policy? "Whatever else may be said of the Truman Doctrine, its words scarcely support the radical position." It didn't speak in terms of capitalism, nor did it identify democracy with openness to American economic penetration. "This is why a radical critique either ignores the Truman Doctrine or insists that it obscures the true nature of America's objectives. But if it is argued that the Truman Doctrine obscures our true objectives, there is no apparent reason for not applying the argument to statements that in the radical view reveal those objectives."

Here Tucker was being willfully obtuse. Historians and other seekers of truth don't have to accept the public statements of elected officials on an all-or-nothing basis. Naturally the radicals exercised selectivity in making their case; in no other way could they, or anyone else, hope to find order in the chaos that characterizes human existence. They judged that the evidence, on balance, revealed that the constellation of values Williams identified with the Open Door outweighed other considerations in official American thinking. Consequently they gave greatest credence to evidence to that effect. In any event, one would hardly expect the president of the United States to declare his intent to secure the world for Wall Street even if – perhaps especially if – such was precisely what he intended.

Despite his belief that the revisionists were fundamentally wrong, Tucker credited them with certain insights. He agreed, for example, with their assertion that the Cold War was more an extension of World War II than a break from it. "The radical critics are quite right in concluding that the reasons that ultimately impelled us to intervene in World War II also impelled us to a course of action that made the cold war inevitable. On both occasions, the prospect was held out of a world outside this hemisphere hostile to American interests and institutions, a world in which America's economic and political frontiers might become increasingly coextensive with its territorial frontiers, and thus a world in which prosperity and democracy in America itself might be imperiled."

On this point, Tucker accepted the hard-leftist view that the Cold War was essentially inevitable. But where Kolko followed Marx in perceiving the inevitability as a product of the clash between capitalism and socialism, Tucker followed Morgenthau in interpreting it as the consequence of the ceaseless, and fundamentally ideology-less, struggle for power among nations. As a thought experiment – again following Morgenthau – Tucker asked whether a hypothetical socialist America would have behaved, and would behave, any differently than the actual capitalist America. He thought not. Ideological quarrels between a United Socialist States of America and the Soviet Union might diminish, although the bitter and recently violent disputes between co-ideologists China and Russia made this no sure thing. But the world surrounding a socialist America would remain as polarized in terms of rich and poor, powerful and weak, as the genuine article. The actions of the Soviets toward the nonaligned countries provided little reason to think socialism rendered states suddenly selfless.

In an argument he would expand later, Tucker contended that the inequality that increasingly marked international relations resulted not from ideological divisions, and even less from the machinations of monopoly capitalists, but from a global order based on national sovereignty. And national sovereignty, in turn, reflected desires and fears rooted in the deepest recesses of human nature. Radical advocates of socialism looked to a transformation of human nature under a socialist form of government. The world had yet to witness such a transformation, and Tucker wasn't holding his breath.[19]

[19] Robert W. Tucker, *The Radical Left and American Foreign Policy* (Baltimore, 1971), 10, 15–16, 57, 65, 89–91, 105, 126, 138–45.

10

The Brief of Norman's Woe: Commentary *and the New Conservatism*

I

In appealing to a changeless human nature, Tucker identified a basic division between the radicalism of the 1960s and early 1970s and the conservatism that characterized the decade that followed (and for that matter between radicalism and conservatism generally). The radicals believed that American society could be changed significantly for the better, by enlightened individual action, in the view of Williams and the near left, or by institutional restructuring, in the opinion of Kolko and the distant left. Conservatives like Tucker had no such faith. They perceived the tragedy of American diplomacy, and of human affairs overall, as originating in the intrinsically flawed character of individuals. Until human nature changed, as it hadn't done during the several millennia people had been keeping track, wisdom resided in making the modest best of a bad situation, which usually meant leaving things alone.

Conservatism has always flourished in the wake of reforms run awry. The 1970s fit the pattern, although not immediately. Lyndon Johnson's Great Society uncovered as many problems as it solved, raising expectations among the dispossessed and their sponsors that would have proved impossible to meet even had the War on Poverty and on other forms of inequality always been fought with exemplary skill and bravery, which it wasn't. The series of leaps in oil prices that began with the 1973 round of Middle East fighting exacerbated inflationary pressures originating in Johnson's double-dipping of dollars to fund both domestic programs and the war in Vietnam while holding taxes down. The protests of the 1960s produced not the new heaven and new earth proclaimed by Theodore Roszak in *The Mak-*

ing of a Counter Culture or the "Consciousness III" heralded by
Charles Reich in *The Greening of America*, but exhaustion and disillusionment.

Ready though the country was for a conservative reaction, two
major hurdles blocked the way. The first was Richard Nixon, who
did his best in the Watergate scandal to discredit what passed for
conservatism in America in the years between Barry Goldwater and
Ronald Reagan. By covering himself in ignominy, Nixon set conservatism back most of a decade. Yet Nixon wasn't an unrelieved disaster for conservatives, for he brilliantly confirmed their argument
about errant human nature.

The second hurdle was Vietnam. Conservatives had never loved
containment; during the early 1950s, many followed James Burnham
in promoting "liberation," an alternative that promised to "roll
back" the red tide. But after the Soviet Union acquired a nuclear
arsenal effectively matching America's, liberation lost its appeal. Eisenhower's refusal to risk war over Hungary in 1956 demonstrated
that, as far as American policy went, liberation was going nowhere.
William F. Buckley Jr. dedicated his 1959 *Up from Liberalism* to
Burnham, but conceded that those conservatives who had denounced
containment as defeatist had failed to make a convincing demonstration of the truth of their case. The Kremlin hadn't conquered the
earth, either by boring from within or assaulting from without. If
conservatives continued to preach the imminence of catastrophe,
Buckley said, "we will, like the Seventh Day Adventists, who close
down the curtain on the world every season or so, lose our credit at
the bar of public opinion or be dismissed as cultists of a terrestrial
mystique." A new conservatism whose message matched present realities must replace the old.[1]

The new conservatism hadn't emerged by the time the Cold War
liberals took the United States into Vietnam, and conservatives were
forced to tag behind. Some complained, as Goldwater did in the 1964
presidential campaign, that the Democrats weren't prosecuting the
war with sufficient vigor, but Johnson's post-election conversion to
escalation silenced all but the most unreconstructed MacArthurites.
As the war went against America, and America increasingly went
against the war, conservatives found themselves in something of a

---

[1] James Burnham, *Containment or Liberation?* (New York, 1952); William F. Buckley Jr., *Up from Liberalism* (New York, 1959), 161.

quandary. On one hand, defending the war required defending policies initiated by and long associated with Democrats and liberals. Eventually conservatives would learn to invoke the spirits of Harry Truman and John Kennedy, but not yet. On the other hand, dissociating from the war weakened what remained of the possibility of preserving South Vietnam from a communist takeover. Whatever political gains conservatives might make from the liberals' failures, preventing the spread of communism continued to be an overriding objective.

The conservatives' Nixon problem solved itself when the siege of the White House ended in surrender in August 1974. Vietnam solved itself too, when the siege of Saigon ended in surrender eight months later. Nixon's departure released conservatives from having continually to explain that he really wasn't one of them. Saigon's capture freed them from such burden of responsibility as they felt toward South Vietnam and allowed them to recriminate to their hearts' content. They capitalized on their opportunity, burying Nixon alive in San Clemente (although he later proved very resourceful in digging himself out) and converting the war in Vietnam into the modern equivalent of the Lost Cause of the American South. In the process, those most energetic in effecting the conversion created the new conservatism William Buckley had called for fifteen years earlier.

II

The origins of the new right of the 1970s lay in the remnants of the old left of the 1930s. The Molotov-Ribbentrop pact of 1939 had shaken the faith of even dedicated American pro-Muscovites, and if the subsequent Grand Alliance restored some of that faith, the unimagined destructiveness of World War II severely challenged the assumptions of human rationality and human goodness upon which socialism and its tamer variants rested. It wasn't coincidence that the ranks of the neoconservatives included a sizable contingent of Jews, for whom the Nazi Holocaust had particular meaning, or that *Commentary* magazine, which provided the principal forum for neoconservative thought on foreign affairs, was published by the American Jewish Committee.

The early years of the Cold War found many future neoconservatives in the ranks of what Norman Podhoretz called "hard anti-Communism." Podhoretz described hard anticommunism as resting on two tenets: that the Soviet Union was a totalitarian state of the same incorrigibly evil character as Nazi Germany, and that the Kremlin aimed at world revolution, by subversion where possible and force where necessary. The proto-neos defended or at least tolerated McCarthyism. Irving Kristol asserted that American interests were safer with the Wisconsin senator than with his critics; Nathan Glazer disagreed with certain aspects of McCarthy's conduct but declared, "I cannot see that it is an imminent danger to personal liberty in the United States."[2]

Vietnam cracked the consensus on which American anticommunism rested, throwing the budding neoconservative movement momentarily into disarray. "All about us canvas tore and cables parted," wrote Daniel Patrick Moynihan, who had urged Irving Kristol and Daniel Bell to name their new journal *Consensus* rather than *The Public Interest*, but changed his mind under the duress of events. The tempest scattered the proto-neos in all directions. Podhoretz, now editor at *Commentary*, moved briefly to the left. Glazer went a bit right, from "mild radical," as he put it, to "mild conservative." Kristol joined the camp of Hubert Humphrey. Moynihan wound up in the Nixon administration.[3]

Yet by the early 1970s, Podhoretz's hard anticommunists were beginning to regroup. They coalesced around the same issue that had brought them together in the first place: relations with the Soviet Union. With increasing loudness, the neoconservatives excoriated the Nixon administration's policy of detente toward Moscow as the Cold War equivalent of appeasement. They denied, indeed ridiculed, the possibility of genuine change within the Soviet Union. The leaders of the world communist movement might engage in a Leninist zigzag, the neocons said, and they might accept an arms-control treaty as a device to lull the West into complacence. But their fundamental objective, world conquest, remained as always.

Theodore Draper, writing a series of articles in *Commentary*, decried detente as "an unmitigated snare and delusion." Draper alleged that detente consisted primarily of American concessions to Soviet demands, with the Russians granting nothing comparable in return. As such, it reiterated the capitulationist policies of Britain during the

---

[2] Peter Steinfels, *The Neoconservatives: The Men Who Are Changing America's Politics* (New York, 1979), 29–30.
[3] Ibid., 44–6.

1930s. "Appeasement was built into detente," Draper wrote, "whenever we adapted ourselves to them but they did not adapt themselves to us." In some respects, the new version was more insidious than that which had produced World War II, for this model worked "silently, automatically, almost unthinkingly." Moscow hardly had to lift a finger. "The cards were stacked in the Soviets' favor without any overt effort on their part." In the "humiliating climate" fostered by detente, Americans ran far greater risks than they knew. "We are faced strategically with a long-term Soviet imperial pressure, now gathering momentum and based, as Soviet spokesmen like to say, on a 'new relationship of forces.' If the Soviets can get the world to accept their version of this 'new relationship of forces,' the consequences will be cumulatively disastrous."[4]

Norman Podhoretz took an equally alarmist view of the situation. The *Commentary* editor described detente and its offshoots as a way of "making the world safe for communism." By 1976, Nixon was comfortably out of range of the guns of the right, but Nixon's accomplice Henry Kissinger remained in office and therefore fair game. Like Draper, Podhoretz hammered on the appeasement theme. Kissinger attempted to disguise soft policy in tough rhetoric, Podhoretz said. The secretary of state "often sounds like Churchill and just as often acts like Chamberlain." The charade fooled Western liberals, who were happy to be deceived, but it didn't fool the Soviets. "When the 'Chamberlain' side of Kissinger asks American critics of the SALT agreements, 'What in the name of God is strategic superiority? What do you do with it?' he might better address the question to the Russians, who seem to know very well both what it is and what you do with it, and who could easily enough give him an answer. What you do with it is intimidate other nuclear powers who might wish to stand in your way when you start to move ahead." And the Russians definitely were moving ahead, Podhoretz asserted, as their actions and those of their Cuban proxies in the civil war in Angola demonstrated.

In Podhoretz's opinion, detente betokened a resurgence of American isolationism. As such, it indicated a failure of American will, the will that had kept the peace in Europe for thirty years and broadly if not entirely prevented communist expansion. Because of Kissinger's large role in designing detente, Podhoretz could not help asking, "Is

---

[4] Theodore Draper, "Detente," *Commentary*, June 1974, and "Appeasement and Detente," *Commentary*, February 1976.

Kissinger then an isolationist?" Podhoretz answered his own question: "The suggestion seems absurd until one coldly considers the actual content of the policy toward Communist power with which he has been associated or over which he has presided for the past seven years. However one might choose to describe this policy, one would scarcely call it a species of anti-Communist interventionism." It was, rather, a policy of "phased American withdrawal" from anticommunist interventionism, occasioned by the trauma of Vietnam.

Podhoretz soon would essay a full-scale rehabilation of the American effort in Vietnam; for now, he merely refused to accept the interpretation of the war that inferred narrow constraints on the ability of the United States to affect the destiny of the planet. Vietnam, he said, demonstrated the limits not of American power but of American will. In the end, the issue of America's global future reduced to a matter of will. "Have we lost the will to defend the free world – yes, the free world – against the spread of Communism? Contemplating the spread of isolationist sentiment in the United States today, one might easily conclude that we have."

The liberal elites had already given up the struggle, Podhoretz claimed, and accepted what he called "Finlandization from within." The populace as a whole hadn't yet succumbed, but he didn't hide his pessimism. That America should have arrived at such a pass in 1976 was tragically ironic. "If it should turn out that the new isolationism has indeed triumphed among the people as completely as it has among the elites, then the United States will celebrate its two-hundredth birthday by betraying the heritage of liberty which has earned it the wonder and envy of the world from the moment of its founding to this, and by helping to make that world safe for the most determined and ferocious and barbarous enemies of liberty ever to have appeared on the earth."[5]

III

The neoconservatives enjoyed making mischief for Nixon and Kissinger, but they positively delighted in tormenting Jimmy Carter. Carter's cardinal sin consisted in attempting to move America away from the vindicationism that had produced Vietnam, toward an exemplar-

[5] Norman Podhoretz, "Making the World Safe for Communism," *Commentary*, April 1976.

ism that better reflected what he – and other chastened liberals – saw as America's true gifts and the contemporary configuration of the world. Nor were liberals the only ones who perceived a new configuration. Walt Rostow, the economic historian and Kennedy-Johnson hawk, described the erosion of the bipolar system which underlay the Cold War as a "diffusion of power." In 1945, Rostow argued, Washington and Moscow had truly bestridden the planet, but with the revival of Europe and Japan, the recovery of China from its forty-year revolution and civil war, and the emergence of the Third World from the ruins of the colonial empires, the United States and the Soviet Union now confronted multiple centers of power.[6]

American leaders during the 1970s recognized this transformation and adjusted their policies accordingly. Nixon and Kissinger acknowledged it by their opening to China. Carter carried the process further. In a widely noted 1977 speech at the University of Notre Dame, the Democratic president announced that his administration wouldn't allow "an inordinate fear of communism" to dictate its actions. "For too many years, we've been willing to adopt the flawed and erroneous principles and tactics of our adversaries, sometimes abandoning our own values for theirs. We've fought fire with fire, never thinking that fire is better quenched with water." This approach had failed, most disastrously in Vietnam. It must be changed. America must recapture the moral high ground that had long made it the beacon of hope to the world. Carter committed himself to reversing the arms race, to promoting human rights around the world, to ameliorating the disparity in wealth between the industrial nations and the less-developed. He didn't deny that military force might occasionally be necessary to defend American interests – no president in the twentieth century could do that. But he left not the slightest doubt that moral example, rather than military force, was his instrument of choice. "We cannot make this kind of policy by manipulation" – here he was referring as well to the dirty tricks of the C.I.A. that had recently come to light. "Our policy is rooted in our moral values. Our policy is designed to serve mankind. And it is a policy that I hope will make you proud to be Americans."[7]

---

[6] Walt W. Rostow, *The Diffusion of Power: An Essay in Recent History* (New York, 1972).

[7] *Public Papers of the Presidents: Jimmy Carter 1977* (Washington, 1977), 1:954–62.

It was a policy that made the neoconservatives ill. In neocon think-ing, any subject that distracted the American people from the over-riding struggle against communism threatened American security. (It also threatened the security of Israel – or so alleged novelist and critic Gore Vidal, whose bare-knuckled brawling with Podhoretz provided one of the more entertaining, if less edifying, aspects of the political debates of the period. Vidal detected a sinister thread linking the understandably pro-Israel position of *Commentary* and the campaign to revive the Cold War. Writing in the *Nation*, which blasted *Com-mentary* as regularly as he pounded Podhoretz, Vidal explained the connection as he read it after several seasons of success by the reviv-alists.

Over the years, Poddy [a typical Vidal snidery] has, like his employers, the AJC, moved from those liberal positions traditionally occupied by American Jews (and me) to the far right of American politics. The reason for that is simple. In order to get Treasury money for Israel (last year five billion dollars [an exaggeration]), pro-Israel lobbyists must see to it that America's "the Russians are coming" squads are in place so that they can continue to frighten the American people into spending enor-mous sums for "defense," which also means the support of Israel in its never-ending wars against just about everyone. To make sure that nearly two thirds of the federal budget goes to the Pentagon and Israel [a wild exaggeration], it is necessary for the pro-Israel lobbyists to make com-mon cause with our lunatic right. Hence the virulent propaganda.[8]

The corollary of the neoconservatives' focus on the Cold War was their resistance to the elevation of the Third World in American di-plomacy. In 1975, even before Carter entered office, Robert Tucker in *Commentary* attacked what he called the "new egalitarianism" in American foreign policy. Tucker denied the significance of the au courant issue of "interdependence," both as it was expressed by Third World leaders and as it was accepted by American liberals. The Third Worlders, Tucker said, in charging that the poverty of the developing nations resulted from exploitation by the developed coun-tries, intended to play on American guilt. That liberals bought the claim and, worse, talked of a global redistribution of wealth, indi-cated that the Third Worlders were succeeding. At the same time,

---

[8] Gore Vidal, "The Empire Lovers Strike Back," *Nation*, March 22, 1986.

Tucker noted hopefully the resistance of the American people to such nonsense. "If a large portion of Western liberal elites finds no more difficulty in distinguishing between the United States and Bangladesh than it does between California and Mississippi, it is safe to say that the general public continues to find a great deal of difficulty."[9]

Tucker expanded the argument of this article into a book entitled *The Inequality of Nations*. "The history of the international system is a history of inequality par excellence," Tucker wrote. The demands of the new egalitarians notwithstanding, he saw little reason to expect the situation to change. Inequality among nations reflected circumstances fundamentally different from those involved in inequality among individuals within a single nation, for while individuals could appeal to an authority higher than all, namely the national government, nations lived in anarchy relative to each other. Tucker noted that the countries demanding greater equality had not volunteered to divest themselves of any portion of their sovereignty, including sovereignty over resources, even though they had no compunctions about insisting that the industrialized divest *them*selves of sovereignty over some of *their* wealth. With most neoconservatives – logic-choppers all – Tucker could spot a double standard at ten thousand paces. He found one here, namely "the insistence of the developing countries that *every* state, by virtue of its sovereign equality, has exclusive control over its own resources and that *some* states have a duty to share their resources with others."

Tucker judged that the essential selfishness underlying the double standard was part of human nature, and that the condition of inequality wouldn't change until human nature changed. The resource-rich countries, notably the oil producers, owed their new influence not only to their possession of what the great powers wanted but to the forbearance of the latter in accepting the producers' conditions of sale. If the producers got too pushy, they might find themselves forcibly divested of their resources. In addition, the power of the producers – OPEC for example – rested to a considerable degree on cooperation among regimes with diverse interests. At the moment, they succeeded in suppressing this diversity, but they couldn't hold the line forever. Although the developing nations might call for a new egalitarianism in international relations, they would more likely get sim-

[9] Robert W. Tucker, "A New International Order?" *Commentary*, February 1975.

ply a new hierarchy. "That the new hierarchy will prove more benign than those of the past can be little more than a profession of hope," Tucker concluded.[10]

As if to ensure the fulfillment of his forecast, Tucker suggested that the petroleum-consuming states of the West needn't meekly accept the quadrupling of oil prices OPEC had recently engineered. In one of the more provocative pieces *Commentary* ran in 1975, Tucker wrote, "We know how the oil crisis would have been resolved until quite recently. Indeed, until quite recently it seems safe to say that it would never have arisen because of the prevailing expectation that it would have led to armed intervention." Outlining a possible military operation against producers in the Persian Gulf, Tucker suggested that a revival of gunboat diplomacy would have a sobering effect on the oil bandits and a salutary influence on the world at large.[11]

Tucker's suggestion provoked outrage in several quarters – which, needless to say, was half the idea. Earl Ravenal, writing in the *New Republic*, denounced demands for military intervention over oil as "proposals of international armed robbery." I. F. Stone in the *New York Review of Books* labeled such talk "criminal nonsense." The *New York Times* carried Anthony Lewis's column asserting that irresponsible calls for gunboat diplomacy simply fostered the "dangerous illusion" that Americans needn't come to terms with the end of the age of cheap energy.[12]

Undeterred, the neoconservatives and *Commentary* sustained the offensive. In the spring of 1975, Daniel Patrick Moynihan called for an end to coddling the Third World. Moynihan, just back at Harvard from two years as American ambassador to India, brought to his analysis a personal experience other neoconservatives usually lacked. The experience moderated the tone of his arguments, but only slightly. Moynihan complained that Third World countries like India had effected an ideological takeover of such international forums as the United Nations. Playing on American liberal guilt, they had put forth the notion that the poor and weak of the world had a valid

[10] Robert W. Tucker, *The Inequality of Nations* (New York, 1977), 3, 68, 201.
[11] Robert W. Tucker, "Oil: The Issue of American Intervention," *Commentary*, January 1975.
[12] Earl Ravenal, "The Oil Grab Scenario," *New Republic*, Jan. 18, 1975; I. F. Stone, "War for Oil?" *New York Review of Books*, Feb. 6, 1975; Anthony Lewis, *New York Times*, Dec. 29, 1974.

claim on the conscience and property of the rich and powerful – especially the United States. American officials had contributed to this development by accepting the Third World claims at face value. This situation must end. American representatives at the U.N. should go frankly into opposition against what he called "the politics of resentment and the economics of envy." They – and all who represented the United States to the world – should speak out forthrightly for the American way of life. "It is past time we ceased to apologize for an imperfect democracy. Find its equal." Americans shouldn't hesitate to defend capitalism, even that most vilified of capitalist inventions, the multinational corporation, which Moynihan described as "arguably the most creative international institution of the 20th century." Americans should reject demands for redistribution of the world's wealth and insist on growth as the answer to poverty. When the gloom-sayers held up Calcutta as an instance of the hopelessness of development under the present global regime, Americans should point to Singapore. When they cited Bangladesh, Americans should counter with Brazil and Nigeria and Taiwan. If they complained of the status quo as inherently repressive, Americans should point to human rights success stories like Costa Rica and Gambia and India. If they asserted that only developed nations benefited from the activities of international organizations, Americans should ask who gained most from the eradication of smallpox.

"Such a reversal of roles would be painful to American spokesmen," Moynihan said, "but it could be liberating also. It is time we grew out of our initial – not a little condescending – supersensitivity about the feelings of new nations. It is time we commenced to treat them as equals, a respect to which they are entitled." Moynihan mentioned meeting an Israeli socialist who remarked that countries that placed liberty before equality generally provided more of both than countries that reversed the order. "This is so," Moynihan agreed, "and being so, it is something to be shouted to the heavens in the years now upon us. *This is our case.* We *are* of the liberty party, and it might surprise us what energies might be released were we to unfurl those banners."[13]

---

[13] Daniel Patrick Moynihan, "The United States in Opposition," *Commentary,* March 1975.

IV

The neoconservative shouting grew louder than ever when revolutions swept radical regimes to power in Iran and Nicaragua. In a job-winning *Commentary* essay – largely on the strength of this article, Ronald Reagan would appoint her ambassador to the United Nations – Jeane Kirkpatrick lambasted the Carter administration in language seldom heard in America since the communist victory in China in 1949. Kirkpatrick catalogued the egregious sins of the Democrats: wrongheaded revision of the Panama Canal treaties, which would deliver the canal to "a swaggering Latin dictator of Castroite bent"; Third World follies that facilitated "a dramatic extension of Soviet influence in the Horn of Africa, Afghanistan, Southern Africa, and the Caribbean, matched by a declining American position in all these areas"; strategic sleepwalking that abetted "a dramatic Soviet military build-up, matched by the stagnation of American armed forces."

But the worst had occurred in Iran and Nicaragua. There governments supportive of American interests, if somewhat less than enamored of American liberal ideals, had fallen to uncooperative and often downright hostile forces. "In each country," Kirkpatrick charged, "the Carter administration not only failed to prevent the undesired outcome, it actively collaborated in the replacement of moderate autocrats friendly to American interests with less friendly autocrats of extremist persuasion." Nor did Kirkpatrick doubt that the new autocrats in Iran and Nicaragua would become more extremist and still less friendly in short order.

Kirkpatrick conceded the faults of the Shah in Iran and Somoza in Nicaragua. Each had ruled with heavy hand, employing martial law and police repression to quell certain forms of dissent. Each created "what the American press termed 'private armies.'" (Kirkpatrick didn't supply a more appropriate term.) But each tolerated limited opposition, including opposition newspapers and political parties. "In short, both Somoza and the Shah were, in central ways, traditional rulers of semi-traditional societies." Each sought to modernize his country, although by means that did not endanger his personal political power.

As for their relations with the superpowers, both the Shah and Somoza "were not only anti-Communist, they were positively friendly to the U.S." They sent their sons to America for education and voted with the United States at the United Nations. Although she gave no examples, Kirkpatrick contended that they regularly supported American interests and positions "even when these entailed personal and political cost." (Kirkpatrick neglected to note that the Shah had been one of the leading price-hawks in OPEC, and that the increases he had persuaded his colleagues to demand had cost Americans hundreds of billions of dollars.) Remarking a circumstance doubtless more significant to a Georgetown University professor than to observers from beyond the Washington beltway, she added, "The embassies of both governments were active in Washington social life, and were frequented by powerful Americans who occupied major roles in this nation's diplomatic, military, and political life." As individuals, the Shah and Somoza "were both welcome in Washington, and had many American friends."

But when the Shah and Somoza ran into trouble, the Carter administration abandoned them, and the Iranian and Nicaraguan people as well, along with American interests. Perceiving "a suggestive similarity to our behavior in China before the fall of Chiang Kai-shek, in Cuba before the triumph of Castro, in certain crucial periods of the Vietnamese war, and, more recently, in Angola," Kirkpatrick asserted that last-minute American efforts to impose liberalizing reforms on Iran and Nicaragua, beset as those countries were by violent internal opposition, "not only failed, but actually assisted the coming to power of new regimes in which ordinary people enjoy fewer freedoms and less personal security than under the previous autocracy – regimes, moreover, hostile to American interests and policies."

Kirkpatrick predicted that such outcomes would recur in American foreign policy until American leaders accepted a fundamental historical truth: that democracy is a rare beast whose progenitors are more often found on the political right than on the left. "Although there is no instance of a revolutionary 'socialist' or Communist society being democratized, right-wing autocracies do sometimes evolve into democracies – given time, propitious economic, social, and political circumstances, talented leaders, and a strong indigenous demand for representative government." Kirkpatrick decried a double standard in the Carter administration's treatment of non-democratic governments around the world. The administration, with its stress on "interdependence" and similar fashionable causes, had demonstrated a disturbing inclination to participate actively in the toppling of non-communist autocracies, while remaining passive in the face of the expansion of far more repressive communist regimes. Although Kirkpatrick was realistic enough (neoconservatives prided themselves on realism) not to expect complete consistency from any government, she thought the Democrats not merely hypocritical but foolishly so. "What makes the inconsistencies of the Carter administration noteworthy are, first, the administration's moralism – which renders it especially vulnerable to charges of hypocrisy; and, second, the administration's predilection for policies that violate the strategic and economic interests of the United States. The administration's conception of national interest borders on doublethink: it finds friendly powers to be guilty representatives of the status quo and views the triumph of unfriendly groups as beneficial to America's 'true interests.' "

The American government must learn to tell friends from enemies, succoring the former and afflicting the latter. It must abandon its current posture of "continuous self-abasement and apology vis-à-vis the Third World." It must be prepared to use force where necessary to secure American interests, and it must always speak out for American ideals. Kirkpatrick denied a disjunction between American interests and ideals. "Liberal idealism need not be identical with masochism, and need not be incompatible with the defense of freedom and the national interest."[14]

V

The animus of the neoconservatives against what they judged the mishandling of American foreign policy spawned a variety of political committees and other activist organizations. The noisiest was the Committee on the Present Danger, a collection of anti-detentists that included Paul Nitze and Podhoretz and dedicated itself to rekindling the Cold War. From the neoconservative perspective, of course, only American participation required rekindling, for the Soviets had never allowed the struggle to die out.

Podhoretz made precisely this point in a book adapted from a *Commentary* article, both bearing the title *The Present Danger*. Podhoretz wrote in 1980, following the Russian invasion of Afghanistan and preceding the American presidential election. Each event shaped the argument. Podhoretz condemned those commentators on international affairs who refused to accept the recent Soviet advance in

[14] Jeane J. Kirkpatrick, "Dictatorships and Double Standards," *Commentary*, November 1979.

Central Asia for what he thought it plainly was, namely a Russian reversion to the form that in 1956 produced the rape of Hungary and in 1968 the crushing of Czechoslovakia. More fundamentally, the attack on Afghanistan signaled that the communist dream of world conquest continued to animate the Kremlin's actions. If Americans read the lesson correctly and reawakened to the global duties they had rightly assumed during the early Cold War, the Afghans' travail might yield some good. But considering the capacity of liberals in the United States for self-deception, one couldn't take even such obvious lessons for granted.

In Podhoretz's thinking, only the first phase of the Cold War had shown America at the country's worthiest. The formulation of the policy of containment by George Kennan – later an apostate from his own doctrine, Podhoretz noted – and its implementation in Europe via the Marshall plan and NATO, and in Asia during the Korean war, demonstrated the willingness of Americans to accept the historic role fate had decreed for them. Yet within a short time the nation's confidence began to slip. Although the Republicans who took office in 1953 promised a dynamic policy of liberating territories fallen to communism, Eisenhower and his advisers soon displayed an aversion to any action carrying the risk of confrontation with Moscow. The Soviet brutalization of Hungary demonstrated the toothless character of the administration's pledges.

For a time during the 1960s, the commitment to Vietnam seemed an indication of renewed resolve. The Johnson-Nixon decision to accept less than victory, though, indicated that the overall trend continued. Nixon attempted to cover the loss of nerve by the so-called Nixon doctrine of reliance on proxies in the Third World and by detente in dealings with the Soviet Union. Podhoretz credited Nixon and Kissinger with diplomatic finesse, but their subtlety couldn't disguise the fundamental fact that containment had now given way to what Podhoretz labeled "strategic retreat." The accompanying cutbacks in defense spending amounted to "unilateral disarmament." Moreover, by failing to take military action against the oil extortionists in 1973 and after, Nixon and Kissinger sent the message that aggression against America entailed no consequences.

Under Carter, the alarming trend turned still more sharply downward. The Carter administration, by its passivity in the face of the 1979 storming of the American embassy in Teheran and the kidnapping of the American diplomats there, confirmed the impression that anti-American aggression was easy and cost-free. Why, Podhoretz asked, did the Iranians not assault the Soviet embassy? "Might it have something to do with a fear of Soviet retaliation as against the expectation that the United States would go to any length to avoid the use of force?" Podhoretz deemed laughable the liberals' notion that Afghanistan would become Moscow's Vietnam. A Vietnam, in the sense Americans used the term, required an independent public opinion, capable of criticizing the government's conduct of the war, as well as an outside supplier of arms to the insurgents.

The announcement of the Carter doctrine, by which the president pledged to defend the Persian Gulf against Soviet aggression, had initially hinted at an end to the decline of American power. "If the President could be believed, the period of strategic retreat was over and a new period of containment had begun." Unfortunately, Podhoretz said, evidence since indicated an election-year conversion of convenience rather than a genuine change of heart. "Yet even if such unkind speculations are dismissed and even if the President is given the benefit of every doubt, a far more ominous question arises. *Is it too late?*" For some time, groups like the Committee on the Present Danger had warned that the Soviets' momentum in building weapons would propel their country past the United States, creating a potentially decisive nuclear advantage for Moscow – a "window of vulnerability." Early projections had identified the year of maximum danger as 1984, but recent events suggested that the Russians' calendar read differently. "The invasion of Afghanistan may mean that the Soviets think the window is open *now*."

What did this portend for the United States? A disarming first strike by Soviet missiles? Probably not. Nuclear blackmail? Perhaps, although a better description would be what Podhoretz again called "the Finlandization of America." Liberals and other blinkered persons might dismiss this possibility, arguing that the situation confronting Americans paralleled in no significant way that of the Finns, who faced the credible threat of absorption into their giant neighbor. While Podhoretz granted part of the objection, he contended that the concept still had meaning for America. "Politicians and pundits would appear to celebrate the happy arrival of a new era of 'peace' and 'friendship' and 'cooperation' between the Soviet Union and the United States. Dissenters from this cheerful view would be castigated as warmongers and ways would be found to silence questions and criticisms, which could, after all, only result in making things worse for everyone."

At the root of America's problem, Podhoretz said, was what he alternately called "the new isolationism" and "the culture of appeasement." Among a people lately traumatized by Vietnam, the new isolationism manifested itself as "a revulsion against the entire policy of containment." The culture of appeasement was evident in recent echoes of the 1930s, such as a statement by Senator Edward Kennedy that "we should not be moving toward the brink of sending another generation of the young to die for the failures of the old."

Compounding the danger was the failure of American leaders to declare unmistakably what they stood for, and what they stood against. Podhoretz found it disturbingly revealing that the term "communism" had, as he put the matter, "quietly disappeared from the discussion of the Soviet-American conflict." One would think from reading liberal papers and magazines that the Soviet Union was a nation like any other and that the United States could deal with Moscow much as with London or Paris or Tokyo. Such a view could lead only to disaster. "The Soviet Union is not a nation like any other. It is a revolutionary state, exactly as Hitler's Germany was, in the sense that it wishes to create a new international order in which it would be the dominant power and whose character would be determined by its national wishes and ideological dictates."

Only by holding this fact uppermost in mind could Americans hope to survive the current crisis – only by this and by rededicating themselves to the struggle George Kennan had identified in 1947 when he described the "implacable challenge" communism posed to the Free World. "In 1947 these words pointed the way to the containment of Soviet expansionism," Podhoretz concluded. "Today, if we but consent, they can energize our resistance to Finlandization and our determination to marshal the power we will need 'to assure the survival and the success of liberty' in the new and infinitely more dangerous age ahead."[15]

VI

In calling for a revival of Cold War vindicationism, Podhoretz and the neoconservatives recognized their need to shake the country out of the exemplarist mood into which it had fallen after Vietnam, and

[15] Norman Podhoretz, *The Present Danger: Do We Have the Will to Reverse the Decline of American Power?* (New York, 1980), 33, 40–9, 53–60, 67, 79, 85, 91, 101.

which the Carter administration had openly embraced. Hence their incessant assaults on Carter, even after the Democratic president, by his Persian Gulf speech, indicated at least a partial reversal of course, and even after he left office. And hence their hammering on the twin themes of isolationism and appeasement.

Charles Krauthammer gave several good blows during the early Ronald Reagan years. Krauthammer, a psychiatrist-turned-political-philosopher whose regular and regularly conservative contributions to the *New Republic* demonstrated the increasingly rightist foreign-policy bent of Walter Lippmann's old journal, offered a guide to the "new isolationism." He identified two predominant classes. "Left isolationism" was the ideology of the Democratic party. Initially confined to the McGovernite fringe, left isolationism had since captured the party's core constituencies. Krauthammer detected what he considered a paradox in left isolationism: It was internationalist but not interventionist. Put otherwise, it set the high standards of democracy as goals the world should strive for, but it refused to adopt measures to require the world to live up.

Put still otherwise, although Krauthammer didn't (if he had, it wouldn't have seemed so paradoxical), left isolationism was essentially the traditional philosophy of American exemplarists. Krauthammer singled out Senator Gary Hart as a spokesman of left isolationism. "American restraint on intervention, military action, and covert operations does not mean American indifference," Krauthammer quoted Hart as saying. "We care about human rights and democratic values and economic development." But the United States could not guarantee these good things around the world, and it ought not try.

Krauthammer disagreed. He discounted non-interventionism, however well-intentioned, as ineffective. He rejected a criticism leveled by Daniel Patrick Moynihan (speaking as an opposition Democrat rather than a neoconservative) against the recent American invasion of Grenada; Moynihan had said, in effect, that democracy never arrived at the point of a bayonet. Krauthammer rejoined, "That idea will come as a surprise to Germans and Japanese." Krauthammer taxed the Democrats for concealing their isolationism behind a smokescreen of multilateralism. To the Democrats' citing of Truman's cooperation with the United Nations regarding Korea as precedent for their insistence on the support of the international community in foreign-policy initiatives, Krauthammer responded that multilateralism meant something different in Truman's time from what it meant at present. "For the strong, multilateralism is a cover for unilateralism. For the rest it is a cover for inaction. Today the United States is part of the rest."

Krauthammer's second kind of isolationism was, predictably, "right isolationism." The right isolationists formed a motley crew, including Henry Kissinger, who had advocated a reduction in American forces in Europe; Irving Kristol, who argued for a complete pullout from that continent; Democrat Sam Nunn, who supported Kissinger from the chair of the Senate armed services committee; and Defense Secretary Caspar Weinberger, who called for a major increase in America's military power but could envision few circumstances requiring the use of that power. Krauthammer held that while the isolationists of the left cloaked their timidity with internationalist multilateralism, the isolationists of the right wrapped themselves in the mantle of nationalist unilateralism. They allowed, theoretically, American intervention overseas, but practically they defined American interests so narrowly and insisted on such unfettered freedom of action as to render unilateralism the equivalent of noninterventionism.

Krauthammer judged right isolationism more defensible logically than left isolationism. Where the latter failed on its own terms, effectively ruling out the measures necessary to achieve the objectives it espoused, the former dispensed with the noble objectives altogether. The right isolationists, by grounding their approach to international affairs solely in what served the United States, didn't need to apologize for refraining from action; they simply claimed that such action didn't serve the national interest and left the matter there.

But internal coherence didn't preserve right isolationism from Krauthammer's disdain. He judged it nearly as misguided and dangerous as the isolationism of the left. Krauthammer didn't think a reduction of the American presence in Germany or East Asia would start an irrevocable unraveling of world peace. "Are American troops in Korea and Berlin there to defend American security?" he asked. "It is not so easy a case to make," he answered. American security, however, wasn't the principal issue. The issue was the welfare of the world. Adopting an exaggeratedly vindicationist approach, Krauthammer contended that the United States must impose its will and values on the rest of humanity, not so much for the good of the United States as for the good of humanity. Internationalists had long contended that freedom was indivisible, that damage done democracy in Europe or Asia would ultimately injure America. Krauthammer dismissed this "woolly Wilsonian claim" as "empirically false and dangerous." Eastern Europe, China, and much of Southeast Asia had been lost to tyranny, but the United States survived. Freedom might fail in Central America and Afghanistan without gravely jeopardizing the American way of life.

The argument for interventionism, Krauthammer said, was properly made in terms broader than what benefited the United States. "A new Wilsonianism must argue not that freedom is indivisible, but that it is valuable. A sustained internationalism rests on a large vision of America, an America that stands for an idea." It was this idea, the idea of democracy and individual liberty, and not merely American self-interest, that American policy must pursue. To be sure, a world of free and democratic states would be a world conducive to American security. Yet achieving such a world might well cost more than the result returned, and, on grounds of narrow self-interest, Americans might reasonably forgo the effort and disengage from the international contest.

Americans must resist this temptation. The idea America uniquely embodied had incalculable value for the world. No other country could take America's place. "To disengage in the service of a narrow nationalism is a fine foreign policy for a minor regional power, which the United States once was and which, say, Canada or Sweden are now. For America today it is a betrayal of its idea of itself."[16]

VII

To the degree isolationism took hold in America during the post-Vietnam era – a degree the neoconservatives overstated – its appeal lay less in the contention that America lacked the *right* to act for democracy abroad than in the claim that it lacked the *ability*. The radical revisionist view that American foreign policy was little more than the expression of the class interests of the American elite always remained a minority position. And even fewer people bought the charges of intentional American genocide in Vietnam that mobilized the most militant of the antiwar cadres. Plenty of people, on the other

---

[16] Charles Krauthammer, "The New Isolationism," *New Republic*, March 4, 1985.

hand, saw Vietnam as a massive snafu, as a story not of sordid conspiracy but of appalling incompetence.

Yet whether dripping blood or merely mummified in red tape, the ghost of Vietnam stalked the landscape of American foreign relations long after the American pullout. Intuitively or otherwise, the neoconservatives and their allies recognized that reviving American vindicationism required putting that ghost to rest. Various authors – academics, professional soldiers, journalists – contributed to the project during the late 1970s and early 1980s. The most energetic statement of the neoconservative position emanated, not surprisingly, from the typewriter of Norman Podhoretz.

During the years of the war itself, Podhoretz, like a number of other neoconservatives-to-be, had placed himself among the dissenters. In 1962, he published in *Commentary* a gloomy article by Hans Morgenthau predicting that if the United States got deeply involved in the conflict in Vietnam, it would win only with great difficulty and would experience serious division at home. During the following years, Podhoretz ran other pieces questioning what seemed an outsized commitment to a cause not vital to American security.[17]

Yet Podhoretz's opposition to the war was tactical rather than ideological. He never wrestled with the morality of the conflict, or if he did, he evinced few signs of the struggle. Although the war was a mistake, he believed, it was not a sin. The government of South Vietnam had a right to request American aid to rebuff communist aggression, and the United States had a right to send such aid, including troops, planes, and anything else suited to the task. America's judgment in the matter proved faulty, but its motives were above reproach.

If a single sentiment could be said to have characterized American opinion regarding the war during the last several years of American participation, Podhoretz's moderate position captured it as well as any. Yet so polarized had the politics of the war grown by the time of the 1973 Paris accords, and so overheated the debate the war aroused, that moderate voices became nearly impossible to hear. Moderation remained a scarce quantity through the rest of the 1970s. Defenders of the war used the fall of Saigon, the flight of the boat people, and the revelations of the Khmer Rouge massacres in Cam-

---

[17] Hans J. Morgenthau, "Vietnam – Another Korea?" *Commentary*, May 1962.

bodia as occasions for finger-pointing. Opponents of the war pointed back, contending that American intervention had prolonged and deepened the agony of Vietnam and spread it across Indochina.

Podhoretz revealed the country's continued sensitivity on the Vietnam issue by sparking a fresh debate with a 1982 book that delivered an essentially unremarkable message, albeit in combative language. Podhoretz sometimes gave the impression that he couldn't order dinner without starting a fight; *Why We Were in Vietnam* showed him at his polemical best. He declared, for example, regarding the coherence of world communism at the time of Mao Zedong's victory in China: "In subsequent years much ridicule came to be heaped upon the idea of an international Communist movement or a monolithic Communist conspiracy, but there was nothing ridiculous or even overstated about this idea in 1949." This remark, which said two quite different things, typified much of Podheretz's argument. Indeed there was nothing ridiculous about the notion of an international communist movement in 1949: Despite Tito's defection the year before, the various parties subscribing to the doctrines of Marx and Lenin possessed sufficient common interests and aims to be considered a movement. But to call the movement a monolithic conspiracy was another matter, and such a label did in fact overstate the situation. Alliances among the communist powers, no less and perhaps more than those among the democracies, were marriages of convenience, as subsequent events demonstrated.

Podhoretz continued in the same vein when he said, "It was obvious, therefore, that the conquest of China represented a major victory for the Soviet Union and an enormous extension of its power. It was equally obvious that this victory would inspire and energize other Communist insurgencies throughout Asia." Again half the statement, in this case the second half, was indisputable. The first half was considerably less so, as became apparent within less than a decade when China began challenging Russia for leadership of the world socialist movement, producing, initially, raucous doctrinal rows and, subsequently, actual shooting matches across the Soviet-Chinese border.

But Podhoretz's central contentions didn't stand or fall on such plays to the gallery. He aimed to demonstrate how thoroughly the war in Vietnam was America's war – not Johnson's war, nor Nixon's, but a war designed and desired by the country as a whole. The task wasn't especially difficult, because the charge was true. Podhoretz took particular pleasure in hanging major responsibility for American involvement on John Kennedy, in the process refuting efforts by keepers of the flame to gloss over their hero's role in the matter. There was no doubt, Podhoretz accurately wrote, "that Kennedy and his people took it as virtually self-evident that the lesson of Munich was as applicable to the war in Vietnam as it had been to the war in Korea." The circumstances differed, but not the basic issue. "The war in Vietnam was a variant, or a mutation, of the pattern of totalitarian aggression, and it called under the tutelage of Munich for the same response as its more conventional predecessor in Korea."

This portion of Podhoretz's argument might have seemed a bit curious, since to all appearances he was criticizing the Democrats for holding views he shared. While in the neighborhood, he launched ad hominem assaults on Kennedy's closest assistants. He described McGeorge Bundy as a man "whose arrogance had been legendary at Harvard" – arrogance "so unshakable that it would survive the debacle of his ideas about Vietnam to shape policies on race relations in his future career as president of the Ford Foundation which would be equally disrespectful of local conditions and difficulties." Regarding Bundy's successor, Podhoretz wrote, "If Bundy's arrogance was an attribute of his personality, Walt W. Rostow's was mainly located in his intellect." Podhoretz's Rostow "was confident that he knew everything," from how to fight and win a guerrilla war to the laws of economic development, "about which he had written a famous book entitled *The Stages of Economic Growth* in whose subtitle, *A Non-Communist Manifesto*, he implicitly claimed to be superseding Marx." The assault continued: "Then there was Robert McNamara, the Secretary of Defense, whose arrogance was a function of his belief that he could devise a system for dealing efficiently and successfully with any enterprise, whether an automobile company (he had been president of Ford in the days when Detroit was still a symbol of the awesome brilliance of American industry), a government bureau (he became instantly famous in the Kennedy Administration for the way he was bringing the Pentagon under control), or a guerrilla war."

And these were the Democratic hawks, the relative good guys. The administration's doves "(including those who when the going got rough in the late sixties would convert to dovishness or claim a dovish past for themselves) were not noticeably less arrogant." John Kenneth Galbraith "was not famous for being humble." George Ball wasn't either. Likewise Arthur Schlesinger and Richard Goodwin, "neither of whom had much influence over policy but both of whom would later exert a great deal of influence in the public debates over Vietnam."

This last comment indicated Podhoretz's purpose in his otherwise irrelevant character assassinations: He didn't intend to let the Kennedyites duck the blame for the fiasco the war became. "The United States, under Kennedy," he wrote, "for all practical purposes and in all but name, went to war in Vietnam." Podhoretz didn't take issue with Kennedy's decision. "To have stayed out obviously would have meant conceding South Vietnam to the Communists, and it would obviously have been a defeat for the United States." But the venture went bad, and Podhoretz wanted to ensure fair apportionment of responsibility. To the just-previous statement, he added that a defeat in 1963 would have been "a lesser defeat than we eventually suffered," and he described what was in some ways the most important contribution of the Kennedy administration to the Vietnam debacle, the overthrow and murder of Ngo Dinh Diem, as a horrible mistake fraught with "unintended consequences: less rather than more political stability in South Vietnam, and more rather than less American responsibility for a war that Kennedy and everyone around him had always made a point of saying was 'their war and not ours to win or lose.' "

Podhoretz contributed nothing original to the debate over whether the war was winnable. For his factual analysis of the fighting, as well as for evidence to rebut charges by the more extreme opponents of the war regarding alleged American atrocities and genocide, he relied on the work of others, particularly Guenter Lewy. Podhoretz concentrated on questions of motive. Why did the United States go into Vietnam? Because, he said, not going in would have handed all of Vietnam over to the tyranny Ho Chi Minh had already imposed on the North. Why did the United States stay in? For the same reason, and to demonstrate American faithfulness in honoring commitments.

But was the war winnable? To put the matter another way: Was the decision to intervene in Vietnam a prudent one? Podhoretz said no, at least given the political and strategic constraints under which American leaders operated. Yet Podhoretz was less interested in refighting the war in Vietnam than in rehabilitating containment as the centerpiece of American foreign policy. If American intervention had been merely imprudent, as Podhoretz held, then Vietnam might be shrugged off as a simple mistake in judgment. Proponents of containment would have to be more careful in the future, but they needn't reexamine their basic premises. If, on the other hand, intervention had been immoral, the result of some fundamental flaw in the character of Americans as individuals or a people, then containment as a whole came into question.

Podhoretz roundly denounced those who attacked the war as immoral, as, for instance, a manifestation of an overweening American will to power. He charged the antiwar movement with McCarthyism of the left – an overheated allegation, but one not entirely unfounded – while himself loosely branding most opponents of the war as "anti-American." Explaining, he wrote, "By anti-Americanism I mean the idea that the United States was a force for evil in Vietnam." This unfair definition included far too many thoughtful and patriotic critics of the war – one didn't have to be anti-American to judge America's actions in Vietnam, even if well-intended, objectively (or perhaps in a Niebuhrian-tragic sense) evil. Podhoretz blasted easy targets like Bertrand Russell and Noam Chomsky, but didn't pay sufficiently serious attention to the far more numerous, if less vocal, moderate dissenters. He defended the morality of America's conduct of the war on the logically shaky grounds that what followed the communist victory was worse. Even then he stretched to make his case, contending, for example, that the indisputable trauma of the boat people constituted "a new form of the Communist bloodbath."

Podhoretz concluded on a conveniently contemporary note. He juxtaposed two comments regarding Vietnam, the first by then-president Carter, the second by then-candidate Reagan. Carter described the intervention in Vietnam as the outgrowth of the "intellectual and moral poverty" of American foreign policy; Reagan called it a "noble cause." History, Podhoretz declared, had proved Reagan right and Carter wrong. The American effort in Vietnam, though ultimately a failure, was on the whole "an act of imprudent idealism" whose moral soundness had been "overwhelmingly vindicated by the hideous consequences of our defeat."[18]

VIII

Ronald Reagan's 1980 election, as it related to foreign affairs, augured a triumph of neoconservative vindicationism. Reagan fully en-

---

[18] Norman Podhoretz, *Why We Were in Vietnam* (New York, 1982, 1983), 21–2, 48, 59–63, 103, 199, 210.

dorsed the Present Dangerist platform of a new Cold War (although he joined Podhoretz, Kirkpatrick, and the others in believing that the old one had never ended). He called for a major military buildup to close the perceived window of U.S. nuclear vulnerability, and he authorized efforts to destabilize pro-Moscow regimes wherever possible. America must stand tall, he argued, not merely to raise the beacon of liberty but to smite liberty's foes.

Americans as a group liked Reagan; his election and reelection demonstrated that. But many, even many of those who voted for him, had doubts about certain of his policies. A majority of the country, for example, refused to endorse the administration's vendetta against the Nicaraguan Sandinistas. A majority looked askance at sending American marines to Lebanon. Popular feeling for patrolling the Persian Gulf during the Iran-Iraq war never approached the temperature of the waters the warships plied.

In one area, American misgivings turned to outright fear. The Republican military expansion – combined with reports that the Pentagon considered nuclear war winnable, with studies describing a life-extinguishing "nuclear winter" that a war between the superpowers might produce, and with some tasteless attempted humor by the president about bombing Moscow – raised popular distress regarding nuclear weapons to levels not seen since the Cuban missile crisis. Antinuclear activists circulated petitions condemning the arms race; communities declared themselves nuclear-free zones; church leaders and other humanitarians, not excluding politicians, demanded a moratorium on assorted combinations of testing, construction, and deployment of weapons. One of the principal television networks, ABC, broadcast a chilling enactment of a nuclear war entitled *The Day After*, and in the process provoked a storm of protest not unlike that which had greeted Herman Kahn's *On Thermonuclear War*.

No published work captured the mood of fear and foreboding better than Jonathan Schell's 1982 *The Fate of the Earth*. Originally serialized in the *New Yorker*, Schell's book examined the nuclear issue from nearly all conceivable angles. He traced the development of the physics that made nuclear weapons possible; he identified the components necessary to produce the weapons; he explained the atomic and sub-atomic reactions involved in the detonation process.

Schell's most affecting passage described the probable results of a nuclear explosion over New York City:

Burst some eighty-five hundred feet above the Empire State Building, a one-megaton bomb would gut or flatten almost every building between Battery Park and 125th Street, or within a radius of four and four-tenths miles, or in an area of sixty-one square miles, and would heavily damage buildings between the northern tip of Staten Island and the George Washington Bridge, or within a radius of about eight miles, or in an area of about two hundred square miles. . . . .

The physical collapse of the city would certainly kill millions of people. The streets of New York are narrow ravines running between the high walls of the city's buildings. In a nuclear attack, the walls would fall and the ravines would fill up. The people in the buildings would fall to the street with the debris of the buildings, and the people in the street would be crushed by this avalanche of people and buildings. . . .

If it were possible (as it would not be) for someone to stand at Fifth Avenue and Seventy-second Street (about two miles from ground zero) without being instantly killed, he would see the following sequence of events. A dazzling white light from the fireball would illuminate the scene, continuing for perhaps thirty seconds. Simultaneously, searing heat would ignite everything flammable and start to melt windows, cars, buses, lampposts, and everything else made of metal or glass. People in the street would immediately catch fire, and would shortly be reduced to heavily charred corpses. About five seconds after the light appeared, the blast wave would strike, laden with the debris of a now nonexistent midtown. . . .

Soon huge, thick clouds of dust and smoke would envelop the scene, and as the mushroom cloud rushed overhead (it would have a diameter of about twelve miles) the light from the sun would be blotted out, and day would turn to night. . . . As at Hiroshima, a whirlwind might be produced, which would sweep through the ruins, and radioactive rain, generated under the meteorological conditions created by the blast, might fall. Before long, the individual fires would coalesce into a mass fire, which, depending largely on the winds, would become either a conflagration or a firestorm. In a conflagration, prevailing winds spread a wall of fire as far as there is any combustible material to sustain it; in a firestorm, a vertical updraft caused by the fire itself sucks the surrounding air in toward a central point, and the fires therefore converge in a single fire of extreme heat. . . .

In this vast theatre of physical effects, all the scenes of agony and death that took place at Hiroshima would again take place, but now involving millions of people rather than hundreds of thousands.

As this passage demonstrated, Schell's account achieved its impact from his clinical detachment, his piling of detail upon detail, to the

point of defining the difference between a conflagration and a firestorm, a matter most authors would have judged academic at this
point in the destruction of Manhattan.

Schell grew less detached, and considerably less effective, in pre-
scribing a way out of the nuclear dilemma. He rejected the doctrine
of nuclear deterrence, contending that retaliation was even more suicidal than a first strike, as striker and retaliator would realize in a
genuine crisis. "Once the action begins," he asserted, "the whole
doctrine is self-cancelling." (This was about the only point on which
he agreed with the neoconservatives, whose argument of a window
of nuclear vulnerability was predicated on just such a realization in
American leaders following a Soviet first strike: that retaliation would
trigger a second strike that would wipe out those Americans who had
survived the first.)

The solution? Schell specified two ultimate requirements for human survival: "global disarmament, both nuclear and conventional,
and the invention of political means by which the world can peace-
fully settle the issues that throughout history it has settled by war."
As an immediate minimum, he advocated a freeze on the deployment
of new nuclear weapons, agreed to both by the nuclear powers and
by those countries on the verge of going nuclear. Better would be a
reduction in superpower arsenals, perhaps by half. Farther down the
future, all inhabitants of the planet must come to recognize their
connectedness to each other and to generations dead and unborn.
Schell remarked that Auden had said humans must love one another
or die; he amended this to: "Let us love one another – in the present
and across the divides of death and birth." Christ had said he came
not to judge the world but to save it. "Let us, also, not judge the
world but save the world."[19]

IX

Not unexpectedly, the neoconservatives lambasted Schell and the
other freezeniks and disarmers as muddleheaded utopians. In *Commentary*, Charles Krauthammer denounced Schell's book as unreal-
istic and uninformed. "It willfully ignores history," Krauthammer
complained. "Deterrence has a track record. For the entire postwar
period it has maintained the peace between the superpowers, pre-

---

[19] Jonathan Schell, *The Fate of the Earth* (New York, 1982), 47–49, 202, 227, 230.

venting not only nuclear war but conventional war as well. Under the logic of deterrence, proxy and brushfire wars are permitted, but not wars between the major powers. As a result, Europe, the central confrontation line between the two superpowers, has enjoyed its longest period of uninterrupted peace in a century." The United States and the Soviet Union, sworn ideological foes locked in a global struggle as profound as any in history, had "not exchanged so much as small-arms fire for a generation."[20]

Krauthammer, like most defenders of deterrence, satisfied himself with this post-hoc-ergo-propter-hoc treatment of the forty years of the nuclear era in superpower relations. He didn't prove, because he couldn't prove, that the nuclear threat had prevented a third world war. He didn't demonstrate that either side would have had sufficient incentive to take the other on directly in the absence of nuclear weapons. Europe had avoided major wars for a hundred years before 1914; perhaps peace was the norm and war the exception – just the opposite of what the deterrence devotees held. An argument could be made, and was made repeatedly by advocates of greater spending on NATO conventional forces, that nuclear weapons didn't decrease, but rather increased, the risk of war in Europe by convincing the members of the Atlantic alliance that they could secure their borders on the nuclear cheap. As for global security, the tens of millions killed, wounded, or rendered homeless in Korea, Vietnam, Cambodia, Laos, Afghanistan, Iran, Iraq, and numerous other countries doubtless took scant solace from the fact that their wars did not rate the label "world."

Krauthammer stood on solid ground, though, in criticizing Schell for unhelpfulness in getting from the dire present to the dreamed-of future. "He does not explain how we are to bring about a lion-and-lamb scenario which even Isaiah had the audacity only to predict and not to mandate," Krauthammer wrote. Schell urged a freeze by all actual and potential possessors of nuclear weapons, but didn't say how the Russians, French, and Chinese, not to mention the Israelis and South Africans, might be persuaded to accept the idea. Schell advocated the discovery of a peaceful method of solving international disputes; he might as well have recommended finding a cure for cancer.

Krauthammer had hardly more patience with those who agitated for a simple freeze in deployment of nuclear weapons. These people,

[20] Charles Krauthammer, "On Nuclear Morality," *Commentary*, October 1983.

he alleged, pandered to fear without proposing a realistic means of dealing with the situation engendering the fear. "The freeze crusade has enlisted hundreds of thousands of Americans by showing what happens if the sword of Damocles ever drops." Krauthammer conceded that fear wasn't an entirely unreasonable response to present circumstances, but he contended that the freezers dealt only selectively with the fear issue. Few of them argued for reducing nuclear forces below "sufficiency" – the minimal level required to retaliate against a first strike – for the good reason that anything less would probably destabilize the international system. Yet sufficiency levels left Americans effectively as threatened as before. "Insofar as people support the freeze because they can't stand the thought of being a target for Soviet missiles, they have joined the wrong movement. The freeze offers no solution to that problem."

"The freeze is not a plan," Krauthammer concluded. "It is a sentiment." Though the freeze proposal reflected the laudable desire of millions of Americans to reduce the danger of nuclear war, it promised little that might accomplish that goal. Indeed, its sloganeering distracted the country from the hard thinking nuclear questions demanded. "The freeze continually fails on its own terms. It seeks safety, but would jeopardize deterrence; it seeks quick action, but would delay arms control; it seeks real reductions, but removes any leverage we might have to bring them about."[21]

Krauthammer likewise attacked a proposal recently forwarded by four individuals who brought to the nuclear debate credentials considerably more impressive than most freeze advocates. During the spring of 1982, George Kennan joined with McGeorge Bundy, Robert McNamara, and former arms negotiator Gerard Smith in publishing an article in *Foreign Affairs* advocating an American commitment to no-first-use of nuclear weapons. Citing recent troubles within the Atlantic alliance, including controversies over intermediate-range nuclear missiles and the neutron bomb, Kennan and the others saw these as symptomatic of a more fundamental problem. "They are rooted in the fact that the evolution of essentially equivalent and enormously excessive nuclear weapons systems both in the Soviet Union and in the Atlantic Alliance has aroused new concern about the dangers of all forms of nuclear war. The profusion of these systems, on both sides, has made it more difficult than ever to construct rational plans for any first use of these weapons by anyone."

[21] Charles Krauthammer, "In Defense of Deterrence," *New Republic*, April 28, 1982.

This difficulty by itself might have prompted the authors to call for abandoning current alliance policy, under which NATO openly planned to respond with nuclear weapons to a major conventional attack by the Warsaw Pact. But their primary complaint was that first use invited second use and worse. "It is time to recognize that no one has ever succeeded in advancing any persuasive reason to believe that any use of nuclear weapons, even on the smallest scale, could reliably be expected to remain limited," they said. "Any use of nuclear weapons in Europe, by the Alliance or against it, carries with it a high and inescapable risk of escalation into general nuclear war which would bring ruin to all and victory to none." The distinction between conventional and nuclear weapons provided an easily understood firebreak against uncontrolled expansion of conflict – as it had since critics of Henry Kissinger's limited-nuclear-war ideas had made the identical point twenty-five years before. "To keep that firebreak wide and strong is in the deepest interest of all mankind."[22]

Krauthammer's opinion of this proposal by what he called "the auxiliary brigade of the antinuclear movement" – alternatively and sarcastically, and unoriginally, "the four wise men" – was that it represented a step in precisely the wrong direction. Although the four acknowledged that a no-first-use policy would require strengthening NATO conventional forces, the realities of politics and economics on both sides of the Atlantic made this improbable. Absent conventional strengthening, a no-first-use policy would be nearly suicidal. "It means the end of the Western alliance and the abandonment in particular of West Germany to Soviet intimidation and blackmail." Indeed, substantial damage had already been done. "The result of their highly publicized, grossly unbalanced proposal is predictable: another support in the complex and highly vulnerable structure of deterrence has been weakened. The world will be no safer for it."[23]

X

Kennan's group didn't really form an auxiliary of the antinuclear movement; Krauthammer exaggerated. George Will, on the other hand, did serve that function for neoconservatism. Will, a lapsed professor of political philosophy whose arch style combined weak-

---

[22] McGeorge Bundy, George F. Kennan, Robert McNamara, and Gerard Smith, "Nuclear Weapons and the Atlantic Alliance," *Foreign Affairs*, Spring 1982.

[23] Charles Krauthammer, "In Defense of Deterrence," *New Republic*, April 28, 1982.

nesses for archaic usages and baseball, brought a distinctive voice to conservative thought during the 1970s and 1980s. Affecting a distaste for most ideas not current at the time Edmund Burke died, he contended that conservatives should not oppose strong government if government action tended to the moral uplift of the community. In his syndicated columns and his books, he combated what he perceived as the moral relativism of modern life and argued that government had an obligation to do likewise, to encourage citizens "to measure up to the better angels of our nature."[24]

While Will endorsed the communitarian aspects of the Western tradition as they related to American politics, he had no sympathy whatsoever for the kind of communitarianism practiced in the Soviet Union and other communist countries. Instead he adopted a position on foreign affairs close to neoconservative orthodoxy. He lionized Russian dissident Alexander Solzhenitsyn for revealing the true nature of Soviet society. He preferred the George Kennan of 1947 to recent revisions. He denounced detente as a fool's game, judging Jimmy Carter the foremost fool. When Carter's supporters, following the president's announcement of the cancellation of the neutron bomb, cited a similar announcement by the Kremlin as evidence of the beneficial effects of the administration's decision, Will offered a contemptuous analogy: "A man plagued by rats considers purchasing a cat. The rats respond that if he will not purchase a cat, they will not purchase a cat." Calling for a more forthright defense of American interests in the western hemisphere, Will asked, "Why is Finland 'Finlandized' but Cuba not 'Cubanized'?" After Ronald Reagan named Jeane Kirkpatrick ambassador to the United Nations, Will declared her "indispensable to American policy-making."[25]

Will criticized the arms control process as "injurious to U.S. interests." With other conservatives, he deemed the phrase "arms race" a misnomer, since he contended that only the Soviets were racing. "During the era of detente and arms control the Soviet nuclear arsenal has grown quantitatively and qualitatively." In the meantime,

[24] George F. Will, *Statecraft as Soulcraft: What Government Does* (New York, 1983), 165.

[25] George F. Will, syndicated column of May 21, 1978, reprinted in *The Pursuit of Virtue and Other Tory Notions* (New York, 1982), 164; columns of Oct. 11, 1982 and Nov. 25, 1984, reprinted in *The Morning After: American Successes and Excesses, 1981–1986* (New York, 1986), 261, 285.

America's nuclear capacity had stagnated. Will noted a recent study showing that while the United States had been ahead in every category of nuclear weapons in 1962, it had fallen behind in all but two by the late 1970s. And since the latter period, which coincided with the negotiation and signing of the SALT II accords, Moscow had added more than three thousand warheads to its stockpile. "Does anyone think the world is safer than it was when the SALT process began?"

The arms control business, Will asserted, tilted unavoidably against the United States. America's allies urged American officials to reach agreements, placing Washington in a no-win position. Rejecting Moscow's proposals antagonized the allies; accepting the proposals, which were framed in full knowledge of the tension within the alliance, damaged American security. Further, while the openness of American society made American cheating on agreements impossible, the Soviets could cheat with impunity. Undiscovered violations aside, the Kremlin recognized that the American political process would restrain Washington from doing anything about those Soviet violations that did come to light. "Because our society invests such hope in arms control, even an administration as starchy as Reagan's is apt to forgive Soviet cheating or mute even required reports of it."

The Russians used arms talks as a cover for continued expansion. "The arms control era has coincided with unparalleled Soviet aggression and threats, from Indochina through Afghanistan. Try to tell victims of 'yellow rain' [an alleged biological weapon] about the wonders of arms control. Biological weapons are controlled – on paper. What has violation of the controls produced? A U.S. clamor for yet more agreements." American security required stilling those voices calling irresponsibly for arms control and for a general improvement in superpower relations. "Such talk worsens the asymmetry in U.S.-Soviet negotiations by building pressure on the U.S. government for concessions to produce 'movement.' An immoderate and unempirical belief in arms control produces a policy of apologetic retreats."

As a confessed authority on matters touching morality and politics, Will took particular umbrage at efforts by members of the clergy, Roman Catholic in particular, to pronounce on the moral consequences of nuclear weapons. Will quoted Augustine: "To maintain peace within the natural order of men, rulers require the power and decision to declare war." Will added Aquinas's comment that rulers must "defend the state against external war weapons." Did the priests and bishops challenge the Church Fathers? Will asked. Some clergy had declared the mere possession of nuclear weapons immoral on grounds that the weapons' only function was to threaten to anni-hilate innocent millions. But what of the alternative the weapons guarded against? "Any of the wide variety of possible uses of nuclear weapons would be dreadful. However, it is reckless to decree that any use, even any possession for deterrence purposes, is necessarily a larger evil than the long night of centuries that would follow the extinguishing of Western cultural values by armed totalitarianism." The cultural values of the West were worth defending, and they wouldn't defend themselves. When evil possessed nuclear weapons, good must too. When evil was prepared to use them, so must good.[26]

[26] George F. Will, columns of Dec. 21, 1982, and June 18, 1984, in *Morning After*, 271–6.

11

It Ain't Over till It's Over – and Not Even Then

I

Ronald Reagan didn't make neoconservatism; the converse was more nearly correct. Yet Reagan gave the constellation of ideas the neoconservatives promoted a genial gloss their hard hearts never could have provided. (He also gave lots of neoconservatives, from Jeane Kirkpatrick down, positions in government.) The wonder of Reagan was his ability to cause Americans to feel warm and fuzzy about a presidency devoted to a crabbed and dismal view of human nature – to a conviction that individuals responded to no higher sentiment than self-interest and that the world would never know peace short of the annihilation of dissent from America's official anticommunist ideology. It was significant that polls regularly showed far higher support for Reagan personally than for his policies.

Mikhail Gorbachev didn't *un*make neoconservatism; the converse was more nearly correct – or at least it would have been if some of the neoconservatives had had their way. The neoconservatives recognized that the urgency of their message depended on a condition of confrontation between the United States and the Soviet Union. Gorbachev, by directing a restructuring of Soviet society away from the Stalinist model and allowing the introduction of pluralism elsewhere in the East bloc, threatened to deprive the neoconservatives of their present-dangerist raison d'tre. Alarmed by the prospect of their wishes coming true, many of the neoconservatives balked at the brink of success.

But after a couple of years of declaring Gorbachev merely a dictator with a tailor, even the neoconservatives conceded that something important was happening beyond the Elbe. "Is it possible we are watching the evolution of totalitarian states into authoritarian regimes?" asked Jeane Kirkpatrick at the end of 1988. The author of the proposition that right-wing dictatorships might democratize but left-wing ones never would wasn't prepared to junk her thesis just yet. Though Gorbachev allowed reform, he hadn't relinquished the power to control that reform. He had loosened the reins but not let go. "While there is evidence to suggest that totalitarian systems are capable of change, there is so far no example of such a regime evolving into something different." All the same, Kirkpatrick said she was observing developments with "rapt attention."[1]

The changes in the Soviet Union and Eastern Europe led to obvious questions, by others in addition to the neoconservatives, about the Cold War. Was it over? If so, who won? If the United States, to what did Americans owe their succes? To the force of America's example? Or to the force of America's force?

George Kennan was willing to call it over by the summer of 1988. But then Kennan had been willing to call it over for many years. The Soviet Union, he said, had never posed a genuine military threat to the United States, except perhaps at the time of the 1948 Berlin blockade. Politically, the Soviets had challenged the West in a meaningful way only during the first few years after World War II, before the Marshall plan put Europe back on its feet. Now, with the Soviets abandoning the teachings of the communist patriarchs, the challenge was less worrisome than ever. "The Marxist-Leninist ideology is a stale and sterile ritual to which lip service must be given because it is the only ostensible source of legitimacy for the Communist Party in Russia. Beyond that, nobody takes it seriously."

Kennan denied that the changes in Soviet policies were the result of the Reagan remilitarization. Recent Soviet acceptance of the intermediate-nuclear-force treaty for Europe and Moscow's decision to evacuate Afghanistan had "very little to do" with American military pressure. Military pressure had been downright counterproductive regarding Russia's domestic mellowing. American leaders had long tended to "over-militarize our relationship with the Soviet Union," and in doing so had been "more of a hindrance than a help" to the reform process, giving a pretext to the militarists in the Soviet Union to stick to their guns, literally and figuratively. Soviet reforms were

---

[1] Jeane J. Kirkpatrick, "The Withering Away of the State?" *New Perspectives Quarterly*, Winter 1988–1989.

essentially an internal matter, "primarily the result of forces operating within Soviet society." Among those forces were disgust at the excesses of Stalinism and dissatisfaction among non-Russian nationalities. To the degree outside influences had an effect, that effect was chiefly exemplary. Western prosperity increasingly contrasted with Soviet stagnation, eliciting a "gradual recognition on the part of many people (outstandingly Gorbachev himself) that the remaining Stalinist rigidities were seriously undermining the Soviet system and making it uncompetitive with the advanced countries."

Containment had grown "irrelevant," asserted containment's coiner. The Cold War mindset was now a barrier to creative American diplomacy – although it still served the psychic requirements of that large segment of American society that demonstrated a "need to cultivate the theory of American innocence and virtue, which must have an opposite pole of evil." Kennan concluded: "The Soviets dropped the Cold War mentality. Now, it's up to us to do the same thing."[2]

Not so fast, responded Charles Krauthammer. "Such thinking is wishful until the Soviets leave not just Afghanistan but Central America, until they not only talk about 'defensive sufficiency' but practice it by making real cuts in defense spending and by reconfiguring their offensive force structure in Europe." Yet even Krauthammer conceded that victory was closer than before. "For the first time in the postwar period it is possible to foresee an end to the cold war – on Western terms."

For precisely this reason, it was necessary to maintain the pressure. Against Kennan's claims to the contrary, Krauthammer and the other neoconservatives judged the Reagan military buildup, the covert war in Afghanistan and Central America, and the other manifestations of American resolve to have been absolutely critical in causing Gorbachev to decide to revamp the Soviet system. To back off now, before the Kremlin's final and definite surrender, risked losing all the progress that had been made to date.

Krauthammer felt mixed emotions about the West's impending triumph. On one hand, the United States would have accomplished great good for humanity. "America's historic role of saving the West after World War II will have been achieved." On the other, the re-

---

[2] George F. Kennan, "Obituary for the Cold War," *New Perspectives Quarterly*, Summer 1988.

mission of the Soviet threat would weaken the cohesion of the free countries. "Nations need enemies. Take away one, and they find another." Americans might well turn on their allies – as some American economic nationalists were already turning on Japan. All the same, Krauthammer allowed himself a certain measure of hope. "As V-CW Day approaches, we should have the confidence to start thinking about the new world on the other side. If we intelligently manage Western integration and resist the more mindless forms of nationalism that are trying to substitute for postwar anti-communism, the next century holds out the promise of a Western Peace as global and secure as any that we have known before."[3]

Zbigniew Brzezinski couldn't wait until the next century. Brzezinski, an academic Soviet-watcher before becoming Jimmy Carter's special assistant for national security affairs, and subsequently an all-purpose big thinker, agreed with Kennan that the Cold War was already over. Taking the long view of world affairs, Brzezinski accounted communism a three-generation wonder. Lenin had seized Marxism – which Brzezinski dismissed as the moribund brainchild of an "emigre German-Jewish librarian" – and converted it into the rationale for one-party rule in Russia. Stalin had transformed that one-party structure into an appalling edifice of state terror. Brezhnev had diminished the terror somewhat but had supplemented it with thoroughgoing corruption and stagnation.

Gorbachev's task, Brzezinski explained, was to peel back oppression. The Brezhnev layer came off easiest, since its failures in terms of shortages of essential goods and overall economic backwardness were unmistakable. The Stalinist layer stuck more tenaciously to the Soviet consciousness, having created a bureaucracy of ponderous weight and a mystique of responsibility for victory in the Great Patriotic War. Yet Stalin's capricious brutality had ravaged so many lives that he too became a symbol of the bad old days. Removing the Leninist layer was the most difficult of all. Leninism served as the foundation of party rule. "Any rejection of it would be tantamount to collective psychological suicide." But Leninism too would go, whether Gorbachev wished it or not, for it embodied a fatal misconception of human nature and a basic misjudgment of history. The misconception was that people would forever tolerate being ordered around; the misjudgment was that a cowed populace could generate

---

[3] Charles Krauthammer, "Beyond the Cold War," *New Republic*, Dec. 19, 1988.

sustainable economic development. History had caught up with communism, and the future had no place for it.[4]

II

Francis Fukuyama carried the notion of the inevitable demise of communism one step further. Fukuyama, deputy director of the State Department's policy planning staff and a former analyst at the Rand Corporation, declared that the bankruptcy of communism signaled "the end of history" itself. For this startling statement, Fukuyama took as his point of departure an 1806 pronouncement by Hegel, the thrust of which was that the victory by Napoleon over Prussia at the battle of Jena amounted to the triumph of the ideals of the French revolution over the outmoded notions that had propped up the defeated autocracy. Fukuyama couldn't pinpoint the recent end of history so precisely, but he cited the travails the 1970s and 1980s had brought to the communist world as evidence of the imminent triumph of the ideals of modern Western liberalism over those of its Marxist competition.

What Fukuyama was really talking about, although he didn't credit Daniel Bell, was the end of ideology rather than the end of what most people would call history. Fukuyama conceded that life after history, at least for some considerable period, would look much like life during history. Individuals and regimes would still vie for power. International conflict would continue, even to the point of war. Yet ideology would no longer drive the struggles of individuals and states, since the principal late challengers to Western liberalism, namely fascism and communism, no longer possessed the ability to inspire. Fascism had failed the material test of World War II (this was a curious position for Fukuyama, a self-proclaimed antimaterialist, to take). Communism had failed the test of the postwar period (again a material test, this one involving the capacity to mobilize productive resources in pursuit of national goals). Whatever the measure of the failures, no one now plausibly promoted the right-wing ultranationalism that had produced Nazi Germany and imperialist Japan, and very soon no one would plausibly promote the left-wing coercive egalitarianism that had produced Bolshevik Russia and Red China.

---

[4] Zbigniew Brzezinski, *The Grand Failure: The Birth and Death of Communism in the Twentieth Century* (New York, 1989), 3, 47–48, 242.

"Those who believe that the future must inevitably be socialist tend to be very old," Fukuyama wrote, "or very marginal to the real political discourse of their societies."

At the end of history, political and ideological strife would largely cease; the principal activity of nations would be economic. This was a blessing, but not an unmitigated one. Fukuyama's remarks on this point recalled some of the gloom of Brooks Adams ninety years before. (At least they did if one took Fukuyama at face value. When a reporter asked him if he believed everything he wrote, Fukuyama replied, "I guess I prefer not to answer that. Leave it ambiguous. All I can say is, if people can't take a joke . . . ") "The end of history," the published Fukuyama predicted, "will be a very sad time." As people around the world devoted their energies chiefly to the pursuit of economic goals, the ennobling virtues that had made possible the rise of civilizations would atrophy. "The struggle for recognition, the willingness to risk one's life for a purely abstract goal, the worldwide ideological struggle that called forth daring, courage, imagination, and idealism, will be replaced by economic calculation, the endless solving of technical problems, environmental concerns, and the satisfaction of sophisticated consumer demands." History ended with neither bang nor whimper, but with the hum of an electronic cash register and a sigh.[5]

Paul Kennedy also recalled Brooks Adams, both in his broad-gauged and decidedly materialist approach to world history and in his pessimistic judgment that America had peaked as an international power. A British-born military and diplomatic historian at Yale, Kennedy analyzed *The Rise and Fall of the Great Powers* in the modern era. He chronicled the emergence of the Hapsburg empire during the sixteenth century, the Hapsburgs' displacement by Britain and France during the seventeenth and eighteenth centuries, the German challenge of the late nineteenth and early twentieth centuries, the creation of the bipolar international order of the mid-twentieth century, and the fragmentation of that bipolar order since about 1960. Kennedy respected history and history-makers sufficiently to allow for the ef-

---

[5] Francis Fukuyama, "The End of History?" *National Interest*, Summer 1989; James Atlas, "What is Fukuyama Saying?" *New York Times Magazine*, Oct. 22, 1989. Fukuyama later expanded his essay into a book: *The End of History and the Last Man* (New York, 1992).

fects of human idiosyncracies, of accidents and nonmaterial influences; but, like Adams, he argued that there existed a definite and ineluctable connection between economic development and national power – "between productive and revenue-raising capacities on the one hand and military strength on the other." Great powers remained great only so long as they could marshal the material resources to defend their turf against encroachers.

In the five centuries he studied, Kennedy found no instance of a country maintaining hegemony over a large portion of the earth for more than a few generations (close to Adams's figure of three generations for the lifespan of each phase of the international system). As power grew, so did the interests power was called upon to secure. Eventually the interests outstripped the power, leaving the country in a position of "imperial overstretch." Spain had confronted the problem in 1600, Britain even more clearly when its time came in the twentieth century. Kennedy saw no reason to expect an exemption for the United States. "Decision-makers in Washington must face the awkward and enduring fact that the sum total of the United States' global interests and obligations is now far larger than the country's power to defend them all simultaneously." The best American leaders could hope for was to manage their decline to a position of comparability to the rest of the world with a modicum of grace and a minimum of disruption.[6]

Kennedy's book became a bestseller, which perhaps demonstrated that the Reaganist admonitions that it was "morning in America" were losing their effect. At the same time, Kennedy's analysis and warnings didn't go unchallenged. Various reviewers took Kennedy to task for accentuating the negative in America's predicament and warned against facile applications of history to current events. Joseph Nye in 1990 devoted a whole book, *Bound to Lead*, to a refutation of the arguments of Kennedy and other declinists.

Actually, Nye didn't so much refute the arguments regarding American decline as put a different spin on them. "There is no doubt that the United States is less powerful now at the end of the twentieth century than it was in mid-century," Nye conceded. "Even conservative estimates show that the U.S. share of global product has de-

---

[6] Paul Kennedy, *The Rise and Fall of the Great Powers: Economic Change and Military Conflict from 1500 to 2000* (New York, 1987), xvi, 515, 534.

clined from more than a third of the total after World War II to a little more than a fifth in the 1980s." The important question, however, was what these and similar numbers meant.

Nye contended that they meant less than Kennedy thought. In the post-industrial age, such traditional measures of national strength as population and natural resources didn't signify as much as they had during earlier periods. For this reason, Nye doubted that the decline of the Spanish or British empires had much to tell Americans on the eve of the third millennium of the modern era. Besides, at each previous power transition, there had existed a likely candidate to supplant the aging hegemon. Who was there to supplant the United States? Nye tested and rejected each obvious successor. "The United States remains the largest and richest power with the greatest capacity to shape the future," he concluded.[7]

III

Briefly, the world at the end of the Cold War appeared willing to let the Americans argue in peace about how the Cold War was won. The neoconservatives, by now not so neo any more, continued to claim credit for what a sympathetic Peter Schweizer straightforwardly and celebratorially called *Victory*. Different authors stressed different aspects of the winning strategy, with some highlighting the Reagan doctrine, others the Star Wars space initiative, still others the modernization of America's nuclear arsenal and the commitment to a six-hundred ship navy. Yet all agreed that Gorbachev had had no choice but to surrender to this overwhelming display of American force and resolve.

Kennan and the exemplarists continued to reject this vindicationist chest-thumping. Speaking at a ninetieth birthday party thrown for him by the Council on Foreign Relations, Kennan pointed out that even if the militarists had been responsible for Moscow's final capitulation – and they hadn't – their victory was awfully slow in coming. Billions of dollars had been wasted; millions of lives had been lost in Korea, Vietnam, and other flashpoints along the superpower front; and Eastern Europe – the cause of the whole thing – had been consigned to forty years of terror, oppression, and poverty. If American

[7] Joseph S. Nye, *Bound to Lead: The Changing Nature of American Power* (New York, 1990), 5, 261.

leaders had been willing to negotiate with Moscow after World War II, instead of insisting on what amounted to the Kremlin's unconditional surrender – in other words, though Kennan didn't say so, if the United States had followed Walter Lippmann's advice instead of his own – these tragic consequences might have been averted.

Looking to the future, Kennan recited John Quincy Adams's classic warning about involvement in the affairs of other people to the detriment of America's domestic concerns. He urged Americans to look within, to examine themselves and their country, building on their strengths and remedying their weaknesses.

And then ask yourselves how such a country ought to shape its foreign relations in such a way as to help it be what it could be to itself and to its world environment, bearing in mind, of course, that it is primarily by example, never by precept, that a country such as ours exerts the most useful influence beyond its borders, but remembering, too, that there are limits to what one sovereign country can do to help another, and that unless we preserve the quality, the vigor and the morale of our own society, we will be of little use to anyone at all.[8]

IV

Yet the world's patience with American retrospection was limited, and the dust from the demolition of the Berlin wall had scarcely settled before the vindicators and exemplarists were required to go at each other again in real time. The Iraqi invasion of Kuwait in the summer of 1990 threw the Persian Gulf into turmoil, disrupted world oil markets, threatened the world economy – and re-posed the perennial question of America's obligation to the world.

Few commentators faulted George Bush for arranging permission to land American soldiers in Saudi Arabia. A defensive disposition of troops would discourage additional Iraqi adventurism, and, assuming Saddam Hussein took the hint and shelved any plans for going beyond Kuwait, it would cost the United States relatively little. Nor did many observers discern much to complain about in Bush's successful diplomatic efforts in the United Nations to have Hussein's actions condemned and punished by economic sanctions, although some querulous voices (updating an argument made by Walter Lippmann and his co-editors at the *New Republic* against the British blockade

[8] *New York Times*, Mar. 14, 1994.

of Germany in World War I) predicted that the sanctions would cause less suffering to Saddam and his cronies than to the Iraqi people at large, who were already suffering from the dictator's everyday despotism.

But when the Bush administration made a conspicuous shift from safeguarding Saudi Arabia to smashing Iraq, a chorus of dissent arose in the United States. Most of the dissenters doubted the administration's claim of attachment to a "new world order" in which small countries would be preserved from depredation by the strong. Why wasn't the administration protesting China's occupation of Tibet? Or Israel's occupation of the West Bank and Gaza? The skeptics suggested that the crux of the issue was oil, a point administration officials didn't bother to deny when promised anonymity. Secretary of State James Baker went so far as to summarize the stakes in the Persian Gulf in a single word, "Jobs." The dissenters demurred from a war to make the world safe for American gas-guzzlers; such a war, they said, would be a shocking waste of American lives and a disgrace to American honor.[9]

Nor, for that matter, was war necessarily the way to secure those American jobs. Charles William Maynes, editor of *Foreign Policy*, asserted that the American huffing and puffing in the Gulf was precisely the wrong approach to calming petroleum buyers and sellers. The United States, Maynes said, had done about all it could do to stabilize prices when it made clear that it would prevent an Iraqi takeover of Saudi Arabia. "Thereafter," he wrote, "the greatest immediate threat to the price or supply of oil became the very war that the United States was threatening to unleash. It was no accident that oil prices fell whenever there was a rumor of peace or that they mounted when war seemed nearer." Maynes went on to predict that a war would wreak havoc on the oil fields and refineries of Kuwait and parts of the surrounding region. And there was little evidence that even if Saddam Hussein acquired control of Saudi Arabia's oil fields, American consumers would be conspicuously worse off. "Saudi Arabia, in fact, has regularly pursued oil-pricing policies as detrimental to U.S. interests as those Saddam Hussein prefers. A war will not solve America's energy dependence problems."

Maynes rebutted other arguments adduced by the hawks for going

[9] James Baker in Lawrence Freedman and Efraim Karsh, *The Gulf Conflict 1990–1991* (Princeton, N.J., 1993), 224.

after Hussein. To the contention that Iraqi forces were brutalizing the population of Kuwait and that this constituted grounds for war, he responded that decency toward those under one's power was indeed a worthy objective, but the Republicans were hardly in a position to make a case from decency, considering their record of support for repressive regimes in other regions – Central America, for example. Besides, a war for Kuwait might well produce more deaths and maimings among the Kuwaitis than the Iraqi occupation was or would. He found equally unconvincing the argument that Iraq was a present or future threat to the United States. A regional nuisance, perhaps; but no strategic threat. He similarly rejected an assertion put forward by some that a war against Iraq was necessary for the safety of Israel. Even if true – which he didn't accept – such an argument was terribly divisive in American politics. (Already the issue had created a rift between Jewish and Christian leaders in the United States, and when more than a dozen spokespersons of various Christian denominations met with President Bush to tell him that war wasn't the answer to the problems of the Gulf, the American Jewish Committee assailed the group for playing into the hands of Saddam Hussein.) Neither would a war set a usable precedent for crises elsewhere. For reasons of "American politics, finances, and common sense," Maynes said, the world couldn't expect the United States to fight every small country's battles. "World order will have to rest on more than the shoulders of the U.S. military."[10]

Norman Podhoretz might have agreed that more shoulders were needed than Uncle Sam's, but he believed that without Uncle Sam's, there wouldn't be any others. Podhoretz had been bothered by Saddam for some years, and as the crisis in the Gulf intensified during the summer of 1990, he began calling for the strongest sanctions against Iraq. He was encouraged by the Bush administration's timely dispatch of troops to Saudi Arabia, but with each indication that the conflict might be resolved by diplomatic means, he began to fret. Podhoretz worried that a coalition of conservative neo-isolationists and liberal anti-militarists would prevent the president from doing his duty to America and the world.

Podhoretz deemed the liberals' dissent simply an aspect of their general woolly-mindedness, and had little to say about it; but for the

[10] Charles Maynes, "Dateline Washington: A Necessary War?" *Foreign Policy*, Spring 1991.

conservative opponents of military action, he had much to say, none of it nice. The most visible of the conservative anti-interventionists was Patrick Buchanan, a former Nixon speechwriter and current columnist. Buchanan had alleged that the primary advocacy of war against Iraq came from Israel and its "amen corner" in the United States. Podhoretz denounced this "brutal allegation," as well as what he asserted was Buchanan's use of the label "neoconservative" as a code word for "Jews." Not only was Buchanan anti-Semitic, Podhoretz said, he was wrong: Both William Buckley's *National Review* and the London *Economist*, "two magazines which could in no sense be characterized as neoconservative (let alone Jewish), and which are not exactly notable for saying amen to everything Israel does," were calling for swift military action against Iraq.

Podhoretz heard echoes of the debate over Vietnam in the current controversy about Iraq and Kuwait. In the 1960s, he explained, Americans had supported the efforts on behalf of South Vietnam until the costs of those efforts had begun to mount. He worried that the same might hold true regarding the Persian Gulf. Americans had endorsed the administration's deployment of American forces to the Gulf, but now that it looked as if those forces might be used in combat, the endorsement was eroding. He feared that this would lead to leaving the job undone, as had happened in Vietnam.

Podhoretz doubted that economic sanctions would drive Iraq out of Kuwait, but even if they did, he said, that wouldn't suffice. "There would still be the problem of how to deal with Saddam's military machine. For if the Iraqi tyrant, or for that matter some thuggish successor who might overthow him, were to withdraw from Kuwait while being allowed to hold onto his missiles and his chemical weapons and his nascent nuclear capability, the threat Iraq poses to our vital interests in the region would remain." Podhoretz granted that in knocking out Hussein, the United States would be doing Israel's work. But that was no reason not to do the work. "The war against Saddam is no more a 'Jewish war' than was the war against Hitler. It is a war to prevent control of a vital resource from falling into the hands of a ruthless aggressor. It is a war to discourage others from engaging in such aggression. It is a war to establish a more peaceful order in the post-cold-war world."[11]

[11] Norman Podhoretz, "A Statement on the Persian Gulf Crisis," *Commentary*, November 1990.

The *New Republic* took much the same position as *Commentary*, which wasn't surprising in that Lippmann's old journal was now nearly as neoconservative in matters of foreign affairs as Podhoretz's present one, and almost as militantly pro-Israel. Like Podhoretz, the editors of the *New Republic* were afraid that the Bush administration would be discouraged from smiting Saddam by assorted Arab and Western critics who pointed out that Kuwait hadn't exactly been a democracy, either. Overstating for polemical purposes their opponents' case, the editors continued: "The idea has been put forth [by whom they didn't say] that the forced exit of the ruling al-Sabah family – to be followed by a plebiscite, open to non-Kuwaitis and to as many imported Iraqis as needed to ensure the result – will somehow promote democracy. This is simply fatuous, a pitiable attempt to obscure the horror that has been unleashed in the Gulf." In any event, the issue in Kuwait had little to do with democracy. "It has to do with order, in the region and in the world." The editors conceded that more was involved than abstract principle. "In recent days we have heard many remarks to the effect that if the sands of Kuwait were dry all the way down, the world would have little trouble controlling its indignation at its conquest. There is some truth in that cynical observation." But petroleum didn't preclude principles. "The United States is not simply defending oil for itself. Every country in the world, rich and poor, depends upon oil. It is the fuel not just of transportation and industry but of civilization." Saddam's assault on Kuwait, therefore, was a blow against civilization. And America's defense of Kuwait was a defense of civilization. "In the Persian Gulf the United States is not merely combating an isolated 'aggression' by one country against another. It is setting a precedent for collective security action for years to come."[12]

V

Many observers joined the *New Republic* in thinking, or at least hoping, that the American stand in the Persian Gulf would set a precedent for collective security. These hopes increased when the war came and proved swiftly successful and remarkably inexpensive in terms of American and allied lives. The easy expulsion of Iraq from

[12] "Fighting Dirty," *New Republic*, Sept. 10 and 17, 1990; "Sand Trap," *New Republic*, Sept. 24, 1990.

Kuwait silenced most of the critics of military action, although Saddam's survival of the war left an unpleasant aftertaste on the lips even of many who toasted Bush on a brilliant victory.

One thing the Gulf war did *not* do was end the debate over the direction of American policy in the post-Cold War period. If anything, the debate grew more intense as the focus of foreign conflict shifted away from areas of obvious material interest to the United States. One area of non-obvious material interest – it would have been more accurate to say obvious *non*-interest – was Bosnia. The trials of Muslims in that post-Tito slice of the former Yugoslavia triggered numerous and loud calls for American intervention. The calls crossed party lines and ordinary divisions between liberals and conservatives – as the exemplarist-vindicator debate often had. For stridency and regularity, none of the callers surpassed Anthony Lewis, the last of the reliable liberals to opine on foreign affairs for the *New York Times*. With calendaric consistency during 1993 and 1994 – if this is Wednesday, the topic must be Bosnia – Lewis excoriated the Clinton administration for ignoring the "screaming truths" of Bosnia and failing to rescue the Muslims from "ethnic cleansing" and other forms of Serb aggression.[13]

Edward Luttwak, a conservative military-affairs analyst who agreed with Lewis on little else, seconded his views on Bosnia. Writing in *Commentary*, Luttwak complained at the inaction of the Clinton administration. He conceded that there existed no groundswell of support in the United States for strong measures, but in circumstances like the present it was up to the White House to summon such support. Indeed, Luttwak said, the confusion attending the end of the Cold War greatly expanded "the potential scope of the moral leadership the President of the United States *could* exercise, for example by persuading the American public that Bosnian Muslims should be actively protected." The United States had the power; it needed only the will.[14]

Richard Falk saw the situation as considerably more complicated. A professor of international law at Princeton, Falk contended that military intervention in Bosnia would be doomed to fail, just as military intervention in those two other current trouble spots – Somalia and Haiti – would be doomed to fail, and as military interventions in

[13] Anthony Lewis, "Principle or Pose?" *New York Times*, Feb. 21, 1994.
[14] Edward Luttwak, "If Bosnians Were Dolphins . . . " *Commentary*, October 1993.

most circumstances was doomed to fail. The recent war in the Persian Gulf was no counterexample, for the war had ended with Saddam Hussein as entrenched as ever in Baghdad. "In some ways," Falk said, "the result of the Gulf War was comparable to ending World War II with Germany devastated but with Hitler and the Nazi Party still in power!" Falk pointed out that Bosnia was essentially a civil conflict: Bosnian Serbs against Bosnian Muslims. Intervention might temporarily halt the fighting in Bosnia, but it couldn't make the two groups (not to mention the Bosnian Croats) want to live together. Until a Bosnian basis for a settlement emerged, intervention would be expensive and probably unproductive – even counterproductive. This might be hard counsel, especially for the Bosnian Muslims. But life was hard. In words that could have been written by Reinhold Niebuhr or Hans Morgenthau, Falk concluded that the Bosnian situation – and others like it – were "tragic in their depth and complexity." For this reason, morality was "a matter of doing better, encouraging what is possible." The possible, in this case, didn't include bringing peace to Bosnia.[15]

VI

That Falk could take the reasoning Morgenthau and Niebuhr had used to justify interventionist foreign policies, and reach an anti-interventionist conclusion, demonstrated, among other things, how thoroughly the end of the Cold War had mixed up American thinking on international affairs. Not since World War II had the politics of the planet changed so dramatically so fast; not since then had the future seemed so unsettled. For forty years, when Americans had peered ahead they had always been able to spy the onion-domes of the Kremlin looming above the diplomatic landscape; now those landmarks were gone. Whether or not one accepted Krauthammer's argument about nations needing enemies, the vanishing of the Soviet Union deprived Americans of something to which they had grown accustomed, even attached in a negative sort of way. (The attachment seemed less negative when more than a few commentators noted that the horrors of Bosnia would never have been allowed to occur in the days when the superpowers insisted on order in Europe.)

That Moscow's disappearing act took place in the lengthening

---

[15] Richard Falk, "Hard Choices and Tragic Dilemmas," *Nation*, Dec. 20, 1993.

shadow of the end of the century – and of the millennium, which exacerbated the tendency – favored the far-sighted among those offering guidance across the suddenly unfamiliar terrain of the years to come. Perhaps unsurprisingly, those who looked farthest into the future did so by looking farthest into the past. Perhaps equally unsurprisingly, given the topic and the times, a significant portion of these wound up sounding like Brooks Adams.

Samuel Huntington certainly did. In the summer of 1993, the Harvard political scientist published a widely noticed article in *Foreign Affairs* whose title and general outlook recapitulated Adams's themes. Huntington's "The Clash of Civilizations?" was less pessimistic than Adams's *Law of Civilization and Decay*, but that wasn't saying a lot, since greater pessimism was hard to imagine. Huntington refused to buy into the end-of-history philosophizing of Fukuyama, and he definitely evinced little sympathy for the triumphalism of Nye. Nor did he think Paul Kennedy's imperial-overstretch analogies offered much guidance for the century about to begin. The problem with all of these approaches, in Huntington's opinion, was that they were too contemporary. They – even Kennedy's five-century survey – didn't delve deeply enough into the past, and consequently missed the big picture.

Huntington's big picture portrayed the world at the dawn of the third millennium as dividing into competing civilizations. These civilizations actually had been competing for many centuries, but their competition had been masked by more ephemeral events. Huntington identified three passing phases in the recent – that is, since the 1648 Peace of Westphalia – evolution of international relations. The first was characterized by contests among monarchs, and included the blossoming of the first European overseas empires. The second was marked by the rise of, and conflicts among, nation-states. The French set the example here, building on what the Bourbons had constructed, but adding the revolutionary fervor that broke open the Bastille and toppled the *ancien régime*. The age of nation-states lasted from 1789 to 1917, when another revolution, this one in Russia, ushered in the third phase. The initial part of this phase of ideology witnessed a three-way struggle among communism, liberal democracy, and fascism, but after fascism failed during World War II, communism and democracy squared off. The ideological phase of international relations continued until the immediate past, when communism lost its ability to inspire and the Soviet system collapsed.

The phase just beginning, Huntington asserted, was the age of civilizations. Yet while this phase was new, it was also, in certain crucial respects, older than the three previous phases. Civilizations were distinguished by common cultures: the mores and institutions they had evolved over dozens of generations to cope with the vicissitudes of life. Huntington's civilizations varied greatly in size. Western civilization included most of the countries of Europe and North America, and the hundreds of millions of their inhabitants. Chinese civilization comprised the billion-plus people living in China, as well as many of those in the Chinese diaspora, but only one country. (Huntington quoted Lucian Pye's definition of China: "a civilization pretending to be a state.") Japanese civilization likewise was confined to a single country. Islamic civilization contained dozens of countries and scores of millions of people. The civilization of the Anglophone Caribbean contained several island-states but not many people.

Huntington predicted that the most important conflicts of the twenty-first century would be between civilizations. He offered several reasons for this. First, civilizations were basic to human existence; they had developed over centuries and millennia and weren't about to disappear. Second, the world was growing smaller; contact, and therefore friction, between civilizations was becoming more frequent. Third, as the process of modernization dissolved local identities, people turned back to their cultural – that is, civilizational – roots. Fourth, the recent and continuing political and economic preeminence of the West was producing a reaction in other civilizations: the "Asianization" of Japan, the "Hinduization" of India, the "re-Islamization" of the Middle East. Fifth, cultural characteristics weren't subject to facile change the way ideological or political characteristics were; a Russian could be a communist one day and a democrat the next, but an Azeri couldn't so easily become an Armenian, nor a Bosnian Muslim a Serb. Finally, economic regionalism was growing more distinct. Intra-regional trade was increasing as a proportion of the total trade of Europe, East Asia, and North America. This was both a testament and a contributor to the rise of civilization-consciousness.

The coming clash of civilizations had already begun, in Huntington's view. All along the boundaries of civilizations, peoples were fighting. Serbs murdered Muslims in Bosnia; Hindus and Muslims exchanged bullets in India; the Turkic peoples of the former Soviet Central Asian republics smote the Slavs who lived next door, and got smitten in return. The clash had ripped apart some countries, with the Soviet Union and Yugoslavia being obvious examples. Other countries – India, Russia, the Philippines, Turkey – were at grave risk.

Huntington didn't have much concrete to offer by way of guidance for American policy, beyond a recommendation not to reduce American military capacity too rapidly in the post-Cold War period lest the West lose its ability to defend its interests against civilizational challengers. The nature of his analysis prevented him from saying a lot more, for the grand forces he dealt in transcended the ability of any one country to control. While the United States was the most powerful of the Western countries, it hardly had a monopoly on Western civilization, and it couldn't defend that civilization alone. Even less could it command the feelings and actions of the billions of people belonging to other civilizations.

To a large extent, Americans would simply have to get used to a world dominated by forces beyond their control. Speaking especially of the rising civilizations of Asia, Huntington wrote, "The West will increasingly have to accommodate these non-Western modern civilizations whose power approaches that of the West but whose values and interests differ significantly from those of the West." To the extent that the expansion of Western influence during the last few centuries had caused Westerners to believe that their civilization was becoming universalized, they would have to alter their thinking. "For the relevant future, there will be no universal civilization, but instead a world of different civilizations, each of which will have to learn to coexist with the others."[16]

Many of Huntington's readers found his gloomy outlook no more persuasive than Theodore Roosevelt had found Brooks Adams's pessimism a century earlier. Fouad Ajami of Johns Hopkins thought Huntington had things backward in elevating civilizations above states in his assessment of the future. "Let us be clear," Ajami wrote. "Civilizations do not control states, states control civilizations." Jeane Kirkpatrick accused Huntington of sloppy civilization-lumping, and she thought he underestimated the irreversibility of the modernization process. Though individuals and groups might wish to return to the past, they couldn't. Robert Bartley adopted much the view

---

[16] Samuel P. Huntington, "The Clash of Civilizations?" *Foreign Affairs*, Summer 1993. This article grew into a book: *The Clash of Civilizations and the Remaking of World Order* (New York, 1996).

Theodore Roosevelt – and more recently Joseph Nye – had taken with respect to predictions of decline. While disputing a few points of Huntington's analysis, Bartley, the editor of the *Wall Street Journal*, took special pains to counter what he saw as the defeatist implications of that analysis. The future remained unformed, he asserted; the forces of disintegration might prevail, or the forces of expanding democracy and personal freedom. "The essence of the task for the new era is to strike a balance between realpolitik and moralism."[17]

VII

Of course, that was precisely the problem, and always had been. But in the mid-1990s it was more acute than at any time in two generations. So long as the Soviet Union had posed a credible threat to the United States, Americans tended to give realpolitik the benefit of the doubt. The existence of the Soviet threat had hardly stifled debate between vindicators and exemplarists. William Appleman Williams and the revisionists of the 1960s had beaten on the Cold War vindicationism of the early Kennan and the other containers, denting their orthodoxy enough to make possible the exemplarism of the early Carter, and to make necessary the vindicationist repairs of the neoconservatives and Reagan. But the debate had always taken place against a background of Soviet power, and all parties knew that whatever else their arguments professed to do, if they did not deal adequately with the Soviet Union, they would be judged abject failures. The Soviets had weapons, and while they did, even the exemplarists acknowledged the necessity of keeping America's powder dry.

With the collapse of the Soviet Union, the other side of Bartley's scales – moralism – received a closer look than it had for half a century. The message it conveyed caused Washington to send troops not simply to Bosnia, as Bill Clinton ultimately did, but to Somalia and Haiti. Unalloyed humanitarianism – inspired by heart-rending television footage of starving children – set the transports in motion to Somalia, where the marines stayed until the local warlords demonstrated that even in the post-Cold War world, humanitarianism

---

[17] Fouad Ajami, "The Summoning," *Foreign Affairs*, September-October 1993; Jeane J. Kirkpatrick, "The Modernizing Imperative," ibid.; Robert Bartley, "The Case for Optimism," ibid.

didn't come free. Humanitarianism joined hands with self-interest – in the shape of a desire to forestall a flood of refugees – to carry marines to Haiti, where they restored the ousted president, Jean-Bertrand Aristide, but otherwise didn't propel the poorest country of the western hemisphere very far along the road toward either democracy or prosperity.

In the cases of both Somalia and Haiti, the same split surfaced between exemplarists and vindicators that had marked the debate over Bosnia – and that, indeed, had marked the debate over nearly ever other important feature of American foreign policy since the French revolution. Yet the debaters of the 1990s had a crucial advantage over those that had gone before: namely, the knowledge of the debate that had gone before, and of its various provisional outcomes. The vindicators of the 1990s, seeking historical support for intervention in Somalia, Haiti, and Bosnia, could recall the arguments of Daniel Webster on behalf of Greek freedom fighters, of Josiah Strong and Albert Beveridge on Americans' Providentially ordained obligation to share American values with such heretofore unfavored places as the Philippines, of the young Walter Lippmann on the need to cease drifting and master the opportunity to stand up to German aggression, of the young Kennan on America's unique capacity to contain totalitarianism in Eastern Europe, of Reinhold Niebuhr on the moral necessity of backing the better when the best wasn't available (as it never was), of Podhoretz and Kirkpatrick on how if Americans didn't resist evil overseas, no one would. (In the case of Podhoretz and Kirkpatrick, these two were able and willing to restate their vindicationist arguments themselves.)

The exemplarists of the 1990s, who held that American troops could bring bread to Somalia but nothing approaching lasting peace, that they could deliver a president to Haiti but not the values prerequisite to democracy and development, that they might momentarily halt the murders in Bosnia but couldn't quell the passions of centuries, likewise had ample precedents for their arguments. They could remember the dying Henry Clay telling Louis Kossuth to find freedom and virtue within himself and his countrymen; the discouraged Carl Schurz seeing a half-century of sacrifice for republicanism being traded for the hollow glory of empire; the outraged Randolph Bourne deriding the rush to World War I; the indignant Charles Beard insisting that there were evils enough at home without chasing after them overseas; the disillusioned William Appleman Williams asking whether it wasn't time for Americans to stop defining their security and happiness in terms of foreign prowess. And, as each generation of exemplarists since the 1820s had done, they could quote John Quincy Adams on America's being the well-wisher of every country's liberty but the vindicator only of her own.

History had proven both parties to the debate right – right at least sufficiently to keep them convinced of their respective rectitudes. The decision to annex the Philippines in 1899 did indeed entangle the United States in the coils of empire, as the exemplarists predicted; yet it didn't destroy democracy at home, and it helped lay the foundation upon which the Filipinos built what was (at least for a time) the most prosperous and progressive country of Southeast Asia. The decision for war in 1917 finished off the liberal spirit in America, as Randolph Bourne said it would; but it also finished off German aggression (again, for a time). The isolationism for which Charles Beard supplied the philosophical justification almost certainly encouraged the militarists of depression-era Germany and Japan; but it also helped guarantee American national unity when the war finally came. Anticommunist containment may have made sense in Europe after World War II, as Kennan and the Cold War vindicators contended; but it proved a disaster when extrapolated to Indochina, as the exemplarists warned. The neo-vindicationism of the neoconservatives, as implemented by the Reagan administration, may have been the straw that broke the Kremlin's back; or it may simply have extended the superpower standoff another decade, as the later Kennan averred.

The exemplarists were surely right in contending that, in the long run, every nation has to solve its own problems itself. And a beneficent example is definitely a more persuasive argument for democracy than bayonets. But as Keynes noted (some years after storming out of the Paris peace conference), in the long run everybody's dead. And a lot more would be dead in the short run, too, if American policy were left entirely to the exemplarists. Sometimes simple humanity cries out for action to stop the brutalization of innocents. This was what Beard couldn't understand in the late 1930s and early 1940s, and what the latter-day opponents of American intervention in Somalia and Bosnia didn't appreciate either. America couldn't save Europe in Beard's day; it couldn't save Somalia and Bosnia in the 1990s. But it *could* save lots of Europeans, and lots of Somalis and Bosnians.

If the two centuries of shouting between the exemplarists and the vindicators demonstrated anything, it was that neither approach to the world suits all situations. This is partly the world's fault, partly Americans'. The world recurrently refuses to find the American example as compelling as the exemplarists do, with different nations insisting on discovering their own paths to heaven. This much is their prerogative; unfortunately, heaven for one country can be hell on the neighbors, at which point third parties, including the United States, may legitimately intervene. But intervention is no permanent solution, either, since much of the world takes even less kindly to American coercion than to American example. A powerful country like the United States can impose its will by main force upon certain regions for particular periods, but not ubiquitously and not indefinitely.

Americans' fault in the matter consists in failing to recognize these limits on both their example and their power. They tend to carry the examplarist and vindicationist positions to alternate extremes. To some degree, this tendency reflects the bipolar imperatives of democratic politics under a constitution that effectively precludes competitive third parties. To a perhaps equal degree, it reflects the moral self-assurance, not to say self-righteousness, that comes with the territory of American exceptionalism and which, at bottom, drives the American desire to improve the world. Moral questions, as contrasted to economic or purely political questions, rarely lend themselves to compromise.

A capacity for compromise between the exemplarists and vindicators almost certainly would improve American foreign policy. In the first place, it would dampen the oscillations between such exaggerated and ultimately destructive approaches as the arch-exemplarism of Beard and the hyper-vindicationism of Vietnam. Any foreign policy that aspires to popular support – in a democracy, the sine qua non of sustained success – must take account of both facets of American thinking about the world.

At a deeper level, an outlook that blends both facets would benefit from the strengths and insights of each. The fundamental truth the exemplarists caught hold of long ago is that people have to save themselves. The fundamental truth the vindicators understood is that people sometimes need help. The exemplarists correctly complained that vindicationism could be an excuse for failing to fix what was wrong at home; the vindicators rightly replied that exemplarism could be a cover for ignoring evil overseas.

In the best of worlds, a blending of the two philosophies would arise from a mutual appreciation of the merits of the opposing argu-

ments. Given the rancorous character of the historical contest between the exemplarists and the vindicators, this hardly appears likely,
and definitely not imminent. Tolerance, in politics at any rate, typically reflects exhaustion rather than appreciation; even after two hundred years, both sides seem to have plenty of energy. This being so,
perhaps the outcome to aim for is what Morgenthau might have
called a balance of intellectual and moral power, with each side keeping its arguments sharp, the better to keep the other honest.

Note on Sources

As remarked in the preface, the pickings are surprisingly slim on the history of the debate over the appropriate American role in world affairs, and regarding the intellectual background of American foreign policy generally. Observations germane to this dearth can be found in Peter Paret, "Assignments New and Old," *American Historical Review*, February 1971; and Gordon Craig, "Political and Diplomatic History," in Felix Gilbert and Stephen R. Graubard, eds., *Historical Studies Today* (New York, 1972). The dearth is manifest in "A Round Table: Explaining the History of American Foreign Relations," *Journal of American History*, June 1990. Norman A. Graebner's 1964 anthology, *Ideas and Diplomacy: Readings in the Intellectual Tradition of American Foreign Policy* (New York), is an invaluable sourcebook, with commentary that is characteristically insightful, but makes no pretense of being a regular history. Arthur A. Ekirch, Jr., *Ideas, Ideals, and American Diplomacy: A History of Their Growth and Interaction* (New York, 1966), is a quick survey – sort of a Graebner without the readings. Dexter Perkins's published series of lectures, *The American Approach to Foreign Policy* (Uppsala, Sweden, 1951), is thought-provoking but impressionistic. Michael H. Hunt, *Ideology and U.S. Foreign Policy* (New Haven, Conn., 1987), and Robert Dallek, *The American Style of Foreign Policy: Cultural Politics and Foreign Affairs* (New York, 1983), are more interested in unspoken and usually unquestioned values than in explicit and explicitly analyzed ideas. Robert W. McElroy, *Morality and American Foreign Policy: The Role of Ethics in International Affairs* (Princeton, N.J., 1992); Judith Goldstein and Robert O. Keohane, eds., *Ideas and Foreign Policy: Beliefs, Institutions, and Political Change* (Ithaca, N.Y., 1993); Tony Smith, *America's Mission:*

The United States and the Worldwide Struggle for Democracy in the Twentieth Century (Princeton, N.J., 1994); and Walter A. McDougall, *Promised Land, Crusader State: The American Encounter with the World Since 1776* (New York, 1997), address aspects of the intellectual and moral debate, but focus on policy outcomes.

Occasionally diplomatic historians have dealt with particular facets of the debate among the thinkers, or with particular intellectuals-cum-policy makers; such works are cited in the notes and in the appropriate paragraphs below, as are books by intellectual historians that cross over into the foreign-policy field. Beyond this, what follows is intended as a – necessarily very selective – guide to useful volumes on the subjects treated in the text. The arrangement is roughly by chapter.

The clearest portrayal of the Jeffersonian position on the French revolution is Lawrence S. Kaplan, *Jefferson and France* (New Haven, Conn., 1967); of the Hamiltonian view, Gerald Stourzh, *Alexander Hamilton and the Idea of Republican Government* (Stanford, Cal., 1970), and Gilbert L. Lycan, *Alexander Hamilton and American Foreign Policy: A Design for Greatness* (Norman, Okla., 1970). The origin and evolution of Washington's farewell address – and much else relating to early thinking on American foreign policy – are elegantly covered in Felix Gilbert, *To the Farewell Address: Ideas of Early American Foreign Policy* (Princeton, N.J., 1961).

The standard source on U.S. reactions to the revolutions in Latin America is Arthur Preston Whitaker, *The United States and the Independence of Latin America, 1800–1830* (Baltimore, 1941). American thoughts and feelings about the Greek war for independence are thoroughly aired in Paul Constantine Pappas, *The United States and the Greek War for Independence, 1821–1828* (Boulder, Colo., 1985). On John Quincy Adams, the place to start is Samuel Flagg Bemis, *John Quincy Adams and the Foundations of American Foreign Policy* (New York, 1949).

The two essential treatments of American expansionist thought during the 1840s, as well as during other decades of the nineteenth century, are Albert K. Weinberg, *Manifest Destiny: A Study of Nationalist Expansionism in American History* (Baltimore, 1935); and Frederick Merk, *Manifest Destiny and Mission in American History: A Reinterpretation* (New York, 1963). On the Kossuth craze, consult Donald S. Spencer, *Louis Kossuth and Young America: A Study of Sectionalism and Foreign Policy* (Columbia, Mo., 1977). Social Darwinism is treated in Richard Hofstadter, *Social Darwinism in American Thought, 1860–1915* (Boston, 1955 ed.).

The standard life of Brooks Adams is Arthur F. Beringause, *Brooks Adams: A Biography* (New York, 1955). On Brooks and Henry, see Timothy P. Donovan, *Henry Adams and Brooks Adams: The Education of Two American Historians* (Norman, Okla., 1961). On Mahan and his influence: William D. Puleston, *Mahan: The Life and Work of Captain Alfred Thayer Mahan* (New Haven, Conn., 1939); William E. Livezey, *Mahan on Sea Power* (Norman, Okla., 1947); and especially Robert Seager II, *Alfred Thayer Mahan: The Man and His Letters* (Annapolis, Md., 1977).

The debate over imperialism is portrayed in Robert L. Beisner, *Twelve Against Empire: The Anti-Imperialists, 1898–1900* (New York, 1968); E. Berkeley Tompkins, *Anti-Imperialism in the United States: The Great Debate, 1890–1920* (Philadelphia, 1970); and (as it touched the Philippines) H. W. Brands, *Bound to Empire: The United States and the Philippines* (New York, 1992).

The definitive (so far) life of Walter Lippmann is Ronald Steel, *Walter Lippmann and the American Century* (Boston, 1980). Charles Forcey, *The Crossroads of Liberalism: Croly, Weyl, Lippmann, and the Progressive Era, 1900–1925* (New York, 1961), treats the trio that established the *New Republic*. On that journal's first quarter century, see David Seideman, *The New Republic: A Voice of Modern Liberalism* (New York, 1986). On Randolph Bourne: Bruce Clayton, *Forgotten Prophet: The Life of Randolph Bourne* (Baton Rouge, La., 1984). The most useful study of the impact of World War I on American life is David M. Kennedy, *Over Here: The First World War and American Society* (New York, 1980).

The best biography of Lincoln Steffens is Justin Kaplan, *Lincoln Steffens* (New York, 1974). The journalist's own account is *The Autobiography of Lincoln Steffens* (New York, 1931). A sympathetic rendering of John Reed is Granville Hicks, *John Reed: The Making of a Revolutionary* (New York, 1936). John P. Diggins, *Mussolini and Fascism: The View from America* (Princeton, N.J., 1972), provides indispensable material on the vogue for Mussolini in the United States. On Ezra Pound and Mussolini, see Tim Redman, *Ezra Pound and Italian Fascism* (Cambridge, Eng., 1991). Ernest Hemingway's journalistic career is revealed in William White, ed., *By-Line: Ernest Hemingway: Selected Articles and Dispatches of Four Decades* (New York, 1967). The troubles of the times for the American left are portrayed in William L. O'Neill, *A Better World: The Great Schism, Stalinism, and the American Intellectuals* (New York, 1982).

Charles Beard is the subject of Thomas C. Kennedy, *Charles A. Beard and American Foreign Policy* (Gainesville, Fla., 1975); Bernard C. Borning, *The Political and Social Thought of Charles A. Beard* (Seattle, 1962); Ellen Nore, *Charles A. Beard: An Intellectual Biography* (Carbondale, Ill., 1983); and Howard K. Beale, ed., *Charles A. Beard: An Appraisal* (Lexington, Ky., 1954). Richard Hofstadter, *The Progressive Historians: Turner, Beard, Parrington* (New York, 1968), places Beard in context. For more context, consult Richard H. Pells, *Radical Visions and American Dreams: Culture and Social Thought in the Depression Years* (New York, 1973). Isolationism is covered in Manfred Jonas, *Isolationism in America, 1935–1941* (Ithaca, N.Y., 1966), and Wayne S. Cole, *America First: The Battle Against Intervention, 1940–41* (Madison, Wis., 1953).

George Kennan's thinking has been studied to death, initially by himself, in his *Memoirs*, 2 vols. (Boston, 1967–1972). Several authors have explored his writings and aspects of his career: Barton D. Gellman, *Contending with Kennan: Toward a Philosophy of American Power* (New York, 1984); David Allan Mayers, *George Kennan and the Dilemmas of U.S. Foreign Policy* (New York, 1988); Anders Stephanson, *Kennan and the Art of Foreign Policy* (Cambridge, Mass., 1989); Walter L. Hixson, *George F. Kennan: Cold War Iconoclast* (New York, 1989); and Wilson D. Miscamble, *George F. Kennan and the Making of American Foreign Policy, 1947–1950* (Princeton, N.J., 1992). Hans Morgenthau has been left more alone; Greg Russell, *Hans J. Morgenthau and the Ethics of American Statecraft* (Baton Rouge, La., 1990), is the only book-length study.

The most illuminating life of Reinhold Niebuhr is Richard Wightman Fox, *Reinhold Niebuhr: A Biography* (New York, 1985). Robin W. Lovin, *Reinhold Niebuhr and Christian Realism* (Cambridge, Eng., 1995), analyzes Niebuhr's thought within the framework of the life. The intellectual atmosphere of the postwar period is examined most perspicaciously in Richard H. Pells, *The Liberal Mind in a Conservative Age: American Intellectuals in the 1940s and 1950s* (New York, 1985). On the resurgence of intellectual conservatism, see Ronald Lora, *Conservative Minds in America* (Chicago, 1971); John P. Diggins, *Up from Communism: Conservative Odysseys in American Intellectual History* (New York, 1975); George H. Nash, *The Conservative Intellectual Movement in America Since 1945* (New York,

1976); and John P. East, *The American Conservative Movement: The Philosophical Founders* (Chicago, 1986).

Gregg Herken, *Counsels of War* (New York, 1985), is an entertaining survey of what the nuclearists, including Herman Kahn, were up to. Fred Kaplan, *The Wizards of Armageddon* (New York, 1983), highlights the people who did the nuclear thinking, while Lawrence Freedman, *The Evolution of Nuclear Strategy* (New York, 1983), concentrates on the thought. Barry H. Steiner, *Bernard Brodie and the Foundations of American Nuclear Strategy* (Lawrence, Kan., 1991), portrays that seminal figure. On the subject of nuclear testing, begin with Robert A. Divine, *Blowing on the Wind: The Nuclear Test Ban Debate, 1954–1960* (New York, 1978), and Howard Ball, *Justice Downwind: America's Atomic Testing Program in the 1950s* (New York, 1986).

The phenomenon of New Left revisionism is examined in Joseph Siracusa, *New Left Diplomatic Histories and Historians: The American Revisionists* (New York, 1973); Robert James Maddox, *The New Left and the Origins of the Cold War* (Princeton, N.J., 1973); and Robert W. Tucker, *The Radical Left and American Foreign Policy* (Baltimore, 1971). An assessment of the significance of William A. Williams's work can be found in Bradford Perkins, " 'The Tragedy of American Diplomacy': Twenty-Five Years After," *Reviews in American History*, March 1984. A brief biographical sketch is William G. Robbins, "William Appleman Williams: 'Doing History Is Best of All. No Regrets'" in Lloyd C. Gardner, ed., *Redefining the Past: Essays in Diplomatic History in Honor of William Appleman Williams* (Corvallis, Ore., 1986); this entire volume reveals Williams's influence on his students and friends. The Madison mafia collectively is the subject of Paul Buhle, ed., *History and the New Left: Madison, Wisconsin, 1950–1970* (Philadelphia, 1990).

Neoconservatism, as it relates to foreign affairs, is the subject of John Ehrman, *The Rise of Neoconservatism* (New Haven, Conn., 1995). Peter Steinfels, *The Neoconservatives: The Men Who Are Changing America's Politics* (New York, 1979), is more gossipy. Norman Podhoretz's personal accounts – *Making It* (New York, 1967), and *Breaking Ranks* (New York, 1979) – describe how things looked to him. Another inside account is Irving Kristol, *Neoconservatism: The Autobiography of an Idea* (New York, 1995).

Evaluations of the end of the Cold War continue to vary, as do assessments of America's obligations to the post-Cold War world.

H. W. Brands, *The Devil We Knew: Americans and the Cold War* (New York, 1993), cautions against excessive celebration. Richard Ned Lebow and Janice Gross Stein, *We All Lost the Cold War* (Princeton, N.J., 1994), is more skeptical still. John Lewis Gaddis, *The United States and the End of the Cold War* (New York, 1992), seems happier; Peter Schweizer, *Victory: The Reagan Administration's Secret Strategy That Hastened the Collapse of the Soviet Union* (New York, 1994), is positively exultant. Richard N. Haass, *The Reluctant Sheriff: The United States After the Cold War* (New York, 1997), is neither happy nor sad, but resigned – and reluctant – in endorsing vindicationism. Zbigniew Brzezinski, *The Grand Chessboard: American Primacy and Its Geostrategic Imperatives* (New York, 1997), embraces vindicationism enthusiastically. Robert D. Kaplan, *The Ends of the Earth: A Journey at the Dawn of the Twenty-First Century* (New York, 1996), suggests that certain problems abroad will defy American amelioration; better to work on America's good example.

Index

Printed in the United States
112191LV00005B/100-114/P

9 780521 639682